Artificial Intelligence in Remote Sensing for Disaster Management

Scrivener Publishing
100 Cummings Center, Suite 541J
Beverly, MA 01915-6106

Publishers at Scrivener
Martin Scrivener (martin@scrivenerpublishing.com)
Phillip Carmical (pcarmical@scrivenerpublishing.com)

Artificial Intelligence in Remote Sensing for Disaster Management

Edited by

Neelam Dahiya

Gurwinder Singh

Sartajvir Singh

and

Apoorva Sharma

Scrivener Publishing

WILEY

This edition first published 2025 by John Wiley & Sons, Inc., 111 River Street, Hoboken, NJ 07030, USA and Scrivener Publishing LLC, 100 Cummings Center, Suite 541J, Beverly, MA 01915, USA

For more information about Scrivener publications please visit www.scrivenerpublishing.com.

Wiley Global Headquarters
111 River Street, Hoboken, NJ 07030, USA

For details of our global editorial offices, customer services, and more information about Wiley products visit us at www.wiley.com.

Library of Congress Cataloging-in-Publication Data

ISBN 9781394287192

Front cover images supplied by Adobe Firefly
Cover design by Russell Richardson

Set in size of 11pt and Minion Pro by Manila Typesetting Company, Makati, Philippines

Printed in the USA

10 9 8 7 6 5 4 3 2 1

Contents

Preface

Natural disasters have been increasing at a very high rate over the Earth's surface in recent decades. This is happening all over the world, and these abrupt changes can lead to natural hazards that have a significant impact on human beings. Monitoring the changes on the Earth's surface for tracking natural disasters poses a huge challenge for researchers. Artificial Intelligence (AI) is acquiring a greater amount of significance these days because it is used in weather prediction, snow detection, and the estimation or prediction of upcoming natural disasters. It has been proven a boon to humanity. To achieve information over a larger area at short intervals of time regarding natural calamities, Remote Sensing(RS) along with AI, has done tremendous work as a vital tool in the prevention and detection of natural calamities.

This book highlights the review of natural disasters, the challenges associated with them, their solutions with AI and the future perspective of numerous researchers. Advanced machine learning and deep learning algorithms play an important role in handling real-time disasters at a rapid rate. This book is not just to showcase technological progress but also to encourage new strategies and collaborations that can improve our capacity to prevent and handle disasters. We aim for this book to be a useful guide for scholars, decision-makers, and professionals in the field, and to ignite more innovation and cooperation.

This book has been carefully compiled to provide our esteemed readers with comprehensive knowledge and insights on AI in disaster management, advanced tools to handle earthquake assessment and the role of integration of AI and remote sensing plays in the real-time monitoring of natural calamities. The goal of this book is to explain and highlight how the synchronization of AI and remote sensing helps in the rapid evaluation and assessment of natural disaster management. This book will help students, beginners, and researchers learn the various tools and technologies to access and prevent the damage caused by natural disasters. We want to convey our deep gratitude to everyone who contributed to bringing this book to reality. Our entire team and family have consistently offered much-needed support and motivation throughout the process. We also want to express our appreciation to the Scrivener Publishing and the entire production team for their significant effort and dedication in ensuring the timely and high-quality printing of this book.

1

Introduction to Natural Hazards, Challenges, and Managing Strategies

Puninder Kaur*, Taruna Sharma, Jaswinder Singh and Neelam Dahiya

Chitkara University Institute of Engineering and Technology, Chitkara University, Punjab, India

Abstract

Natural disasters are unforeseen events that spread danger to human existence and have major effects on our ecosystem. It includes volcanic eruptions, floods, earthquakes, wildfires, tsunamis, droughts, and extreme climate changes. To prevent and manage natural disaster has become a critical issue; if not resolved on time, it can lead to severe injuries and even death. On the basis of origin, these are categorized into various forms such as biological, geological, and hydrological. These hazards are life threatening; thus, early detection and management is necessary to resolve the issue. Remote sensing plays an important role in managing natural disaster. In the current work, a detailed review of natural disaster, challenges, and its possible managing strategies has been discussed. This research work will help the beginners, researchers, and human beings for early detection of natural hazards and also to implement effective solutions to resolve the issue.

Keywords: Disaster, flood, hazards, remote sensing

1.1 Introduction

Natural hazards are defined as the phenomena that can become disastrous when they cause significant casualties and property damage, impeding social and economic growth. If occurring on a worldwide scale and

**Corresponding author*: puninder.k@chitkara.edu.in; ORCID: 0000-0003-3959-593X
Taruna Sharma: ORCID: 0000-0002-2647-1332
Jaswinder Singh: ORCID: 0000-0003-1343-4740
Neelam Dahiya: ORCID: 0000-0003-1839-9040

Neelam Dahiya, Gurwinder Singh, Sartajvir Singh and Apoorva Sharma (eds.) Artificial Intelligence in Remote Sensing for Disaster Management, (1–20) © 2025 Scrivener Publishing LLC

with great frequency, these endanger human society, environmental systems, and critical infrastructures [1]. Earthquakes, floods, cyclones, volcanic eruptions, and landslides are natural events that have shaped the Earth's terrain over millennia. These natural processes can result in natural catastrophes when they interact with man-made elements such as towns, agriculture, and infrastructure [2].

India's unique geoclimatic circumstances have made it prone to catastrophic calamities. Floods, droughts, cyclones, earthquakes, and landslides have been common occurrences. Approximately 60% of the landmass is prone to earthquakes of varying intensities, over 40 million hectares is prone to flooding, approximately 8% of the total area is prone to cyclones, and 68% of the territory is vulnerable to drought [3]. The loss of individual, municipal, and governmental assets has been massive. India has been struck by numerous disasters in recent years, including, among the major ones, the Bangalore circus tragedy (1981), Bhopal gas tragedy (1984), Gujarat cyclone (1998), Orissa super cyclone (1999), Gujarat earthquake (2001), annual flooding in large parts of the country during the monsoon, and tsunami.

In 2016, natural disasters caused up to 520 billion USD in worldwide losses, which was 60% more than previously estimated losses. China is one of the countries that have suffered significant losses due to natural calamities. The significant loss can be due to its broad region, complex and diversified ecological environment, and high frequency [4].

To successfully mitigate natural catastrophes, it is crucial to understand the predicted frequency, type, and severity of hazardous events in a certain location. Natural disaster management relies heavily on geographical information. Spatial data includes maps, aerial photography, satellite images, GPS, rainfall data, borehole data, and other geographic information. To superimpose data from disparate projections and coordinate systems, they must be converted to a common map basis. Remote sensing and geographic information systems (GIS) are effective tools for disaster management. Satellite remote sensing data can quickly map disaster-related data distributions [5]. Satellite systems vary in terms of geographic, temporal, and spectral resolution.

To analyze catastrophes, remote sensing data should be combined with other data sources such as mapping, measuring networks, or sample locations to determine valuable parameters. There are two methods for image linkage: visual interpretation and categorization.

The main focus of this chapter is to provide an overview of the numerous natural processes that have the potential to trigger natural catastrophes [6]. It comprises of an introduction section which describes about the natural hazards, which is further followed by a section on the terminologies used, classification, challenges of natural hazards, and possible solution via remote sensing. The chapter finishes with a discussion of obstacles in coping with catastrophes caused by natural hazards and suggests new directions in improving the ability to mitigate the harmful impact of natural disasters on vulnerable sections.

1.2 Terminology Used

Natural disaster have been continuously changing during the last decades. There are some important key terminologies used for natural disaster prediction which are mentioned below.

1.2.1 Hazard

Hazard has the capability to occur, change the lives of people, and has greater impact on people or places. The main reason for their occurrence is due to the interaction of social, technological, and natural systems. This idea of hazard implies that the interaction of natural and social systems is the crucial aspect in changing a natural activity into a threat. It is also vital to recognize that a "hazard" is not always dangerous; rather, it is a "threat" with the potential to do harm. The Federal Emergency Management Agency (FEMA) defines hazards as "events or physical conditions capable of causing fatalities, injuries, property damage, and infrastructure" [7].

1.2.2 Mitigation

The mitigation sector "mitigates or prevents the adverse effects of natural hazards with measures, activities, and actions taken by humans and communities". It employs an integrated strategy that includes land use planning, infrastructure development, ecosystem restoration, and public awareness, all of which are critical for risk reduction and resiliency [8]. Mitigation is primarily beneficial for reducing the likelihood and severity of such accidents. It is unavoidable because it develops various techniques to limit human life losses, lessen the destruction of personal property, and lessen the intervention from communities.

1.2.3 Vulnerability

Vulnerability in hazardous areas refers to the link between people, infrastructure, assets, and ecosystems that are considered targets for these hazards. It may have adverse impacts on the planet due to ecological conditions, socioeconomic and structural factors, and lack of access to the necessary infrastructures and resources [8]. There is a need for holistic approaches to protect, especially for developing economies, from natural risks such as incorporating socio-economic improvement, infrastructure development, risk-lowering measures, and community empowerment. The vulnerability of poor people to the aftermath of disasters can be minimized by diagnosing the reasons for their vulnerability and by improving their resilience to prevent it.

1.2.4 Disaster

Disaster refers to any activity that foreshadows negative consequences and is a one-of-a-kind event that affects the natural environment. Disasters have a wide-ranging impact on people, property, and the environment, causing both short- and long-term harm. Natural occurrences can be complicated or benign, and they can be caused completely by people or by a combination of the two [9]. Disasters vary in severity, ranging from a few individuals or houses to the entire country, and can occur simultaneously. While individuals cannot predict catastrophes, anticipatory efforts can assist to mitigate the impacts by making the impact less severe and decreasing the danger to vulnerable populations.

1.2.5 Risk

Risk is the possibility of an unintentional action occurring, and there may be a variety of harmful behaviors that result in individuals losing their lives, damaging the beauty of the environment, and incurring economic losses. It considers the probability of the event's occurrence as well as the extent of its impact when determining the hazard's risk level. After all assessments from 2013 to 2020, the natural risk is continuously increasing [9]. The formula is provided in Equation 1.1 [10].

$$R = H * V \tag{1.1}$$

R stands for risk, and it may be calculated using the multiplication factor of *H* and *V*. *H* stands for hazards (disaster), and *V* is for vulnerability. If the value of dangers and vulnerabilities raises, so is the likelihood of risk.

1.3 Classification of Natural Hazards

Natural disasters encompass a wide range of occurrences that pose dangers to human life, transportation, and ecosystems. Some typical forms of natural hazards are shown in Figure 1.1.

1.3.1 Biological Natural Hazards

Biological risks are those that result from numerous biological processes. It includes some variants of disease which can spread from person to person and also has the capability to infect human beings at a large scale [11]. Biological natural hazards are events or phenomena that come from the stable probiotic that exists in animals, plants, and other organisms—for instance, viruses, bacteria, parasites, insects, and pathogens—which present health and wellness challenges, decline in agriculture, damage to ecosystems, and undermining of economies. Apart from human health systems, biological hazards have the potential of affecting agriculture and ecosystem health by bringing diseases in farm or aquatic animals [12]. Plant diseases, such as leaf porings, stem cankers, head rot, and bud blindness, which may be caused by rusts, blights, and wilt diseases, may completely destroy crops and reduce food production. Animals' diseases, such African face fever, foot and mouth disease, and white nose syndrome, cause severe economic and ecological interrupts. Human activities had a crucial role in both the

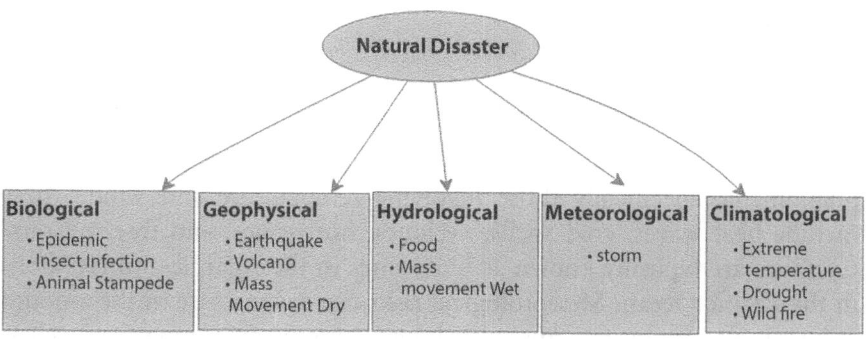

Figure 1.1 Classification of natural disaster.

propagation and control of the virus. While biological dangers are unquestionably relevant, they are not addressed in depth in this session.

1.3.2 Geological Hazards

Volcanoes, earthquakes, and landslides are all examples of spectacular and violent natural disasters with far-reaching and catastrophic consequences. The effects on human health might still be noticed years after the incident has occurred [13]. Geologic hazards are the cause of significant loss of life and property. As a result of earthquakes, more than a million people have died.

1.3.3 Hydrological Hazards

Hydrological catastrophes are dramatic and have damaging changes to the quality of water on Earth as well as changes in how water is dispersed under the surface or in the atmosphere. It can be induced by severe weather events such as droughts, tornadoes, mudslides, landslides, or flooding [14]. A true example of a hydrological disaster is the 2018 Kerala flood, which was the worst scenario in a century and displaced over 1 million people. Hydrological risks of different forms provide a plethora of technical and public policy challenges across the world. Hydrological hazards are defined as severe occurrences linked with the occurrence, movement, and distribution of water. They include droughts, flooding, and related phenomena (e.g., landslides, river scour, and deposition). Hydrological risks and their consequences are linked to climatic variability, population trends, land cover change, and other causal variables, which may be exacerbated by global climate change [15]. The rise in greenhouse gases in the atmosphere will continue to cause global warming and an intensification of the hydrological cycle, making hydrological extreme research increasingly complicated and hard.

1.3.4 Meteorological Hazards

Meteorological risks are those caused by meteorological (i.e., weather) phenomena, specifically those involving temperature and wind. These include heat waves, cold spells, cyclones, hurricanes, and freezing rain. Cyclones are typically known as hurricanes in the Atlantic and typhoons in the Pacific Ocean. Meteorological risks can cause a rise in the amount of heat waves, intense storms, and climatic extremes, in general, as well as changes in hydrological systems [16].

1.4 Challenges and Risks of Natural Hazards

"Natural catastrophe" refers to an extreme catastrophic occurrence or loss of a natural phenomenon such as an earthquake, wildfire, flood, or drought. These events foreshadow the potentially terrible repercussions for human civilization, including infrastructure, the economy, and the environment. In contrast to disease outbreaks and other pandemic scenarios, natural catastrophes are frequently characterized by abrupt breakouts, weak or non-existent warning systems, and powerful damage. There are numerous challenges associated with natural disaster which are mentioned in Figure 1.2.

1.4.1 Loss of Life

Natural catastrophes inflict not just death and injury but also devastation through collapsed buildings, flooding, flying debris, and landslides. The danger of death and injury is enhanced in densely populated places that lack adequate infrastructure or early warning systems. Disasters result in fatalities and injuries; therefore, comprehensive integrated disaster risk

Figure 1.2 Risks of natural disaster.

reduction strategies will be developed, with a focus on increased preparedness, improved infrastructure adaptability, enhanced early warning systems, and the development of community engagement and building activities. Resolving these critical difficulties can reduce the likelihood of emergency circumstances occurring, which is beneficial to the public and allows them to continue with their usual lives [15].

1.4.2 Property Damage and Economic Losses

Natural disasters can cause massive devastation of houses, businesses, structures, and other investment sources, resulting in a severe drop in the economy. The rebuilding and rehabilitation procedures may result in a financial burden for impacted persons, the government, and the society. Natural disasters typically result in property loss and economic losses, necessitating the development of an alternative comprehensive risk reduction and management strategy that aims to build resilience, promote mitigation measures, increase building structure safety, weave coverage through insurance, and improve local development sustainability [17]. By implementing these methods, communities have the potential to reduce their vulnerability to a reduction in economic performance as a result of natural catastrophes affecting individuals, businesses, and society.

1.4.3 Disruption of Critical Infrastructure

Several cataclysmic events turn the infrastructure systems from critical into a mess, whether it is the health security or transportation network, communications systems, or healthcare. The consequences of this may include difficulties in passing through disaster areas, a lack of crucial services, and more prolonged time frames in which to rehabilitate the region [10].

1.4.4 Health Risks and Disease Outbreaks

Disasters can, in turn, be advantageous to the spread of diseases particularly from contaminated water sources, shelters that are crowded to an extreme, and in cases of lack of health facilities. This affects the increasing possibility of spread of such diseases like cholera, dengue fever, and respiratory infections as well as other health complications and disease outbreaks during and after natural disasters which demand innovative, holistic, and integrated measures, which involves work on public health preparedness, emergency response, and recovery forces [18]. Strategies that could be used involve providing access to clean water and sanitation facilities, carrying out awareness programs on hygiene practices, increasing disease surveillance and monitoring, ensuring fast medical care and treatment, and providing psychosocial support. One of the critical factors to consider in an emergency preparedness plan is to give first priority to health protection and prevention measures [19]. This will help reduce the impact of natural disasters on public health and thus help the affected population to even out.

1.4.5 Environmental Degradation

Natural disasters often bring very severe environmental problems, such as falling trees, deterioration of soil, and pollution of rivers as well as the large-scale destruction of habitats. Changes of environmental conditions can result in the degradation of ecosystems, obstacles to ecosystem balance, and, as a consequence, the impact on biodiversity and umbrella services in the environment.

1.4.6 Social and Economic Disparities

Natural disasters, in most cases, deliver blows to the downtrodden and vulnerable in excess, thereby heightening the already existing social and economic differences. Disasters even more tend to aggravate the social exclusion of vulnerable communities by their limited availability of means, information, and support [20]. Consequently, they may also prevent these groups from coping with disasters. Social and economic disparities require a multi-dimensional approach that is based on the identification of interconnected measures which can be adopted to minimize inequality and enhance social inclusion in the community. Through perceiving the needs of vulnerable segments of society and by attacking the factors which give rise to disparity, communities can increase their ability to deal with the aftermath of natural disasters and to establish a fair and properly functioning society [21].

1.4.7 Psychosocial Impacts

Psychosocial effects involve emotional, psychological, and social processes in individuals and the communities used to affected disaster victims. These consequences may be so long trailed affecting the mental condition, the quality of life, and the social interactions. The disaster manifests itself in the way of psychosocial impact on the persons who took part in it as well as the community [22]. Trauma, stress, anxiety, grief, and loss are some of the effects that commonly occur in such cases. Ensuring availability of sufficient mental health support and psychosocial services is required to make an action toward these outcomes and to promote the residents' resilience. There is a need to prioritize the mental health and affected individuals. Disaster response and recovery efforts can promote resilience, foster social cohesion, and mitigate the long-term psychological effects of natural disasters [23].

1.5 Strategies to Prevent Natural Hazards

Despite the fact that getting rid of a natural disaster is impracticable because it is an unidentified event that can happen anytime, but there are a few strategies to eliminate the impact and risk of natural hazards which are mentioned below.

1.5.1 Planning and Regulation for Reducing Risk on Land

Introduce zoning ordinances and planning protocols that disallow or curb the development of high-risk sites like the floodplains, fault areas of earthquakes, and sites that have vulnerability to landslides or wild fires. A building code should be put on to establish that indeed structures are developed and built to resist potential threats [24].

1.5.1.1 Zoning Regulations

Land is zoned according to different criteria such as height and landform (a higher risk of hazards) or native vegetation, etc. Environmental sensitivity as well as intended use determines the zoning. Furthermore, in the case of danger zones subjected to risks such as flooding, landslides, or earthquakes, these areas are usually approached as restricted to any development or sometimes totally prohibited [25].

1.5.1.2 Building Codes and Standards

Building codes and standards need to be followed to ensure that structures can stand and be designed and built to combat the hazards coming toward them. These standards could be formulated to cover areas as seismic resistance, wind loads, flood-proofing, and fire prevention measures. Follow the strict performance requirements, and the construction of buildings and infrastructure will get less prone to disasters caused by nature [26].

1.5.1.3 Setback Requirements

As setback requirements demand the minimum distance between building hazardous areas like coastline, river bank, or steep slope, they are supposed to be maintained. Those measures are installing dikes, embankments, and protective structures which reduce the influence of floods, coastal erosions, and landslides and also provide spaces for buffers and protection of natural elements [5].

1.5.1.4 Erosion Control Measures

Regulations that require riverbank protection measures may be designed in the high-risk areas like hill slopes and coastal areas. The slop stabilization practice includes managing the vegetation as well as construction of the retaining walls, terracing, and slope stabilization methods to protect the soil from being removed and prevent landslides [27].

1.5.1.5 Floodplain Management

Regulations of floodplain management deny development in flood-prone areas and require measures such as elevating buildings, providing flood proofing and storm-water pipeline management to reduce the chances of flood. Concurrently, regulations could incorporate the conditions of keeping the natural flood plains that are used as a flood control tool [28].

1.5.2 Environmental Conservation and Restoration

It also plays an important role in managing natural hazards. The two issues of ecosystem preservation and restoration are among the key ones in the process of minimizing the impact from natural hazards and ensuring the sustainability of communities. Some vital key components are given below.

1.5.2.1 Protecting Natural Ecosystems

Conservation efforts are dedicated to safeguarding ecosystems from environments like wetlands, mangroves, forests, or coral reefs by their conservation. These systems deliver very crucial services to humans through storm surge management, flood control, erosion prevention, and, consequently, living space for nature and animals. Combating disasters through those people protects the existence of the nature conservation that can suppress natural hazards by providing its own defense mechanism and enabling the ecosystem's resilience [29].

1.5.2.2 Restoring Degraded Ecosystems

Restoration work is all about returning and restoring the ecosystems, which are at risk because of the degradation to their original or functional shape. It could include planting trees, developing or creating habitats, remedying and bringing back marshes or swamps, and similar processes to achieve a better state of the Earth and improve the ecosystem efficiency. On the contrary, repaired ecosystems will be healthier and provide essential services such as flood mitigation, wind erosion inhibition, and biodiversity conservation. This means that they will be more resistant to hazards [30].

1.5.2.3 Floodplain Management

This floodplain conservation and restoration purpose is provided in terms of absorbing floodwaters, minimizing the risk of flood, and low rising level of inundation in the downstream communities. The existing project to restore riparian green vegetation as well as the preservation of native wetlands minimizes flooding and increases biodiversity; therefore, a positive impact on water quality is ensured [31].

1.5.2.4 Coastal Protection

Preserving mangrove forests, salt marshes, and dunes, besides many other ecosystems, is one of the easiest initiatives that acts as natural defense against erosion, surge of storms, and tsunamis. Healthy and stable coastal ecosystems make it possible for them to cope with storm energy, reduce the level of uplands by stabilizing shorelines, and diminish coastal breach impacts on local residents and built infrastructure [32].

1.5.2.5 Sustainable Land Management

Supportive measures that include a lot of agro-forestry, soil conservation, and erosion control practices would contribute to the prevention of soil erosion, landslides, desertification, and many other land degradation or land sickness. Soil fertility improves with these production techniques, soil moisture is encouraged to stay, and the level of risk of natural hazards is reduced [33].

1.5.3 Early Warning Systems and Preparedness

Installing and implementing early warning systems would cover different types of hazards, like tsunami, hurricane, flood, wildfires, and volcanic eruptions. This will be followed by constant drills and exercises to check the existing emergency response plans in place and improve community preparedness [34]. Warning systems and preparedness contribute to preventing natural hazards in the following manner.

1.5.3.1 Hazard Monitoring and Forecasting

The early warning systems look out for natural catastrophes like hurricanes and floods aside from predicting earthquakes and wildfires for an extended time of the disasters so that people have a little bit time to stay safe. They monitor changes of weather conditions and forecast emergencies for the purpose of providing proper precautionary actions before disaster can reach its peak [35].

1.5.3.2 Risk Assessment and Planning

Hazard mapping and risk assessment which help in determining the highly vulnerable areas and populations in the hazards of natural disasters are done by the warning systems. This data is used in land development planning, infrastructure improvement, and emergency response efforts which, in turn, can aid in mitigating dangers and minimizing disasters [36].

1.5.4 Education and Awareness

The community should be educated about natural hazards including their possible effects through public approaching events, workshops and training programs. In order to brief the community, general problems on safety techniques and practicing protection for self and personal property are discussed below.

1.5.4.1 Understanding Hazards and Risks

Integral parts of education programs are those that disclose information about various natural risks, their triggers, and the associated hazards. Through knowing the possible perils due to, e.g., floods, volcanic eruptions, hurricanes, wildfires, and landslides, people can get the information they need to reduce the impact of a hazard and protect those they care about [37].

1.5.4.2 Promoting Risk Reduction Measures

Health and safety awareness through education enables people to know the risks and have the right skills and knowledge to respond to hazard situations and minimize dangers. This includes providing individuals with the technical knowledge regarding securing their homes, how to assemble emergency plans, assemble or purchase a disaster kit, and safe evacuation during emergencies. Thus, education enables people to increase their awareness and ability to protect from natural disasters due to acquisition of practical skills and knowledge [38].

1.5.4.3 School Curriculum Integration

Educating young people about hazards and disaster resilience using school curriculum and other educational activities in the form of regular hazard awareness and preparedness gives room to the youth of the future generations. Through the provision of essential information concerning risk, emergency respond correction, and environmental conservation, schools act as a pillar in molding traits, behaviors, and values which deal with disaster avoidance and preparedness [30].

1.5.5 Climate Change Mitigation

The root causes behind natural phenomenon like climate change are tackled through measures that mitigate global warming, including cutting the worldwide emissions of greenhouse gases and stimulating the trend to renewable energy. Control and adaptation of climate change are concerning parts of the action plan which mainly looks at the prevention of more frequent disaster types and their escalated deaths. Here is how mitigation and adaptation strategies contribute to managing natural disasters.

1.5.5.1 Reducing Greenhouse Gas Emissions

Mitigation actions target at subduing the release of greenhouse gases on the local, regional, national, and global levels such as carbon dioxide, methane, and nitrous oxide that leads to climate change. Through the adoption of cleaner forms of energy, enhancement of energy efficiency, and applying policies that reduce discharges from industry, transport sectors and land use, the mitigation measures control the climate change growth rate.

1.5.5.2 Promoting Renewable Energy

The greater use of renewable energy, e.g., solar, wind, hydroelectric, and geothermal, is one of the options that may decrease CO_2 emissions and directly enhances air quality by reducing regular greenhouse gas emissions. Not only does the shift to renewable energy resources combat climate change but also energy independence is promoted and air pollution is reduced [36].

1.5.5.3 Enhancing Energy Efficiency

Actions such as making houses and buildings, industries, and transportation more energy efficient cut energy consumption to the barest minimum, resulting in reduced man-made emissions. Energy efficiency steps are based on installing insulation in buildings, energy-efficient lightings, fuel-saving/efficient cars, and industrial process optimization, thus resulting in both cost savings and environmental advantages [38].

1.6 Role of Remote Sensing Device to Prevent Natural Disasters

Remote sensing can help risk reduction programs by identifying danger zones linked with floodplains, coastal flooding and erosion, and active faults. It may also be used to validate hazard models by assessing the location and size of real incidents. There are key features that are used to revoke a natural disaster by providing some warnings by detecting information via sensors.

1.6.1 Hazard Detection and Monitoring

With the help of remote sensing instruments, different types of hazardous natural-composition activities like hurricanes, floods, wildfires, earthquakes, landslides, and volcanic eruption could be monitored and detected. Through satellite, aviation, drones, and ground sensors, these devices collect data on the probable hazards and at the same time provide timely or nearly real-time information about the position, length, and intensity of a potential hazard [5].

1.6.2 Early Warning Systems

Remote sensing information is incorporated into early warning systems so as to be able to send timely alerts and notifications to those near the danger zones during natural disasters. As an example, satellite imagery can determine shifts of weather over trend forecasts, document progress of water bodies like rivers and lakes, and identify areas that are at risk of flooding; these can enable authorities to protect and save lives by issuing warnings and evacuating people in advance if they will be likely affected [25].

1.6.3 Risk Assessment and Vulnerability Mapping

Sensors of remote sensing are helpful in determining community and infrastructure disaster risks and vulnerabilities. These experts study satellite data, elevation, land cover maps, and other geospatial data sets to determine high-risk regions. They also consider communities that are exposed to risks on a particular territory. Furthermore, they can distribute resources according to their necessities [8].

1.6.4 Environmental Monitoring

The remote sensing devices continuously undergo trend monitoring so that they can develop a solution to the environmental conditions and the changes by providing the inputs of the factors that lead to the natural disasters. These cover instances such as satellite imagery that can monitor the loss of forests, urban development, soil erosion, and changes in land use trends, thus identifying the causes and warning signs of environmental degradation which are based on disasters [7].

1.6.5 Mapping and Damage Assessment

After a disaster has happened, the data from remote sensing is observed to determine the amount of destruction made and provide support to disaster response and recovery processes. The use of aerial and geo-spatial imagery can speed up the assessment of affected areas, give indications of infrastructures that have been destroyed, and provide estimates of the number of people who have been made homeless and the consequences for ecology and agriculture.

1.7 Conclusion

Natural disaster is defined as an unexpected event that totally destroys our surroundings and creates a dangerous threat for an individual in terms of expected life span, their property, and atmosphere. There are various kinds of natural hazards like biological, hydrological, geological, meteorological, etc., which directly or indirectly damage the beauty of the environment, too. The prevention of such kinds of natural disaster is one of the crucial tasks for everyone. To avoid these issues, remote sensing is the vital tool used in natural disaster management. It is the most effective and advance tool that analyzes, pre-monitors, and responds on time about upcoming natural disasters. It uses various kinds of sensors to mitigate or provide advance intimations to the users that are used to reduce the impact of natural hazards and to protect people's lives. Flooding is a regular concern in this region; thus, it needs extra attention. GIS technology is useful for monitoring and assessing flood danger. This technology can help planners develop successful catastrophe prevention strategies. It can also assist policymakers in making pre-flood decisions to minimize economic and social losses.

Acknowledgments

The authors would like to thank the anonymous reviewers and the editor/associate editor for their critical feedback and helpful ideas.

References

1. Okuyama, Y., Economics of natural disasters: A critical review, 2003.
2. DeMarco, M.J., SenGupta, A.K., Greenleaf, J.E., Arsenic removal using a polymeric/inorganic hybrid sorbent. *Water Res.*, 37, 1, 164–176, 2003.
3. Gill, J.C. and Malamud, B.D., Reviewing and visualizing the interactions of natural hazards. *Rev. Geophys.*, 52, 4, 680–722, 2014.
4. Guo, B., Lu, M., Fan, Y., Wu, H., Yang, Y., Wang, C., A novel remote sensing monitoring index of salinization based on three-dimensional feature space model and its application in the Yellow River Delta of China. *Geomatics Nat. Hazards Risk*, 14, 1, 95–116, 2023.
5. Chuvieco, E., Aguado, I., Salas, J., García, M., Yebra, M., Oliva, P., Satellite remote sensing contributions to wildland fire science and management. *Curr. For. Rep.*, 6, 81–96, 2020.

6. Estoque, R.C., A review of the sustainability concept and the state of SDG monitoring using remote sensing. *Remote Sens. (Basel)*, 12, 11, 1770, 2020.
7. Chai, J. and Wu, H.-Z., Prevention/mitigation of natural disasters in urban areas. *Smart Constr. Sustain. Cities*, 1, 1, 4, 2023.
8. Kamran, M. and Yamamoto, K., Evolution and use of remote sensing in ecological vulnerability assessment: A review. *Ecol. Indic.*, 148, 110099, 2023.
9. Ge, J., Tang, H., Yang, N., Hu, Y., Rapid identification of damaged buildings using incremental learning with transferred data from historical natural disaster cases. *ISPRS J. Photogramm. Remote Sens.*, 195, 105–128, 2023.
10. Krichen, M., Abdalzaher, M.S., Elwekeil, M., Fouda, M.M., Managing natural disasters: An analysis of technological advancements, opportunities, and challenges. *Internet Things Cyber-Phys. Syst.*, 4, 99–109, Jan. 2024. doi: 10.1016/j.iotcps.2023.09.002.
11. Fahad, S., Hossain, M.S., Huong, N.T.L., Nassani, A.A., Haffar, M., Naeem, M.R., An assessment of rural household vulnerability and resilience in natural hazards: evidence from flood prone areas. *Environ. Dev. Sustain.*, 25, 6, 5561–5577, 2023.
12. Al Mamun, A., *et al.*, Livelihood vulnerability of char land communities to climate change and natural hazards in Bangladesh: an application of livelihood vulnerability index. *Nat. Hazard.*, 115, 2, 1411–1437, 2023.
13. Barquet, K., Englund, M., Inga, K., André, K., Segnestam, L., Conceptualising multiple hazards and cascading effects on critical infrastructures. *Disasters*, 48, 1, e12591, 2024.
14. Gupta, V., *et al.*, Hydrometeorological analysis of July-2023 floods in Himachal Pradesh, India. *Nat. Hazard.*, 120, 7549–7574, 2024. https://doi.org/10.1007/s11069-024-06520-5.
15. Enderami, S.A. and Sutley, E., Social vulnerability score: a scalable index for representing social vulnerability in virtual community resilience testbeds. *Nat. Hazard.*, 120, 6457–6480, 2024. https://doi.org/10.1007/s11069-024-06499-z.
16. Debele, S.E., *et al.*, Nature-based solutions can help reduce the impact of natural hazards: A global analysis of NBS case studies. *Sci. Total Environ.*, 902, 165824, 2023. doi: 10.1016/j.scitotenv.2023.165824.
17. López-Saavedra, M. and Martí, J., Reviewing the multi-hazard concept. Application to volcanic islands. *Earth Sci. Rev.*, 236, 104286, 2023. doi: 10.1016/j.earscirev.2022.104286.
18. Ma, Y., Chen, S., Ermon, S., Lobell, D.B., Transfer learning in environmental remote sensing. *Remote Sens. Environ.*, 301, 113924, 2024.
19. Amen, A.R.M., *et al.*, Mapping of flood-prone areas utilizing GIS techniques and remote sensing: a case study of Duhok, Kurdistan Region of Iraq. *Remote Sens. (Basel)*, 15, 4, 1102, 2023.
20. Munawar, H.S., Hammad, A.W.A., Waller, S.T., Remote sensing methods for flood prediction: A review. *Sensors*, 22, 3, 960, 2022.

21. Barmpoutis, P., Papaioannou, P., Dimitropoulos, K., Grammalidis, N., A review on early forest fire detection systems using optical remote sensing. *Sensors*, 20, 22, 104286, 6442, 2020.
22. Khan, A., Gupta, S., Gupta, S.K., Multi-hazard disaster studies: Monitoring, detection, recovery, and management, based on emerging technologies and optimal techniques. *Int. J. Disaster Risk Reduct.*, 47, 101642, 2020.
23. Merz, B., *et al.*, Impact forecasting to support emergency management of natural hazards. *Rev. Geophys.*, 58, 4, e2020RG000704, 2020.
24. Lucas, R., *et al.*, Structural characterisation of mangrove forests achieved through combining multiple sources of remote sensing data. *Remote Sens. Environ.*, 237, 111543, 2020.
25. Liu, Z., *et al.*, Remote sensing and geostatistics in urban water-resource monitoring: A review. *Mar. Freshwater Res.*, 74, 10, 747–765, 2023.
26. Zhao, X., *et al.*, Drought monitoring over Yellow River basin from 2003–2019 using reconstructed MODIS land surface temperature in Google Earth Engine. *Remote Sens. (Basel)*, 13, 18, 3748, 2021.
27. Harsimran, S., Santosh, K., Rakesh, K., Overview of corrosion and its control: A critical review. *Proc. Eng. Sci.*, 3, 1, 13–24, 2021.
28. Meechang, K., Leelawat, N., Tang, J., Kodaka, A., Chintanapakdee, C., The acceptance of using information technology for disaster risk management: A systematic review. *Eng. J.*, 24, 4, 111–132, 2020.
29. Kumar, P., *et al.*, An overview of monitoring methods for assessing the performance of nature-based solutions against natural hazards. *Earth Sci. Rev.*, 217, 103603, 2021.
30. Ward, P.J., *et al.*, Natural hazard risk assessments at the global scale. *Nat. Hazards Earth Syst. Sci.*, 20, 4, 1069–1096, 2020.
31. Wickramasinghe, D., Ecosystem-based disaster risk reduction, in: *Oxford Research Encyclopedia of Natural Hazard Science*, 2021.
32. Mochizuki, J. and Naqvi, A., Reflecting disaster risk in development indicators. *Sustainability (Switzerland)*, 11, 4, 996, Feb. 2019, doi: 10.3390/su11040996.
33. da Silva, V.S., Salami, G., da Silva, M.I.O., Silva, E.A., Monteiro Junior, J.J., Alba, E., Methodological evaluation of vegetation indexes in land use and land cover (LULC) classification. *Geol. Ecol. Landscapes*, 4, 2, 159–169, 2020, doi: 10.1080/24749508.2019.1608409.
34. Dewan, A.M. and Yamaguchi, Y., Land use and land cover change in Greater Dhaka, Bangladesh: Using remote sensing to promote sustainable urbanization. *Appl. Geogr.*, 29, 3, 390–401, 2009, doi: 10.1016/j.apgeog.2008.12.005.
35. Cerulli, D., *et al.*, The role of education in increasing awareness and reducing impact of natural hazards. *Sustainability (Switzerland)*, 12, 18, 7623, Sep. 2020, doi: 10.3390/su12187623.
36. Jia, H., Chen, F., Du, E., Adaptation to disaster risk—An overview. *Int. J. Environ. Res. Public. Health*, 18, 21, Art. no. 21, Jan. 2021, doi: 10.3390/ijerph182111187.

37. Ghaffarian, S., Kerle, N., Filatova, T., Remote sensing-based proxies for urban disaster risk management and resilience: A review. *Remote Sens.*, 10, 11, Art. no. 11, Nov. 2018, doi: 10.3390/rs10111760.
38. van Zelst, V.T.M., *et al.*, Cutting the costs of coastal protection by integrating vegetation in flood defences. *Nat. Commun.*, 12, 1, 6533, 2021.

2

Role of Remote Sensing for Emergency Response and Disaster Rehabilitation

Mochamad Irwan Hariyono[1,2*] and Aptu Andy Kurniawan[3]

[1]*Research Center for Geoinformatics, National Research and Innovation Agency (BRIN), Cibinong, Bogor, Indonesia*
[2]*School of Environmental Science, University of Indonesia Jl. Salemba Raya, Kenari, Senen, Jakarta, Indonesia*
[3]*Environmental Science, Padjajaran University, Dipati Ukur 1 Bandung, West Java, Indonesia*

Abstract

Remote sensing data is crucial for monitoring environmental conditions and topography, aiding in the mitigation of natural disaster risks. Remote sensing data is valuable for emergency response in disaster rehabilitation and mitigation efforts because of its ability to be rapidly acquired and tailored to specific requirements. The diverse resolutions of remote sensing data have both benefits and limitations in catastrophe mitigation. The article seeks to present the public with a comprehensive analysis of the advantages and disadvantages of using remote sensing data for disaster mitigation efforts. It also summarizes the results of studies that specifically investigated the use of data at various resolutions for emergency response activities during disasters.

***Keywords*:** Remote sensing, mitigation, disaster, emergency response, rehabilitation, resolution

2.1 Introduction

The frequency of natural disasters is increasing, and one of the negative aspects of these events is the loss of lives as well as material and immaterial

**Corresponding author*: moch053@brin.go.id; m.irwanhariyono@gmail.com
Mochamad Irwan Hariyono: ORCID: 0000-0002- 4003-1528
Aptu Andy Kurniawan: ORCID: 0000-0003-0996-7085

Neelam Dahiya, Gurwinder Singh, Sartajvir Singh and Apoorva Sharma (eds.) Artificial Intelligence in Remote Sensing for Disaster Management, (21–34) © 2025 Scrivener Publishing LLC

damages. One effort to reduce risks and facilitate disaster rehabilitation is the optimal utilization of remote sensing technology [1, 2]. Therefore, it is essential to conduct research and development on remote sensing data. Several remote sensing applications have been extensively developed, including analysis, disaster emergency response [3, 4], detection of disaster-induced damage [5], rehabilitation and reconstruction of disaster-related damage [6–8], and assessment of disaster hazards and risks [9, 10]. However, when utilizing remote sensing data, it is crucial to consider the strengths and weaknesses of the characteristics of the data being used.

A region may be prone to earthquakes and tsunamis if it is located near tectonic plate fault lines and the sea. However, that is not the only concern, as the area may also be vulnerable to land movements and landslides. Apparently, these disasters alone are not enough to cover all potential threats, as sometimes floods, volcanic eruptions, and droughts can also menace the same region. Reducing the risk of disasters through preparedness and early warning systems requires substantial resources. Among them is advanced technology to carry out these activities—for example, well-functioning earthquake and tsunami detection devices. However, this alone is not sufficient, as these devices must be connected to information dissemination mechanisms that function effectively so that the community can be informed early if there is a tsunami threat post-earthquake. Another example is the integration of technologies for high-water-level monitoring that can provide early warnings before floods occur.

The crucial aspect in utilizing remote sensing technology for disaster mitigation lies in the challenges arising from spatial and temporal resolution. Each type of resolution has its own advantages and disadvantages—for instance, satellite data with high temporal resolution (per hour) can provide rapidly changing information about weather conditions and smoke distribution every hour. However, this data tends to have low spatial resolution, making it unable to detect surface details effectively.

On the other hand, satellites with high spatial resolution can be used to identify damage caused by disasters, but they require more time in the temporal aspect, making rapid disaster damage mapping more challenging. To address these limitations, some countries have developed satellite constellation systems by combining multiple satellites for collaborative purposes. Consequently, quick data acquisition with high spatial resolution can be achieved.

In addition to spatial and temporal resolution aspects, another consideration that becomes more significant is the type of satellite sensor, whether optical or radar. The drawback of optical sensors lies in cloud interference, which is a major constraint in tropical regions like Indonesia. In some emergency response cases during the rainy season, optical data cannot be used to detect disaster-affected areas due to cloud coverage. As an alternative, the use of radar data becomes another option. However, currently, radar data tends to be relatively expensive, its availability is not as good as optical data, and the complexity of its processing makes its use less common. Some studies have successfully utilized radar data to detect disaster-induced damages [11]. While this writing does not delve into the weaknesses and limitations of each satellite, its focus is on providing insights into the utilization of remote sensing satellite data in disaster mitigation efforts. Explanations regarding errors and uncertainties in the use of remote sensing data will be elaborated upon, allowing readers to understand how to judiciously utilize available data for disaster mitigation purposes.

Importantly, "disaster" and "hazard" are not interchangeable. If a potentially dangerous occurrence, such an earthquake, happens in a region without any people living there, it is not considered a disaster. When such an occurrence occurs in populated regions and causes damage, loss, or devastation, it is classified as a disaster. While most of the world is vulnerable to natural catastrophes, some areas are more prone to particular kinds.

There are several ways by which disasters can be characterized [12]. Natural disasters, which include things like hurricanes, earthquakes, and volcanic eruptions, are those that have their origins in the natural world yet have the potential to harm human civilizations. Air pollution, industrial chemical accidents, big-armed wars, nuclear catastrophes, and oil spills are all examples of man-made disasters. On the other hand, human influence can speed up or worsen natural disasters, which are known as human-induced disasters.

This classification method, which incorporates intermediate groups, is used to categorize different disasters (Table 2.1). A landslip, for instance, might be considered entirely natural because it was brought about by things like earthquakes or severe rainfall. It could also be a result of human actions, like the over-steepening of highways.

This paper aims to demonstrate the potential utilization of various resolutions in remote sensing (multi-resolution) for disaster mitigation activities. This can be employed to ensure that the community is well informed about the proper use of remote sensing data by understanding the errors and uncertainties associated with the data used.

Table 2.1 Disaster classification in a gradual range from wholly natural to purely human-made (modified from Cees (2000)).

Natural	Mixed natural/ human influence	Some natural influence	By human
Seismic activity large ocean wave caused by an earthquake explosive release of molten rock and gas from a volcano, Blizzard/avalanche, glacial lake outburst, electric discharge in the atmosphere, typically occurring during thunderstorms, characterized by a bright flash of light and a loud sound. A windstorm is a weather phenomenon characterized by strong and gusty winds. A thunderstorm is a weather phenomenon characterized by the presence of thunder and lightning, often accompanied by heavy rain, strong winds, and sometimes hail. A hailstorm is a weather phenomenon characterized by the falling of ice pellets, known as hailstones, from the sky. A tornado is a violent and destructive weather phenomenon characterized by a rapidly rotating column of air that is in contact with both the surface of the Earth and a cumul. Tropical cyclone Collision with an asteroid The phenomenon known as the Aurora Borealis	Flooding, landslides, subsidence, erosion, desertification, coal fires, coastal erosion, weather conditions, greenhouse effect, sea level increase	Plant pathology, entomological infestation, wildfire, decline in mangrove ecosystems, decline of coral reefs, acid rain, ozone depletion	War, explosive devices buried in the ground, collision on the road, radiological/ hazardous materials incident, incidents resulting in unintended harm or damage, spillage of oil, environmental contamination caused by harmful substances or activities, contamination of underground water sources, electric power, chemical substances used to kill or control pests, such as insects, weeds, or fungi

2.2 Method

Literature review is the initial phase conducted to evaluate the extent to which remote sensing data has been utilized in disaster mitigation activities. Limitations of remote sensing data can be identified through a review of various applied applications. The next step involves evaluating models developed concerning the utilization of remote sensing data in disaster mitigation. This will provide insights into research and development experiences in the use of remote sensing for disaster mitigation. Limitations will also be revealed through the evaluation of experiences with developed models. In this paper, models such as fire hazard rating systems, daily flood potential models, hotspot monitoring models, drought potential models, and disaster quick response systems will be assessed.

The evaluation results will be categorized into subsections according to the types of disasters that commonly occur—for instance, in flood mitigation applications, the use of high temporal resolution remote sensing data can provide information on hourly rainfall potential but may not be sufficiently effective in detecting flood-affected areas due to its limited spatial resolution.

2.3 Disaster Management

One approach to addressing natural hazards is to disregard them. In numerous regions, both the populace and authorities opt not to consider the peril posed by natural hazards seriously, influenced by various factors. The most recent significant destructive event may have occurred a long time ago, remembered merely as a historical narrative. Individuals might have recently settled in the area, lacking awareness of potential hazards.

On the other hand, as a result of the many problems that individuals encounter on a daily basis, the danger posed by natural disasters may be underappreciated. Skeptical authorities may choose to ignore dangers rather than quietly allocate funding for catastrophe mitigation in the hopes of garnering more attention from voters in the aftermath of a calamity. An all-encompassing disaster management plan, the disaster management cycle (Figure 2.1), is necessary to successfully lessen the consequences of natural catastrophes.

Disaster management consists of five stages [13]: prevention, preparation, relief, rehabilitation, and reconstruction. The first two stages occur before a disaster occurs. Disaster management views events like these as

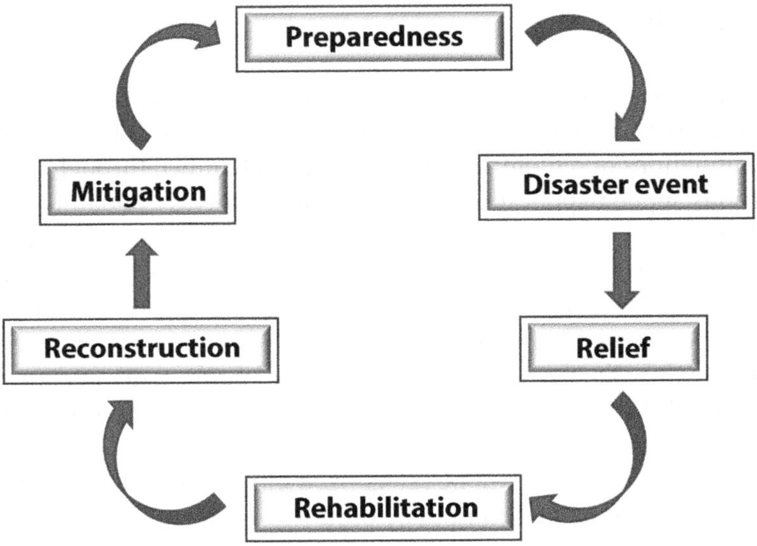

Figure 2.1 The disaster management cycle (modified from Cees (2000)).

part of a continuous cycle, where the results of one impact the way people and communities get ready for the next.

2.4 Result and Discussion

Various kinds of natural disasters can occur at any time, and the use of remote sensing data is to assist in disaster management efforts, namely, in mitigation and rehabilitation efforts. Disaster mitigation is carried out as an effort to minimize the risks, losses, and impacts caused by natural disasters or disasters caused by human activities. Rehabilitation efforts are carried out to restore physical, social, economic, and environmental conditions resulting from a disaster.

2.4.1 Floods

The use of remote sensing technology to comprehend floods has been widely conducted with various resolutions and types of satellites. Several activities, such as determining potential hazard and flood risk areas, identifying land changes that can lead to floods, detecting areas affected by floods, and modeling flood simulations, are frequently applied in flood mitigation efforts. Each stage in flood disaster management can leverage remote sensing data, including hazard and risk analysis before the disaster, early warning systems, and flood simulation models for disaster prevention. Additionally, during a disaster, the rapid detection of flooded or impacted areas can be achieved using specific methods. Post-disaster damage analysis is also another application that can utilize remote sensing data.

Stream floods, sudden floods, dam burst floods, and floods on the coast are distinct from one another in terms of when they occur, how big they are, how long they last, how fast they flow, and how much space they cover. Floods can be caused by a wide variety of things, including heavy and prolonged rainfall, snowmelt, deforestation, land-use patterns, riverbed sedimentation, and both natural and man-made impediments. Important factors to consider when calculating flood risk include flood depth, flood duration, flow velocity, rate of rise and fall, and frequency of occurrence.

During both the warning and response stages, as well as monitoring, Earth observation satellites are utilized extensively. Cloud cover is common during flood occurrences, which greatly limits the application of optical instruments for mapping floods. Because it can function in bad weather, Synthetic Aperture Radar (SAR) from satellites like RADARSAT and ERS has been very useful in mapping areas that have been inundated by floods. Since 1993, ERS-SAR and Radarsat have been utilized effectively for flood monitoring in India [14]. Removing speckles is a standardized approach that makes use of piecewise linear stretching and median filtering algorithms. Then, using both the flood data and the pre-flood SAR photos, color composites are made.

The current satellite systems face limitations in disaster relief operations, primarily attributed to their inadequate spatial resolution and challenges related to cloud cover. It is anticipated that the introduction of a series of high-resolution satellites will address these issues. To identify flood-affected areas, multi-resolution can be employed through various satellites such as MODIS, Landsat, IKONOS, QuickBird, and SAR data. The differences lie in spatial resolution and model accuracy. The accuracy of flood detection using MODIS tends to be lower compared to Landsat, IKONOS, or SAR. Although an accuracy of 60% in detecting inundated areas using MODIS data may be considered acceptable, it is preferably used for global estimates or as an initial step in the detection process. The advantage of MODIS data lies in its speed, enabling faster information delivery and making it more effective in emergency disaster response activities.

2.4.2 Earthquakes

The evaluation of faults responsible for seismic activities can be effectively conducted using remote sensing data of medium to high resolution. However, medium resolution is often deemed more efficient due to its wider coverage in a single capture compared to higher-resolution datasets. High-resolution imagery and Synthetic Aperture Radar (SAR) can be utilized to examine structural distortions caused by earthquakes. The impacted areas by seismic events are typically expansive, albeit confined to known regions such as plate boundaries. Earthquakes usually occur with recurrence intervals spanning from decades to centuries. Observable indicators associated with seismic activities encompass fault ruptures, structural damages resulting from ground vibrations, occurrences of liquefaction, landslides, conflagrations, and inundations. Principal determinants influencing the consequences of earthquakes encompass the proximity to active fault lines, geological formations, soil compositions, groundwater levels, terrain features, and the architectural design of infrastructures.

Seismic hazard zoning primarily relies on data obtained from seismic networks. Seismic microzonation, on the other hand, integrates information from accelerometers, geotechnical surveys, groundwater modeling, and large-scale topographic mapping. Although satellite remote sensing is not playing an important part in earthquake evacuation activities operations, it can contribute significantly during the disaster prevention phase. In this context, satellite remote sensing aids in mapping lineaments and faults, analyzing the tectonic characteristics of an area and conducting neotectonic investigations [15]. Typically, visible and infrared images having spatial resolutions that vary from 5 to 20 m are used for these objectives.

Satellite remote sensing has a limited role during the disaster response phase, especially in detecting significant features like landslides, which can be delineated using medium-detail imagery from platforms such as SPOT, IRS, etc. Nevertheless, the limited resolution of existing systems poses challenges in discerning structural damage to buildings. The introduction of the first commercial very high resolution (VHR) optical purpose, IKONOS-2, has enhanced the potential for assessing damage and pinpointing potential victims in near real-time. However, its effectiveness hinges on achieving sufficient temporal resolution, swath coverage, and convenient data accessibility.

2.4.3 Drought

The development of drought monitoring using remote sensing data has made significant progress. Various indices that can serve as indicators of drought, such as NDVI, SAVI, and VHI, have been developed to detect drought conditions in vegetation within a specific region. Additionally, monitoring land drought has been advanced by utilizing thermal data from satellites to calculate drought fractions through energy balance.

Remote sensing applications for drought monitoring typically rely on low- to medium-resolution data and are monitoring-oriented. Data from sources like NOAA AVHRR, Terra/Aqua MODIS, and MTSAT have proven effective in drought monitoring due to their high temporal resolution. Drought conditions usually cover extensive areas due to their correlation with the climatology of a region. Drought monitoring at the national or regional district scale has been conducted using remote sensing satellite data. However, the results of this monitoring may be influenced by errors and uncertainties originating from the models or methods used as well as the spatial resolution of satellite images.

Several models have been developed, including models for monitoring drought in paddy fields, the standardized precipitation index (SPI), and the vegetation health index (VHI). These models are used to assess drought levels in a region using low-resolution satellite data. Therefore, errors and uncertainties in drought monitoring are significantly influenced by spatial resolution, in addition to the models used. Specifically, for monitoring drought in paddy fields, errors and uncertainties are also highly influenced by the thematic maps of the paddy fields used.

2.4.4 Landslides

Even though particular landslides tend to be rather modest, they occur regularly, especially in mountainous areas. Depending on the material (rock, debris, soil), the speed (millimeters per year to meters per second), the type of movement (sliding, overturning, flowing, falling, spreading), and the triggering mechanism (earthquake, rainfall, human activity), landslides can take on various forms. During the mitigation phase, satellite imagery is primarily used for two purposes: first, to keep track of the number of landslides and, second, to create maps of the lithology, geomorphology, faults, land use, vegetation, and slope that are known to be linked with the occurrence of landslides.

The ratio of landslide feature size to surface quality of satellite imagery data is a significant aspect to consider when creating landslide inventory maps. Measurements of 20 × 20 pixels on a SPOT panoramic image and 10 × 10 pixels on SPOT multispectral images represent a normal 40,000-m^2 landslide, for instance. For a comprehensive examination of the factors linked to failure and the identification of landslide types and characteristics, this may be adequate, but it is inadequate when the landslide is highly contrasted with its environment, like exposed slopes in forested areas.

To build a generic inventory of previous landslides, images with enough spatial resolution and stereo capabilities, as those from SPOT or IRS, can be utilized. However, it is not uncommon for them to miss important details that are needed to accurately map all landslides. In this case, aerial photo interpretation is still crucial.

The ideal scale for interpreting landslides from aerial photos is somewhere between 1:15,000 and 1:25,000 [16]. Landslide detection may be feasible with appropriate great size and contrast when using smaller scales. Eventually, landslide inventory could be a viable use of VHR photography, like that from IKONOS-2.

Obtaining data on important characteristics including soils, geology, slope, geomorphology, land use, hydrology, precipitation, and faults is made much easier with satellite images. Classification of land uses, vegetation, and lithology are all areas that benefit from multispectral photography. Stereo SPOT imagery is employed for the purposes of geomorphological mapping and terrain classification [17]. Various InSAR methods, including those used in the air or space, can be used to create digital elevation models. These methods include SPOT and IRS imaging.

Measurements taken on the ground, photogrammetry, global positioning systems, and radar interferometry are just a few of the tools available to disaster preparedness teams for tracking the progress of landslides. Only in areas with a lot of data is there a landslide warning system in place (for example, knowing when landslides have occurred and how much rain has fallen each day is crucial for setting appropriate safety zones) [18]. Predicting these thresholds using Metaset and NOAA data combined with rain gauge data is presently under investigation.

2.4.5 Land/Forest Fire

Significant growth has occurred in the application of remote sensing for monitoring land/forest fires, especially in contexts not related to drought. Hotspot monitoring activities and the identification of areas affected by fires have become common practices in various countries, including Indonesia.

Hotspot monitoring utilizes low-spatial-resolution data (approximately 1 km^2), but with high temporal resolution. Satellite data with low temporal resolution cannot effectively monitor hotspots, as land fires may conclude within a specific time frame.

Visual analysis of smoke distribution due to fires can be generated using high resolution. Errors and uncertainties in hotspot monitoring are influenced by the model or method used, geometric correction, and spatial resolution. The coordinates of hotspots may have errors of around 1–3 km from their actual locations. Additionally, heat sources other than land fires can be detected as hotspots, posing a potential source of error in hotspot monitoring.

High-resolution data can be used to detect areas affected by past fires. Several studies have utilized data from Terra/Aqua MODIS, Landsat TM/ETM, and SPOT 4/5/6 for this purpose. Errors that may occur depend on the spatial resolution and the method used. Nevertheless, MODIS data has the advantage of high temporal resolution and broad coverage, making it the most suitable choice for global monitoring. An accuracy of 60% in detecting areas affected by fires with MODIS is considered adequate for rapid mapping of fire-affected areas.

2.4.6 Volcanic Eruption

High-spatial-resolution data and digital elevation models (DEMs) are more commonly utilized for applications in volcanic areas, such as determining hazard zones, conducting volcanic risk analysis, and assessing areas affected by volcanic eruptions. Low-spatial-resolution data is less effective in monitoring volcanoes. Some literature also highlight the potential for monitoring volcanic temperatures using high-temporal-resolution thermal channels. However, operationalizing this remains challenging due to its low spatial resolution, causing the summit temperature to blend with its surrounding environment. Additionally, monitoring the temperature of a volcano's summit can be difficult when the peak is consistently covered by clouds.

In order to map the location and types of deposits from volcanic, Earth observation satellites are important throughout the hazard preventive phase. Additional data including morphological examination, tephra timeline, and lithological content are necessary for a thorough understanding of volcanic activity. Fumarolic action, earthquake vibrations, and deformation of the surface (bulging) are often audible precursors to volcanic eruptions, which can happen between minutes to hours.

Standard analysis of stereo aerial images remains the go-to method for (detailed to semi-detailed) modeling of volcanoes and landforms. In addition to clearly showing the various materials and geomorphological features of volcanic topography, stereo imagery is useful for illustrating the possible routes of various flow patterns.

One very helpful application of remote sensing is the capacity to differentiate between vegetated and fresh rock surfaces using visible and infrared radiation. Vegetation quickly covers most regions, with the exception of those impacted by volcanic activity or other disturbances (urban growth, etc.); therefore, this distinction is useful. Predicting when volcanoes will erupt relies heavily on topographic measures, particularly those that show changes in topography. Using SAR or synthetic aperture radar, sensors are enabled.

Multiple sensors, including TOMS (Kruger *et al.*, 1994) [19], AVHRR (infrared), comprehensive sensors on meteorological satellites, microwave or radar, and sensors that detect gas absorption within the cloud, can be used to identify volcanic clouds. A system of volcanic ash advisory centers (VAACs) and meteorological watch offices (MWOs) has evolved to identify and track the airborne by-products of explosive volcanic eruptions, and remote sensing has become an essential component of this system. The present coverage, height, velocity, and mass of ash clouds can be greatly improved with the use of satellite data.

2.5 Conclusion

The findings of this study suggest that remote sensing satellite data can be customized to meet specific requirements in disaster mitigation. If the main focus is on quickly obtaining information, then it is possible to accept a lower level of precision by utilizing data with a high temporal resolution. However, this knowledge continues to be significant for practical purposes and global planning. High-resolution data has demonstrated significant use in identifying structural damage to buildings and dwellings as well as assessing the impact on important land resources such as farms, ponds, plantations, and forests. While it may be tolerable to have a longer acquisition time, the primary focus is on attaining a greater level of information precision. Acquiring photographs without clouds for the purpose of assessing damage is a significant obstacle in numerous weather-related disasters. Synthetic Aperture Radar (SAR) proves to be a practical solution in scenarios such as floods, debris flows, or oil spills. However, when it comes to disasters such as landslides, earthquakes, and wildfires, precise optical images are generally more appropriate. Satellite remote sensing can assist in identifying large impacted areas during the disaster response phase. In order for this upgrade to be successful, it is necessary to have adequate time resolution, swath coverage, and data accessibility. Consequently, efforts to enhance technology and research on remote sensing persist.

References

1. Khan, A., Gupta, S., Gupta, S.K., Multi-hazard disaster studies: Monitoring, detection, recovery, and management, based on emerging technologies and optimal techniques. *Int. J. Disaster Risk Reduct.*, 47, 101642, Aug. 2020, doi: 10.1016/j.ijdrr.2020.101642.
2. Kucharczyk, M. and Hugenholtz, C.H., Remote sensing of natural hazard-related disasters with small drones: Global trends, biases, and research opportunities. *Remote Sens. Environ.*, 264, 112577, Oct. 2021, doi: 10.1016/j.rse.2021.112577.
3. Hoque, M.A.-A., Phinn, S., Roelfsema, C., A systematic review of tropical cyclone disaster management research using remote sensing and spatial analysis. *Ocean Coastal Manage.*, 146, 109–120, Sep. 2017, doi: 10.1016/j.ocecoaman.2017.07.001.
4. Joyce, K.E., Wright, K.C., Samsonov, S.V., Ambrosia, V.G., Remote sensing and the disaster management cycle, in: *Advances in Geoscience and Remote Sensing*, 2009.
5. Foulser-Piggott, R., Spence, R., Saito, K., Brown, D.M., Eguchi, R., The use of remote sensing for post-earthquake damage assessment: lessons from recent events, and future prospects, in: *15 WCEE, Lisboa*, 2012.
6. Luo, Z., Yang, J., Huang, B., Chen, W., Gao, Y., Meng, Q., Reconstruction and Visualization of Landslide Events Based on Pre- and Post-Disaster Remote Sensing Data. *Water*, 15, 11, 2023, May 2023, doi: 10.3390/w15112023.
7. Asăndulesei, A., Tencariu, F.A., Nicu, I.C., Pars pro toto—Remote Sensing Data for the Reconstruction of a Rounded Chalcolithic Site from NE Romania: The Case of Ripiceni–Holm Settlement (Cucuteni Culture). *Remote Sens.*, 12, 5, 887, Mar. 2020, doi: 10.3390/rs12050887.
8. Brown, D., *et al.*, Indicators for Measuring, Monitoring and Evaluating Post-Disaster Recovery, in: *6th International Workshop on Remote Sensing for Disaster Applications*, Sep. 2008.
9. Sousa, J.J., *et al.*, Geohazards Monitoring and Assessment Using Multi-Source Earth Observation Techniques. *Remote Sens.*, 13, 21, 4269, Oct. 2021, doi: 10.3390/rs13214269.
10. Samarasinghe, S.M.J.S., Weliwitiya, D.P., Nandalal, H.K., Fowze, J.S.M., Hazarika, M.K., Samarakoon, L., Application of Remote Sensing and GIS For Flood Risk Analysis: A Case Study at Kalu- Ganga River, Sri Lanka,

in: *International Archives of the Photogrammetry, Remote Sensing and Spatial Information Science*, Kyoto Japan, vol. XXXVIII, Part 8, 2010.
11. Brunner, D., Lemoine, G., Bruzzone, L., Earthquake Damage Assessment of Buildings Using VHR Optical and SAR Imagery. *IEEE Trans. Geosci. Remote Sens.*, 48, 5, 2403–2420, May 2010.
12. Van Westen, C.J., Remote Sensing For Natural Disaster Management. *Int. Arch. Photogramm. Remote Sens., XXXIII*, 259–298, Part B7. Amsterdam, 2000.
13. United Nations Disaster Relief Office (UNDRO), *Mitigating Natural Disasters: Phenomena, Effects and Options*, p. 164, United Nations Disaster Relief Co-ordinator, United Nations, New York, 1991.
14. Chakraborti, A.K., Satellite remote sensing for near-real-time flood and drought impact assessment-Indian experience, in: *Workshop on Natural Disasters and their Mitigation - A Remote Sensing & GIS perspective*, Dehradun, India, Oct. 1999.
15. Milovsky, G.A. and Belyakov, A.A., Applying Remote Sensing to the Detection of Tectonic Structures and Localization of Ore Deposits within Biryusa and Krepskii-Tumanshet Ore Clusters (Eastern Sayan). *Izv. Atmos. Ocean. Phys.*, 55, 9, 1362–1371, Dec. 2019, doi: 10.1134/S0001433819090275.
16. Wróbel, M., *et al.*, Integrated Geophysical Imaging and Remote Sensing for Enhancing Geological Interpretation of Landslides with Uncertainty Estimation—A Case Study from Cisiec, Poland. *Remote Sens.*, 15, 1, 238, Dec. 2022, doi: 10.3390/rs15010238.
17. Kassouk, Z., Thouret, J.-C., Gupta, A., Solikhin, A., Liew, S.C., Object-oriented classification of a high-spatial resolution SPOT5 image for mapping geology and landforms of active volcanoes: Semeru case study, Indonesia. *Geomorphology*, 221, 18–33, Sep. 2014, doi: 10.1016/j.geomorph.2014.04.022.
18. Liao, Z., *et al.*, Prototyping an experimental early warning system for rainfall-induced landslides in Indonesia using satellite remote sensing and geo-spatial datasets. *Landslides*, 7, 3, 317–324, Sep. 2010, doi: 10.1007/s10346-010-0219-7.
19. Kruger, F.J., *et al.*, The Sr-isotopic stratigraphy of the western Bushveld Complex. *S. Afr. J. Geol.*, 97, 4, 393–398, 1994.

3

Fundamentals of Disaster Management Using Remote Sensing

Garima[1]* and Narayan Vyas[2]

[1]*Department of Computer Science and Engineering, Vivekananda Global University, Jaipur, India*
[2]*Department of Computer Science and Application, Vivekananda Global University, Jaipur, India*

Abstract
Natural disasters are extreme events within the Earth's ecosystem, causing loss of life and damage to infrastructure. These calamities pose a serious threat to humankind, flora, and fauna worldwide. Therefore, it is necessary to mitigate and brainstorm strategies to minimize its impact effectively. This chapter navigates through the potential of remote sensing in the domain of disaster management and recovery. Utilizing various available techniques in remote sensing along with its collaboration with advanced data analytics and geographic information system (GIS), a holistic solution can be offered for damage assessment, rescue proposals, and sustainable rehabilitation for the victim area. By analyzing the scope of visualization for better grasping of the landscape shift before and after the calamity struck, different feature considerations can give details for the rescue planning and aid the segregation needed in a particular region.

Keywords: Remote sensing, disaster management, emergency response, disaster rehabilitation

3.1 Introduction

The introduction of remote sensing has turned over a new leaf in the realm of observing and investigating Earth's topography. Leveraging satellites,

**Corresponding author*: garimalakhera04@gmail.com; ORCID: 0009-0001-4970-8638
Narayan Vyas: ORCID: 0000-0003-4225-0764

Neelam Dahiya, Gurwinder Singh, Sartajvir Singh and Apoorva Sharma (eds.) Artificial Intelligence in Remote Sensing for Disaster Management, (35–58) © 2025 Scrivener Publishing LLC

drones, and aircraft with a varied range of sensors, remote sensing collects ample data across varied scales and parameters. Thus, it enhances our comprehension of a wide range of subjects, including plants, building constructions, landforms, and the atmosphere. The ability to measure electromagnetic radiation emitted or reflected by objects on the surface of the Earth is the building block of remote sensing. The detection of natural radiation by passive sensors like optical and infrared sensors reveals information about surface temperatures, vegetation health, and urban development. High-resolution data that can penetrate clouds and darkness and measure surface elevations and structures are provided by active sensors, such as radar and lidar systems, which emit their signals and measure the echoes that are returned [1].

Remote sensing can be utilized across diverse fields due to its critical insights such as environmental monitoring, disaster management, urban planning, and agriculture. It draws the opportunities for the ongoing perception of normal disasters and permits brief reactions and help support. Agriculture benefits greatly from remote sensing's topographic insights and abundance of data. It gives you all the tools you need to do precision farming, increase yield, and be sustainable. Urban planners use remote sensing to evaluate changes in land use and infrastructure development to make better decisions.

Advanced data analytics and the integration of data from remote sensing with GIS have further expanded their applications, making it possible to perform sophisticated modeling and forecasting. Remote sensing has become an essential tool for addressing global issues like climate change and resource management as technology continues to advance. This will ultimately lead to more informed and efficient decision-making processes.

3.2 Importance of Remote Sensing in Disaster Management

Disaster mitigation institutes work closely with the space technology in developing effective solution for catastrophe management and prevention. Disaster prevention is a long-term goal, which can only be accomplished by rigorous and established study of earth landscape and satellite monitoring for relevant feature changes. The following section talks about how remote sensing improvises and aids the disaster management and help moving on to steps like rehabilitation and to minimize reoccurrence of the event [2].

3.2.1 Role in Emergency Response

The efficiency of disaster management operations has drastically improved due to remote sensing technologies. The potential of remote sensing to offer accurate and immediate information on the extent and impact of a disaster allows for a more informed and coordinated response.

1. Damage assessment
Damage assessment is an integral application of remote sensing in terms of emergency response. Aerial and satellite imagery helps the identification of regions that are being struck by calamities, the high-resolution images from satellites give extensive insight into land deformation, infrastructure disruption, or vegetation erosion. All of these can be taken into consideration to draw an analysis between the pre-and post-disaster images and thereby draw a conclusion on the severity of the situation at hand and release the relief efforts.

2. Prioritizing relief efforts
Once there is a clear picture of the damage that has struck, it is, in turn, to move on to the next step of relief operations. At the damage assessment stage, we have the data that provides insights on the level of damage encountered, thus taking into consideration the rest of the social and economic parameters such as population density, food availability, and medical supplies through a spatial region, a dedicated response and rescue operation shall be designed. The figures aid the operational effectiveness and logistical planning.

3. Coordinating rescue operations
During such calamities, the communication infrastructure fails as soon as the disaster hits remote sensing brings in real-time support with UAVs that offer live feeds from the disaster-stricken area. These instruments can be utilized to keep track of the resources deployed for relief and maintain cohesive communication among the various response teams. Geographic Information System offers the flexibility to track in real time and thereby monitor and manage the evacuation routes and assess conditions.

4. Monitoring hazard spread

During calamities that bear a dynamic behavior, for instance, wildfires, floods, etc., remote sensing provides a bright outlook in keeping the dynamic nature in check. Satellites and aerial images deliver continuous updates regarding the reach and intensity of the damages. In the case of flood-struck areas, remote sensing helps keep a record of the extent of floodwater invasion and potential movement prediction. In the case of forest fires, keeping a check on the speed of expansion and perimeter and thereby predicting regions with the most risk is likewise essential for timely evacuation and issuing warnings [3].

3.2.2 Impact on Disaster Rehabilitation

After the immediate response phase: Remote sensing plays a vital role in the rehabilitation stage by providing distinctive details regarding the post-disaster scenario and spatial dynamics which can be further utilized for effective rehabilitation and lasting resilience building.

Monitoring and assessing damage: Remote sensing can be employed to deal with the consequences of calamities by keeping a check on changes in land cover. Remote sensing plays a vital role in keeping an eye on the topography changes that arise after a disaster. These can be judged by monitoring deforestation land, eroded soil, and modified water bodies. Apart from the vegetation damage, remote sensing works fine for the urban areas as well and gives information regarding the infrastructural damage that has happened—for instance, the collapsed buildings, bridges, and deformed roads.

Mitigating future risks and re-establishing: Remote sensing can be employed to generate a hazard pattern by analyzing historical events or previous images over a period of time. Besides the visual analysis, figures from auxiliary parameters that are responsible for calamities to occur can be kept in check as well. These secondary parameters include the stability of land, moisture content, and soil health. Therefore, the data obtained can facilitate a strategic outcome for reconstruction. and long-term community resilience. Some common taxonomies used in remote sensing are mentioned in Table 3.1.

3.2.3 Remote Sensing Taxonomy

Table 3.1 Remote sensing taxonomy.

Taxonomy criteria	Category	Description
Data acquisition	Passive	Sensors detect natural radiation emitted or reflected from the Earth's surface (e.g., optical, infrared, microwave)
	Active	Sensors emit energy and measure the returned signal (e.g., radar, lidar)
Platform	Satellite	Sensors are mounted on artificial satellites orbiting the Earth
	Aerial	Sensors are mounted on aircraft or drones
	Ground-based	Sensors are located on the Earth's surface (e.g., terrestrial lidar)
Spatial resolution	High	Detailed images with fine spatial resolution (e.g., aerial photography)
	Medium	Moderate level of detail (e.g., Landsat)
	Low	Broad overview with coarse spatial resolution (e.g., MODIS)
Spectral resolution	Multispectral	Images captured in multiple spectral bands (e.g., visible, near-infrared, shortwave infrared)
	Hyperspectral	Images captured in hundreds of narrow spectral bands

(*Continued*)

Table 3.1 Remote sensing taxonomy. (*Continued*)

Taxonomy criteria	Category	Description
Temporal resolution	High	Frequent data acquisition (e.g., weather satellites)
	Medium	Moderate revisit time (e.g., Landsat)
	Low	Infrequent data acquisition (e.g., some radar satellites)
Application	Land cover/land use	Mapping and monitoring land cover types (e.g., forests, agriculture, urban areas)
	Atmosphere	Studying atmospheric conditions (e.g., temperature, humidity, pollution)
	Ocean/coastal	Monitoring ocean dynamics, coastal processes, and marine resources
	Disaster management	Assessing damage, monitoring relief efforts, and supporting recovery
	Agriculture	Monitoring crop growth, yield estimation, and disaster assessment

3.3 Remote Sensing Applications in Emergency Response

3.3.1 Damage Assessment

Remote sensing plays a critical role in emergency response by providing timely and accurate information for assessing damage, coordinating relief efforts, and supporting decision-making processes. This section explores the application of remote sensing in damage assessment, focusing on the techniques and methods used as well as case studies and examples that illustrate its effectiveness.

3.3.1.1 *Techniques and Methods*

To measure the severity of the damage caused by calamities, remote sensing offers a large variety of techniques that can be utilized to facilitate a comprehensive damage assessment in real-time.

1. Optical and Multispectral Imaging
Both optical and multispectral sensors work on different wavelength bands such as visible and infrared light to capture images. These images can be brought into use to identify overall damage to infrastructure, vegetation, and topography. Each sensor produces an image that can be utilized to dig out a detailed analysis for a particular aspect. For example, optical images can be used to draw a comparison between pre-disaster images and post-disaster images, whereas multispectral data uses spectral signatures to draw differential conclusions between damaged and undamaged areas. Thus, with such imaging, it gets easier to identify the areas that are severely struck with the disaster concerning the significant changes that are being observed by the images [4].

2. Synthetic Aperture Radar (SAR)
For natural hazards like earthquakes and landslides, SAR seems to be an optimal technique. SAR systems work on the principle of measurement of backscattered signals [5]. These systems emit microwave pulses and the received signals are then used to create high-resolution images of the land masses. These systems are efficient irrespective of weather constraints and light availability. InSAR or interferometric SAR gives precise results for land mass deformation. Thus, it can be utilized to investigate urban destruction post-disaster.

3. Lidar (Light Detection and Ranging)
Unlike SAR, Lidar offers 3D models as output. Lidar works with laser pulses and overworks on elevation detection. Thus, any difference in the elevation or infrastructural damage can be easily pointed out using these techniques. Lidar also concludes the damages that occurred due to natural calamities by making a pre-disaster and post-disaster comparison of elevation data of the topography.

4. Thermal Infrared Imaging
In case of calamities like wildfires, thermal infrared sensors are utilized. These sensors detect emitted heat and other thermal entities. Therefore, these can be a useful asset to detect potential wildfire and hotspot identification in a disaster-stricken area. This technique is used to facilitate the monitoring of any potential or otherwise heat-related calamities.

3.3.1.2 Integration with Other Data Sources

Remote sensing alone does accumulate a lot of data but that stand-alone does not bring the solution to the actual problems that are encountered once a natural calamity hits. Thus, utilizing this data with a combination of socio-economical figures and front-line observation can give a comprehensive understanding of the problem at hand and potential solution as per requirement.

Combination with ground-based observations: Backing up the data from the remote sensing devices with ground-level observations can give a holistic picture of the crisis at hand. The field survey reports along with the remote sensing data deliver a deeper study of the issues that localities are facing and the support community needs.

Integration with social and economic data: Utilizing the remote sensing data along with the socioeconomic parameters helps a better insight into the needs and grants of the people in the region. Taking demographic factors into consideration, namely, the economic background, population density, social vulnerabilities, and funds, a better judgment is to prioritize areas with relief support. For example, any area with high population density and low socioeconomic status needs to be considered on priority for aid.

Collaboration with health and emergency services data: Integration of health and emergency services along with remote sensing data is a major requirement as it helps to keep a check on the potential disease outbreak that might happen based on geographical and other environmental criteria. Another reason is to know how well equipped the medical backup available in the area, whether or not it can accommodate a calamity for initial response at least. This collaboration can also help in making decisions to regulate emergency services for medical interventions [6].

Use of Geospatial Information Systems (GIS): Data can be insightful and can be brought into use for a better analysis of the issues, but having a tool that can offer a visualization for the data along with the other information that can be put to use is a plus. GIS possesses the capability to integrate the data mentioned in the previous sections and deliver detailed maps as per requirement. It provides the user with an extensive spatial distribution for the requirements and resource deployment for the given area.

3.3.1.3 *Feature Extraction from Pre- and Post-Disaster Imagery*

India, in terms of geographical landscape, has it all, from high-ranging mountains to a large number of rivers, foothills, plains, and plateaus, thus making it susceptible to diverse catastrophic events. The diversity of topography includes Himalayan mountains in the north, which are prone to hazards like landslides and earthquakes, while the plains consist of vast spread river basins which hold the potential of devastating floods. While these subside, being a peninsula country, its coastlines are always vulnerable to cyclones and tsunamis.

This section consists of a visual walkthrough of various tragedies over the last decade in India and how remote sensing has been utilized to study the topographical shift.

1. Lakhimpur Assam Flood
   Assam is one of the few states in India to receive the highest rainfall. Lakhimpur, a district in Assam, is prone to flood every time the rainfall record is high. Sentinel-1 images are utilized to grasp an idea regarding the changes in the Earth's topography before and later after the flood hit the Lakhimpur district of Assam, India. Due to the heavy rainfall and high cloud cover in the area, it is difficult to utilize Sentinel-2 to fetch the image and study the region [7]. Below are the images from the pre-flood image covered on April 26, 2022, while the during/post-flood image spanned

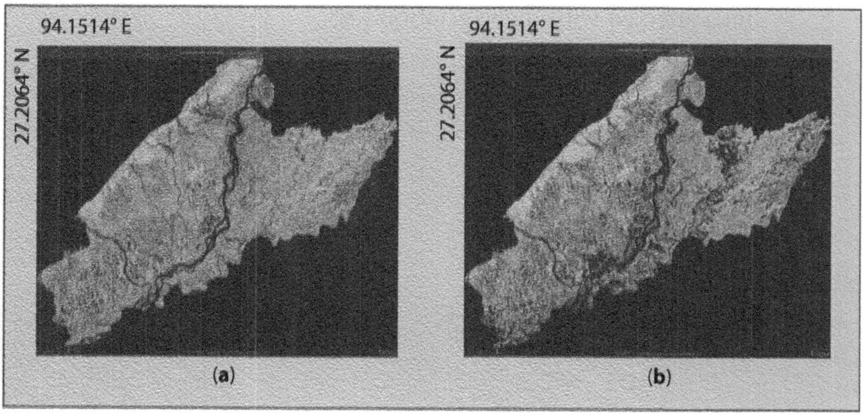

Figure 3.1 Comparison of satellite imagery: (a) Sentinel-1 imagery of Lakhimpur, India (VV+VH Polarization) on April 25 before the flood hit and (b) Sentinel-1 imagery of Lakhimpur, India (VV+VH Polarization) on May 20 after the flood hit.

May 26, 2022, to compare and grasp the surface level changes. The satellite imagery of Lakhimpur district is close to a month apart. Images are derived from Sentinel-1 utilizing dual vertical polarization and RGB ratio. Within the image, the yellow color depicts the urban land, while blue depicts the water; turquoise, on the other hand, shows the vegetation. Comparing the two images, as depicted in Figure 3.1, it is evident that inbound flood coverage has been huge.

2. Fani Cyclone Puri Odisha
   Cyclone Fani 2019 was the most destructive cyclone to hit Odisha since 1999, classified as an extremely severe cyclonic storm (ESCS) that emerged in the Bay of Bengal with its speed ranging between 185 to 215 km/h. Fani led to a significant loss of agriculture and infrastructure. Below are the images taken via Sentinel-2-2 NDVI layer to visualize the significant eradication of vegetation from the regions closer to the coastline [8]. The satellite imagery for Puri district is taken 2 weeks apart. Images are derived from Sentinel-2 utilizing the NDVI (Normalized Difference Vegetation Index) band combination to identify loss to vegetation that occurred due to cyclone Fani. The greener areas depict the vegetation while the white regions depict the barren areas or the areas with no vegetation. Comparing the two images the conclusion can be drawn that cyclone Fani drastically affected the vegetation cover in the Puri district, as shown in Figure 3.2. Majority of the land closer to the coastline have been affected with the vegetation loss.

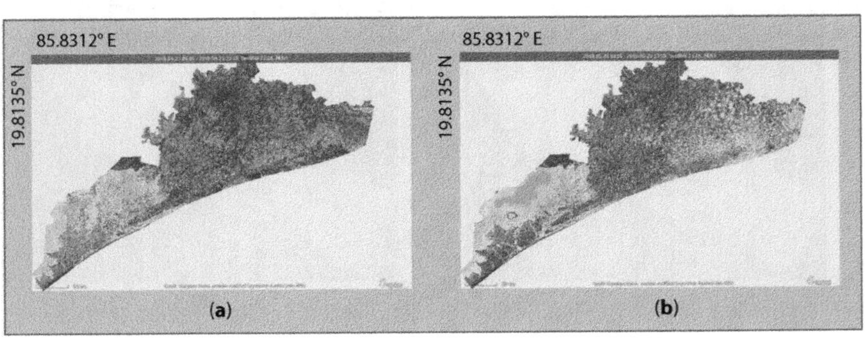

Figure 3.2 Comparison of satellite imagery: (a) Sentinel-2 imagery of Puri, India (NDVI band combination) before the cyclone hit and (b) Sentinel-2 imagery of Puri, India (NDVI band combination) after the cyclone hit.

3.4 Acquisition of Disaster Features

3.4.1 Acquisition of Tsunami Features with Remote Sensing

A tsunami is a large series of waves that are caused because of underwater disturbances. These disturbances may be due to volcanic eruptions, underwater landslides, or meteorites crashing the ocean surface. Since the trigger events occur underwater, the acquisition of tsunami gets tricky. Thus, with the penetration on land, its characteristics significantly change from that of a water wave to a strong inundation flow [9]. Remote sensing allows for the measurement of several key parameters that are useful in characterizing the overland flow of a tsunami. The latter include tsunami inundation extent, which indicates how far the wave travels inland, and flow velocities. Aerial videos can help understand how the tsunami moves and spreads inland.

The Sentinel Asia initiative in the Asia-Pacific region, the UN-SPIDER, the Copernicus Emergency Management Service—European Commission, and other emergency operational frameworks still use this method to rapidly map out areas following a variety of disasters, including meteorological hazards, geophysical hazards, intentional and unintentional man-made disasters, etc. Aerial pictures and optical satellite images are crucial instruments in tsunami damage estimates. These photos are used to extract inundation zones and categorize locations damaged by tsunamis. More specifically, optical satellite photos enable detailed spatial resolution to precisely designate impacted places, while aerial shots offer a wide viewpoint that facilitates the assessment of the overall influence on the environment.

Similarly, visual interpretation is used to evaluate and categorize building damage using high-resolution optical pictures taken both before and after the tsunami occurrence. By methodically comparing pre- and post-event pictures, structural damage may be identified, allowing for a thorough assessment of the disaster's effects on built environments. This method is essential for creating efficient plans for disaster response and recovery, as well as for supplying information for damage estimation and resource distribution.

Table 3.2 provides the summarized details regarding different platforms and sensors that are utilized to collect information across multiple features of tsunami.

Table 3.2 Acquisition of tsunami features with remote sensing platforms.

Feature	Remote sensing platform	Sensor type	Description
Wave height measurement	Satellites, buoys	Radar altimeters, optical	Measures the height of tsunami waves using radar altimeters on satellites and buoys, providing real-time data on wave amplitude and propagation
Wave speed and direction	Satellites, buoys	Radar altimeters, optical	Tracks the speed and direction of tsunami waves to predict their arrival times and impact locations using data from radar altimeters and optical sensors
Coastal inundation	Satellites, UAVs, aircraft	Optical, LiDAR	Maps areas inundated by tsunami waves using high-resolution optical imagery and LiDAR data to assess the extent and impact of flooding
Sediment transport	Satellites, UAVs, aircraft	Multi-spectral, LiDAR	Monitors the movement and deposition of sediments carried by tsunami waves using multi-spectral imagery and LiDAR to study changes in coastal and seabed morphology
Damage assessment	Satellites, UAVs, aircraft	Optical, thermal infrared	Evaluates structural damage in coastal areas using high-resolution optical imagery and thermal infrared sensors to detect heat anomalies related to fires or other impacts

(*Continued*)

Table 3.2 Acquisition of tsunami features with remote sensing platforms. (*Continued*)

Feature	Remote sensing platform	Sensor type	Description
Water quality changes	Satellites, UAVs	Multi-spectral, thermal infrared	Detects changes in water quality such as turbidity and temperature anomalies caused by tsunami waves using multi-spectral and thermal infrared sensors
Vegetation damage	Satellites, UAVs, aircraft	Optical, multi-spectral	Assesses damage to coastal vegetation and habitats using high-resolution optical and multi-spectral imagery to detect changes in vegetation cover and health
Post-tsunami recovery	Satellites, UAVs, aircraft	Optical, LiDAR	Monitors the recovery and rebuilding process in affected areas using optical and LiDAR data to track changes in infrastructure and natural landscapes over time
Wave propagation modeling	Satellites, buoys	Radar altimeters, optical	Provides data for modeling the propagation of tsunami waves across the ocean using radar altimeter measurements and optical imagery to improve prediction models
Coastal erosion	Satellites, UAVs, aircraft	Optical, LiDAR	Observes changes in coastal erosion and morphology caused by tsunami waves using high-resolution optical imagery and LiDAR data

3.4.2 Acquisition of Earthquake Features with Remote Sensing

Table 3.3 provides the summarized details regarding different platforms and sensors that are utilized to collect information across multiple features of earthquake.

Table 3.3 Acquisition of earthquake features with remote sensing platforms.

Feature	Remote sensing platform	Sensor type	Description
Surface deformation	Satellites, UAVs, aircraft	Synthetic Aperture Radar (SAR), optical, LiDAR	Measures the deformation and movement of the ground before, during, and following an earthquake. With the use of methods like SAR, it offers comprehensive deformation maps.
Fault rupture mapping	Satellites, UAVs, aircraft	Optical, LiDAR	Locates and charts the surface fissures and fault lines brought on by earthquakes. To identify changes in the terrain, LiDAR data and high-resolution optical pictures are employed.
Ground shaking intensity	Satellites, seismic networks	Optical, seismometers	Evaluate the strength of ground trembling by comparing damage patterns with shaking intensity using picture analysis and data from seismometers

(*Continued*)

Table 3.3 Acquisition of earthquake features with remote sensing platforms. (*Continued*)

Feature	Remote sensing platform	Sensor type	Description
Building damage assessment	Satellites, UAVs, aircraft	Optical, thermal infrared	Uses thermal infrared sensors and high-resolution optical imaging to assess structure damage in metropolitan areas and identify heat anomalies caused by fires or other effects
Landslides and rockfalls	Satellites, UAVs, aircraft	Optical, LiDAR	Uses optical imaging and LiDAR data to identify changes in topography and land cover that result from earthquakes, which cause landslides and rockfalls
Liquefaction mapping	Satellites, UAVs	Optical, multi-spectral	Uses optical and multispectral data to analyze changes in plant patterns and land surface to identify regions of soil liquefaction
Groundwater changes	Satellites, UAVs	SAR, optical, thermal infrared	Uses optical and thermal sensors to identify anomalies in moisture and temperature and SAR to detect subsidence and to monitor variations in surface moisture and groundwater levels

(*Continued*)

Table 3.3 Acquisition of earthquake features with remote sensing platforms. (*Continued*)

Feature	Remote sensing platform	Sensor type	Description
Crustal movement	Satellites	GPS, InSAR	Uses GPS units and Interferometric Synthetic Aperture Radar (InSAR) to measure strain build-up and release as it tracks both horizontal and vertical crustal motions
Tsunami detection	Satellites, buoys	Radar altimeters, optical	Uses optical sensors for visual confirmation and radar altimeters aboard satellites to measure sea surface height to detect and track tsunamis caused by undersea earthquakes
Coastal changes	Satellites, UAVs, aircraft	Optical, LiDAR	Observes how seismic activity affects the topography and erosion of the shore by employing LiDAR and high-resolution optical imaging

3.4.3 Acquisition of Wildfire Features with Remote Sensing

Wildfire hazards are a combination of multiple subtopics, namely, weather, fuel, and human factors. Thus, detection and prediction for wildfires are relatively tricky and multivariate. In this assistance, remote sensing has majorly contributed to the characterization of fuel state and conditions, taking into consideration features like biomass, horizontal–vertical continuity, FMC, and canopy cover. FMC abbreviates for fuel moisture content which is a ratio of water contained in a plant to its total dry mass. Research has shown that there are clear thresholds of FMC (in both dead and live fuels) associated with the occurrence of wildfires [10].

The Moderate Resolution Imaging Spectroradiometer (MODIS) on NASA's Terra and Aqua satellites provides daily global coverage, making it a valuable tool for detecting and monitoring fires. MODIS can capture both VNIR and TIR data, enabling the identification of active fires and the assessment of fire-affected areas. Another significant satellite is the Visible Infrared Imaging Radiometer Suite (VIIRS) on the Suomi National Polar-orbiting Partnership (Suomi NPP) satellite. VIIRS, on comparison, in terms of the images it delivers, surpasses MODIS due to its higher spatial resolution. It facilitates image irrespective of the day or night and still can grasp even a minute fire outbreak.

A combination of color, motion, spectral, spatial, temporal, and textural characteristics as well as information about the physical properties of smoke and flame are utilized by optical sensors and RGB cameras, which are essential components of fire detection systems. These frameworks utilize a variety of spaces like RGB, YCbCr, CIELAB, YUV, and HSV to distinguish possible fires. Every one of these variety spaces offers extraordinary benefits in featuring explicit elements of smoke and flares, supporting the early identification process. Due to its simplicity and widespread use in digital imaging, RGB, or red-green-blue, is one of the most widely used color spaces [11]. By separating the luminance and chrominance of an image, YCbCr improves fire detection in a variety of lighting conditions [12]. Because CIELAB is designed to be perceptually uniform, it can be used to distinguish subtle color variations that are typical of smoke and flames [12]. Similar to YCbCr, YUV effectively divides the image into luminance and chrominance components and works well in a variety of lighting conditions. Hue-saturation-value, HSV, is a way to show colors in a way that is closer to how people see them. This can be especially useful for figuring out the different colors of fire and smoke.

A major drawback of color-based fire detection models is their susceptibility to high false alarm rates. Relying solely on color information often proves inadequate for robust and early fire detection, as many objects or conditions can produce colors similar to those of fire. To address this issue, many advanced techniques incorporate both motion and color information from images and videos. By analyzing the dynamic properties of potential fire sources, such as the flickering motion of flames and the spread of smoke, these systems can more accurately distinguish real fires from false positives, thereby improving detection reliability and reducing false alarms.

In contrast to these approaches, the deep learning models seem to provide an additional hand on feature extraction or by automatically extracting and learning complex feature representations [13]. Through the connection of the vegetation backscatter water cloud model with the bare soil backscatter linear model, [14] demonstrated the potential of C-band Sentinel-1A data for forest FMC retrieval. [15] used the soil moisture conditions estimated by the Soil Moisture Active Passive (SMAP) L-band radiometer to develop a novel multivariate regression model to estimate FMC in the Mediterranean environment of Southern California. In addition to being able to trace in detail the evolution of the fire line and fire radiative power, the current generation of geostationary satellites delivers measurements every 10 to 15 min at an increased spatial resolution (2 to 3 km). This allows for the detection of short-lived fires that are undetectable by polar-orbiting satellites.

The latest advancement included a network of nanosatellites with multispectral (visible to infrared) cameras, in addition to a ground station, which was the basis for a system created by [16]. With this configuration, all points on Earth's surface are guaranteed to be visited at least once per hour. The device can precisely estimate the heat output of certain locations by taking high-resolution pictures in the mid-wave infrared (MWIR) and long-wave infrared (LWIR) spectra. A multispectral infrared camera that detects incoming power in two thermal infrared bands was used in simulations to show that the device could detect flames as tiny as 400 m^2. The onboard data processing capabilities lessen the requirement for a lot of bandwidth and allow for early wildfire alerts within 30 min. It is also possible to send compressed raw photos to the ground.

Table 3.4 provides the summarized details regarding different platforms and sensors that are utilized to collect information across multiple features of wildfire.

Table 3.4 Acquisition of wildfire features with remote sensing.

Feature	Remote sensing platform	Sensor type	Description
Fire detection	Satellites, UAVs, aircraft	Thermal infrared, optical	Thermal infrared sensors are utilized to identify heat signatures, which deliver high-resolution images for the potential fire outbreak

(Continued)

Table 3.4 Acquisition of wildfire features with remote sensing. (*Continued*)

Feature	Remote sensing platform	Sensor type	Description
Fire intensity	Satellites, UAVs, aircraft	Thermal infrared	Takes infrared sensors into use to detect the intensity of flames record the temperature and deliver the report for severity of burning in a particular area
Burned area mapping	Satellites, UAVs, aircraft	Optical, multi-spectral, SAR	Collaborated the data from three different sensors, namely, optical, multispectral, and SAR to conclude changes in vegetation cover
Smoke and air quality	Satellites, UAVs	Optical, multi-spectral	Evaluate the quality of the air, monitor smoke dispersion, and measure aerosol concentrations and particle matter using optical and multispectral sensors
Vegetation health	Satellites, UAVs, aircraft	Multi-spectral, hyperspectral	Multispectral and hyperspectral sensors help evaluate vegetation health based on pre- and post-shifts in stress levels to assess the health of the vegetation both before and after wildfires to identify shifts in plant vigor and stress levels

(*Continued*)

Table 3.4 Acquisition of wildfire features with remote sensing. (*Continued*)

Feature	Remote sensing platform	Sensor type	Description
Fuel load assessment	Satellites, UAVs, aircraft	LiDAR, optical	Employing LiDAR to measure biomass and optical imaging for vegetation to figure out the amount of substances available to fuel the fire
Fire behavior modeling	Satellites, UAVs, ground stations	Thermal infrared, optical, Weather stations	Provides information for simulating the behavior and spread of fires by combining meteorological, thermal, and optical data from several sources
Post-fire recovery	Satellites, UAVs, aircraft	Optical, multi-spectral, LiDAR	In-depth topography evaluation to keep check on the recovery of ecosystems and vegetation regrowth after wildfires
Fire risk assessment	Satellites, UAVs	Multi-spectral, SAR	These sensors analyze terrain and vegetation dryness to determine the potential threat of wildfire
Soil and water impact	Satellites, UAVs, aircraft	Multi-spectral, SAR	Study the changes in soil moisture and water quality and conclude wildfire repercussions on soil and water characteristics

Conclusion

Remote sensing has been a valuable tool for disaster management due to its capability in supporting early detection, real-time monitoring as well as damage assessment and recovery operations after natural disasters such as floods, wildfires, or earthquakes. LiDAR, SAR, hyperspectral imaging, and other sensor technologies have drastically improved remote sensing skills. Furthermore, cloud computing and machine learning have enhanced the data processing capacities of an organization. This also gives you a competitive advantage by connecting it with big data, IoT, and GIS. Automated alarms during catastrophes and edge computing, real-time data transfer support better decision-making for resilience in cyber-physical systems. Most importantly, though, is the nuances of using technology responsibly such as ethical and policy factors, i.e., data protection compliance. Integration of advanced remote sensing technologies in the disaster management processes may hence lead to improved situational awareness, accurate prediction, and a more viable response plan.

Collaborating GIS with remote sensing enhances the capabilities of emergency response teams for disaster occurrence, response and recovery. Remote sensing platforms enable immediate and precise decision making, effective coordination, and calculated resource allocation, thereby saving collateral deaths and helping in catastrophe management. The development of intricate models and algorithms that enhance the capacity for risk assessments and prediction should be the primary focus of any subsequent research. It is basic to examine the combination of remote detecting with state-of-the-art innovations like blockchain for information security, man-made consciousness, and modern IoT organizations. Plans for disaster management can be improved in the future thanks to studies on long-term monitoring that can shed light on the recovery procedures. This multifaceted approach guarantees that remote sensing will continue to advance as an essential component of effective disaster management.

References

1. Ahmadian, N., Sedaghat, A., Mohammadi, N., Building Footprint Extraction from Remote Sensing Images with Residual Attention Multi-Scale Aggregation Fully Convolutional Network. *J. Indian Soc. Remote Sens.*, 52, 11, 2417–2429, Springer Science and Business Media LLC, Jul. 31, 2024, doi: 10.1007/s12524-024-01961-8.

2. Yadav, S., The Role of GIS and Remote Sensing in Disaster Response and Management, Geographic Book, Accessed: Aug. 06, 2024. [Online]. Available: https://geographicbook.com/the-role-of-gis-and-remote-sensing-in-disaster-response-and-management/.
3. Khan, A., Gupta, S., Gupta, S.K., Multi-hazard disaster studies: Monitoring, detection, recovery, and management, based on emerging technologies and optimal techniques. *Int. J. Disaster Risk Reduct.*, 47, 101642, Aug. 2020, doi: 10.1016/j.ijdrr.2020.101642.
4. Hasanlou, M., Shah-Hosseini, R., Seydi, S.T., Karimzadeh, S., Matsuoka, M., Earthquake Damage Region Detection by Multitemporal Coherence Map Analysis of Radar and Multispectral Imagery. *Remote Sens.*, 13, 6, 1195, MDPI AG, Mar. 20, 2021. doi: 10.3390/rs13061195.
5. Applications of Synthetic Aperture Radar Satellites to Environmental Monitoring, Strategic Technologies Blog | CSIS, Accessed: Aug. 06, 2024. [Online]. Available: https://www.csis.org/blogs/strategic-technologies-blog/applications-synthetic-aperture-radar-satellites-environmental.
6. Loos, S., Levitt, J., Tomozawa, K., Baker, J., Lallemant, D., Efficacy of Damage Data Integration: A Comparative Analysis of Four Major Earthquakes. *Nat. Hazards Rev.*, 23, 4, American Society of Civil Engineers (ASCE), Nov. 2022. doi: 10.1061/(asce)nh.1527-6996.0000581.
7. Halder, B. *et al.*, Large-Scale Flood Hazard Monitoring and Impact Assessment on Landscape: Representative Case Study in India. *Sustainability*, 15, 14, 11413, MDPI AG, Jul. 23, 2023. doi: 10.3390/su151411413.
8. Nandi, G., Neogy, S., Roy, A.K., Datta, D., Immediate disturbances induced by tropical cyclone Fani on the coastal forest landscape of eastern India: A geospatial analysis. *Remote Sens. Appl.: Soc. Environ.*, 20, 100407, Elsevier BV, Nov. 2020. doi: 10.1016/j.rsase.2020.100407.
9. Koshimura, S., Moya, L., Mas, E., Bai, Y., Tsunami Damage Detection with Remote Sensing: A Review. *Geosciences*, 10, 5, 177, MDPI AG, May 12, 2020. doi: 10.3390/geosciences10050177.
10. Luo, K., Quan, X., He, B., Yebra, M., Effects of Live Fuel Moisture Content on Wildfire Occurrence in Fire-Prone Regions over Southwest China. *Forests*, 10, 10, 887, MDPI AG, Oct. 08, 2019. doi: 10.3390/f10100887.
11. Dimitropoulos, K., *et al.*, Flame Detection for Video-Based Early Fire Warning for the Protection of Cultural Heritage, in: *Progress in Cultural Heritage Preservation*, M. Ioannides, D. Fritsch, J. Leissner, R. Davies, F. Remondino, R. Caffo (Eds.), pp. 378–387, Springer, Berlin, Heidelberg, 2012, doi: 10.1007/978-3-642-34234-9_38.
12. Celik, T., Fast and Efficient Method for Fire Detection Using Image Processing. *ETRI J.*, 32, 6, 881–890, Wiley, Dec. 06, 2010. doi: 10.4218/etrij.10.0109.0695.
13. Barmpoutis, P., Stathaki, T., Dimitropoulos, K., Grammalidis, N., Early Fire Detection Based on Aerial 360-Degree Sensors, Deep Convolution Neural

Networks and Exploitation of Fire Dynamic Textures. *Remote Sens.*, 12, 19, 3177, MDPI AG, Sep. 28, 2020, doi: 10.3390/rs12193177.
14. Wang, L., Quan, X., He, B., Yebra, M., Xing, M., Liu, X., Correction: Wang, L., *et al.* Assessment of the Dual Polarimetric Sentinel-1A Data for Forest Fuel Moisture Content Estimation. Remote Sensing 2019, 11(13), 1568. *Remote Sens.*, 12, 2, 206, MDPI AG, Jan. 07, 2020. doi: 10.3390/rs12020206.
15. Jia, S., Kim, S.H., Nghiem, S.V., Kafatos, M., Estimating Live Fuel Moisture Using SMAP L-Band Radiometer Soil Moisture for Southern California, USA. *Remote Sens.*, 11, 13, 575, MDPI AG, 2019. https://doi.org/10.3390/rs11131575.
16. N. Earth Science Data Systems, Moderate Resolution Imaging Spectroradiometer (MODIS), Earthdata, Accessed: Aug. 05, 2024. [Online]. Available: https://www.earthdata.nasa.gov/learn/find-data/near-real-time/modis.

4

Remote Sensing for Monitoring of Disaster-Prone Region

Navdeep Singh Sodhi* **and Sofia Singla**

University Institute of Computing, Chandigarh University, Mohali, Punjab, India

Abstract

In today's era, remote sensing has become a commendable mechanism of monitoring and detecting the multiple characteristics of any disaster and disaster-prone region with the help of effective measurement of emitted and reflected radiations. Many of the researchers had already proposed their work regarding remote sensing by collecting clear images using special cameras. However, it has also been noticed that many of the earlier proposed works lack rationale. This book chapter has compared and reviewed the multiple artificial intelligence-driven remote sensing framework with respect to some defined objectives. A foolproof comparison has been performed based on the proposed framework, advantages, disadvantages, and accuracy. Numerous recent frameworks proposed for different types of disasters like wildfires, earthquakes, landslides, floods, and oil spills are analyzed. It is also seen that the accuracy of proposed frameworks is improving year by year and reached 94% in 2024, but still it needs to be improved consistently and exponentially as compared to the occurrence of disasters across the globe. No doubt it is always expected that relief organizations as well as emergency services must be able to provide accurate and quick information regarding the areas where a disaster has happened. In this book chapter, some possible key takeaways are introduced so that rescue teams can be able to provide quick and authentic emergency response and disaster rehabilitation.

***Keywords*:** Remote sensing, disaster rehabilitation, artificial intelligence, accuracy

**Corresponding author*: ns826653@gmail.com; ORCID: 0009-0006-7371-6204
Sofia Singla: ORCID: 0009-0007-2123-4913

Neelam Dahiya, Gurwinder Singh, Sartajvir Singh and Apoorva Sharma (eds.) Artificial Intelligence in Remote Sensing for Disaster Management, (59–78) © 2025 Scrivener Publishing LLC

4.1 Introduction

Remote sensing is defined as a process of monitoring as well as detecting the various physical characteristics of any targeted region with the help of aircraft, satellites, and other mechanisms. In this process, images of distant regions are gathered by using some special type of camera [1]. It would not be wrong to say that all of the remotely sensed results are entirely based on the emitted radiations before, during, and after the happening of disaster. This kind of result helps the researchers and derived software or other platforms to analyze nature as well as the basic composition of the surface of the earth. Some of the basic examples of remote sensing can be:

- Analyzing the variations in oceans' temperature with the help of cameras deployed on the satellites. These special cameras are providing the images so that any researcher can effectively achieve the results.
- Capturing the images of oceans' floor by deploying the frequently used sonar systems on the targeted ships.
- Predictions related to volcanic eruptions as well as the weather just by analyzing the images of dust storms and clouds by using special cameras.

In the traditional era, researchers had shown a great emphasis on the structured disaster management cycle in the case of any kind of hazard or disaster. The disaster management cycle mainly consists of four different stages such as reduction, readiness, response, and recovery. Reduction provides different planning practices to reduce the overall likelihood of any kind of disaster. Readiness ensures the planning of residual risk that can cause a negative impact on the disasters. The response accepts planning, funding, and recognition efforts in the disasters. Recovery focuses on the reconstruction of lives, buildings, and utilities [2]. It helps in providing good decision-making scenarios as well as spatial phenomena to the respective authorities as well as scientists. However, it was not able to provide better remote capturing as well as predictability of disasters. To consider the complete coverage of disaster management for the emergency response, explainable artificial intelligence technologies must be considered in readiness and reduction activities.

Remote sensing is considered a geospatial technology that can be utilized in several possibilities [3]. Moreover, it has replaced the entire world into the smart world. It seems like remote sensing is one of the most convincing ways to introduce more and more technological advancements and artificial intelligence strategies just with the help of generating sensed images associated with remote areas. In today's era, remote sensing has been introduced in many areas such as estimation of agricultural production, determining weather, planning related to land usage or land coverage, studies related to demography, archeology, hydrological models, monitoring of the environment, disaster predication and further management of disasters. For instance, remote sensing has shown a drastic change in the field of agriculture. Indeed, remote sensing always helps in providing data from remote sources by sensing it by using special devices like cameras. It has been seen that data must be cleaned or processed before getting final results. In the case of agriculture, aircraft or satellites are major moderators to sense the data remotely. It helps in providing the terrain scenarios, atmospheric profiles of targeted regions, and many other scenarios [4]. This remote sensing technique has generally generated a demand for data related to atmospheric conditions for image gathering. No doubt variations in data are very normal as per atmospheric conditions in the field of agriculture. This is a very concise instance of agriculture, but nowadays remote sensing techniques are utilized in numerous applications.

Artificial intelligence has also ensured the most effective growing role concerning remote sensing. Many approaches are improved by artificial intelligence including accurate classification as well as detection of remotely sensed data. Existing research has shown that AI is involved in all of the applications of remote sensing. For instance, convolutional neural networks, active learning, merged deep neural networks, and multiview learning are some of the artificial intelligence approaches involved in animal detection, identification of drug crop sites, detection of hail storms, classification of land utilization, etc. [5]. Furthermore, artificial approaches related to non-linear or autoregressive networks, back-propagation artificial neural networks, and spiking neural networks are also seen in providing their applications in optical depth analysis of aerosol, estimation of crop yield, and estimation of leaf areas. The demand for accurate state prediction has kept on increasing day by day to have a clean analysis of any disaster before the occurrence of any kind of real damage. That is why support vector machines, deep belief networks, and recurrent neural networks are more effectively used in the prediction of rainfall, frequent temperature forecasting, and detection of earthquakes. Furthermore, artificial-intelligence-driven remote sensing frameworks are also utilized as well as frequently developed by researchers in the case of earth sciences. Artificial intelligence has made remote sensing more comprehending. It is now able to approach the multiple sections of atmospheric windows as well as electromagnetic spectrums to analyze emergent variations. It is not wrong to say that artificial intelligence is extremely associated with sensors including both passive sensors and active sensors. Passive sensors help in the overall detection of the natural energy reflected by surfaces of the Earth, whereas active sensors help in the emission as well as the measurement of backscattered or reflected signals [6]. In this manner, these types of sensors have shown major applications in drones, aircraft, satellites, etc., for better resolution, data collection, and global coverage. It is seen that optical remote sensing, radar remote sensing, LiDAR, thermal remote sensing, multispectral, and hyperspectral imaging are more utilized techniques to consider emergent response and better disaster rehabilitation. For instance, optical remote sensing is more focused on the interpreting as well as collecting of optical data that are mainly clearly visible in the infrared sections of the spectrum. The main objective of optical remote sensing is to collect satellite or aerial data in the form of images from different locations. Talking about other sections of the electromagnetic spectrum, radar remote sensing is one of the techniques that effectively works with the reception as well as transmission of microwave waves. No doubt monitoring of the weather patterns, detection of vehicles and buildings, mapping of the land surfaces, and analysis of the ocean currents are usually performed by remote sensing techniques [6]. This is mainly done by radar remote sensing technique with the help of radar antennas. Despite all aspects, meteorological disaster monitoring is considered one of the major research directions in remote sensing. It can help in other practices such as disaster relief, disaster resistance, disaster control, disaster prevention, etc. Disaster rehabilitation includes the perfect timescale, characteristics of disasters, state change of disaster, etc. Meteorological disaster monitoring includes all of these characteristics of disaster rehabilitation [7]. To analyze emergency response and rehabilitation for disasters using remote sensing, the main objectives of the book chapter are:

- To analyze the applications of proposed AI-driven remote sensing frameworks concerning disaster rehabilitation
- To compare the proposed remote sensing frameworks for quick emergency responses considering advantages, disadvantages, and performance accuracy
- To provide a graphical analysis of the accuracy or performance of the proposed remote sensing framework to ensure disaster rehabilitation
- To provide possible as well as required key takeaways for the betterment of remote sensing

This book chapter is entirely drawn on secondary data, existing articles by researchers, press articles, etc. It includes five sections: 1) related existing work, 2) comparison among reviewed existing frameworks, 3) graphical analysis related to emergency response of existing technologies, 4) solutions for better disaster rehabilitation, and 5) conclusion and future scope.

4.2 Related Existing Work

There are many frameworks existing to rationalize the applications and related utilization of remote sensing techniques for quick emergency response and disaster rehabilitation. Some of those earlier proposed frameworks are discussed below.

Natural disasters like landslides are considered one of the most life-threatening disasters that have the potential threat to introduce severe human life loss, degradation in the socio-economic development, and other severe damages to the infrastructures. To minimize or discard such issues completely, a preparedness plan must be ensured by the disaster management team. Moreover, mapping between the vulnerable regions and the occurrence of natural disasters must be considered so that the threat of natural disasters can be reduced and removed. Researchers proposed a study to ensure a better solution in the case of accurate susceptibility of the disaster as well as its respective preparedness plans using moth flame optimizer as well as swarm intelligence algorithm [8] as discussed in Table 4.1. It is found that the usage of convolutional neural network approach helped in providing best susceptibility analysis by taking advantage of geospatial information technology as well as other machine learning approaches. This entire research is based on real-time data sets but still, the preparedness plans could be provided to further researchers for accurate and quickest response. It was also found that researchers had not talked about disaster rehabilitation in this particular type of research.

Sensing an event or disaster before its actual occurrence is really important. In this respect, researchers had proposed a spatiotemporal aware event investigation (SEIS) framework to analyze all different types of disaster-related deadlines and urgency [9]. It is seen that this particular type of framework has completely provided good control or accuracy over the incoming signals, and better event estimation by the deployment of unmanned aerial vehicles [9]. Moreover, SEIS has overcome the major challenge of analysis as well as extraction of semantic features of disasters. However, it was found that the SEIS framework had not been approached for better and more productive disaster response in an emergency as discussed in Table 4.1. Remote sensing has always been considered as a commendable mechanism in the overall detection and monitoring of any kind of disaster with the help of the physical characteristics of a region. With this approach, a framework named GLNet (global to local network) was proposed by researchers to detect objects with the help of remote sensing images as discussed in Table 4.1. This research was concentrating on complex backgrounds, insufficient information, and multi-scaled targets among the remote sensing images. The self-adaptive anchor along with the Clip LSTM module used in the framework helped in the overall extraction and correlation of all features involved in the images [10]. Besides all of these positive features of the framework, it is detected that the accuracy of the framework while detecting a disaster is required to be up to the mark. Moreover, some of the deep learning models could also be utilized to have a better understanding of disaster recovery as well as management. Disasters like floods are very frequent in some of the areas of the globe. It affects the entire ecosystem as well as its living organisms. No doubt that if the occurrence of this type of disaster is detected previously, then many lives and other related losses can be saved. Accurate flood delineation is one of the most crucial tasks for efficient reduction in the entire risk of the disaster. In this regard only, the researcher proposed a framework named multimodal flood delineation, i.e., MMFLood [11]. The major challenges faced by researchers were unbalancing among the datasets and the effectiveness of the datasets. In this research, data were gathered regarding the flood regions in the form of images to have a comparison between the hazardous areas and non-hazardous areas. Across all this collected data, proper segmentation and classification mechanisms were performed using deep learning techniques [11]. It is seen that this proposed framework can provide constant growth in the overall performance of disaster management and recovery without any failure. However, it is also seen that this framework could more exponentially with the usage of large-scale models.

Furthermore, earthquakes are mainly considered great destructive disasters that need to be detected or monitored previously before their actual occurrence to minimize their respective negative impact on urban areas. Researchers had proposed XAI explainable AI and machine learning techniques to have an accurate estimation of earthquake hazard assessment and spatial probability assessment [12]. It is identified that the LightGBM (light gradient boosting machine) model, RNN (recurrent neural networks) model, smart explainer, smart predictor, and LIME (local interpretable model agnostic explanation) model had been utilized to find the accuracy of the proposed study [12]. In the overall analysis, it is found that some of the areas are considered high, moderate, and low hazardous areas as discussed in Table 4.1. Forests play an important role in the overall maintenance of ecological balance. Forest fires are a very common and unpredictable disaster. It mainly affects the climate, lives surviving on the planet, and the entire planet. Therefore, it is very important to track disasters like forest fires using enhanced technologies like remote sensing. In this regard only, researchers had proposed a study including intelligent scheduling algorithms comprised of decreasing total flying time algorithm, increasing total flying time algorithm, half-region algorithm, and half regions assignment algorithm, quarter regions assignment algorithm, tier region assignment algorithm, and randomly iteratively drone algorithm. An analysis was performed among all of these six intelligent scheduling algorithms [13]. It is found that drone tasks were scheduled to complete the detection of forest fires and life-threatening disasters in a more precise and quickest way as discussed in Table 4.1. Among all of the algorithms, it was found that randomly iteratively drone algorithms had been able to provide remarkable and promising results. Rather than achieving results, it is seen that it would be better to test all of the algorithms in the case of large-scale datasets. Floods, a life-threatening natural disaster, have shown devastating impacts on the environment. It had been analyzed that the occurrence of floods since 2008 had already been able to affect nearly 40 million of the population [14]. To discuss remote sensing of floods, a smart integrated risk management framework was proposed as discussed in Table 4.1. Three different methods including nearest neighbors classification, artificial neural network, and support vector machine based on artificial intelligence technology were utilized to classify and predict the consistent occurrence of flash floods [14]. Rather than better efficiency, it met with multiple limitations as well that could be modified in further research. For instance, the combination of the classic Delphi method as well as risk analysis could be able to provide a more fruitful flood-controlling framework. Furthermore, decision systematic dynamic models can be utilized to ensure better dynamic knowledge management.

Later on, researchers proposed multi-modal mining to analyze the remote areas that are badly impacted by any of the natural disasters. In this regard, a framework named BERT, i.e., bidirectional encoder representations from transformers, was proposed [15]. This framework helps in providing the overall demonstration as well as classification of the humanitarian aid. It utilized the pre-processing of images as well as text and OCR (optical character recognition) including the quickest RCNN, RegNet, ConvNeXt, and other approaches [15]. No doubt that better accuracy levels were received by researchers, but still it is lacking in many of the areas. Data limitation is found to the one of the most impactful limitations in the entire study as it was completely dependable on the public social media rather than collecting the data from multiple primary data sources. Moreover, it is seen that classification using multi-modal datasets was performed but it diminishes the entire performance of the study. It would be better if different types of natural disasters like earthquakes, floods, wildfires, etc., were involved. In the end, the prediction of natural disasters using deep learning techniques by effectively generating the text and images could help show better accuracy as well as performance. In past natural disasters, it is not wrong to say that wildfires have always been the most dangerous disaster for both the ecological environment and the entire atmosphere. In the earlier scenarios, deep learning technology and machine learning technology had shown a great impact on the remote sensing framework. Despite of all machine learning and other deep learning technologies have made a great advancement in the respect of wildfire identification frameworks including TIR (thermal infrared) images and RGB (optical) images [16]. This respective wildfire identification framework was proposed by considering the modality-specific shared features. It utilized the two different parallel encoders to retrieve multi-level features including thermal infrared and optical image [16]. Furthermore, all of these TIR and RGB features are integrated into the single fusion layer. Researchers proposed this framework by considering both qualitative as well as quantitative analysis. The performance of the proposed framework was analyzed on different factors such as object scale, monitoring source, and light conditions. Despite this commendable performance shared by researchers in this study, it also addressed many of the limitations. First and foremost, the dataset taken by the researcher is very concise and it needs to be expanded further. Secondarily, the performance of the proposed framework named wildfire identification must be analyzed based on the real-time scenarios seen in wildfires.

It is very crucial to assess risk before the happening of a disaster rather than just the detecting disaster and its quick emergency response. Earlier researchers had studied the risks in the coastal areas of Jiaozhou Bay in China by considering its ground observations as well as habitat information about the existing marine species [17]. With the help of this entire data, environment vulnerability-related maps were introduced. This entire risk assessment framework ensured that oil spills could occur in the upcoming years. Moreover, it also generated observations related to the more vulnerable regions of the coast by considering satellite images and a deep learning-based network detection model as discussed in Table 4.1. However, the major key takeaway is an assessment of ecological risk over the coastal areas along with the consideration of different marine zones and their related species.

Researchers proposed a deep learning framework to have automatic detection of landslides and remote sensing of landslides regions by providing highly resolution images. This framework uses visual saliency algorithms to extract the features of the region [18]. It helps in achieving an overall 94% accuracy as compared to other conventional frameworks that do not use deep learning methods [18]. It is seen that this framework of landslide identification is more effective as it helps in acquiring the data from the borders on the ground including its related displaced mass and surface deformation as discussed in Table 4.1. In the context of images used in this particular framework, only labeled data is used [18]. This framework could improve or approach to non-labeled data.

Furthermore, despite these disasters like landslides, earthquakes, floods, and many more, researchers conducted a study in Thailand for the analysis of air pollution that has completely degraded the quality of air pollution [19]. In this study, a hybrid model consisted of a classification part and an estimation part for the air quality. It is further found that air quality can be improved by just using regression models [19]. However, classification models are degrading the overall performance of the hybrid model but still provide the best results as compared to the traditional models. Deep learning and artificial intelligence technology play an important role in the representation of remote images of any kind of disaster. In this respect only, researchers had proposed a U-net technique based on deep learning to extract effective information of glacial lakes using satellite image [20]. It is seen that this study focused on the monitoring of glacial lakes in terms of global warming and climate change. Overall, promising results, i.e., accuracy at 97.32%, precision at 95.98%, and recall at 95.23%, have been found [20]. No doubt it would not be wrong to say that more disaster management strategies could be ensured and applied just by improving the understanding regarding dynamic environments.

Despite just using enhanced computing advancements along with artificial intelligence and unmanned aerial vehicles, the usage of unmanned aerial vehicles and artificial intelligence photogrammetry for the analysis of the accurate impact of disasters remains undiscovered. In this regard, researchers proposed a debris and damage analysis framework for the disasters. Researchers have recommended effective disaster response efforts along with the 3D capturing of incidents rather than 2D images [21]. To monitor environmental changes, researchers have carried forward their research based on earth observation data by using C2A-DC, i.e., context-aware adaptive data cube. It helps monitor the overall effect of climate change on the environment. The effectiveness of this framework has been measured in the post-disaster assessment, crisis management, and environmental monitoring [22]. It is seen that this framework needs to be improved more along with the consideration of explainable AI methods. Unmanned aerial vehicles are found as most advantageous technology to monitor disasters remotely as they carry various sensors to gather the data. Researchers have discussed how effectively monitoring flood, mudslides, and earthquakes can be performed by high-resolution videos and images obtained by using drones [23]. It is identified that the progress of disaster monitoring can be exponentially improved with the help of explainable artificial intelligence technology, range extension, sensor technology, etc.

Rather than just monitoring disasters, it is very important to ensure the instant rehabilitation of disaster victims. It is not wrong to state that orthodox methods of disaster management need to be updated to achieve effectiveness to some certain extent [24]. Earthquakes cause life-threatening damage across the entire world. Strategies like seismic vulnerability assessments can help facilitate the quickest recovery and effective planning initiatives for disaster rehabilitation. Researchers proposed a framework to evaluate both pre-earthquake and post-earthquake data by considering the case of the Gorkha earthquake that occurred in 2015 [25]. In this research, a random forest classifier is used to observe the accuracy of data gained from respective cases. It is seen that accuracy can be improved with the usage of recent computing technologies. In this respect only, researchers have proposed a novel methodology for the reparability after earthquakes by using MRFs , i.e., moment resisting frames [26]. It is found that this respective framework can help achieve cost-effective post-effective reparability. Other disasters like floods have also become a major cause of life-threatening damage to the lives on earth. Recently, researchers have proposed a framework including the macro scale heterogeneity induced channeling and small-scale molecular diffusion for intensifying the miscible floods. It has utilized a neural network proxy and genetic algorithm model to decrease the overall cost of computation [27]. Furthermore, researchers have proposed a multi-layer model involving optimization technology and engineering theory for rehabilitation from floods [28].

4.3 Comparison Table

In this section, a comparison among multiple proposed frameworks considering remote sensing for quick emergency response and rehabilitation for disasters is discussed. It is completely based on three parameters, i.e., advantages, disadvantages, and accuracy as discussed in Table 4.1.

Table 4.1 Comparison among proposed frameworks for quick emergency response and disaster rehabilitation using remote sensing.

Framework	Advantages	Disadvantages	Accuracy (%)
Moth Flame Algorithm	Real time data utilized. Surrounding impact of landslides are also considered by utilizing around 12 variables. Sensing of landslides areas are considered with the integration of two conventional technologies i.e. machine learning and geospatial information technology itself [8].	No such preparedness or rehabilitation plane are actually proposed by the framework [8].	80.1056
SEIS	Proposed framework has address three different challenges such as effective utilization of social signals in order to deal with unmanned aerial vehicles, identification as well as computation of correlations across all type of events extracting from the sensors' data, and concluding the urgency of disaster or event with the help of semantic features [9].	Some of the data patterns are still unrecognized, hidden, and unseen. Furthermore, human opinions can be utilized for better results.	80.4
GLNet	This proposed framework has effectively integrated the global context and local context extracted by MSP (Multi Scale Perception) module and Clip LSTM (Clip Long Short Term Memory). It has concentrated on the challenges associated with target information, non-understandable backgrounds, and blurry targets [10].	No such preparedness or rehabilitation plans are actually proposed by the framework.	70.7

(Continued)

Table 4.1 Comparison among proposed frameworks for quick emergency response and disaster rehabilitation using remote sensing. (*Continued*)

Framework	Advantages	Disadvantages	Accuracy (%)
Machine learning and XAI	Significant hazard estimation has performed just with the help of deep learning models and machine learning based applications [12]. Overall twelve different factors including all non-earthquake and earthquake factors are used to have better probability assessment and prediction model.	Training data sets treated with the respected models are not must vast. It must be vast enough for better accuracy results. No security and other privacy frameworks associated to propose framework has seen. Further, development of Smart Predictor has shown a great demand to bring a satisfying change in the remote sensing of disasters [12].	89
Intelligent Scheduling algorithm	Results have found by developing six different algorithms such as decreasing total flying time algorithm, increasing total flying time algorithm, half-region algorithm and half regions assignment algorithm, quarter regions assignment algorithm, tier region assignment algorithm, randomly iteratively drone algorithm [13]. Overall, time consumption got minimized to have precised and quickest detection of disaster.	No such heuristics are considered to have genuine formulation of problem [13]. Moreover, this study is completely based on the small scale instances.	90.3

(*Continued*)

Table 4.1 Comparison among proposed frameworks for quick emergency response and disaster rehabilitation using remote sensing. (*Continued*)

Framework	Advantages	Disadvantages	Accuracy (%)
Neural Network	Challenge of data imbalance has resolved by developed framework [14].	Limitation in data, and dependency of accuracy on just type of disaster are found as major disadvantages of study.	86.3
Ecological Risk Assessment	Real time data of risk on Jiaozhou Bay has utilized [17]. Different vulnerability scenarios area seen using ground data, and other habitat information.	No such network model for the future prediction or preparedness plans related to oil spill risks is discussed.	80.95
Visual Saliency landslide identification	Usage of visual saliency for the detection of landslides [18]. Real time datasets are used in the proposed study.	No such preparedness or rehabilitation plans are actually proposed by the framework.	94

SEIS: Spatiotemporal aware Event Investigation, GLNet: Global to Local Network

4.4 Graphical Analysis

In this section, a graphical analysis of the compared framework based on accuracy is discussed. It is seen that accuracy is facing huge variations in the overall performance and response of frameworks in an emergency.

This graphical analysis mentions that the GLNet framework provides the least performance accuracy as compared to other frameworks. However, this accuracy percentage has increased exponentially with the proposal of remote sensing frameworks. It is seen that the latest framework used for landslide identification with the help of visual saliency has become able to provide the best accuracy, i.e., 94% as discussed in Figure 4.1. In order to improve the accuracy with quickest and precised emergency response and disaster rehabilitation, some of the possible key takeaways are discussed below:

1. Possible key takeaways for quick emergency response and disaster rehabilitation
Multiple frameworks are compared and analyzed graphically in order to present its actual performance accuracy. However, it is seen found that these frameworks must be improved so that remote sensing can be predict accurately and efficiently in order to best response and rehabilitation. There can be many key takeaways that must be followed by researchers while proposing any of the remote sensing frameworks for natural disasters.

i. Enhancement in early warning systems:
Artificial intelligence plays an important role in identifying the potential threats related to natural disasters. However, enhancement in early warning systems is really required. Researchers can treat the

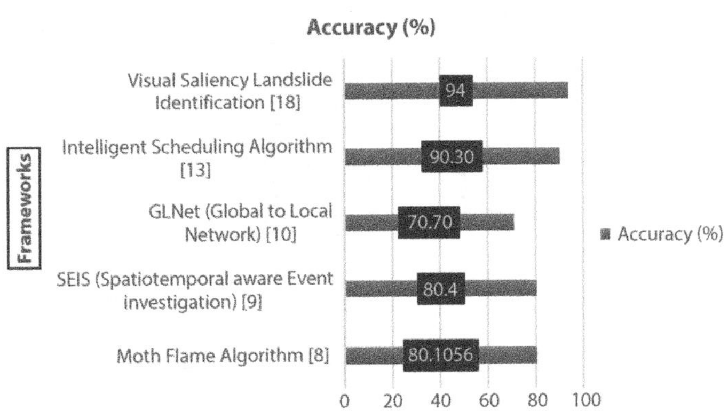

Figure 4.1 Graphical analysis to compare the proposed frameworks' accuracy from 2020 to 2024.

warning systems with the huge chunk of data related to adverse disaster. Furthermore, identification of trends can be possibly performed from the prepared data. AI can help in extracting and analyzing the satellite images to provide early indication of disasters and respective quick responses. This early detection further can help in providing the potential life-saving and disaster rehabilitation

ii. Regular assessment of disaster rehabilitation strategies:
No doubt that many of the disaster rehabilitation strategies are already developed and proposed by the researchers, but still some of those are lacking in its rationale. Those strategies can actually change the response in disaster with the effective association of artificial intelligence algorithms. AI can help in analyzing overall weak as well as strong points of the developed strategies. Furthermore, researchers can operate inefficiencies of previously proposed algorithms and apply the smart artificial technology systems in the respect of quick response.

iii. Smart identification of needed aid:
Disasters are always hazardous and unpredictable, but artificial intelligence can help in analyzing the past occurrence of the natural disasters. Moreover, the rate of impact on the habitat can also be identified. In this regard, artificial-intelligence-based remote sensing frameworks must be working in such a manner so that actual data related to the displacement of the people and potential needs of natural resources can be predicted and circulated among authorities just before the occurrence of the disaster.

iv. Smart navigation by response team:
Researchers can propose smart and non-dischargeable devices embedded with the navigating chips so that rescue teams can help all of the victims quickly and provide them with real-time possible updates.

v. Raising awareness for all vulnerable regions using smart expert systems:
No doubt that some of the regions are often vulnerable regions in the case of a happening of the natural disasters. It is also seen that some of the natural disasters are very destructive and even those vulnerable regions are not able to take their original states. In this regard, smart expert systems can be developed to promote the vulnerable regions rather than just using traditional approaches.

vi. Answering of distress calls or other help calls by AI:
Citizens are very habitual to proceed with distress and help calls in the case of any emergency. During natural disasters, it is very difficult to handle all of the calls manually as it is very cost ineffective and time consuming. In such cases, artificial intelligence assistance can be used to gather all data and assigning the respective manpower or any other

help according to the distance of region suffered a disaster. These AI systems can help in analyzing the overall tone of voice of speaker in the case of any urgency and further all of the calls can be prioritize with the help of effective mechanisms.

4.5 Conclusion and Future Scope

The occurrence of any kind of disaster is unpredictable, and remote sensing is considered an essential approach for all aspects including disaster management, disaster relief, disaster resistance, disaster control, and disaster prevention. This book chapter entirely focuses on comparing and analyzing the different remote sensing frameworks in combination with artificial intelligence technology based on advantages, disadvantages, and accuracy. The entire study is completely based on the applications of proposed AI-driven remote sensing frameworks for disasters like landslides, floods, earthquakes, and forest fires. The discussed comparison shows how much remote sensing frameworks have enhanced the responses as well as rehabilitation in the case of any kind of disaster. Graphical analysis concluded that the performance accuracy of proposed frameworks has improved from 70% to 94%. Furthermore, possible key takeaways are also introduced for the further improvement of accuracy in quick emergency response and disaster rehabilitation. All of the mentioned objectives are discussed and it is found that many of the further enhancements need to be considered by the researchers for emergency response and disaster rehabilitation. Researchers need to consider recent computing technologies and advancements including artificial intelligence, machine learning, and deep learning techniques. This advancement can help in the identification of areas, and assessment of damage caused to infrastructure, buildings, utilities, and lives on Earth. Moreover, frameworks must be proposed to ensure as well as guide the respective individuals regarding the implementation and planning of post-disaster strategies for recovery.

Acknowledgments

The authors would like to thank the University Institute of Computing, Chandigarh University, Mohali. We truly appreciate the encouragement and guidance provided by the institute throughout the study. Furthermore, all of our fellow research scholars have supported to propose this study successfully.

References

1. Read, J.M. and Torrado, M., Remote Sensing, in: *International Encyclopedia of Human Geography*, pp. 335–346, 2009, doi:10.1016/b978-008044910-4.00508-3.
2. K.E., K.C., S.V., V.G., Remote Sensing and the Disaster Management Cycle, in: *Advances in Geoscience and Remote Sensing*, Oct. 2009, doi:10.5772/8341.
3. Anyamba, A., Estes, J., Kline, K., Collins, E., Remote Sensing, in: *International Encyclopedia of the Social & Behavioral Sciences*, pp. 419–424, 2015, doi:10.1016/b978-0-08-097086-8.72046-0.
4. Huang, Y., Chen, Z., Yu, T., Huang, X., Gu, X., Agricultural Remote Sensing Big Data: Management and Applications. *J. Integr. Agric.*, 17, 9, 1915–1931, Sep. 2018, doi: 10.1016/s2095-3119(17)61859-8.
5. Zhang, L. and Zhang, L., Artificial Intelligence for Remote Sensing Data Analysis: A review of challenges and opportunities. *IEEE Geosci. Remote Sens. Mag.*, 10, 2, 270–294, Jun. 2022, doi: 10.1109/mgrs.2022.3145854.
6. Janga, B., Asamani, G., Sun, Z., Cristea, N., A review of practical AI for Remote Sensing in Earth Sciences. *Remote Sens.*, 15, 16, 4112, Aug. 2023, doi: 10.3390/rs15164112.
7. Ye, P., Remote Sensing Approaches for Meteorological Disaster Monitoring: Recent achievements and new challenges. *Int. J. Environ. Res. Public Health*, 19, 6, 3701, Mar. 2022, doi: 10.3390/ijerph19063701.
8. Pham, V.D., *et al.*, Convolutional neural network—optimized moth flame algorithm for shallow landslide susceptible analysis. *IEEE Access*, 8, 32727–32736, 2020, doi: 10.1109/access.2020.2973415.
9. Rashid, M.T. and Wang, D., Seis: A spatiotemporal-aware event investigation framework for Social Airborne Sensing in disaster recovery applications. *Pervasive Mob. Comput.*, 87, 101717, Dec. 2022, doi: 10.1016/j.pmcj.2022.101717.
10. Teng, Z., Duan, Y., Liu, Y., Zhang, B., Fan, J., Global to local: CLIP-LSTM-based object detection from remote sensing images. *IEEE Trans. Geosci. Remote Sens.*, 60, 1–13, 2022, doi: 10.1109/tgrs.2021.3064840.
11. Montello, F., Arnaudo, E., Rossi, C., MMFlood: A Multimodal dataset for flood delineation from satellite imagery. *IEEE Access*, 10, 96774–96787, 2022, doi: 10.1109/access.2022.3205419.
12. Jena, R., *et al.*, Earthquake spatial probability and hazard estimation using various explainable AI (XAI) models at the Arabian Peninsula. *Remote Sens. Appl.: Soc. Environ.*, 31, 101004, Aug. 2023, doi: 10.1016/j.rsase.2023.101004.
13. Jemmali, M., Loai Kayed, B.M., Boulila, W., Amdouni, H., Alharbi, M.T., Optimizing Forest Fire Prevention: Intelligent Scheduling algorithms for drone-based Surveillance System. *Procedia Comput. Sci.*, 225, 1562–1571, 2023, doi: 10.1016/j.procs.2023.10.145.

14. Nakhaei, M., *et al.*, Enhancing community resilience in arid regions: A smart framework for flash flood risk assessment. *Ecol. Indic.*, 153, 110457, Sep. 2023, doi: 10.1016/j.ecolind.2023.110457.
15. Khanmohammadi, S., *et al.*, Multi-modal mining of crowd-sourced data: Efficient provision of humanitarian aid to remote regions affected by natural disasters. *Int. J. Disaster Risk Reduct.*, 96, 103972, Oct. 2023, doi: 10.1016/j.ijdrr.2023.103972.
16. Rui, X., Li, Z., Zhang, X., Li, Z., Song, W., A RGB-thermal based adaptive Modality Learning Network for day–night wildfire identification. *Int. J. Appl. Earth Obs. Geoinf.*, 125, 103554, Dec. 2023, doi: 10.1016/j.jag.2023.103554.
17. Ma, X., Wang, Z., Liu, Y., Ecological risk assessment of a coastal area using multi-source remote sensing images and *in-situ* sample data. *Ecol. Indic.*, 158, 111470, Jan. 2024, doi: 10.1016/j.ecolind.2023.111470.
18. Sreelakshmi, S. and Vinod Chandra, S.S., Visual saliency-based landslide identification using super-resolution remote sensing data. *Results Eng.*, 21, 101656, Mar. 2024, doi: 10.1016/j.rineng.2023.101656.
19. Jitkajornwanich, K., Vijaranakul, N., Jaiyen, S., Srestasathiern, P., Lawawirojwong, S., Enhancing risk communication and environmental crisis management through satellite imagery and AI for Air Quality Index Estimation. *MethodsX*, 12, 102611, Jun. 2024, doi: 10.1016/j.mex.2024.102611.
20. Sharma, A., Prakash, C., Thakur, D., Glacier Lake Detection utilizing remote sensing integration with satellite imagery and advanced deep learning methods. *Appl. Geomat.*, 16, 829–850, 2024, doi: 10.21203/rs.3.rs-3963695/v1.
21. Cheng, C.-S., Luo, L., Murphy, S., Lee, Y.-C., Leite, F., A framework to enhance disaster debris estimation with AI and aerial photogrammetry. *Int. J. Disaster Risk Reduct.*, 107, 104468, Jun. 2024, doi: 10.1016/j.ijdrr.2024.104468.
22. Temenos, A., *et al.*, C2A-DC: A context-aware adaptive data cube framework for environmental monitoring and Climate Change Crisis Management. *Remote Sens. Appl.: Soc. Environ.*, 34, 101171, Apr. 2024, doi: 10.1016/j.rsase.2024.101171.
23. Chen, Z., Application of UAV remote sensing in natural disaster monitoring and early warning: An example of flood and mudslide and earthquake disasters. *Highl. Sci. Eng. Technol.*, 85, 924–933, Mar. 2024, doi: 10.54097/zak5hp77.
24. Chandra, R. and Lakshmi, D., Application of artificial intelligence in disaster management and their challenges, in: *Internet of Things and AI for Natural Disaster Management and Prediction*, pp. 1–27, Mar. 2024, doi:10.4018/979-8-3693-4284-8.ch001.
25. Gautam, D., Bhattarai, A., Rupakhety, R., Machine learning and soft voting ensemble classification for earthquake induced damage to bridges. *Eng. Struct.*, 303, 117534, Mar. 2024, doi: 10.1016/j.engstruct.2024.117534.

26. Hu, S., Zhou, X., Ke, K., Alam, M.S., Shi, T., Post-earthquake repairability-based methodology for enhancing steel mrfs. *Eng. Struct.*, 308, 117898, Jun. 2024, doi: 10.1016/j.engstruct.2024.117898.
27. Ogbeiwi, P. and Stephen, K.D., Assisted upscaling of miscible CO2-Enhanced Oil Recovery Floods using an artificial neural network-based optimisation algorithm. *Transp. Porous Media*, 151, 3, 495–531, Jan. 2024, doi: 10.1007/s11242-023-02049-6.
28. Guo, J., *et al.*, A new method for optimizing water-flooding strategies in multi-layer sandstone reservoirs. *Energies*, 17, 8, 1828, Apr. 2024, doi: 10.3390/en17081828.

5

Artificial Intelligence Tools in Disaster Risk Reduction and Emergency Management

Rupinder Singh[1]*, Manjinder Singh[2] and Jaswinder Singh[1]

[1]*Chitkara University Institute of Engineering and Technology, Chitkara University, Punjab, India*
[2]*Govt. Ranbir College Punjabi University Patiala, Punjab, India*

Abstract
The paper explores the use of AI tools and technologies in disaster risk reduction and emergency management, highlighting their potential to enhance community resilience to both man-made and natural disasters. The study examines how artificial intelligence (AI) tools and technologies are used in emergency preparedness and disaster risk reduction, emphasizing how they might increase community resilience to both natural and man-made disasters. The principles and challenges of disaster preparedness and response are the starting point of our discussion. This will be followed by AI amplification of the efforts. The different kinds of artificial intelligence helpers such as predictive analytics, prevention early warning systems, remote sensing, natural language processing, geographic information systems, simulation models, and remote assistance make the decision-making process easier by forecasting, preventing disaster, and making accurate, fit-for-purpose reaction and response plans at the time of disasters. Moreover, AI apps are fraught with ethical conflicts and data security as well as tragic algorithmic bias which are stumbling blocks for the evolution of the app. This study not only unveils the relevant trends and technologies but also offers advice to policymakers, practitioners, and researchers about AI tools as an effective solution for disaster risk reduction.

***Keywords*:** DRRM, artificial intelligence, disaster management, geographic information systems, natural disasters, natural language processing, remote sensing

**Corresponding author*: rupinder.1153@chitkara.edu.in; ORCID ID: 0000-0002-7553-8759
Manjinder Singh: ORCID: 0009-0001-5003-9857
Jaswinder Singh: ORCID: 0000-0003-1343-4740

Neelam Dahiya, Gurwinder Singh, Sartajvir Singh and Apoorva Sharma (eds.) Artificial Intelligence in Remote Sensing for Disaster Management, (79–98) © 2025 Scrivener Publishing LLC

5.1 Introduction

Disaster risk reduction and management (DRRM) are cardinal pillars of the resilience program which are vital for guarding and, hence, saving the structures of the communities, economies, and ecosystems from the devastating impacts posed by natural and human-made hazards [1]. These tragic events span a wide array, which include seismic motions, massive floods, alarming hurricanes, panicky man-made fires, worrisome pandemics, threatening technology disasters, and many others. They bring never-ending human suffering, loss of properties, relocations, and the disruption of essential services, thus calling for solid DRRM plans.

A comprehensive understanding of and proactive aapproach to the root causes of disaster risk is the essence of effective disaster risk management [2]. A range of preventive measures tailored to specific hazards and contexts are implemented to identify vulnerable populations, critical infrastructure, and environmentally sensitive areas. Besides that, beefing up emergency preparedness and response competencies will become a priority, which requires the establishment of structured linkage networks, timely evacuation systems, and quick and efficient response techniques that will allow the timely delivery of necessary resources and the organization of coordinated relief attempts in emergencies [3].

The aim of DRRM projects is not only to set up measures that decrease the immediate impacts but also to help society transform itself into a robust one that supports larger societal resilience as well as sustainable development. Via smart investments in infrastructures, education, health, and environmental plans, communities can support one another to withstand and get back easily from adversity and thus create a way for a more equal and robust future. Thus, DRRM remains on the side of light as a beacon of the collective sense of humanity who will never surrender in the long confront of calamity with resilience, solidarity, indomitable will, and endurance.

5.1.1 Role of AI Tools and Technologies

Figure 5.1 shows Aritificial Intelligence (AI) inventions and technologies are, to some extent, a paradigm shift in the sense that they give out things that were interesting to think about while civilization was lagging in disaster risk reduction and management (DRRM) and yet they are completely excellent approaches to resilience and responsiveness in the face of calamity. Thanks to neurocomputing that can process different, huge data from

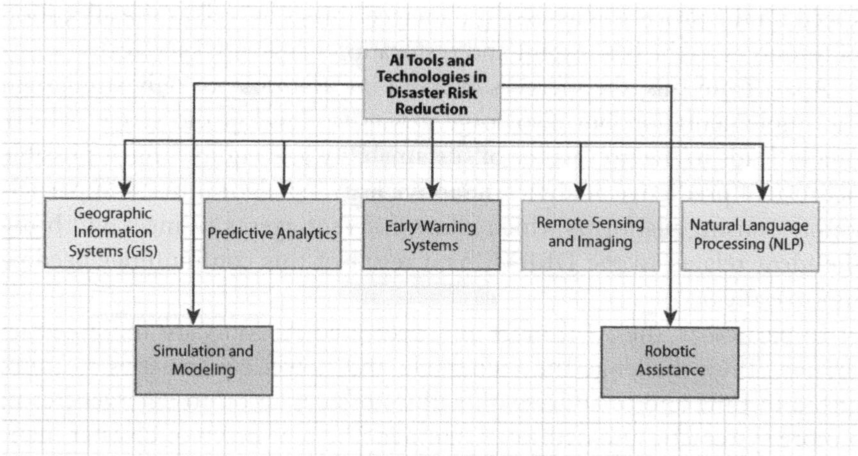

Figure 5.1 AI tools and technologies.

disparate sources [4] (images from satellites, the further flow of info from social networks, sensor bridges, and old documents) which are highly useful to everyone involved in the disruption efforts from commencement to conclusion. The AI-driven predictive analytics have indeed become an essential part of the disaster preparedness [5]. Using the predictive method aids in forecasting the possibility and severity of a forthcoming hazard, which, in turn, provides authorities the time to mobilize resources, apply evacuation measures, and reinforce critical infrastructure. This is only possible through the application of machine learning algorithms that use past data and real-time sensor readings as information. In the phase when the disaster response is carried out, AI technologies [6] help to quickly comprehend the current issues of the environment and then make sure that the decision is based on their devotion. This is what guides emergency responders to the right choices as well as the allocation of resources. Fast-paced data fusion and its predictive analytics capabilities are the perks of AI systems that help predict the affected places, test them for damages, and mark the dangerous regions and persons in vulnerable conditions needing help.

Although AI-powered devices also enable, in post-disaster recovery and reconstruction processes, people to be more productive and their abilities to improve, they will make the things mentioned earlier above faster. It is by the application of such things as sophisticated image manipulation [7], natural speech processing, and positional mapping techniques that can speed up the process of assessing damaged things as well as the allocation of resources to the best extent and restoration of essential services.

Apart from this, the mergers of AI to innovations not only strengthen the implementation but also forge a way to develop the scope, which, finally, leads to the prevalence of sustainability and equity. This is possible because of predictive analytics, adaptive learning algorithms, and participatory sensing platforms which allow different agents to meet and bring the ideas related to the DRRM. As a result of this communities become more resilient.

In particular, the AI devices and dedicated AI tools are the potential drivers. They challenge the vulnerable and powerless societies to think ahead in time and to address difficulties of adaptation to emergencies in a more systematic and dedicated manner. The new dawn of disaster management comes and it comes with the possibility that AI promises. It brings the message of hope that tomorrow will be both safe and resilient, where the environment can recover.

5.1.2 Purpose and Objectives of the Research Paper

Through this research, we intend to figure out the place of artificial intelligence (AI) software and hardware in disaster risk reduction and management (DRRM). By looking at the positive side of AI, this paper will explain the ways AI can help during the different phases of disaster management and how AI can aid the disaster management sector to become more reliable and faster.

Firstly, the paper will look at how disaster preparedness efforts using AI tools and technologies are being deployed. Such means as predictive analytics to indicate and forecast emergent hazards, advanced early warning systems to inform risk groups, and area identification using risk mapping to find both places and members of the community who are in danger are a few examples. Through the analysis of these technologies, the paper will underline that AI can take at least one head of the issues of suffering and damages leading to the reduction of negative impacts that occurred before the disasters. Secondly, this section will investigate the place of AI through assisting and helping in the process of disaster. In the first place, the emphasis is given to the aspect that AI-driven decision-making systems provide real-time support for quick decisions, resource allocation, and coordination of the corresponding response in the disaster scenario. It will also give insights into the utilization of image analysis AI and remote sensing technologies to detect damage [8], prioritize responses, and simplify recovery operations. Yet, on the side of this divisional, this article will also deal with the challenges and the ethical questions involved in the use of AI in the context of disasters. This could include issues associated with data privacy, biased algorithms, and accountability as well as the possibility that AI systems might lead to unintentional outcomes or be subject to misuse in crisis management situations with sensitive distracters.

Therefore, the paper is dedicated to discovering ways to innovate and collaborate in the branch of artificial intelligence-powered disaster management. Through this paper, it is intended to spotlight emerging trends, make recommendations, and identify areas needing additional research. This will help policymakers, practitioners, and researchers with the necessary tools for harnessing AI for better and risk-adaptive approaches to future disasters.

5.2 AI Tools and Technologies in Disaster Risk Reduction

Disaster risk governance has emerged from the evaluation of vast amounts of information derived from various sources such as technology, media, and so on [6]. Disaster risks include both the pre-disaster state as well as the post-disaster stage [8].

- Pre-disaster stage: The pre-disaster period includes risk mitigation and preparation activities as a preemptive measure against disasters to reduce their impact or, at the very least, increase resilience among affected populations.
- Mitigation: Hence, the resilience phase involves work on reducing the impact of the disasters that take place. The government in the process is using geo-information data to furnish response systems that can lead to the least possible loss of lives and property. The essence of the mitigation is to offer maximum benefit of the use of the GIS technology which involves the establishment of an awareness program. This is the simple form—to develop mitigation programs to minimize the effect of the disaster.
- Preparedness: It contains a step in creating a disaster response plan. The plan encompasses a people checklist as the feats can be conveyed from one settlement to another whereby only medical supplies, construction tools, and other equipment can be shared among the affected areas.

- Disaster management done correctly leads to disaster size reduction, and in rebuilding from this disaster, the affected people will be helped.
- Post-disaster stage: This step is an active one where a swift reaction together with recovery options will be deployed to create a conducive environment on the scene of the disaster.
- Response: These are among the essential functions for crisis management operation, which involves the provision of emergency assistance to the victims. In times of natural disaster, people need emergency help after the disaster takes place, and public health centers start using mapped geospatial data to answer the following questions—where are health centers operating and shelter places available in the meantime? Authorities from the government can use GIS data to manage or to provide responses and accurate information to people and this can make them proactive.
- Recovery: humanization: There is assistance for those local people to lead their life back to normal after the accident by providing emergency steps for others. During disasters, there is support from government bodies that make it easy for the victims to lead their day-to-day lives. The underlying factor is to separate aid from political strains and provide economic support to affected states [9].

In disaster risk management, the first and foremost step is to address the gap between the preparedness, response, as well as recovery efforts, and artificially intelligent technologies are one of the important ones that can be used as a tool in the process of improvement.

Following are the AI tools and techniques used in disaster risk reduction and management:

i. Predictive analytics: Effective disaster risk governance has emerged from the evaluation of vast amounts of information derived from various sources such as technology, media, and so on. Disaster risks include both the pre-disaster state as well as the post-disaster stage.

The use of AI algorithms is necessary to provide an analysis of past climatic routes like everyday weather, geological-based information, natural disasters, and so forth as inputs for prediction. Having both information with big-scale insight leads AI systems to be more functional and precise [5]. Predictive models serve their purpose for risk-favored areas to be identified and resources allocated based on their priority. Predictive analytics require the help of various statistical algorithms along with machine learning techniques [10] to analyze historical data to lay foundations that can predict future risks. As a crucial tool in the disaster management arsenal, predictive analytics is employed to produce a simulation of how disastrous an event such as a hurricane, earthquake, flood, wildfire, or pandemic may prove.

The initial move in the efficient utilization of predictive analytics in risk reduction consists of collecting data related to past disasters, including such details as about previous weather conditions, geological situations, social and economic factors, as well as case histories related to disasters. This information should come from different sources, e.g., federal agencies, institutions, non-governmental organizations, and satellite images. These zags may be either rainfall patterns, population density, infrastructure vulnerability, historical disaster records, land use, etc. After that, you need to train the machine learning algorithms; examples are regression, decision trees, and neural networks to perform learning of patterns and regularities [11]. These models are AI systems that can predict outcomes by using what they have previously learned. Usually, in the final stage, the predictive models are applied to analyze real-time data to predict upcoming disasters. Risk assessment [12] of diverse danger zones coupled with geographical areas will help to determine the requirement of resources and alleviate the impact of disasters to the possible level. Authorities can use their findings from risk analysis to make timely decisions to stop or reduce the effect of disasters on losing lives people and property.

Some well-known predictive modeling methods often used in disaster risk reduction and crisis management are regression analysis [13] which aims to develop multiple linear relationships between dependent variables (like, for example, failure of preventive actions or disaster occurrence, damage intensity), and some independent variables (e.g., set environmental factors or socio-economic indicators), logistic regression which is a type of regression analysis for predicting arrivers. Every node in the tree stands for one of the decision variables, based on which the branch develops. However, there can be multiple branches where different outcomes correspond. Fitting together many decision trees increases the quality of prediction as well as robustness. Every tree that is within the forest is presented randomly in terms of the sample and predictor variables, thereby preventing bias and increasing accuracy. A supervised learning algorithm [14, 15] is utilized for classification and regression problems. SVMs are methods that find a hyperplane that best separates the data into different classes or estimates the value of a continuous variable. The neural network class of machine learning can learn complex patterns and relationships being nonlinear and appropriate for modeling complicated disaster scenarios. Time series analysis techniques are used for modeling the temporal behavior of the variable; interesting examples are weather forecasting, seismic activities, or disease spreading. Spatial analysis such as spatial autocorrelation, spatial regression, and geo-statistics are used to model the spatial distribution of hazards, vulnerability, and exposure.

ii. Early warning systems: Sensors, satellites, social media, and news sources are only a few of the three in which real-time data enables the early warning system monitors [16, 17]. This system uses the data to detect disasters. Such informational systems can serve as a utility for timely and direct notification of authorities and populations living at risk to safeguard themselves. Real-time data is provided from different sources depending on the targets of warning systems: images from satellites, weather stations, and social media feeds; afterward, the system processes manifested data with some analytic tools to find different patterns of past disasters. Speech recognition is for the early identification of the signals of coming disaster and normal conditions. But first comes the data computation. After analysis, prospective danger is evaluated and scale in terms of impending disasters is estimated. Consequently, all essential warnings must be provided to people in advance. Through these alerts, vulnerable people have to be alerted through the means of broadcasting messages via mobiles, radios, television, and through social media. The basic duty is to incorporate the message to as many people as possible who are within that risk-prone area and able to provide clear instructions necessary for the safety of the people. The main purpose of this motive is for early warning disaster, tipping off the public, and taking some proactive steps that are meant to minimize causalities and reduce property damage.

iii. Remote sensing and imaging: Having machine learning models, artificial intelligence includes satellite images and aerial photographs as required. This will enable the evaluation of damage and allocation of resources to specific needs [18]. The sensing of distance is attained through data collection from far off by connection to sensors fitted on satellites, planes, or drones or to stationed ground-based instruments. This data then is used to calculate the level of destruction, find the impacted region, and support case-making during and after disasters. It compiles input data from many different radar sources, imagery data as well as LiDAR data that provides details about Earth's surface, atmosphere, and oceans. These inputs are used to identify various features and changes during different periods. We could apply software with AI algorithms to obtain data and find information related to disaster management. The tool can be used to apply the user's fingerprint to access some websites and programs. Artificial intelligence algorithms have discovered the areas damaged; this information is forwarded directly to funding and planning for recovery activities. The purpose of such a mission is a continuous measurement of the environmental variables like air quality, water quality, and land degradation before a disaster, during a disaster, and after the disaster as well. AI systems identify pollution, track changes, and measure the consequences of natural disasters on ecosystems. The data gathered from people's experiences is key to long-term environmental management and conservation and rehabilitation of disaster-stricken regions.

iv. Natural language processing (NLP): Natural language processing, also known as NLP, is a fundamental element in the technology innovation that will be useful in disaster management and reduction of risk. NLP has already found its way to operational life and is increasingly being used in many areas, whether in external affairs like commerce and retail (for example, with the help of customer service chatbots) or in medicine (for instance, in electronic health record interpretation or summarization). NLP algorithms can help us to have access to information in social media articles, newspapers, and so on. In this way, we are made aware of difficult times, new developments, and activities in projects or campaigns [19].

The starting point is an extraction of information from unstructured sources such as social media posts, newspapers, and reports produced by varying government departments. It can manage the names of places, more of occurrences, time, and others because of disaster relatives' concepts. NLP algorithms can automatically examine the flow of data in real time, picking out and monitoring disaster-related information. Therefore, latent semantics analysis (LSA), through the recognition of specific disaster-related words and other language patterns linked with disasters, can help relevant authorities with early warning disaster information. Today social media is very useful for information gathering. People use it as a platform for sharing updates, videos, as well as photos of the disaster. As a result, the NLP algorithms process the information and extract critical information for the relevant authorities. NLP-based chatbots and virtual assistants serve as assistants and authoritative experts during crises. These respondents will be able to provide some answers to questions of a routine nature, give emergency instructions, and help authorities in times of crisis. The NLP system performs the gathering of necessary data from the people that have a different language than the communicating authority and in exchange of information, it does it all from language barriers.

v. Geographic Information Systems (GIS): What we can do with technology is to endeavor to imitate and sort of copy other things bringing us a step closer to technological revolution. However, humans and other naturally made creations are of greater importance than technological progress. A disaster may be challenged with more or less time to prepare, or it could be a natural, man-made, or accidental occurrence. The elephant in the room—i.e., the catastrophic climate change attributed to human actions like air, water, and soil pollution—is the most identifiable one. Management of such disasters is tightly connected with Geographic Information System (GIS) technology which performs an important function therein.

The geographic information systems along with remote sensing can be used in the victory from disaster management itself, no matter which stage and the crucial phases of the process are disaster mitigation or recovery. This repository of the technical systems is the container for the communications as well as the analysis and display of data. Disaster prediction studies using huge data sets were launched. This data contains information about several disasters for services, population, and age, gender details, land details, and the whole state. Natural catastrophes are hazardous phenomena that are related to the nature and formation of the Earth's crust. A case in point would be natural disasters such as flooding, earthquakes, typhoons, volcanic eruptions, and other geological phenomena. Anthropogenic or man-made disasters are those human implying human involvement. The use of remote sensing and GIS technology becomes a means for predicting floods. Disaster responders are likely to turn up technologies that are remote sensing-based, like GIS/photogrammetry to effectively and economically get rid of disasters. The main function of GIS technology is to determine places of emergency and provide humanitarian accommodations for people in difficult situations. To be concrete, the two major places should be identified for installing the wall structure and the alternate road is a necessity to drain the water. In addition, the process of tailoring various levels of the flood vulnerability maps is also done which indicate the areas with more frequency of occurrence of the flood and also the base maps which depict the setup of boats and location of the rescue squad. GIS facilitates national, regional, and local crisis management entities to plan and manage these programs preparatory to the disasters. Discover additional engineering essays on our blog.

Human-based GIS-based urban information systems together display data on demographics and infrastructure covering the area to be developed. The use of remote sensing and GIS technology makes it possible to get the location of the historical site exactly (the spatial dataset) about its place. One aim of remote sensing and GIS technology is the ability to map changes in the environment that find the location of the most severe damage and its potency to lessen these consequences. Disaster prompt GIS Tech can flag up the areas affected with no less time. Locational tracking platforms and GIS/web-based software can provide real-time location information, including the details of the earthquake location, nearby health facility, the base camp, and the assessment of the damages. The digital map-based analysis also provides the situation picture to the incident management teams who collect data on infrastructure damage or fire and share information with relief teams aimed at the employment of appropriate relief measures for the victims. Remote sensing and GIS technology are one of the greatest tools in many occurring disasters like dryness, heatwaves and cold waves, climate change, and global warming. Through disasters such as air pollution, water pollution, and soil pollution, which have climate and global warming impacts many pollutions to occur. These disasters are considered common in places where there are unregistered meteorological events and conditions. The cyclones that have struck our region before have been dealt with by properly utilizing geographic information systems (GIS) technology, which has entailed both planning and preparedness, thereby saving human lives. It has aided and assisted by way of exceeding potentials in environmental comprehension, strategic making and execution, monitoring a climate change impact, and ensuring future challenges. Additionally, it is the role of Mathematics to carry out a functioning algorithm to analyze geospatial data and the output of it is having a visual format. The data is visualized, and then distinguishing patterns and interconnections among them become possible. The information obtained from this intelligence will not only shorten the time of these bodies but also give them enough information that would help them in their disaster management of particular regions [20].

By way of GIS technology, the historical data will be available to the community. The weather agencies and rescue teams will show evidence of vulnerability through maps and the risk time display. COVID-19 stands for instance that one shall learn how important is infographics and maps. These days, geographical information system (GIS) technology has come to the assistance of the healthcare industry in response to the worldwide outbreak of COVID-19. It is fought through mapping pre-existing data such as current COVID-19-positive cases, quarantine center locations, hospital infrastructure capabilities, and identifying hotspots via a GIS-based COVID-19 monitoring and response solution. Vaccination coverage, as well as spatial mapping, and analysis skills are the key roles with positive yields based on the spatial mapping, and GIS can play in efficiently distributing the vaccines [21].

vi. Simulation and modeling: AI-based simulation along with modeling methods is used for ascertaining the influences of specific factors on the infrastructure, humans, and the environment by offering various disaster scenarios. It supports the decision-makers and offers an opportunity to test various strategies, measure the impact, and finally find out the prone areas where improvements are required before the lapse of the disaster. AI systems make it possible to simulate an entire series of extreme natural disaster scenes that are determined by the content of available historical data, environmental factors, and socio-economic conditions. One of the major benefits to the decision makers of tackling spatial data; they can efficiently deploy space-based mitigation measures and allocate the resources with precision. Among the operational apps, simulation and optimization algorithms are being used to search and optimize the fittest response strategies and resource allocation charts to counter the disasters and minimize the impact of it. AI methods such as genetic algorithms, neural networks, and reinforcement learning that optimize evacuation routes contribute to decision-makers understanding human wants and behaviors. They also help to determine emergency communication strategies further. AI-inner HTML servers simulate platforms used for training purposes by emergency responders. The platforms deliver response processes that can be tested for interoperability, effectiveness, and suitability of different approaches when using them in a safe structured environment. These trainings, aimed at building resiliency, improving coordination, and enhancing capabilities among the response teams and the stakeholders are also essential elements. Simulation and modeling technologies let the companies create preparedness plans that assist the operation of vital links during disasters. AI algorithms examine organizational frameworks and lines of dependence as well as essential operations that can be impacted by a disruption. This helps identify the core areas where mitigation measures can be taken and business continuity systems can be enhanced [22].

vii. Robotic assistance: AI-enhanced robots and drones perform after disasters for rescue and injury assessment, infrastructural inspection, and personal safety, all at once. AI-powered chatbots and digital assistants give humans a plenitude of help in an emergency setting. Through these AI-powered systems, people will have access to crucial information, assistance, and support that will be made available to them before, during, and after disasters. Such data will enable response teams to carry out their roles seamlessly with service delivery being prioritized. While these assistants are there whenever you need them and as much time as it takes, it can run millions of operations at the same time relative to different persons by keeping a record of information in such a manner that everyone can have that [23]. This is where the NLP system comes help because the chatbots can communicate and respond to the users' inquiries in multiple languages providing the information to people belonging to different nations. Thus, the assistant parser is quite useful when medical care access is compromised by delivering first aid instructions supplemented with remote medical assistance as well as telemedicine services in line with individual demands. It encourages vulnerable individuals to learn to cultivate stress and anxiety tolerance after disasters. Chatbots are being used to generate comprehensive two-way communication across the authorities and affected communities through the provision of information for individuals to report emergencies and request aid and feedback when it comes to response efforts. Instances that involve message interaction between the disaster response organizations and victims as well as those who reside in the affected areas can be successfully carried out through the use of chatbots and voice assistants [24].

5.3 Ethical and Social Implications of Using AI Tools in Disaster Management

The use of AI tools in disaster management raises several ethical and social implications that must be carefully considered. While most technologies give great potential benefits, they also come with a huge number of risks and difficulties that need to be addressed.

Bias and fairness: One major issue is the capabilities of AI systems to preserve or boost existing biases. If the training data used to expand these AI tools is bent or lacks diversity, the following models and predictions may give unfair treatment to certain groups or communities [28]. This could lead to uneven distribution of assets, aid, or categorization during disaster response efforts.

Privacy and data protection: AI tools in disaster management often rely on piling and processing large amounts of private data, such as GPS information, social network data, and other responsive information. This raises privacy concerns and the need to certify proper data safety measures are in place [29]. Strict data governance and security protocols must be carried out to prevent unofficial access, misuse, or taking advantage of personal data.

Transparency and accountability: Many AI systems, especially deep learning models, operate as "black boxes," making it hard to understand how they reach their choices or predictions. This lack of translucency can be awkward in disaster management layouts where essential decisions are made [30]. There is a need for definable AI techniques and procedures that ensure accountability and enable human oversight [25].

Human agency and control: There are questions surrounding the potential for human autonomy and decision-making in disaster response as AI assistance becomes more commonplace. AI can support decision-making but the individual decision-maker should always have control of AI actions or extensive discretion in high-risk decisions [32].

Public trust and acceptance: This necessitates the public's trust and acceptance of these AI tools in the domain of disaster management to be a success. It states that if these technologies are perceived by the public as being non-transparent, unreliable, and a potential threat to privacy or health, this could lead to rejection or fear of AI-based solutions [33].

5.4 Impact and Effectiveness of AI Tools and Technologies

a) Disaster preparedness

Predictive analytics and risk assessment: AI-driven predictive analytics systems help to pinpoint threats and spur preparedness proactively before a crisis rather than booting up immediately after the disaster.

Early warning systems: AI-powered early warning systems, such as those mentioned, impose alerting of exposed communities and create possibilities for actions taken before to be lived through, thus making cases relating to disaster preparedness, relief, and response extra protected.

Risk mapping techniques: AI-driven risk mapping helps to identify populations and vulnerable areas and therefore the authorities can not only give the resources and interventions but can also go a step ahead to identify such areas before the disaster occurs [26, 27].

b) Disaster response

Decision support systems: The AIs supplier system is the most critical factor that makes possible, rapid decisions, next it allows the allocation of resources and also the coordination of the response in emergencies which ends up boosting the effectiveness of disaster response [31].

c) Disaster recovery

Data analytics and machine learning: When implemented as model enhancements of the hectic nature of post-disaster data analytics and machine learning algorithms help expedite the process of assessment, reconstruction, and planning thus contributing to shortening the period of recovery and reducing the impacts in the long run.

Risk management strategies: AI-based risk management approaches framework ensures us to experience firstly effects reduction and secondly, improves resilience by identifying and remedying system weaknesses.

d) Disaster mitigation

Predictive modeling and optimization algorithms: Next-gen AI-aided predictive models and optimization algorithms help plan land use, infrastructure design, and ecosystem restoration which indirectly results in less vulnerable buildings against disasters. Therefore, the community resilience is enhanced [34].

Early warning systems and real-time monitoring: Such emergent AI-equipped early warning systems and real-time monitoring technology have demonstrated their potential efficiency in timely communication of hazards, risk mitigation and adaptively responding in disasters leading to fewer effects on the affected population.

Following the discussion on the key success factors and best practices for the implementation of AI, it can be concluded that:

> Data quality and accessibility: Establish the availability of high-quality, credible data from different sources and adopt strong data governance systems with an emphasis on the security and privacy of the content.
> Interdisciplinary collaboration: Leverage the expertise and resources of partners from different stakeholders, such as government agencies, academia, NGOs, and the private sector which promote the integration of different sections.
> Ethical and transparent AI deployment: Ensure adherence to ethical guidelines and principles to AI development deployment where transparency, accountability, and fairness are observed during the decision-making process.
> Continuous learning and adaptation: Fostering a learning culture that inculcates adaptation, relying on the loop learning experience and mistakes to make the AI algorithms and decision support tools better.
> Community engagement and empowerment: The incorporation of communities in the development, roll-out, and assessment of AI-based initiatives, paying attention to their top priorities, outlooks, and concerns as a must in local disaster management.

Through adopting these critical practical steps and best practices in AI-based disaster management, stakeholders are afforded the capabilities to gain considerable efficiency and high impacts of these AI tools and technologies in improving disaster preparedness, response, recovery, and mitigation, resulting in the surge of overall resilience among the affected communities and reduced impacts of disasters on the populations as a whole [35].

5.5 AI for Dismantling Difficulties in Disaster Management

However, the contribution of the artificial intelligence technology systems is highly significant but the challenges accompanying AI systems cannot be ignored.

- Data collection and handling: Any data collection and uses of AI systems involve one of the main issues, i.e., data collection proper and handling. A lack of well-trained models even if the testing is not properly conducted may lead to the diminishing of the entire AI-powered system's reliability.
- Computational and transparency issues: Automated systems usually have to process a large amount of the information which complicates the whole process, making it obscure and very difficult to master.
- Operational implementation: The results from all AI systems need to be in line with users' requests and will be translated into terms that users can comprehend and process. The user needs to be encompassed in the majority of the stages of implementation which means that it will be too hard for implementation.
- Privacy and security: The data used in artificial intelligence systems needs to be collected through liaisons with safe and secure sources. Besides the datum processing as the law dictates, it has to be stored properly. Some secure systems may meet security and privacy issues because it has to deal with so much data.
- Data quality and quantity: This data may be incorrectly collected and hence not relevant to teach the AI algorithms that may eventually give rise to faulty predictions [36].

- Cost: The construction of human intelligent systems that can provide risk reduction and management in natural disasters needs high expenses which are impossible to bear by people in affected areas.
- Technical experts: The engineering of artificial intelligence is an indispensable part of technical expertise.

5.6 Future Directions and Recommendations

The integration of AI-based tools into disaster risk reduction and emergency preparation processing approaches has a big opportunity. On the contrary, the main challenge lies in the joining effort of the different disciplines. Future missions must prioritize the establishment of cooperation networks among stakeholders, including the policymakers, scientists, humans, and AI experts, to design and use AI-based solutions together. A key element of the sensible use of AI and robotics is the creation of ethical guidelines and governance frameworks to ensure that they are used responsibly and transparently. Investments in data infrastructure, data interoperability, and capacity building are essential that will make AI possible as intelligent management of data. Conducting pilots and evaluating targets based on different storm kinds will improve reliability and performance. Public–private joint ventures bring into play the private sector's competence and resources, while international cooperation and knowledge sharing are vital in the role of experience exchange. Continuous study, interdisciplinary approach, and community organizing are three main ingredients to ensure ethical, practical, and socio-cultural considerations and to enhance the context-specific and sustainable solution. The maximum possible effect of AI by handling the recommendations will be the decrease of lives lost, reduction of economic losses, and improving the resilience of the communities at the global level.

5.7 Conclusion

The results of the presented research demonstrate the undoubted capabilities of AI-based tools and technologies to support disaster risk reduction and emergency preparedness efforts. AI adapts these advanced analytical methods such as predictive analytics, early warning systems, remote sensing, natural language processing, and geographic information systems, and simulation models to intervention and response processes during disasters.

This will enable decision-makers to be able to come up with reliable forecasts, effective, preventative measures, and timely and well-informed responses during a disaster. In the end, the study reveals that policymakers, practitioners, and scientists have to cooperate to investigate and set up AI-based solutions to cope with the challenges of it. AI can be a game changer when it comes to saving precious lives, reducing economic losses, and ensuring sustainability and resilience for communities at different corners of the world by applying its powers at the right time and right place.

Acknowledgments

The authors would like to thank the anonymous reviewers and the editor/associate editor for their critical feedback and helpful ideas.

Funding

The authors wish to declare that they have not received any funding for this research.

References

1. Taub, A., Baiocchi, D., Rajaratnam, B., Leveraging machine learning for disaster risk prediction: A review. *Int. J. Disaster Risk Reduct.*, 48, 101660, 2020.
2. Nguyen, T., Pham, T., Dinh, T., Artificial intelligence in disaster risk management: A systematic literature review. *Int. J. Disaster Risk Reduct.*, 54, 102042, 2021.
3. Fountoulakis, I., Moschoyiannis, S., Askoxylakis, I., Early warning systems for natural disasters: A review. *Sensors*, 19, 15, 3369, 2019.
4. Meroni, A.N., Calvani, G., Musacchio, A., A review of remote sensing technologies for disaster management. *Sensors*, 20, 3, 823, 2020.
5. Li, J., Wang, D., Lu, Y., A survey on decision support systems for disaster management: Past, present, and future trends. *Inf. Syst. Front.*, 22, 5, 1199–1219, 2020.
6. Fernandez, R., Calvino, A., Alesanco, A., A review of decision support systems based on artificial intelligence for disaster management. *Sustainability*, 13, 1, 217, 2021.
7. Hu, H., Xu, X., Chen, Y., A review of image analysis and machine learning techniques for automatic detection of building damages in post-earthquake

remote sensing imagery. *ISPRS J. Photogramm. Remote Sens.*, 147, 289–307, 2019.

8. Khan, S., Abbasi, M., Mahmood, A., Applications of artificial intelligence for the assessment of post-disaster damages: A review. *Sustainable Cities Soc.*, 55, 102057, 2020.
9. Zhang, L., Guo, W., Xu, H., A review of data analytics and machine learning approaches in disaster response and recovery. *Sustainability*, 13, 8, 4607, 2021.
10. Du, H., Zhang, X., Zhang, H., Big data analytics and machine learning in disaster management: A systematic review and future directions. *Sustainable Cities Soc.*, 54, 101975, 2020.
11. Zheng, J., Duan, Z., Yin, J., A review of artificial intelligence applications in disaster management: Opportunities and challenges. *Saf. Sci.*, 117, 170–184, 2019.
12. Wang, X., Liu, Z., Yu, Y., A systematic review of artificial intelligence applications in risk management of natural hazards. *Sustainability*, 13, 12, 6524, 2021.
13. Lee, S., Kim, S., Kim, K., A review of artificial intelligence techniques in disaster management: Recent trends and future perspectives. *Sustainability*, 12, 7, 2945, 2020.
14. Liu, Y., Li, M., Chen, S., A survey of artificial intelligence applications in disaster risk reduction and management: Techniques and methods. *Nat. Hazard.*, 106, 2, 1245–1274, 2021.
15. Smith, J. and Johnson, A., Role of Artificial Intelligence in Disaster Management. *J. Disaster Manag.*, 5, 2, 123–135, 2023.
16. Garcia, M. and Patel, R., Leveraging Predictive Analytics in Disaster Preparedness. *International Conference on Disaster Risk Reduction Proceedings*, pp. 45–56, 2022.
17. Chen, L. and Wang, Q., Early Warning Systems for Disaster Risk Reduction. *J. Risk Anal.*, 8, 3, 210–225, 2021.
18. Rodriguez, P. and Martinez, S., Remote Sensing and Imaging Techniques in Disaster Management. *J. Remote Sens. Appl.*, 15, 78–92, 2020.
19. Lee, H. and Kim, D., Ethical Considerations in AI Deployment for Disaster Management. *IEEE Conference on AI Ethics Proceedings*, pp. 112–125, 2019.
20. Tanaka, Y. and Suzuki, T., Addressing Algorithmic Bias in Disaster Response Systems. *International Workshop on Ethical AI Practices*, pp. 30–45, 2018.
21. Li, X. and Wu, Z., Challenges of Data Privacy in AI-driven Disaster Management. *J. Priv. Prot.*, 12, 4, 320–335, 2017.
22. Brown, K. and Wilson, M., Innovative Practices in AI-driven Disaster Response. *Int. J. Disaster Recov.*, 25, 2, 156–170, 2016.
23. Patel, R. and Garcia, M., Opportunities and Challenges in AI-driven Disaster Management. *Proceedings of the International Symposium on Disaster Risk Reduction*, pp. 88–102, 2015.

24. Rajendran, N., *et al.*, Secured control systems through integrated IoT devices and control systems. *Meas.: Sens.*, 24, 100487, 2022, https://doi.org/10.1016/j.measen.2022.100487.
25. Wang, Q. and Chen, L., Strategies for Responsible AI Deployment in Disaster Contexts. *J. Ethical Technol.*, 7, 1, 45–60, 2014.
26. Kumar, A., *et al.*, 'Secure and energy-efficient smart building architecture with emerging technology IoT. *Comput. Commun.*, 176, 207–217, https://doi.org/10.1016/j.comcom.2021.06.003, 2021.
27. Khattar, N., Sidhu, J., Singh, J., Toward energy-efficient cloud computing: a survey of dynamic power management and heuristics-based optimization techniques. *J. Supercomput.*, 75, 8, 4750–4810, 2019, https://doi.org/10.1007/s11227-019-02764-2.
28. Andersen, L., Kaplan, J., Merlino, L., Artificial intelligence and climate change: Opportunities, considerations, and policy levers to mitigate risk, Brookings Institute, 2021.
29. Jiang, H., Qin, S., Wang, J., Lu, Y., Privacy-preserving AI-enabled IoT for disaster management. *IEEE Internet Things J.*, 9, 3, 1625–1636, 2022.
30. Zhang, Y., Luo, Z., Li, M., Explainable AI for disaster relief logistics: A survey. *IEEE Access*, 10, 19193–19216, 2022.
31. Alhaidari, H., Santos, E., Tannous, W.K., Cai, X., Explainable AI for post-disaster damage assessment. *IEEE Access*, 9, 152673–152688, 2021.
32. Verma, S., Singh, R., Yalcin, G.S., Designing trustworthy AI for humanitarian assistance and disaster relief. *Proceedings of the 52nd Hawaii International Conference on System Sciences*, 2019.
33. Crawford, K. and Calo, R., There is a blind spot in AI research. *Nature*, 538, 7625, 311–313, 2016.
34. Dogra, R., Rani, S., Sharma, B., A Review to Forest Fires and Its Detection Techniques Using Wireless Sensor Network, in: *Advances in Communication and Computational Technology.* ICACCT 2019. Lecture Notes in Electrical Engineering, vol. 668, G.S. Hura, A.K. Singh, L. Siong Hoe, (Eds.), Springer, Singapore, 2021.
35. Rani, S., Ahmed, S.H., Rastogi, R., Dynamic clustering approach based on wireless sensor networks genetic algorithm for IoT applications. *Wirel. Netw.*, 26, 2307–2316, 2020.
36. Kumar, Y., Garg, P., Moudgil, M.R., *et al.*, Enhancing parasitic organism detection in microscopy images through deep learning and fine-tuned optimizer. *Sci. Rep.*, 14, 5753, 2024.

6

AI Tools and Technologies in Disaster Risk Reduction and Management

Alisha Sinha* **and Laxmi Kant Sharma**

Department of Environmental Science, Central University of Rajasthan, Ajmer, Rajasthan, India

Abstract

Natural disasters have the capacity to cause severe destruction as well as significant loss of economy and human life. The rapid uncontrolled development and the changing climate have extensively increased the risk of disasters across the world. As a result, disaster management is an important tool to ensure the well-being of humanity as well as prevent them from serious consequences. The increasing incidence of disasters highlights the crucial need for modern technologies in disaster risk reduction and management. Nowadays, artificial intelligence (AI) is an innovative approach, increasingly being used in disaster risk management, ranging from disaster prediction to response optimization. The AI approach not only may provide the quick outputs but also can significantly reduce the risk related with the human and economic resources at the various phases of disaster. The study emphasized on the application of AI in effective disaster management and attempts to present example applications of several AI algorithms and their utilization for managing disaster risk at different phases. The study also addressed complex challenges and envisioned future directions.

***Keywords*:** Artificial intelligence, disaster risk assessment, mitigation, risk reduction, natural hazards, disaster

**Corresponding author*: alishasri2018@gmail.com; ORCID ID: 0000-0003-2911-2893
Laxmi Kant Sharma: ORCID: 0009-0004-5255-8441

Neelam Dahiya, Gurwinder Singh, Sartajvir Singh and Apoorva Sharma (eds.) Artificial Intelligence in Remote Sensing for Disaster Management, (99–124) © 2025 Scrivener Publishing LLC

6.1 Introduction

Disaster risk management is an important sector that needs robust and effective policy framing, quick action, and comprehensive preparedness. With the rise in disaster frequency and intensity [1] of late, the role of disaster management bodies has become more important. In the purview of changing climate and intensified population growth, the impacts of disasters have grown significantly in the past few decades. Disasters like flash floods, cloud bursts, droughts, cyclones, storm surges, floods, landslides, subsidence, wildfires, urban flooding, urban heat hazards, and pollution episodes may be linked with uncontrolled anthropogenic activities and climatic changes; on the other hand, episodes which are generally not triggered by humans, like volcanic eruptions and earthquakes, also cause greater loss to humans and the economy due to population explosion. [2] mentioned that there is approximately $1 trillion of loss due to disasters, led by the United States, followed by China, Japan, and India in just two decades (1998–2017). On the perusal of the aforementioned, a question arises to formulate a solution to meet the exigency of proactive measures.

Traditionally, hazard and risk factors were identified using several methods such as experts' survey, multi-criteria decision making, field monitoring as well as various physics-based models, while these approaches were human-based having a significant chance of false alarm [3]. In the light of technical advances, the utilization of AI is providing new insights and paving new pathways even in the concern of disaster management. The field of AI has recently become in mode with the advent of popular large language models or LLMs; however, the actual potential and application of AI is many times greater than this.

The AI and Geographic Information Systems (GIS) can provide unprecedented results by working together. Machine learning (ML) is one of the most important tools in the context of AI and disaster management, as it can be used in the interpretation of thousands of satellite imagery in a short time. Through the use of convolutional neural network (CNN) which is a type of artificial neural network (ANN) mostly used in image recognition, AI can save hundreds of hours of image processing time, and through fast data dissemination modules, AI can, in turn, save millions of lives by providing fast and accurate automated results. With the increase in urbanization, climate change, and other human-induced pressures, the intensity and reoccurrence of hazards have increased. In such scenarios, the role of AI increases manifolds with its ability in prediction, data analysis, and pattern identification.

By examining current advancements and envisioning future directions, this chapter aims to shed light regarding how AI can enhance our capabilities to reduce the impacts of disasters and build resilient communities.

6.2 AI Tools in Different Phases of Disaster Management

Disaster management can roughly be categorized into three phases, *viz.*, i) before disaster, ii) during disaster, and iii) after disaster (Figure 6.1). In every single phase, AI has a significant role to play [2, 4].

6.2.1 Before Disaster

The stage before the occurrence of any disaster involves three steps, namely, prevention, mitigation, and preparedness. The major part of this stage is for risk assessment, which means to analyze the extent of risk that could be associated with a future disaster. AI models are used for the sensitivity assessment of any area and the disaster risk associated. It includes collecting data through past events and also with sensors for early detection [5]. The data through the sensors comes from the information collected by

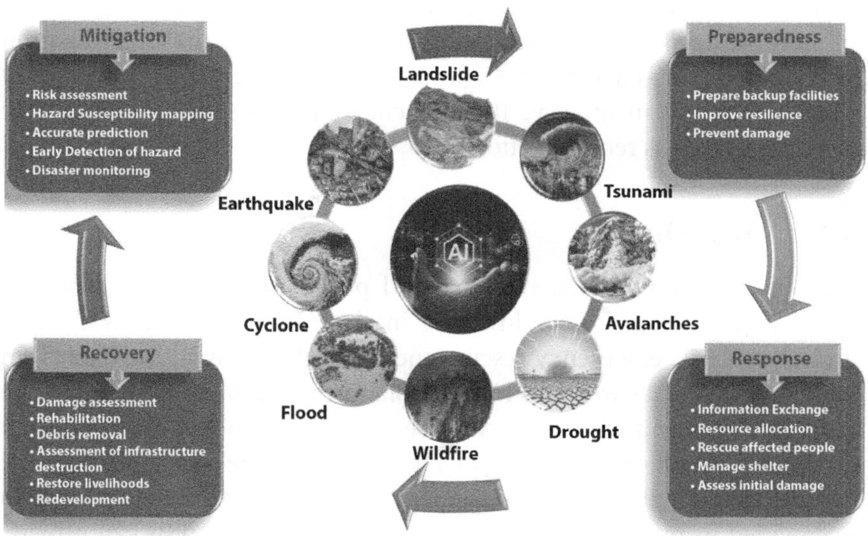

Figure 6.1 An overview of the application of artificial intelligence (AI) in various phases of disaster risk reduction and management.

remote sensing techniques, monitoring equipment, and the Internet. This data is updated at regular periods to mark the sensitive zones and to get informed about disaster-prone scenarios. This is a crucial stage for reducing the expected deaths and property damage. Predicting and modeling tools that incorporate AI methods help in developing mitigation measures. Multi-source data from various sources like satellites, social media, and IoT sensors, when combined with historical data and real-time information and machine learning models, can detect the early warning signs of disasters like forest fires, floods, etc. The significant advancements in AI experienced in the recent decade have substantially improved to predict these catastrophic events and aid in calamities [6–8].

6.2.2 During Disaster

The major step involved in this phase is the response to the disaster by making precise emergency decisions. These decisions are taken by various decision-makers which can be influenced by each other [9]. At this stage, timely coordinated steps are very important for rescue and recovery. The AI tools at this stage are used for the decision-making for the rescue process which has to be time-constrained. The process of evacuation from the affected area is carried out using Markov decision-making as well as a case-based reasoning method [10]. So, it is important to search for hierarchical reinforcement learning with an analytic hierarchy process and other processes to define the steps and objectives of this phase which would support the decision makers for taking further actions. The amalgamation of AI and cutting-edge technologies such as the Internet of things (IoT) and blockchain can improve the efficiency and transparency of disaster response as well as recovery efforts.

6.2.3 After Disaster

Once the disaster occurs, recovery and post-disaster needs assessment (PDNA) are the processes involved in that stage. It includes disaster impact analysis, emergency rescue, and evacuation. Real-time data from satellites, sensors as well and Internet platforms can measure the damage caused to lives and property, prioritize the rescue process, and efficiently distribute the resources needed [11]. AI algorithms are also applied for the logistics and supply chain management to ensure that the necessary help is provided in required areas. The post-disaster data analysis can provide insight regarding damage caused by the disaster. It includes identification of vulnerable areas and affected zones so that necessary steps and measures could be taken.

In addition, pertinent policy support can be developed for such industries and regions in order to minimize financial losses during the recovery and reconstruction phase following a disaster. Additionally, it helps on how to identify and address the issue of low disaster management efficiency, such as through optimized data analysis following a disaster, and confirm the effectiveness of emergency response. Furthermore, a challenge that must be overcome during the disaster recovery stage is how to assess the impact of emergency actions using post-disaster data analysis, identify and tackle the issue of low disaster management efficacy, such as optimum resource allocation, and improve the disaster emergency management effectiveness. During disaster response operations, AI-powered optimization algorithms can help with the effective distribution of resources like food, medical supplies, and rescue workers. AI-enabled robots and drones can be used for infrastructure inspection, search and rescue operations, and relief delivery in locations that are inaccessible to people.

6.3 Use of Geospatial Technologies and AI in Disaster Management

The use of geospatial technologies with AI has evolved the process of disaster risk management by integrating different models for disaster simulation, assessment, and response. The geographic information system and remote sensing can work as support tools as the geospatial datasets obtained from these technologies have a major importance in the field of disaster management and disaster risk reduction. Different modern datasets are capable of monitoring different parameters as potential precursors of any anticipated disasters. AI can monitor the datasets to give a prediction of any occurrence of disasters. In a study conducted by [12], AI algorithms that process seismic data with satellite imagery were used to measure the extent of damage and plan rescue operations in case of an earthquake disaster. The AI-based tools can monitor, generate, and integrate several geospatial parameters, such as land cover data, slope, and aspect data from digital elevation model outputs, weather data including precipitation data from various satellite, and ground-based sources over the area of interest. Using ML and decision-making tools like analytic hierarchy process (AHP), these tools can prepare real-time hazard maps or can project the risk of hazard in future (using numerical weather prediction (NWP) outputs). These AI outputs can be disseminated to the concerned stakeholders, policymakers, disaster rescue teams, and general public for saving thousands of human lives. Several urban disasters, namely, urban heat vulnerability and urban flood management, can be easily done in the AI environment. The satellite-based heat and emissivity data, climate and weather model outputs, satellite-based precipitation data, and stormwater management models integrated in an AI environment can prepare a comprehensive urban management system, which can save lives during flood-like disasters and in heat-wave-related health hazards. To evaluate potential repercussion and assess susceptibility to predict possible structural damage during natural hazard(s) using seismic fragility curves, [13, 14] used Lasso regression, [15–18] used neural network, and [19] used SVM. Natural disaster, i.e., flooding, has caused significant economic loss as well as loss of life worldwide over the past few decades [20]. Although significant efforts have been embraced to prevent flood, the consequent destruction of human life and assets remain at high level [21]. Precipitation datasets like PERSIANN-CDR are already using ANN for dataset preparation. These datasets along with decision-making tools in AI-based platforms not only can save lives but also may provide significant improvements in the field of food security. The analysis of forecasts, identifying precursors, hazard risk reduction during the event, and management during the PDNA phase can all be done using AI- and ML-based tools.

Using vegetation classification, soil moisture, and meteorological datasets, the AI can also save thousands of floras and fauna by automated data creation and dissemination to the concerned personnel. Geospatial data and AI tools can also provide real-time fire detection and mapping which can help in the evacuation and allocation of resources [22]. These technologies, when coupled together, are also capable of early detection of flood, helping rescue actions and mitigation measures [23]. Such collaborative approaches help decision-makers with profound information enhancing disaster resilience and reducing human and economic losses. The AI can provide round-the-clock analysis of different parameters and disseminate the information to different platforms. To enrich the system further, data from citizen scientists and LLMs can also be incorporated. Table 6.1 represents studies, where AI-based technologies have been used for disaster risk reduction and management.

Table 6.1 An overview of the different applications of AI and geospatial data in disaster risk reduction and management reported globally.

Disaster type	Objective	AI algorithm	Geospatial data	References
Landslide	Landslide prediction	Multilayer perceptron (MLP)	Satellite images	[24]
	Landslide vulnerability	Naïve Bayes tree (NBT), logistic model tree (LMT) and random forest (RF)	Landslide conditioning factors	[25]
	Landslide susceptibility assessment	NBT-RS (Naıve Bayes trees and random subspace)	Elevation, slope, aspect stream power index (SPI), topographic wetness index (TWI), lithology, land use, distance to road, fault, stream, fault density, stream density, and rainfall	[26]
	Landslide susceptibility	Support vector machines (SVM), artificial neural networks (ANN), logistic regression (LR), and reduced error-pruning tree (REPT)	Satellite images of conditioning factors	[27]

(*Continued*)

Table 6.1 An overview of the different applications of AI and geospatial data in disaster risk reduction and management reported globally. (*Continued*)

Disaster type	Objective	AI algorithm	Geospatial data	References
	Landslide susceptibility assessment	NBT, MLP, kernel logistic regression (KLR),	DEM derivatives, plan curvature, SPI, TWI, rainfall, sediment transport index (STI), land use, lithology, distance to faults, roads, rivers	[28]
	Landslide susceptibility assessment	LR, convolutional neural network (CNN), logitboost, random Forest (RF),	-	[29]
Urban hazard	Susceptibility of urban infrastructure to catastrophic weather events urban flood mapping	Deep neural network (DNN)	Satellite data demographic attributes	[30]
	Identifying survival in debris earthquake-hit smart urban settlements	Residual patch similarity convolutional neural network (ResPSNet)	-	[31]

(*Continued*)

Table 6.1 An overview of the different applications of AI and geospatial data in disaster risk reduction and management reported globally. (*Continued*)

Disaster type	Objective	AI algorithm	Geospatial data	References
	Fire hazard detection in smart	CNN, ANN and SVM	Images	[32]
	Urban flood risk mapping	Deep belief network (DBN) with recurrent LSTM neural network (R-LSTM-NN)	Big data	[33]
	Heat wave risk assessment	Fuzzy logic	Thermal infrared satellite data	[34]

(*Continued*)

Table 6.1 An overview of the different applications of AI and geospatial data in disaster risk reduction and management reported globally. *(Continued)*

Disaster type	Objective	AI algorithm	Geospatial data	References
Drought	Drought prediction	ANN	Temperature, wind speed, precipitation, relative humidity, and sun hours (monthly)	[35]
	Drought monitoring	RF, SVM, and MLP-NN	SPI (standardized precipitation index)	[36]
	Long-term prediction of drought	Deep belief network (DBN)	Standardized streamflow index (SSI)	[37]
	Drought monitoring	Deep learning	Satellite data	[38]
	Drought risk mapping for mitigation	Fuzzy logic	Precipitation slope, soil data	[39]
	Forecast drought	Adaptive Neuro Fuzzy Inference System (ANFIS)	Rainfall, SST anomalies, temperature	[40]

(Continued)

Table 6.1 An overview of the different applications of AI and geospatial data in disaster risk reduction and management reported globally. (*Continued*)

Disaster type	Objective	AI algorithm	Geospatial data	References
Flood	Flood prediction	DNN	Temperature and rainfall intensity	[41]
	Flood susceptibility mapping	Rotation forest (RF), nearest shrunken centroids (NSC), k-nearest neighbor (KNN), boosted regression tree (BRT), and LogitBoost	Flood conditioning parameters	[42]
	Flood vulnerability assessment	ANN	-	[43]
	Flood affected area Classification	SVM	Drone images	[44]
	Relief supplies in affected area	MLP-NN	Baidu big data	[45]
	Relief operations	AWS (Amazon Web Services)	Satellite images data	[46]

(*Continued*)

Table 6.1 An overview of the different applications of AI and geospatial data in disaster risk reduction and management reported globally. (*Continued*)

Disaster type	Objective	AI algorithm	Geospatial data	References
Cyclone/ hurricanes/ typhoon	Prediction of daily precipitation during typhoons	Fuzzy NN—locally linear embedding algorithm	-	[47]
	Assessment of damage for response and relief	CNN	Aerial images	[48]
	Solve the issues of effective rescue scheduling during disaster.	Bi-directional LSTM (bi-LSTM) and CNN	Twitter data	[49]
	To detect communications and power disruptions	SVM and LR	Twitter data	[50]
	Infrastructure damage assessments, caused due to the disaster	Deep neural network	Social media image	[51]
	Identified the highly affected area with most affected people and damaged infrastructure.	LSTM	Tweets	[52]

(*Continued*)

Table 6.1 An overview of the different applications of AI and geospatial data in disaster risk reduction and management reported globally. (*Continued*)

Disaster type	Objective	AI algorithm	Geospatial data	References
Tsunami	Early warning system	TUNAMI F1 mode	Historical earthquake data	[53]
	Forecasting to provide accurate and early warning	CNNs	Geodetic data	[54]
	Maximum tsunami prediction	Bayesian neural networks (BNN)	-	[55]
	The arrival time for prediction of tsunamis in the Indian ocean	ANN	-	[56]
	Maximum height and arrival time prediction	NN	-	[57]

(*Continued*)

Table 6.1 An overview of the different applications of AI and geospatial data in disaster risk reduction and management reported globally. *(Continued)*

Disaster type	Objective	AI algorithm	Geospatial data	References
Avalanches	Snow avalanche predictions	Logistic regression (LR)	Water equivalent, air temperatures (mean, maximum, and minimum), wind speed, and direction	[58]
	Snow avalanche predictions	SVM	Slope, precipitation, topographic position index, and TWI	[59]
	Snow avalanche susceptibility maps	NN	Snow and weather condition	[60]
	Snow avalanches forecasting	SVM, KNN, classification and regression tree (CART), MLP	Average temperature and average annual snowfall	[61]
	Search and rescue operation	SVM	Avalanches' historical data, meteorological conditions, and snowpack data	[62]
	Snow avalanche modelling	CNN, SVM	UAV imagery	[63]

(Continued)

Table 6.1 An overview of the different applications of AI and geospatial data in disaster risk reduction and management reported globally. (*Continued*)

Disaster type	Objective	AI algorithm	Geospatial data	References
	Avalanches forecasting	ANN	Air temperature, snow surface temperature, snowpack depth	[64]
	Snow avalanches monitoring	CNN	DEM derivatives, distance from stream, relative slope position (RSP), TWI, WEI, land use, lithology	[65]
Wildfires	Early fire detection	CNN	Camera images	[66]
	Wildfire risk assessment	RF, Bayesian optimization (BO), extreme gradient boosting (XGBoost)	Duff moisture code, fine fuel moisture code, drought code, initial spread index (ISI)	[67]
	Burnt area mapping	Artificial neural network (ANN)	Landsat Thematic Mapper	[68]
	Wildfire susceptibility assessment	RNN and LSTM	Forest coverage ratio, humidity, maximum and average temperatures	[69]
	Duration of fire spread and burn area analysis	RNNs	Temperature and precipitation	[70]

(*Continued*)

Table 6.1 An overview of the different applications of AI and geospatial data in disaster risk reduction and management reported globally. (*Continued*)

Disaster type	Objective	AI algorithm	Geospatial data	References
	Prediction of fire behavior	RNN	-	[71]
	Fire occurrence prediction	DNN	Evapotranspiration, heat flux, maximum temperature, solar irradiation, soil moisture, vapor pressure	[72]
Earthquakes	Prediction of the potential seismic moment for the next earthquake	ANFIS	Seismic data	[73]
	Predict earthquakes before 12 h of its occurrence	Expert system	Satellite images	[74]
	Predict the aftershock of an earthquake	PR-KNN (polynomial regression and k nearest neighbor)	Time interval data	[75]
	Earthquake timing and its energy prediction	Neural network	Magnitude and distance to the fault line and from the epicenter	[76]
	Earthquake magnitude prediction	RNN, RF	Seismic parameters	[77]

(*Continued*)

Table 6.1 An overview of the different applications of AI and geospatial data in disaster risk reduction and management reported globally. (*Continued*)

Disaster type	Objective	AI algorithm	Geospatial data	References
	Earthquake damage detection	CNN	3D point cloud	[78]
	Damage assessment and loss map	Latent Dirichlet allocation (LDA)	Social media data	[79]
	To identify survivors in debris	CNN, ANN, and SVM	-	[80]

6.4 Future Challenges and Goals with AI

Every step involved with disaster management is significant because of the risk involved in it.

The people responsible for risk assessment and management should have a clear understanding of the techniques and process. AI tools have not been implemented up to their potential as they involve computational processes that lack explanatory results and validity [81]. There is a need to explore current AI tools for its multi-source data representation and analysis [82]. To get a piece of authentic and complete information, continuous updates in AI tools along with developing more features for prediction, identification, and classification are essential. There is a prevalence of multi-source data analysis and data fusion that includes increased data types and sources such as social media that help to enhance the efficiency of AI models in the management of disasters. Still there is an opportunity to research AI and big data for this purpose since there are times when the data for disaster management carries misleading information that reduces the precision of data extraction. The present studies on disaster assessment encompass many single and hybrid methods, but there is still a need for such studies using hybrid tools for better results. The focus should be on the difference in the performances of single as well as hybrid techniques and also to improve their feasibility, effectiveness, speed, and accuracy. There are many data-related challenges, such as accessibility, security, and ethical concern in the application of AI for disaster management. In the future, the development of AI involves using IoT devices sensing, multi-source data analysis, and machine learning technologies. Multilateral collaboration between the stakeholders, administration, and researchers is also required along with keeping the integrity and ethics of AI intact. Furthermore, AI technologies with the technologies of edge computing and block chain have the potential to improve data extraction and resilience in areas prone to disasters.

6.5 Conclusions

The present research explores the potential of AI tools that have been employed in different disaster risk reduction and management. By enabling early warning, damage assessment, and community engagement, AI tools and technologies have a significant role in improving disaster management processes. The application of AI along with technology can enhance the clarity in steps taken by stakeholders at the level of preparedness, response, and recovery. AI has the potential to assist, avert, mitigate, and monitor natural calamities by analyzing large numbers of datasets; however, responsible deployment of AI is required. AI applications in disaster management face challenges with data and processing as well as the inability to separate and replicate analysis results. However, this needs continuous efforts from policymakers, researchers, and technicians to take the challenges involved with AI application in disaster management and risk assessment. The present study describes various AI tools and methods required for various phases of disaster management. We also tried to explore the different types of disasters and the AI tool applications associated with them in previous studies. This chapter concludes that AI is very important and useful in natural as well as man-made disaster management. Its effectiveness, however, is linked with data extraction and analysis. Geospatial technology is also a powerful tool that provides useful information on the geographical front required in responding to and mitigating a disaster. GIS and RS, when coupled with AI models, provide vital information for disaster risk management. The innovation in AI technology, with multiple data, would contribute toward risk analysis and early warning systems. Extensive research and interdisciplinary collaboration in the field of disaster predictive models could also help the stakeholders get involved in various steps by extracting the necessary information. Furthermore, it may be concluded that incorporation of AI tools for disaster risk assessment and management has the potential to improve decision-making efficiency by reducing the risks associated with disasters.

Acknowledgment

The author would like to express their gratitude to DST-FIST Lab, Central University of Rajasthan, India, for providing all the help to access the data and remote sensing and GIS software facilities for carrying out this research.

References

1. Tan, L., Guo, J., Mohanarajah, S., Zhou, K., Can we detect trends in natural disaster management with artificial intelligence? A review of modeling practices. *Nat. Hazards*, 107, 3, 2389–2417, Jul. 2021, doi: 10.1007/s11069-020-04429-3.

2. Kamolov, S., Machine learning methods in civil engineering: a systematic review. *Ann. Math. Comput. Sci.*, 21, 181–191, 2024.
3. Bellaire, S., van Herwijnen, A., Mitterer, C., Schweizer, J., On forecasting wet-snow avalanche activity using simulated snow cover data. *Cold Reg. Sci. Technol.*, 144, 28–38, 2017.
4. Ghaffarian, S., Taghikhah, F.R., Maier, H.R., Explainable artificial intelligence in disaster risk management: Achievements and prospective futures. *Int. J. Disaster Risk Reduct.*, 98, 104123, 2023.
5. Khosravi, K., Panahi, M., Tien Bui, D., Spatial prediction of groundwater spring potential mapping based on an adaptive neuro-fuzzy inference system and metaheuristic optimization. *Hydrol. Earth Syst. Sci.*, 22, 9, 4771–4792, 2018.
6. Ivić, M., Artificial intelligence and geospatial analysis in disaster management. *Int. Arch. Photogramm. Remote Sens. Spat. Inf. Sci.*, 42, 161–166, 2019.
7. Sun, W., Bocchini, P., Davison, B.D., Applications of artificial intelligence for disaster management. *Nat. Hazards*, 103, 3, 2631–2689, Sep. 2020, doi: 10.1007/s11069-020-04124-3.
8. Zabihi, O., Siamaki, M., Gheibi, M., Akrami, M., Hajiaghaei-Keshteli, M., A smart sustainable system for flood damage management with the application of artificial intelligence and multi-criteria decision-making computations. *Int. J. Disaster Risk Reduct.*, 84, 103470, 2023.
9. Tissera, P.C., Printista, A.M., Luque, E., A hybrid simulation model to test behaviour designs in an emergency evacuation. *Procedia Comput. Sci.*, 9, 266–275, 2012.
10. Ramchurn, S.D., *et al.*, Human–agent collaboration for disaster response. *Auton. Agents Multi-Agent Syst.*, 30, 1, 82–111, Jan. 2016, doi: 10.1007/s10458-015-9286-4.
11. Fan, X., Earthquake-Induced Chains of Geologic Hazards, in: *AGU Fall Meeting Abstracts*, pp. EP53B–02, 2019, Accessed: Aug. 07, 2024. [Online]. Available: https://ui.adsabs.harvard.edu/abs/2019AGUFMEP53B.02F/abstract.
12. Zhu, W., Allison, K.L., Dunham, E.M., Yang, Y., Fault valving and pore pressure evolution in simulations of earthquake sequences and aseismic slip. *Nat. Commun.*, 11, 1, 4833, 2020.
13. Kameshwar, S. and Padgett, J.E., Multi-hazard risk assessment of highway bridges subjected to earthquake and hurricane hazards. *Eng. Struct.*, 78, 154–166, 2014.
14. Mangalathu, S., Heo, G., Jeon, J.-S., Artificial neural network based multi-dimensional fragility development of skewed concrete bridge classes. *Eng. Struct.*, 162, 166–176, 2018.
15. Lagaros, N.D. and Fragiadakis, M., Fragility Assessment of Steel Frames Using Neural Networks. *Earthq. Spectra*, 23, 4, 735–752, Nov. 2007, doi: 10.1193/1.2798241.
16. Mitropoulou, C.C. and Papadrakakis, M., Developing fragility curves based on neural network IDA predictions. *Eng. Struct.*, 33, 12, 3409–3421, 2011.

17. Liu, Z. and Zhang, Z., Artificial neural network based method for seismic fragility analysis of steel frames. *KSCE J. Civ. Eng.*, 22, 2, 708–717, Feb. 2018, doi: 10.1007/s12205-017-1329-8.
18. Mangalathu, S., Jeon, J., DesRoches, R., Critical uncertainty parameters influencing seismic performance of bridges using Lasso regression. *Earthq. Eng. Struct. Dyn.*, 47, 3, 784–801, Mar. 2018, doi: 10.1002/eqe.2991.
19. Mahmoudi, S.N. and Chouinard, L., Seismic fragility assessment of highway bridges using support vector machines. *Bull. Earthq. Eng.*, 14, 6, 1571–1587, Jun. 2016, doi: 10.1007/s10518-016-9894-7.
20. Gaume, E., *et al.*, A compilation of data on European flash floods. *J. Hydrol.*, 367, 1–2, 70–78, 2009.
21. Wang, Z., Lai, C., Chen, X., Yang, B., Zhao, S., Bai, X., Flood hazard risk assessment model based on random forest. *J. Hydrol.*, 527, 1130–1141, 2015.
22. Kamilaris, A., Filippi, J.B., Padubidri, C., Koole, R., Karatsiolis, S., Examining the potential of mobile applications to assist people to escape wildfires in real-time. *Fire Saf. J.*, 136, 103747, 2023.
23. Mousavi, F.S., Yousefi, S., Abghari, H., Ghasemzadeh, A., Design of an IoT-based flood early detection system using machine learning, in: *2021 26th International Computer Conference, Computer Society of Iran (CSICC)*, IEEE, pp. 1–7, 2021, Accessed: Aug. 07, 2024. [Online]. Available: https://ieeexplore.ieee.org/abstract/document/9420594/.
24. Yuan, C. and Moayedi, H., Evaluation and comparison of the advanced metaheuristic and conventional machine learning methods for the prediction of landslide occurrence. *Eng. Comput.*, 36, 4, 1801–1811, Oct. 2020, doi: 10.1007/s00366-019-00798-x.
25. Nsengiyumva, J.B. and Valentino, R., Predicting landslide susceptibility and risks using GIS-based machine learning simulations, case of upper Nyabarongo catchment. *Geomat. Nat. Hazards Risk*, 11, 1, 1250–1277, Jan. 2020, doi: 10.1080/19475705.2020.1785555.
26. Shirzadi, A., *et al.*, Shallow landslide susceptibility assessment using a novel hybrid intelligence approach. *Environ. Earth Sci.*, 76, 2, 60, Jan. 2017, doi: 10.1007/s12665-016-6374-y.
27. Phong, T.V., *et al.*, Landslide susceptibility modeling using different artificial intelligence methods: a case study at Muong Lay district, Vietnam. *Geocarto Int.*, 36, 15, 1685–1708, Sep. 2021, doi: 10.1080/10106049.2019.1665715.
28. Hong, H., Liu, J., Zhu, A.-X., Landslide susceptibility evaluating using artificial intelligence method in the Youfang district (China). *Environ. Earth Sci.*, 78, 15, 488, Aug. 2019, doi: 10.1007/s12665-019-8415-9.
29. Wang, H., Zhang, L., Luo, H., He, J., Cheung, R.W.M., AI-powered landslide susceptibility assessment in Hong Kong. *Eng. Geol.*, 288, 106103, 2021.
30. Sriram, L.M.K., Ulak, M.B., Ozguven, E.E., Arghandeh, R., Multi-network vulnerability causal model for infrastructure co-resilience. *IEEE Access*, 7, 35344–35358, 2019.

31. Peng, B., Liu, X., Meng, Z., Huang, Q., Urban Flood Mapping with Residual Patch Similarity Learning, in: *Proceedings of the 3rd ACM SIGSPATIAL International Workshop on AI for Geographic Knowledge Discovery*, Nov. 2019, ACM, Chicago IL USA, pp. 40–47, doi: 10.1145/3356471.3365235.
32. Chaudhuri, N. and Bose, I., Exploring the role of deep neural networks for post-disaster decision support. *Decis. Support Syst.*, 130, 113234, 2020.
33. Zhang, Y., Geng, P., Sivaparthipan, C.B., Muthu, B.A., Big data and artificial intelligence based early risk warning system of fire hazard for smart cities. *Sustain. Energy Technol. Assess.*, 45, 100986, 2021.
34. Keramitsoglou, I., *et al.*, Heat wave hazard classification and risk assessment using artificial intelligence fuzzy logic. *Environ. Monit. Assess.*, 185, 10, 8239–8258, Oct. 2013, doi: 10.1007/s10661-013-3170-y.
35. Azizi, E., Tavakoli, M., Karimi, H., Faramarzi, M., Evaluating the efficiency of the neural network to other methods in predicting drought in arid and semi-arid regions of western Iran. *Arab. J. Geosci.*, 12, 15, 489, Aug. 2019, doi: 10.1007/s12517-019-4654-z.
36. Feng, P., Wang, B., Li Liu, D., Yu, Q., Machine learning-based integration of remotely-sensed drought factors can improve the estimation of agricultural drought in South-Eastern Australia. *Agric. Syst.*, 173, 303–316, 2019.
37. Agana, N.A. and Homaifar, A., A deep learning based approach for long-term drought prediction, in: *SoutheastCon 2017*, IEEE, pp. 1–8, 2017, Accessed: Aug. 07, 2024. [Online]. Available: https://ieeexplore.ieee.org/abstract/document/7925314/.
38. Shen, R., Huang, A., Li, B., Guo, J., Construction of a drought monitoring model using deep learning based on multi-source remote sensing data. *Int. J. Appl. Earth Obs. Geoinf.*, 79, 48–57, 2019.
39. Dayal, K.S., Deo, R.C., Apan, A.A., Spatio-temporal drought risk mapping approach and its application in the drought-prone region of south-east Queensland, Australia. *Nat. Hazards*, 93, 2, 823–847, Sep. 2018, doi: 10.1007/s11069-018-3326-8.
40. Nguyen, V., Li, Q., Nguyen, L., Drought forecasting using ANFIS- a case study in drought prone area of Vietnam. *Paddy Water Environ.*, 15, 3, 605–616, Jul. 2017, doi: 10.1007/s10333-017-0579-x.
41. Sankaranarayanan, S., Prabhakar, M., Satish, S., Jain, P., Ramprasad, A., Krishnan, A., Flood prediction based on weather parameters using deep learning. *J. Water Clim. Change*, 11, 4, 1766–1783, 2020.
42. Prasad, P., Loveson, V.J., Das, B., Kotha, M., Novel ensemble machine learning models in flood susceptibility mapping. *Geocarto Int.*, 37, 16, 4571–4593, Aug. 2022, doi: 10.1080/10106049.2021.1892209.
43. Akshya, J. and Priyadarsini, P.L.K., A hybrid machine learning approach for classifying aerial images of flood-hit areas, in: *2019 International conference on computational intelligence in data science (ICCIDS)*, IEEE, pp. 1–5, 2019, Accessed: Aug. 07, 2024. [Online]. Available: https://ieeexplore.ieee.org/abstract/document/8862138/.

44. Lin, A., *et al.*, A big data-driven dynamic estimation model of relief supplies demand in urban flood disaster. *Int. J. Disaster Risk Reduct.*, 49, 101682, 2020.
45. Nagendra, N.P., Narayanamurthy, G., Moser, R., Management of humanitarian relief operations using satellite big data analytics: the case of Kerala floods. *Ann. Oper. Res.*, 319, 1, 885–910, Dec. 2022, doi: 10.1007/s10479-020-03593-w.
46. Huang, Y., Jin, L., Zhao, H., Huang, X., Fuzzy neural network and LLE Algorithm for forecasting precipitation in tropical cyclones: comparisons with interpolation method by ECMWF and stepwise regression method. *Nat. Hazards*, 91, 1, 201–220, Mar. 2018, doi: 10.1007/s11069-017-3122-x.
47. Presa-Reyes, M. and Chen, S.-C., Assessing building damage by learning the deep feature correspondence of before and after aerial images, in: *2020 IEEE conference on multimedia information processing and retrieval (MIPR)*, IEEE, pp. 43–48, 2020, Accessed: Aug. 07, 2024. [Online]. Available: https://ieeexplore.ieee.org/abstract/document/9175304/.
48. Kabir, Md.Y. and Madria, S., A Deep Learning Approach for Tweet Classification and Rescue Scheduling for Effective Disaster Management, in: *Proceedings of the 27th ACM SIGSPATIAL International Conference on Advances in Geographic Information Systems*, Nov. 2019, ACM, Chicago IL USA, pp. 269–278, doi: 10.1145/3347146.3359097.
49. Paul, U., Ermakov, A., Nekrasov, M., Adarsh, V., Belding, E., #Outage: Detecting Power and Communication Outages from Social Networks, in: *Proceedings of The Web Conference 2020*, Apr. 2020, ACM, Taipei Taiwan, pp. 1819–1829, doi: 10.1145/3366423.3380251.
50. Alam, F., Imran, M., Ofli, F., Image4Act: Online Social Media Image Processing for Disaster Response, in: *Proceedings of the 2017 IEEE/ACM International Conference on Advances in Social Networks Analysis and Mining 2017*, Jul. 2017, ACM, Sydney Australia, pp. 601–604, doi: 10.1145/3110025.3110164.
51. Sit, M.A., Koylu, C., Demir, I., Identifying disaster-related tweets and their semantic, spatial and temporal context using deep learning, natural language processing and spatial analysis: a case study of Hurricane Irma, in: *Social Sensing and Big Data Computing for Disaster Management*, Routledge, pp. 8–32, 2020, Accessed: Aug. 07, 2024. [Online]. Available:https://www.taylorfrancis.com/chapters/edit/10.4324/9781003106494-2/identifying-disaster-related-tweets-semantic-spatial-temporal-context-using-deep-learning-natural-language-processing-spatial-analysis-case-study-hurricane-irma-muhammed-ali-sit-caglar-koylu-ibrahim-demir.
52. Wibowo, M., *et al.*, Tsunami Database Development in the Sunda Arc Indonesia to Support Early Warning through Artificial Intelligence Technology. *Int. J. Adv. Sci. Eng. Inf. Technol.*, 13, 5, 1635–1644, 2023.
53. Makinoshima, F., Oishi, Y., Yamazaki, T., Furumura, T., Imamura, F., Early forecasting of tsunami inundation from tsunami and geodetic observation data with convolutional neural networks. *Nat. Commun.*, 12, 1, 2253, 2021.

54. Song, M.-J. and Cho, Y.-S., Modeling maximum tsunami heights using bayesian neural networks. *Atmosphere*, 11, 11, 1266, 2020.
55. Kumar, B.P., *et al.*, Tsunami Early Warning System — An Indian Ocean Perspective. *J. Earthquake Tsunami*, 02, 03, 197–226, Sep. 2008, doi: 10.1142/S1793431108000311.
56. Rodríguez, J.F., Macías, J., Castro, M.J., de la Asunción, M., Sánchez-Linares, C., Use of neural networks for tsunami maximum height and arrival time predictions. *GeoHazards*, 3, 2, 323–344, 2022.
57. Gauthier, F., Germain, D., Hétu, B., Logistic models as a forecasting tool for snow avalanches in a cold maritime climate: northern Gaspésie, Québec, Canada. *Nat. Hazards*, 89, 1, 201–232, Oct. 2017, doi: 10.1007/s11069-017-2959-3.
58. Choubin, B., Borji, M., Mosavi, A., Sajedi-Hosseini, F., Singh, V.P., Shamshirband, S., Snow avalanche hazard prediction using machine learning methods. *J. Hydrol.*, 577, 123929, 2019.
59. Dekanová, M., Duchoň, F., Dekan, M., Kyzek, F., Biskupič, M., Avalanche forecasting using neural network, in: *2018 ELEKTRO*, IEEE, pp. 1–5, 2018, Accessed: Aug. 07, 2024. [Online]. Available: https://ieeexplore.ieee.org/abstract/document/8398359/.
60. Wen, H., Wu, X., Liao, X., Wang, D., Huang, K., Wünnemann, B., Application of machine learning methods for snow avalanche susceptibility mapping in the Parlung Tsangpo catchment, southeastern Qinghai-Tibet Plateau. *Cold Reg. Sci. Technol.*, 198, 103535, 2022.
61. Pozdnoukhov, A., Matasci, G., Kanevski, M., Purves, R.S., Spatio-temporal avalanche forecasting with Support Vector Machines. *Nat. Hazards Earth Syst. Sci.*, 11, 2, 367–382, 2011.
62. Bejiga, M.B., Zeggada, A., Nouffidj, A., Melgani, F., A convolutional neural network approach for assisting avalanche search and rescue operations with UAV imagery. *Remote Sens.*, 9, 2, 100, 2017.
63. Singh, A. and Ganju, A., Artificial Neural Networks for snow avalanche forecasting in Indian Himalaya, in: *Proceedings of 12th international conference of international association for computer methods and advances in geomechanics, IACMAG*, p. 550, 2008, Accessed: Aug. 07, 2024. [Online]. Available: https://www.researchgate.net/profile/Amreek-Singh-4/publication/263651736_Artificial_Neural_Networks_for_Snow_Avalanche_Forecasting_in_Indian_Himalaya/links/00b7d53b69391e4fa6000000/Artificial-Neural-Networks-for-Snow-Avalanche-Forecasting-in-Indian-Himalaya.pdf.
64. Chen, Y., *et al.*, Toward the development of deep learning analyses for snow avalanche releases in mountain regions. *Geocarto Int.*, 37, 25, 7855–7880, Dec. 2022, doi: 10.1080/10106049.2021.1986578.
65. Muhammad, K., Ahmad, J., Baik, S.W., Early fire detection using convolutional neural networks during surveillance for effective disaster management. *Neurocomputing*, 288, 30–42, 2018.

66. Xie, L., *et al.*, Wildfire risk assessment in Liangshan Prefecture, China based on an integration machine learning algorithm. *Remote Sens.*, 14, 18, 4592, 2022.
67. Petropoulos, G.P., Kontoes, C., Keramitsoglou, I., Burnt area delineation from a uni-temporal perspective based on Landsat TM imagery classification using Support Vector Machines. *Int. J. Appl. Earth Obs. Geoinf.*, 13, 1, 70–80, 2011.
68. Cao, Y., Wang, M., Liu, K., Wildfire Susceptibility Assessment in Southern China: A Comparison of Multiple Methods. *Int. J. Disaster Risk Sci.*, 8, 2, 164–181, Jun. 2017, doi: 10.1007/s13753-017-0129-6.
69. Liang, H., Zhang, M., Wang, H., A neural network model for wildfire scale prediction using meteorological factors. *IEEE Access*, 7, 176746–176755, 2019.
70. Kozik, V.I., Nezhevenko, E.S., Feoktistov, A.S., Adaptive prediction of forest fire behavior on the basis of recurrent neural networks. *Optoelectron. Instrum. Data Process.*, 49, 3, 250–259, May 2013, doi: 10.3103/S8756699013030060.
71. Dutta, R., Aryal, J., Das, A., Kirkpatrick, J.B., Deep cognitive imaging systems enable estimation of continental-scale fire incidence from climate data. *Sci. Rep.*, 3, 1, 3188, 2013.
72. Mirrashid, M., Givehchi, M., Miri, M., Madandoust, R., Performance investigation of neuro-fuzzy system for earthquake prediction, 2016.
73. Ikram, A. and Qamar, U., Developing an expert system based on association rules and predicate logic for earthquake prediction. *Knowledge-Based Syst.*, 75, 87–103, 2015.
74. Li, A. and Kang, L., Knn-based modeling and its application in aftershock prediction, in: *2009 International Asia Symposium on Intelligent Interaction and Affective Computing*, IEEE, pp. 83–86, 2009, Accessed: Aug. 07, 2024. [Online]. Available: https://ieeexplore.ieee.org/abstract/document/5376072/.
75. Cheraghi, A. and Ghanbari, A., Study of risk analysis and earthquake magnitude and timing prediction via tectonic and geotechnical properties of the faults and identifying risky areas in terms of seismicity in Larestan city using artificial neural network. *QUID: Investig., Cienc. y Tecnol.*, 1, 1137–1142, 2017.
76. Asim, K.M., Martínez-Álvarez, F., Basit, A., Iqbal, T., Earthquake magnitude prediction in Hindukush region using machine learning techniques. *Nat. Hazards*, 85, 1, 471–486, Jan. 2017, doi: 10.1007/s11069-016-2579-3.
77. Vetrivel, A., Gerke, M., Kerle, N., Nex, F., Vosselman, G., Disaster damage detection through synergistic use of deep learning and 3D point cloud features derived from very high resolution oblique aerial images, and multiple-kernel-learning. *ISPRS J. Photogramm. Remote Sens.*, 140, 45–59, 2018.
78. Resch, B., Usländer, F., Havas, C., Combining machine-learning topic models and spatiotemporal analysis of social media data for disaster footprint and damage assessment. *Cartogr. Geogr. Inf. Sci.*, 45, 4, 362–376, Jul. 2018, doi: 10.1080/15230406.2017.1356242.

79. Chaudhuri, N. and Bose, I., Application of Image Data Analytics for Immediate Disaster Response, in: *Proceedings of the 21st International Conference on Distributed Computing and Networking*, ACM, Kolkata India, pp. 1–5, Jan. 2020, doi: 10.1145/3369740.3372729.
80. Kundu, S., Srijith, P.K., Desarkar, M.S., Classification of short-texts generated during disasters: A deep neural network based approach, in: *2018 IEEE/ACM International Conference on Advances in Social Networks Analysis and Mining (ASONAM)*, IEEE, pp. 790–793, 2018, Accessed: Aug. 07, 2024. [Online]. Available: https://ieeexplore.ieee.org/abstract/document/8508695/.
81. Nweke, H.F., Teh, Y.W., Mujtaba, G., Al-Garadi, M.A., Data fusion and multiple classifier systems for human activity detection and health monitoring: Review and open research directions. *Inf. Fusion*, 46, 147–170, 2019.
82. Stieglitz, S., Mirbabaie, M., Ross, B., Neuberger, C., Social media analytics–Challenges in topic discovery, data collection, and data preparation. *Int. J. Inf. Manage.*, 39, 156–168, 2018.

7

AI-Based Landslide Susceptibility Evaluation

Amanpreet Singh* **and Payal Kaushal**

Chitkara University Institute of Engineering and Technology, Chitkara University, Punjab, India

Abstract

An important output variable in the landslide susceptibility prediction (LSP) model is the landslide inventory. Still the impact of incomplete inventory of landslides on LSP and fault propagation in the model has not been extensively examined. Using Xunwu County, China, as a case study, we first obtain an existing landslide inventory, assuming that it represents all potential landslide samples under ideal conditions. We then simulate different missing sample conditions using random sampling. These conditions include random omission of samples from the landslide inventory in the research area by rates of 10%, 20%, 30%, 40%, and 50% as well as scenarios in which the samples are missing. LSP is implemented using five ML models, such as RF and SVM. The LSP results are evaluated for uncertainty analysis under different conditions. Furthermore, we examine modifications in the RF model's decision-making process under these circumstances using a variety of machine learning model interpretation techniques. The findings indicate that LSP results in local regions are impacted by random missing landslide inventory samples, with rates ranging from 10% to 50%. Clustered missing samples can cause a significant bias in LSP, especially in under-sampled regions. When 50%of the landslide samples are missing, two crucial steps in the RF model's decision-making process change (random or clustered): first, the components' respective rankings of importance. There are minor variations in environmental influences and factors. Second, the weights of individual factors in the LSP model can vary significantly within the same experimental grid unit. By combining data from earlier studies, aerial photographs, and field observations, a comprehensive landslide inventory map was created. The researchers then imported data into ArcGIS about unstable components including land cover pattern, slope angle, soil

**Corresponding author*: amanpreet.singh@chitkara.edu.in; ORCID: 0000-0002-3409-9833
Payal Kaushal: ORCID: 0000-0001-5235-9566

Neelam Dahiya, Gurwinder Singh, Sartajvir Singh and Apoorva Sharma (eds.) Artificial Intelligence in Remote Sensing for Disaster Management, (125–138)

type, soil erodibility, soil fluidity index, rainfall, and range close to water source. These elements are ranked on a numerical scale based on their physical conditions in the area. The numerical data set was analyzed using bivariate and multivariate models in order to determine the contribution of each element to the regulation of the geographical distribution of landslides. According to research, the most significant elements influencing slope movement are slope angle, proximity to streams, soil erosion, and soil type. These results can inform strategies to reduce landslide risks and protect the region's infrastructure and ecosystems.

***Keywords*:** Machine learning, deep learning, artificial intelligence, landslides

7.1 Introduction

Landslides are a dangerous natural hazard in karst areas that often result in significant damage [1, 2]. Recently, the recurrence, measure, and damaging tendency of landslides have expanded due to heightened human exercises and more visits on extraordinary climate occasions [3, 4]. In China alone, landslides threaten 74 million people and cause annual economic damages amounting to hundreds of millions of dollars [5]. While completely preventing landslides is impossible, effective mitigation strategies can be developed by studying the factors that contribute to landslides, modeling landslide risk, and identifying and interpreting areas prone to such hazards. These landslide helplessness evaluations are pivotal for calamity anticipation, relief management, and hazard assessment in landslide-prone regions.

Assessing a landslide's susceptibility involves calculating its probability both geographically and quantitatively within a certain range [6]. This handling process considers different contributing components such as topographic highlights, fabric properties [7], and natural variables like climate, hydrology, environment, human exercises, and seismic movement [8]. Progress in farther detecting innovation and spatial datasets has essentially upgraded the geographical risk observation and LSM [9]. Inaccessible detecting procedures give broad information, counting optical and microwave perceptions, which offer experiences into normalized contrast vegetation list (NDVI) and soil dampness substance [10, 11]. The work of Authors emphasizes the importance of vegetation distribution on LSM and shows how Interferometry Engineered Opening Radar systems help improve LSM accuracy [12, 13]. The nature of drivers along with regional variations in geography, topography and climate remains a primary challenge. In this manner, variables affecting landslides must be chosen concurring to the particular characteristics of the considered range.

Scientists employ various methods to assess landslide susceptibility, including physical models, measurable examination, and ML methods [14–21]. Numerical recreation strategies, such as limited component models and restrain balance strategies, are utilized to assess slope steadiness [14]. However, these strategies include rearranged presumptions, almost natural conditions, and landslide structures, requiring costly field investigations and making large-scale territorial checking challenging [15]. Statistical techniques are objective and repeatable; popular methods include the index of entropy and logistic regression (LR) [16–18]. Currently, ML is an overwhelming strategy for LSM, altogether improving the precision and exactness of LSM. Well-known machine learning strategies incorporate SVM, irregular woodland (IW), and profound neural systems [19–21].

Landslide risk assessment includes assessing the probability of landslides happening and the potential dangers they may pose. These hazards include injuries, loss of life, and damage to assets that could affect communities or societies over time [22]. The soft approach focuses on regional landslide risks, while the hard approach emphasizes the risk of individual landslides [23].

In recent decades, research has largely concentrated on developing knowledge-driven expert systems for landslide risk assessment [24–27]. These systems frequently rely on senior engineers' subjective experience, which produces outcomes that are strongly impacted by individual opinion. Furthermore, there is uncertainty and unpredictability in landslides across various places because of the large geographical heterogeneity of rocks and soils [28, 29]. Consequently, expert systems are typically confined to specific survey areas and depend heavily on manual labor and engineers' subjective experience. There is a growing need for semi-automated and automated methods capable of representing the complex nonlinear connections of soil structures.

AI excels at characterizing the inherent nonlinear relationships within large datasets, particularly in geotechnical contexts [30]. However, in the quest for higher accuracy, researchers have often ignored how these models explain their predictions. Because these methods are like "black boxes", it is hard to understand how different factors contribute to landslides in a specific area. The absence of interpretability is a key issue, especially for high-risk events like landslides and earthquakes, where decisions can impact lives and property [31]. This method combines landslide-related factors and explains how they influence predictions.

In this study, we utilized today accessible detecting information and topographical data to recognize components influencing avalanches. DEM information gives data on landscape height, slant, viewpoint, and ebb and flow. The normalized contrast vegetation record (NDVI) measured vegetation cover, demonstrating soil dampness substance and soil sort, which influence soil solidness. Lithology was moreover considered for soil quality. Overwhelming precipitation, mining exercises, streets, and streams were also contributing components.

The GAMI-net demonstration utilized these components to form landslide susceptibility models and gave a clear translation of landslide risk. We compared the execution of conventional models with the GAMI-net demonstration.

7.2 Principle of Support Vector Machines (SVM)

A lot of inquiries have been undertaken on the use of SVMs to produce landslide propensity charts (LSMs) by applying different ways, including separate SVM models, combining SVM models, and comparisons [32–36]. The foundation of statistical learning theory is the basic supervised machine learning technique known as SVM, which incorporates the structural risk minimization concept [37, 38]. The purpose of SVM is to map future spatial dimensions depending on the initial input space by identifying the best separating hyperplane. To distinguish between regions that are at risk for landslides, SVM looks for the best separation hyperplane within the framework of LSM.

As stated by Lee *et al.* [38], SVM is a popular method for producing LSM since it gives excellent performance and requires little setup. The optimal classification hyperplane and the application of kernel functions determine where to position the SVM models. Two different forms of data are shown by the dots and squares in Figure 7.1. Line H is the classification line; the parallel outlines H1 and H2, which cross the data items nearest to the arrangement line, creating the classification margin. As shown in Figure 7.2, the kernel function transforms the input samples into a space with greater dimensions and classifies them linearly. The margin of that specific hyperplane is the shortest path from the data vector for each layer. The SVM model's accuracy will increase with an increase in the classification margin [39, 40]. In SVM, the kernel's main job is to make it possible to transform input data into spaces with greater dimensions so that the best-separating hyperplane may be found [41]. SVM uses a variety of kernel function types, and choosing the right one is crucial because it affects the algorithm's performance significantly [42].

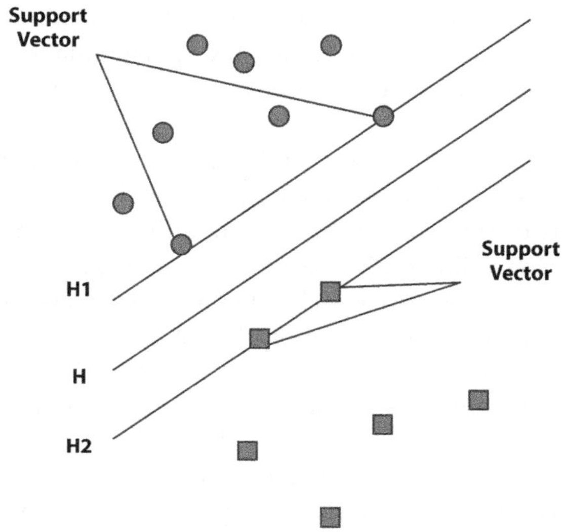

Figure 7.1 Dimensional hyperplane: showing the hyperplane that optimally separates two classes by maximizing the margin between them.

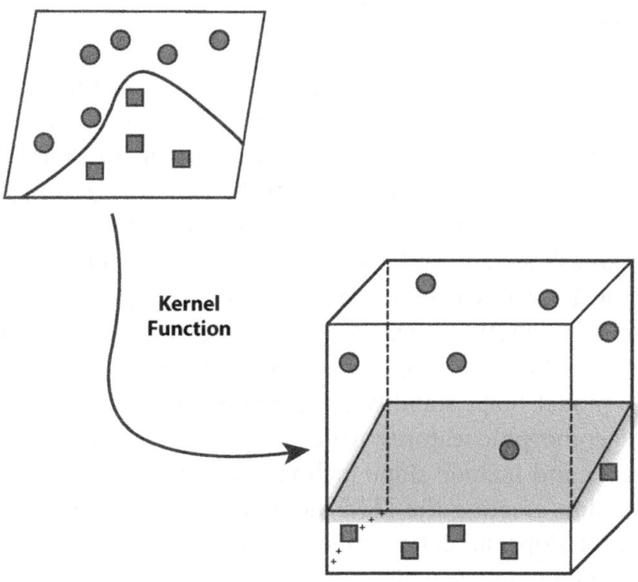

Figure 7.2 A situation where classes cannot be separated linearly is demonstrated, introducing slack variables to allow for some misclassifications.

Despite the fact that other kernel functions have been presented in earlier research, four types—linear kernel (LN), polynomial kernel (PL), and others—are frequently employed because of their efficacy in various applications [43, 44].

Using the SVM in ML to map landslide risk has become more prominent. For instance, 354 landslide data points with seven causative components and two triggering elements were utilized to create the LSM in Wencheng, China, utilizing SVM as the only model [45].

This study does not separate each data sample into sets for training and testing, contrary to common opinion. It instead removes the impact of creating training data sets via a fivefold cross-validation technique. LSM achieved an AUC score of 96%, demonstrating exceptional performance, according to the data. The ability of the SVM model to generate localized surface models (LSMs) for restricted regions vulnerable to certain trigger events, such as typhoons Trami and Kong-Re, was also evaluated in the study. The maps with significant chance values that are limited to a narrow area show the stability and great generalization capabilities of the SVM method. Future landslide mitigation efforts in high-risk locations may discover that substituting projected excessive rains for past triggers makes LSM more dependable and beneficial.

Using the SVM model, a research by Lee *et al.* [38] produced LSM for Pyeong Chang and Inje. In both cases, the same landslide causation factors were used. The results show that Inje's AUC value is 77.39%, whereas Pyeong Chang's is 81.36%. The small variations in the model's performance might be caused by differences in the geographic distribution of events occurring in the two sites. Another method employed in this study to identify landslide-causing factors that are strongly correlated and have an impact on LSM is sensitivity analysis. The topography of the region, comprising slope length, slope, and water energy index (SPI), topographic wetness index (TWI), and slope, was found to have a substantial influence on the LSM model. Slope stability and the possibility of mudslide initiation depend on geomorphic features, which are impacted by the topography of a specific area and include slope inclination and exposure. SPI and TWI were essential in creating the LSM model because of how important soil moisture is for slope stability. Feizizadeh *et al.* [46] investigated the performance of SVM models while constructing an LSM with several kernel functions.

Furthermore, Xu *et al.* [42] showed that a PL and RBF may be used to produce any input for the training data set. Higher landslide probabilities can be estimated using RBF and PL as they are intended for nonlinear modeling. The choice of landslide-causing elements can affect how differently a model performs in different research. This choice might affect the performance of the SVM model when using four different types of kernel functions to create the LSM. AUC values more than 80% were obtained for nearly all of the evaluated SVM models, indicating strong performance in LSM development. In order to improve LSM output, Lai SVM Dou *et al.* [47] conducted a study in a Japanese mountain watershed using SVM in combination with bagging, boosting, and stacking approaches. The findings demonstrated that while the SVM-boosted and SVM-bagging models were successful in raising the SVM model's predictive capacity, the SVM-stacked model did not have an enhanced performance. Combining SVM with boosting and bagging strategies improved the performance of the model by reducing bias, outliers, and overfitting problems.

Kumar *et al.* [36] compared the traditional SVM model with two hybrid SVM models, PSVM and Modified L2-Finite Newton SVM, for LSM generation in river basins in Mandakini, Garhwal Himalayas, India. Three additional statistical metrics—true negative rate, average percentage correct, and true prediction rate—were used in calculation to the AUC metric to assess how well these models performed. The L2-SVM-MFN model performs better than the other models across all validation measures, according to the results. Compared to the normal SVM model, the hybrid PSVM model performs somewhat differently across all validation criteria. When comparing the L2-SVM-MFN model to PSVM and SVM, it has the greatest true negative rate and the lowest false negative rate for correctly classifying landslide and non-landslide pixels. This suggests that the L2-SVM-MFN model produces superior outcomes and accuracy and is especially useful in lowering false alarms. It also performs better in areas with a deficiency of training data.

In two different studies, Kong *et al.* [48] and Zhang *et al.* [12] compare several hybrid machine learning methods for generating LSM. With an AUC of 97.6%, Zhang *et al.* [12] discovered that the hybrid fuzzy and support vector machine (F-SVM) outperformed the other hybrid and non-hybrid models in their investigation. According to Kong *et al.* [48], the PSO-RF model performs better than the SVM and (PSO-SVM) models combined. All of the study's models achieved outstanding to exceptional AUC values, ranging from 86% to 93%, despite variations in performance. Compared to the first machine learning model, the hybrid model demonstrated a significant improvement in overall performance. The superior performance of landslide susceptibility maps (LSMs) is attributed to the amalgamation of many learning methodologies, which surpasses the capabilities of a solitary learning model.

7.3 Conclusion

The use of support vector machines (SVM) in the creation of landslide susceptibility maps (LSM) is investigated in this work. Drawing from the literature review, the subsequent deductions can be made:

Chen *et al.*, Nhu *et al.* [49], Ortiz and Martínez-Graña [50], Yu and Chen [51], and Zare *et al.* [52] demonstrated that SVM and its hybrid models work well for LSM development. Even in regions with little landslide data, these models usually achieve good accuracy, frequently above 80%. While SVM works well, a number of studies have shown that a slightly greater performance is achieved by ADT, BT, LR, RF, and RL, among other machine learning techniques. SVM works extremely well for producing stable and objective LSMs, especially when working with high-dimensional and constrained nonlinear training data. It works effectively in places where there is a dearth of geoenvironmental data, like underdeveloped nations where data may be stale or lacking. When choosing the causal factors to develop LSM, there is no set standard. Diverse studies employ diverse parameters, indicative of a range of methodologies. Data sets regarding the origins of instability, encompassing causal or triggering events, exhibit notable variations contingent upon the nature, extent, and methodology of data gathering. Model performance is not significantly affected by the quantity and distribution of data samples used for training and validation. However, machine learning models' ability to generate LSM can be enhanced by choosing causal factors with greater weights and removing less significant components. The AUC approach is frequently used to assess the performance of LSM generated by machine learning models in order to gauge prediction success and accuracy. Additional quantitative and qualitative metrics, like the Statistical Index and Kappa Index, have been used in recent trends to assess LSM performance [53–56].

Acknowledgments

The authors would like to take this opportunity to express our deep gratitude to the reviewers of the book chapter. They played a crucial role in guiding us with our book chapter work. Their invaluable support and encouragement were especially helpful during difficult times.

References

1. Wistuba, M., Malik, I., Gärtner, H., Kojs, P., Owczarek, P., Application of eccentric growth of trees as a tool for landslide analyses: The example of Picea abies Karst. in the Carpathian and Sudeten Mountains (Central Europe). *Catena (Amst.)*, 111, 41–55, Dec. 2013, doi: 10.1016/j.catena.2013.06.027.
2. Chen, L., *et al.*, Deformation monitoring and failure mode research of mining-induced Jianshanying landslide in karst mountain area, China with ALOS/PALSAR-2 images. *Landslides*, 18, 8, 2739–2750, Aug. 2021, doi: 10.1007/s10346-021-01678-6.
3. Guzzetti, F., Landslide fatalities and the evaluation of landslide risk in Italy. *Eng. Geol.*, 58, 2, 89–107, Nov. 2000, doi: 10.1016/S0013-7952(00)00047-8.
4. Gariano, S.L. and Guzzetti, F., Landslides in a changing climate. *Earth Sci. Rev.*, 162, 227–252, Nov. 2016, doi: 10.1016/J.EARSCIREV.2016.08.011.
5. Zheng, H., *et al.*, Research on landslide hazard spatial prediction models based on deep neural networks: a case study of northwest Sichuan, China. *Environ. Earth Sci.*, 81, 9, 258, 2022.
6. Yong, C., Jinlong, D., Fei, G., Bin, T., Tao, Z., Hao, F., Qinghua, Z., Review of landslide susceptibility assessment based on knowledge mapping. *Stoch. Environ. Res. Risk Assess.*, 36, 9, 2399–2417, 2022.
7. Dikshit, A., Sarkar, R., Pradhan, B., Acharya, S., Alamri, A.M., Spatial landslide risk assessment at Phuentsholing, Bhutan. *Geosci. (Switzerland)*, 10, 4, 131, Apr. 2020, doi: 10.3390/geosciences10040131.
8. Chen, X. and Chen, W., GIS-based landslide susceptibility assessment using optimized hybrid machine learning methods. *Catena (Amst.)*, 196, 104833, Jan. 2021, doi: 10.1016/J.CATENA.2020.104833.
9. Kalantar, B., Ueda, N., Saeidi, V., Ahmadi, K., Halin, A.A., Shabani, F., Landslide susceptibility mapping: Machine and ensemble learning based on remote sensing big data. *Remote Sens. (Basel)*, 12, 11, 1737, Jun. 2020, doi: 10.3390/rs12111737.
10. Yang, W., Wang, M., Shi, P., Using MODIS NDVI time series to identify geographic patterns of landslides in vegetated regions. *IEEE Geosci. Remote Sens. Lett.*, 10, 4, 707–710, 2013, doi: 10.1109/LGRS.2012.2219576.
11. Zhao, F., Meng, X., Zhang, Y., Chen, G., Su, X., Yue, D., Landslide susceptibility mapping of karakorum highway combined with the application of SBAS-InSAR technology. *Sensors (Switzerland)*, 19, 12, 2685, Jun. 2019, doi: 10.3390/s19122685.
12. Zhang, Y., Shen, C., Zhou, S., Luo, X., Analysis of the Influence of Forests on Landslides in the Bijie Area of Guizhou. *Forests*, 13, 7, 1136, Jul. 2022, doi: 10.3390/f13071136.
13. Shen, C., *et al.*, Refinement of landslide susceptibility map using persistent scatterer interferometry in areas of intense mining activities in the Karst region of Southwest China. *Remote Sens. (Basel)*, 11, 23, 2821, Dec. 2019, doi: 10.3390/rs11232821.

14. Bai, D., Lu, G., Zhu, Z., Zhu, X., Tao, C., Fang, J., Using Electrical Resistivity Tomography to Monitor the Evolution of Landslides' Safety Factors under Rainfall: A Feasibility Study Based on Numerical Simulation. *Remote Sens. (Basel)*, 14, 15, 3592, Aug. 2022, doi: 10.3390/rs14153592.
15. Sengani, F., Mokibelo Mashao, F., Allopi, D., An integrated approach to develop a slope susceptibility map based on a GIS-based approach, soft computing technique and finite element formulation of the bound theorems. *Transp. Geotech.*, 36, 100818, Sep. 2022, doi: 10.1016/J.TRGEO.2022.100818.
16. Yan, F., Zhang, Q., Ye, S., Ren, B., A novel hybrid approach for landslide susceptibility mapping integrating analytical hierarchy process and normalized frequency ratio methods with the cloud model. *Geomorphology*, 327, 170–187, Feb. 2019, doi: 10.1016/J.GEOMORPH.2018.10.024.
17. Mondal, S. and Mandal, S., Landslide susceptibility mapping of Darjeeling Himalaya, India using index of entropy (IOE) model. *Appl. Geomatics*, 11, 2, 129–146, Jun. 2019, doi: 10.1007/s12518-018-0248-9.
18. Das, G. and Lepcha, K., Application of logistic regression (LR) and frequency ratio (FR) models for landslide susceptibility mapping in Relli Khola river basin of Darjeeling Himalaya, India. *SN Appl. Sci.*, 1, 11, 1–22, Nov. 2019, doi: 10.1007/s42452-019-1499-8.
19. Azarafza, M., Azarafza, M., Akgün, H., Atkinson, P.M., Derakhshani, R., Deep learning-based landslide susceptibility mapping. *Sci. Rep.*, 11, 1, 24112, Dec. 2021, doi: 10.1038/s41598-021-03585-1.
20. Sun, D., Wen, H., Wang, D., Xu, J., A random forest model of landslide susceptibility mapping based on hyperparameter optimization using Bayes algorithm. *Geomorphology*, 362, 107201, Aug. 2020, doi: 10.1016/J.GEOMORPH.2020.107201.
21. Z.S., Y.M., Z.Z., M.L., P.J., Luo, X., Lin, F., Mine landslide susceptibility assessment using IVM, ANN and SVM models considering the contribution of affecting factors. *PLoS One*, 14, 4, 1–18, Aug. 2019, doi: 10.1371/journal.pone.0215134.
22. Guo, Z., Chen, L., Gui, L., Du, J., Yin, K., Do, H.M., Landslide displacement prediction based on variational mode decomposition and WA-GWO-BP model. *Landslides*, 17, 3, 567–583, 2020, doi: 10.1007/s10346-019-01314-4.
23. Y.C., S.-H.J., S.W., Lei, Y., Huang, J., Ching, J., Time capsule for landslide risk assessment. *Georisk: Assess. Manage. Risk Eng. Syst. Geohazards*, 17, 4, 613–634, 2023, doi: 10.1080/17499518.2023.2164899.
24. Althuwaynee, O.F., Pradhan, B., Lee, S., Application of an evidential belief function model in landslide susceptibility mapping. *Comput. Geosci.*, 44, 120–135, Jul. 2012, doi: 10.1016/J.CAGEO.2012.03.003.
25. Kayastha, P., Dhital, M.R., De Smedt, F., Application of the analytical hierarchy process (AHP) for landslide susceptibility mapping: A case study from the Tinau watershed, west Nepal. *Comput. Geosci.*, 52, 398–408, Mar. 2013, doi: 10.1016/J.CAGEO.2012.11.003.

26. Pourghasemi, H.R., Mohammady, M., Pradhan, B., Landslide susceptibility mapping using index of entropy and conditional probability models in GIS: Safarood Basin, Iran. *Catena (Amst.)*, 97, 71–84, Oct. 2012, doi: 10.1016/J.CATENA.2012.05.005.
27. Tien Bui, D., Pradhan, B., Lofman, O., Revhaug, I., Dick, O.B., Landslide susceptibility mapping at Hoa Binh province (Vietnam) using an adaptive neuro-fuzzy inference system and GIS. *Comput. Geosci.*, 45, 199–211, Aug. 2012, doi: 10.1016/J.CAGEO.2011.10.031.
28. Li, J., Cassidy, M.J., Huang, J., Zhang, L., Kelly, R., Probabilistic identification of soil stratification. *Géotechnique*, 66, 1, 16–26, 2016, doi: 10.1680/jgeot.14.P.242.
29. Liu, W.F. and Leung, Y.F., Characterising three-dimensional anisotropic spatial correlation of soil properties through *in situ* test results. *Géotechnique*, 68, 9, 805–819, 2018, doi: 10.1680/jgeot.16.P.336.
30. Baghbani, A., Choudhury, T., Costa, S., Reiner, J., Application of artificial intelligence in geotechnical engineering: A state-of-the-art review. *Earth Sci. Rev.*, 228, 103991, May 2022, doi: 10.1016/J.EARSCIREV.2022.103991.
31. Yin, Z. and Xu, M., Explainable Neural Network Cancer Diagnosis of Unstained Tissue Samples Measured by Chemometric Microscope, in: *Biophotonics Congress 2021*, Optica Publishing Group, p. NM1C.5, 2021, doi: 10.1364/NTM.2021.NM1C.5.
32. Ballabio, C. and Sterlacchini, S., Support Vector Machines for Landslide Susceptibility Mapping: The Staffora River Basin Case Study, Italy. *Math. Geosci.*, 44, 1, 47–70, 2012, doi: 10.1007/s11004-011-9379-9.
33. E.L., P.C.K., C.D.W., G.R., F.J.U., V.M.R., Chaytor, J.D., Geist, Source Characterization and Tsunami Modeling of Submarine Landslides Along the Yucatán Shelf/Campeche Escarpment, Southern Gulf of Mexico, in: *Global Tsunami Science: Past and Future*, vol. I, H.M., R.A.B., T.Y., L. Geist Eric, Fritz (Eds.), pp. 4101–4116, Springer International Publishing, Cham, 2017, doi: 10.1007/978-3-319-55480-8_22.
34. Chen, W., Chai, H., Zhao, Z., Wang, Q., Hong, H., Landslide susceptibility mapping based on GIS and support vector machine models for the Qianyang County, China. *Environ. Earth Sci.*, 75, 6, 474, 2016, doi: 10.1007/s12665-015-5093-0.
35. Faming Huang Chi Yao, W.L.Y.L. and Liu, X., Landslide susceptibility assessment in the Nantian area of China: a comparison of frequency ratio model and support vector machine. *Geomatics Nat. Hazards Risk*, 9, 1, 919–938, 2018, doi: 10.1080/19475705.2018.1482963.
36. Kumar, D., Thakur, M., Dubey, C.S., Shukla, D.P., Landslide susceptibility mapping & prediction using Support Vector Machine for Mandakini River Basin, Garhwal Himalaya, India. *Geomorphology*, 295, 115–125, Oct. 2017, doi: 10.1016/J.GEOMORPH.2017.06.013.
37. Abedini, M., Ghasemian, B., Shirzadi, A., Bui, D.T., A comparative study of support vector machine and logistic model tree classifiers for shallow

landslide susceptibility modeling. *Environ. Earth Sci.*, 78, 18, 560, 2019, doi: 10.1007/s12665-019-8562-z.

38. Lee, S., Hong, S.M., Jung, H.S., A support vector machine for landslide susceptibility mapping in Gangwon Province, Korea. *Sustainability (Switzerland)*, 9, 1, 48, 2017, doi: 10.3390/su9010048.
39. Huang, Y. and Zhao, L., Review on landslide susceptibility mapping using support vector machines. *Catena (Amst.)*, 165, 520–529, Jun. 2018, doi: 10.1016/J.CATENA.2018.03.003.
40. Lee, S., Lee, M.J., Jung, H.S., Data mining approaches for landslide susceptibility mapping in Umyeonsan, Seoul, South Korea. *Appl. Sci. (Switzerland)*, 7, 7, 683, Jul. 2017, doi: 10.3390/app7070683.
41. Tien Bui, D., Tuan, T.A., Klempe, H., Pradhan, B., Revhaug, I., Spatial prediction models for shallow landslide hazards: a comparative assessment of the efficacy of support vector machines, artificial neural networks, kernel logistic regression, and logistic model tree. *Landslides*, 13, 2, 361–378, 2016, doi: 10.1007/s10346-015-0557-6.
42. Xu, C., Dai, F., Xu, X., Lee, Y.H., GIS-based support vector machine modeling of earthquake-triggered landslide susceptibility in the Jianjiang River watershed, China. *Geomorphology*, 145–146, 70–80, Apr. 2012, doi: 10.1016/J.GEOMORPH.2011.12.040.
43. Ercanoglu, M. and Gokceoglu, C., Assessment of landslide susceptibility for a landslide-prone area (north of Yenice, NW Turkey) by fuzzy approach. *Environ. Geol.*, 41, 6, 720–730, 2002, doi: 10.1007/s00254-001-0454-2.
44. Shirzadi, A., *et al.*, A comparative study between popular statistical and machine learning methods for simulating volume of landslides. *Catena (Amst.)*, 157, 213–226, Oct. 2017, doi: 10.1016/J.CATENA.2017.05.016.
45. Su, C., Wang, L., Wang, X., Huang, Z., Zhang, X., Mapping of rainfall-induced landslide susceptibility in Wencheng, China, using support vector machine. *Nat. Hazard.*, 76, 3, 1759–1779, 2015, doi: 10.1007/s11069-014-1562-0.
46. Feizizadeh, B., Roodposhti, M.S., Blaschke, T., Aryal, J., Comparing GIS-based support vector machine kernel functions for landslide susceptibility mapping. *Arabian J. Geosci.*, 10, 5, 122, 2017, doi: 10.1007/s12517-017-2918-z.
47. Dou, J., *et al.*, Improved landslide assessment using support vector machine with bagging, boosting, and stacking ensemble machine learning framework in a mountainous watershed, Japan. *Landslides*, 17, 3, 641–658, 2020, doi: 10.1007/s10346-019-01286-5.
48. Kong, C., Xu, K., Wang, J., Wu, C., Liu, G., Landslide susceptibility assessment based on different machine-learning methods in Zhaoping County of eastern Guangxi. *Nat. Hazards Earth Syst. Sci. Discuss.*, 2020, 1–41, 2020, doi: 10.5194/nhess-2020-251.
49. Nhu, V.H., *et al.*, Comparison of support vector machine, bayesian logistic regression, and alternating decision tree algorithms for shallow landslide susceptibility mapping along a mountainous road in the west of Iran. *Appl. Sci. (Switzerland)*, 10, 15, 5047, Aug. 2020, doi: 10.3390/app10155047.

50. Ortiz, J.A.V. and Martínez-Graña, A.M., A neural network model applied to landslide susceptibility analysis (Capitanejo, Colombia). *Geomatics Nat. Hazards Risk*, 9, 1, 1106–1128, 2018, doi: 10.1080/19475705.2018.1513083.
51. Yu, C. and Chen, J., Landslide susceptibility mapping using the slope unit for southeastern Helong city, Jilin province, China: A comparison of ANN and SVM. *Symmetry (Basel)*, 12, 6, 1–23, Jun. 2020, doi: 10.3390/sym12061047.
52. Zare, M., Pourghasemi, H.R., Vafakhah, M., Pradhan, B., Landslide susceptibility mapping at Vaz Watershed (Iran) using an artificial neural network model: a comparison between multilayer perceptron (MLP) and radial basic function (RBF) algorithms. *Arabian J. Geosci.*, 6, 8, 2873–2888, 2013, doi: 10.1007/s12517-012-0610-x.
53. Lee, D.H., Kim, Y.T., Lee, S.R., Shallow landslide susceptibility models based on artificial neural networks considering the factor selection method and various non-linear activation functions. *Remote Sens. (Basel)*, 12, 7, 1194, Apr. 2020, doi: 10.3390/rs12071194.
54. Dahiya, N., *et al.*, Detection of Multitemporal Changes with Artificial Neural Network-Based Change Detection Algorithm Using Hyperspectral Dataset. *Remote Sens. (Basel)*, 15, 5, 1326, Mar. 2023, doi: 10.3390/rs15051326.
55. Bajaj, J.S., Kumar, N., Kaushal, R.K., AI Based Novel Approach to Detect Driver Drowsiness. *ECS Trans.*, 107, 1, 4651, Apr. 2022, doi: 10.1149/10701.4651ecst.
56. Fallah-Zazuli, M., Vafaeinejad, A., Alesheykh, A.A., Modiri, M., Aghamohammadi, H., Mapping landslide susceptibility in the Zagros Mountains, Iran: a comparative study of different data mining models. *Earth Sci. Inf.*, 12, 4, 615–628, 2019, doi: 10.1007/s12145-019-00389-w.

8

Navigating Risk: A Comprehensive Study of Landslide Susceptibility Mapping and Hazard Assessment

Gaurav Kumar Saini* **and Inderdeep Kaur**

Department of Computer Science and Engineering, Chandigarh University, Mohali, Punjab, India

Abstract

Landslides are one of the most destructive natural disasters in the world, causing significant damage to the property and fatalities all around the world. The use of remote sensing has emerged as a boon for observing landslides at a large scale. Soil naturally has some binding forces created by microorganisms' excreta, hyphae (filaments of fungi), and some oxides that hold all the particles together. Landslides occur when external forces exceed these binding forces. In this chapter, all the existing machine learning methods for detecting landslides are examined in detail. A fully convolutional neural network (FCN) architecture is suggested to perform image segmentation after comparing with the already existing state-of-the-art models like PSPNet, ContextNet, DeepLab-v2, DeepLab-v3+, LinkNet, and FCN. For benchmarking, landslide4sense data is used which has 3,799 high-resolution images from sentinel-2 sensors taken from ALOS PALSAR from areas like Hokkaido, Japan's Iburi-Tobu Area, Kodagu District, Karnataka, and Taiwan. The suggested approach uses U-net architecture which can identify landslides with an accuracy of 98.6%, precision of 79.29, recall of 66.02%, and f1 score of 72.04% on the given dataset. U-net in landslide detection can be very useful for researchers and policymakers in predicting future risk assessment and management.

Keywords: FCN, hyphae, landslides, PSPNet, ContextNet, DeepLab-v2, Linknet, ALOS PALSAR

**Corresponding author*: mailgaurav77@gmail.com; ORCID: 0009-0003-4644-9102
Inderdeep Kaur: ORCID: 0009-0005-8345-0676

Neelam Dahiya, Gurwinder Singh, Sartajvir Singh and Apoorva Sharma (eds.) Artificial Intelligence in Remote Sensing for Disaster Management, (139–160) © 2025 Scrivener Publishing LLC

8.1 Introduction

Humans, animals, and natural vegetation are largely affected by landslides. Landslides can also lead to other natural calamities like floods. If the population density in a particular region is high, there will be more chances of the destruction of infrastructure, landscapes, and fatalities in that area [1].

A lot of advancements have been made on both national and international levels. The methods takes into account all the bands in images. The landslide4sense dataset has 14 bands in total. To calculate the probability of a landslide in a particular area, we need to take into account several factors such as climate, vegetation index, the population of humans and animals in that area, infrastructure, weather, and water level. Earlier GIS-based methodologies were really popular when it came to quantitative evaluations [2]. To perform the predictions, we can choose the combination of various machine learning algorithms with statistical methods and some strategies that are data-driven such as Shannon entropy and frequency ratio.

Using advanced technologies like GIS and remote sensing, this chapter has explained the various methods used in calculating the probability of landslides at a particular location. We have also discussed the old machine learning methods and the current deep learning methods used for the mapping of landslides.

Classical machine learning techniques were used earlier for the mapping of landslides. Logistic regression (LR) is mostly used for binary classification problems. It operates on a sigmoidal curve whose value is limited between 0 and 1 [3]. There is a threshold value that decides whether the calculated probability will fall in category A or category B (landslide or non-landslide). Support vector machines (SVM) have one hyperplane and two support vectors. The core idea is to maximize the gap between the hyperplane and the supporting vectors. The hyperplane and both of the vectors should be parallel to each other. Random forest is a kind of optimization algorithm which operates on decision trees. Decision trees of depth 1 are also called as stumps. The result from all of the stumps is gathered, and a final decision is made by taking the average or maximum vote (most repetitive value) in case of regression and classification, respectively.

We can use some semi-qualitative methods like the analytic hierarchy process (AHP). AHP is mainly used for applications where group decision-making is required such as decisions related to business, government policies, and healthcare industries. Fuzzy logic is used where the decision is non-binary. Weighted linear combination (WLC) is mostly used in decision-making situations where more than one attribute are involved, and we take a weighted sum of all the variables to make the final decision [4]. These techniques take both qualitative and quantitative approaches into account.

Many studies worked on comparing the methodologies mentioned above. The sole purpose of these studies was to determine the best method for landslide detection and mapping.

8.1.1 Challenges in Factor Selection and Weighting

In the given landslide4sense dataset, 14 bands are present. Based on the combination of these bands, we can calculate various factors such as elevation, slope, normalized difference vegetation index (NDVI), etc., to perform a probability assessment. This can be done through classical machine learning, deep learning, semi-qualitative methods and weighted linear methods, etc.

8.1.2 Combination of Subjective and Objective Approaches

The objective weighting methods derive weights by mathematical procedures and decision-makers, whereas the subjective weighting methods rely on the preferences of decision-makers to generate criteria weights. Though the objective approach gives better results, but still both types of approach are considered in some weightage for the final calculation of probability.

8.2 Factors Responsible for Landslides

8.2.1 External

a) Undercutting of hill slopes' feet:

Undercutting happens when the base of the soil is removed by some natural or man-made phenomena like infrastructure such as buildings, canals, and water bodies like rivers. It results in reducing the resistance of soil against the gravitational force.

b) External loads:

Along with the gravitational force, the soil has to deal with external loads such as different structures, stockpiles of rocks, vehicles, reservoirs, and roads [5]. This external load combines with gravity and puts more load on the soil, which may cause landslides.

c) Increase in the weight of the material comprising the slope:
The soil is a clay-bearing material that contains clay minerals such as smectite, chlorite, and micas [6]. An increase in the water levels inside the soil reduces the cohesion and the angle of internal friction which leads to a decrease in the resisting force of the soil against the external loads. Heavy rainfall, melting snow, and poor drainage systems are the major reasons of additional water in the soil.

d) Vibrations:
There can be several causes that create vibrations like road traffic, earthquakes, construction, and mining activities. These vibrations increase the shear stress on the soil, decrease the resistance to external forces, and may result in landslides.

e) Deforestation:
Roots of vegetation hold the soil and help in increasing the cohesive and tensile strength of soil [6]. It also prevents erosion of the soil because of rainfall, snow melt, gully erosion, and sheet erosion which can ultimately cause landslides.

f) Undermining:
Undermining results in damaging the structures (man-made or natural) that are supporting a slope [5]. It can cause, due to some reasons, erosion of seepage, tunneling, collapse of caverns, and some other underground actions.

8.2.2 Internal

a) Increase in water pressure:
The void spaces between the grains of soil or rocks are called pores. Additional water in the soil by activities like poor drainage systems, rainfall, and snowmelt increases the water pressure [5, 6]. This pressure decreases the resistive strength of soil against the external load and may become one of the reasons for landslides.

b) Decrease in cohesive strength:
Lateralization leads to a decrease in the cohesive strength of soil. This makes it more vulnerable to landslides [5]. It is simply the dissolution of rocks and aluminum oxides which leads to the formation of soil nearby it. A decrease in cohesive strength leads to the reduced shear strength of soil.

c) Hairline cracks:
Sequential occurrence of processes like freezing, wetting, and heating results in the expansion and contraction of soil frequently. The soil is in the form of sheets placed over each other [6]. The gap between them is

filled when water flows inside. Due to the increase in heat, the soil gets dry, which leads to the removal of water from the empty spaces. If the bonds of the soil are not strong enough, the dryness may lead the soil to lose its resistance against external forces.

d) Weathering due to cycles of freezing and thawing:
This may lead to the formation of cracks, fractures, and fissures. When water freezes in the pore spaces of rocks or soils, it expands and exerts pressure on the surrounding material. The material is stressed when it thaws because this pressure is released. Over time, the material may deteriorate due to these frequent cycles of freezing and thawing, increasing its susceptibility to landslides.

e) Earth material's physical characteristics:
Its inherent features, which include cohesiveness, compressive strength, shearing strength, and internal friction angle, dictate characteristics like its compressive and shearing strengths and the resistance of soil or rock to deformation and failure. Poor strength properties make rocks and soils more prone to damage [3].

8.3 Types of Landslides

a) Slides: Slides are used to transport a discrete mass of soil, rock, or debris down a distinctly defined surface or plane of weakness [7]. As illustrated in Figure 8.1, there are two primary types of slides:

   i) Slump formations: These are also known as rotating slides or slump blocks, which are the result of material sliding over a curved surface. One feature of the material's rotating movement is backward tilting.
   ii) Translational slides: These are typically parallel to the ground's slope and transport material along a planar surface. These slides through cohesive soils or fractured rock formations may move swiftly or slowly, depending on the conditions and initial causes.

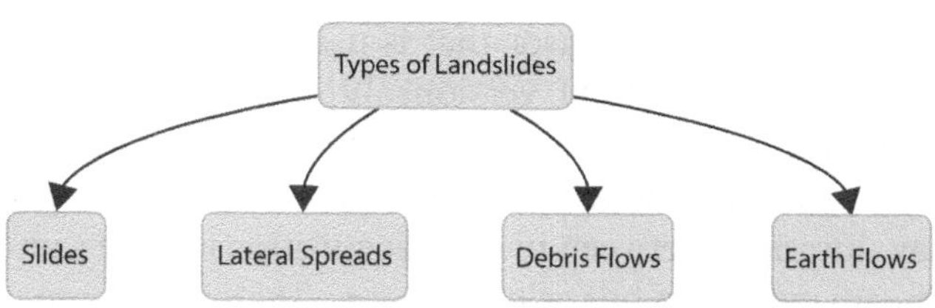

Figure 8.1 Different types of landslides.

b) Lateral spreads: The characteristic that distinguishes lateral spreads is the lateral movement of soil or rock over a relatively flat area. These events often occur in areas with saturated soils or weak sedimentary deposits, particularly in response to groundwater fluctuations or seismic activity. Lateral spreads can result in considerable damage to buildings, roadways, and utilities. They can also cause deformation and movement of infrastructure.

c) Debris flows: Debris flows, also called mudflows or lahars, are fast-moving masses of rock, soil, and water. These incredibly fluid mass movements can go large distances downward, usually with fatal consequences for the people they come in contact [8]. Debris flows are typically caused by intense rainfall, rapid snowmelt, or volcanic activity. Debris flows pose a particular threat because of their rapid velocity and high water content, which enable them to engulf and demolish any object in their path [7].

d) Earth flows: Earth flows are the gradual to rather rapid downslope movement of saturated soil or worn rock. These movements are typified by their viscous or plastic behavior and usually take place in fine-grained soils. Prolonged rainfall or soil saturation can cause earth flows by weakening the soil and allowing it to flow downslope [7].

8.4 Landslide Detection Techniques

a) Remote sensing: Remote sensing has significantly advanced since the Landsat satellite's first flight in 1972 and is now a crucial tool for tracking and identifying landslides [8]. It comprises using sensors to track radiation emitted and reflected from the Earth's surface by spacecraft, unmanned aerial vehicles, and ground-based platforms. There are instruments for both active and passive remote sensing; active sensors generate signals, while passive sensors measure solar radiation that is reflected into space. Passive sensors, found on satellites like Landsat, SPOT, and Sentinel, provide multispectral and hyperspectral images, while active sensors, like Synthetic Aperture Radar (SAR), gather microwave data. LiDAR is another active sensor that is used to measure in both aerial (ALS) and terrestrial (TLS) versions [9]. Unmanned aerial vehicles (UAVs) provide flexibility in gathering data, particularly in isolated or dangerous locations. The temporal, spectral, radiometric, geographical, and delay durations between picture acquisitions of the same area vary across the images taken by various sensors. These developments make it easier to recognize, track, and identify landslides and enable the evaluation of surface alterations over time.

b) Geotechnical: Geotechnical monitoring is necessary to detect and evaluate landslide movement and slope displacement [10]. Numerous geotechnical sensors, including tiltmeters, extensometers, geophones, and inclinometers, are used to monitor landslides. Inclinometers monitor horizontal subsurface deformation and track displacement normal to the casing axis when they are installed in vertical boreholes. Because tiltmeters detect the angle between the instrument body and the plumb line and provide high-resolution data, they are ideal for tracking rotating landslip processes. Extensometers measure the relative displacement between sites to detect landslide activity. Geophones use microseismical monitoring techniques to detect vibrations associated with landslide movement to identify landslides based on the features of their vibration signals [11]. Geotechnical monitoring data are essential for stability analysis and landslip prediction modeling.

c) Geodetic techniques: These are crucial for monitoring point displacements in landslide-prone areas, both absolute and superficial. These methods are often used in conjunction with geotechnical monitoring to provide precise information on the movements of landslides. Traditionally, terrestrial surveyors have used total stations equipped with geodetic reflecting prisms to measure the absolute displacements of object points. GNSS monitoring offers more flexibility and precision because it allows for the installation of permanent GNSS stations for multiple surveys of benchmarks or real-time monitoring. High-resolution digital elevation models (DEMs) and orthophotos produced by photogrammetry and terrestrial laser scanning (TLS) are further tools used in geodetic procedures [12]. TLS quickly gathers dense 3D point clouds of object surfaces, making it possible to measure volumes and displacement rates. Near real-time change detection is made easier by Automated Terrestrial Laser Scanning (ATLS), and although photogrammetry offers more affordable surface data collecting, it is less effective in densely vegetated areas. In areas with a high density of vegetation, LiDAR surveys are useful for producing high-resolution DEMs. To effectively manage risk, it is essential to comprehend and track the dynamics of landslides using geodetic methods.

d) Hydrological: Understanding slope instability requires hydrogeological monitoring since water plays a crucial role in the onset and movement of landslides. Gaining knowledge of the dynamics of landslides can be achieved by measuring water-related parameters in landslide-prone areas. Water changes the effective stress condition of slopes and weakens geological materials when they are saturated. Hydrogeological parameters like precipitation, soil moisture, pore water pressure, snow cover thickness, and water discharge are frequently observed [11].

e) Mapping: Landslide detection is a type of image segmentation problem. Image segmentation includes dividing an image into more than one part. In our case, we can take it as a binary segmentation problem where we need to divide the entire image into landslide and non-landslide parts. Geomorphological mapping includes studying the land, which involves the study of its dynamics, creation and how it evolved around time. Scientists use contemporary technology to analyze the soil and discover several factors that can lead to the formation of landslides. Mapping is very useful in studying the behavior of slopes. Vegetation, shape of the surface, level of groundwater, and study of tectonic plates and other materials in soil are the major factors to be studied in geological mapping. Scientists create several management plans to avoid risk by working on datasets related to water level, structure of soil and various lithological attributes [10]. Improvement in the technology related to satellite images and aerial photography has improved the mapping image quality skills also. By using various geological factors and applying various machine learning techniques, we can map the landslides and predict the risk metrics in the current situation.

8.5 Landslide Monitoring Techniques

Remote sensing methods such as LiDAR (ALS) are widely employed for landslide detection, especially for earth flows, while radar imagery is more commonly used for debris slides, earth slides, rock slides, and complex landslides [13]. In geotechnical monitoring, inclinometers are frequently used to track different types of landslides, while extensometers and crack-meters are helpful for tracking rock falls, landslides, and slides. Rock falls, debris slides, earth flows, and complex landslides are commonly tracked with geodetic methods such as GPS. For all kinds of landslides, hydrogeological monitoring is essential because it sheds light on the water-related factors that affect slope stability. This is mainly achieved through the use of piezometers and precipitation data. For many different kinds of landslides, mapping techniques such as engineering geological mapping, geomorphological mapping, and geological mapping are frequently used [14].

Geographically, mapping is mostly utilized at the local level, whereas remote sensing and mapping techniques are utilized for monitoring at the regional level [13]. The examination of temporal resolution is crucial, as remote sensing and mapping methods generally display varying degrees of temporal resolution. Only 38% of the techniques are still in use, with hydrogeological and geotechnical approaches remaining the most prevalent in terms of operational condition. The majority of monitoring methods are implemented following a landslide, suggesting that landslide investigations take a reactive rather than a proactive strategy. Furthermore, the fact that only a small portion of techniques are included in early warning systems emphasizes the difficulty and complexity of both their conception and application [15].

8.6 Use of Machine Learning in Landslide Mapping

Two types of approach are followed for image segmentation object-based and pixel-based [16]. These two methods can be implemented with the help of machine learning methods. Machine learning methods are used to check the textural features for the mapping of landslides. There are a number of machine learning algorithms such as random forest (RF), which utilizes many decision trees to make the final decision. This is one of the ensemble methods used in machine learning. Random forest is widely utilized in landslide detection in satellite photography [17]. Using kernelization techniques we can increase the dimensionality of the dataset, which makes the segmentation process very easy [16]. Support vector machine (SVM) algorithms use the method of kernelization while performing segmentation in complex datasets. Support vectors in the SVM algorithm help to separate the landslide and non-landslide data with maximum margin. Logistic regression (LR) has a sigmoidal curve which is used to separate two classes. Firstly, a threshold value is decided. If the probability of a point lying in a particular class is above the threshold value, then the point is assigned to that class [17]. This algorithm is easy and simple to understand and it works well on small datasets also. There are a variety of machine learning algorithms like multilayer perceptron neural networks (MLP), kernel logistic regression (KLR), and radial basis function neural networks (RBFNN) [18]. Each algorithm has some distinct quality that can help in detecting the potential of landslides and contribute to decreasing the risk and potential damage.

8.7 Use of Deep Learning in Landslide Mapping

There are three most important sub-topics in remote sensing. Object detection, transformation recognition and surface classification are the three most important sub-topics in remote sensing [19]. In deep learning, we use computer vision (CV) algorithms to analyze the images taken by the satellite. Earlier it was done with the help of classical machine learning algorithms. Deep learning has taken the process of landslide detection to a whole new level. The simplest and the first architecture in deep learning was the convolutional neural network (CNN). After CNN, we got other architectures like autoencoders and deep belief networks (DBN) [20]. Deep belief networks can easily learn from complex data, while on the other hand, autoencoders are more useful when the complexity is at an intermediate level. CNN was found to be very successful in removing the abstract part of the image which led to a more generalized deep learning model [21]. Satellite images have a number of bands which are difficult for segmentation tasks. If you try to do it with the help of CNN, it will require a huge number of neurons. The combination of topographic data with the bands is used to perform risk analysis using deep learning techniques [22]. There are some pre-trained models which are already trained on huge datasets. They can be fine-tuned and can be used directly in our dataset. This is called transfer learning. Transfer learning is very useful in cases where the dataset we are having is small.

8.8 Use of Ensemble Techniques

When we use more complex and multi-dimensional data, the deep learning models start giving limited performance. In such cases, we can use ensemble learning techniques. These techniques combine several weak learning models to create a strong model that gives higher accuracy and resilience. Bagging, AdaBoost, Logit boost, Multiboot, random forest, etc., are few of the examples of ensemble learning techniques [23]. In bagging, we do bootstrap sampling. Bootstrap sampling includes randomly picking a sample of rows with replacements. These samples will be trained on different models and finally, we will combine the results of all the models to give the final output. In AdaBoost, we create classifier series by doing the precise analysis of data [6]. LogitBoost is an extension of AdaBoost in which we use Bernoulli-likelihood loss to perform additive logistic regression. Multiboot is the combination of bagging and boosting algorithms.

To reduce variance, we use models with varying bases for the segmentation of images [23]. Random forest is a kind of bagging algorithm that uses multiple decision trees and combines the output on the basis of average results given by decision stumps. Ensemble methods are very powerful tools when it comes to increasing the performance of the model [24] in the case of complex datasets.

8.9 Limitations of Existing Algorithms

A detailed review was done on the existing image segmentation and object detection algorithms and the following shortcomings were observed:

a) PSPNet (Pyramid Scene Parsing): The aim of PSPNet is to do multi-scale feature learning by putting features under four pyramid scales. It uses a pyramid pooling strategy and does regional aggregation which results in learning the global context. It has observed limited performance of this model in landslide detection and achieved an f1 score of only 56.39%. The model struggles to capture contextual information and abilities at different scales.
b) ContextNet: The model can work very well in resource constraint conditions and work in real-time environments because of very low memory consumption. It expands a shallow network at a very high resolution that concentrates on semantic features which are at very low resolution. The performance of this model is suboptimal having a precision of 70.77% and a very low recall of 49.29%, respectively.
c) Deeplabv3+: This model uses an innovative encoder and decoder structure to capture object boundaries that are more distinct. Algorithm fails to capture landslide pixels properly and classifies some non-landslide pixels as regions of landslides.
d) Linknet: This model bypasses the spatial information from the encoder to the required decoder, reducing latency and increasing accuracy. Bypassing features may lead to decrease in accuracy in identifying landslide regions.

8.10 Dataset Used

For the benchmarking of machine learning models, this chapter has used the landslide4sense dataset. The dataset is available at https://github.com/

iarai/Landslide4Sense-2022. The dataset recognizes that not all scenarios may be covered by even enormous volumes of labeled data, which could result in limited performance when new examples are encountered during model inference. Because of the wide variations in landslides' sizes, forms, and geographical characteristics, this problem is most noticeable in them. To address this, the study expands and diversifies the Landslide4Sense benchmark dataset by purposefully choosing landslide-prone sites from four distinct geographical regions. The landslides in these chosen places are caused by a variety of variables, which increases the likelihood that DL models trained on this dataset may generalize to other areas [25]. This section delineates the following: a) the selected case study regions, b) the attributes of Sentinel-2 and ALOS PALSAR sensors, c) the landslide inventory annotation methodology, and d) the dataset statistics and shapes.

Based on a global landslide susceptibility map created by [25] using a heuristic fuzzy approach incorporating several explanatory variables, the study is focused on four main study areas, which are as follows:

1. Hokkaido, Japan's Iburi-Tobu Area: This southern Hokkaido region was struck by a powerful 6.6-magnitude earthquake in 2018, which resulted in several shallow-sliding landslides, valley damming, and the creation of quake lakes. Typhoon Jebi's intense rains ahead of the earthquake resulted in over 5,600 landslides and significant damage to public facilities.
2. Kodagu District, Karnataka, India: Severe landslides and flash floods were caused by unusually high rainfall in the Kodagu District of Karnataka, India, during the late monsoon season of 2018. The rainfall total exceeded 1,200 mm over a month.

The explanations included background information on the landslide instances, emphasizing the specific reasons and regional environmental elements that each location's unique geological events owed. In the Kodagu District of Karnataka, India, heavy rainfall during the late monsoon season of 2018 resulted in numerous landslides, many of which were debris flows. These catastrophes resulted in the death of 16 people and caused damage to about 200 communities. The region's structurally split and sloping hill ranges make up its geomorphological features. The majority of the land cover consists of dense woods with agroforestry crops like cardamom and pepper, and farmed valleys with fields of rice and coffee. The land cover and use of the area have changed significantly in the last 20 years.

Taiwan Province: The county of Western Taitung is situated inside the province. In this region as well as other sections of the province, landslides are mostly caused by typhoons and earthquakes. The region receives 2,500 mm of mean annual precipitation from the summer and winter monsoons, with some locations receiving as much as 6,700 mm [25]. Typhoon Morakot in August 2009 brought Western Taitung County and surrounding counties a record 2,884 mm of rain in just 5 days. Numerous floods and landslides brought on by this intense rainstorm resulted in serious property damage as well as fatalities. Over 50 persons were reported missing, and about 400 people were slain. Larger, deeply seated landslides were mainly caused by Typhoon Morakot, although small-scale, shallow-sliding landslides were more common in Western Taitung County, Taiwan Province. Numerous research works have investigated supervised and unsupervised deep learning (DL) methods for identifying typhoon-related landslides in different regions of Western Taitung County. Notably, DL techniques for landslide identification in this region have been studied by Ghorbanzadeh *et al.* and Shahabi *et al.* The information used to inventory landslides in this study area was assembled through a combination of prior research and a visual analysis of Google Earth archival pictures taken between 2011 and 2013.

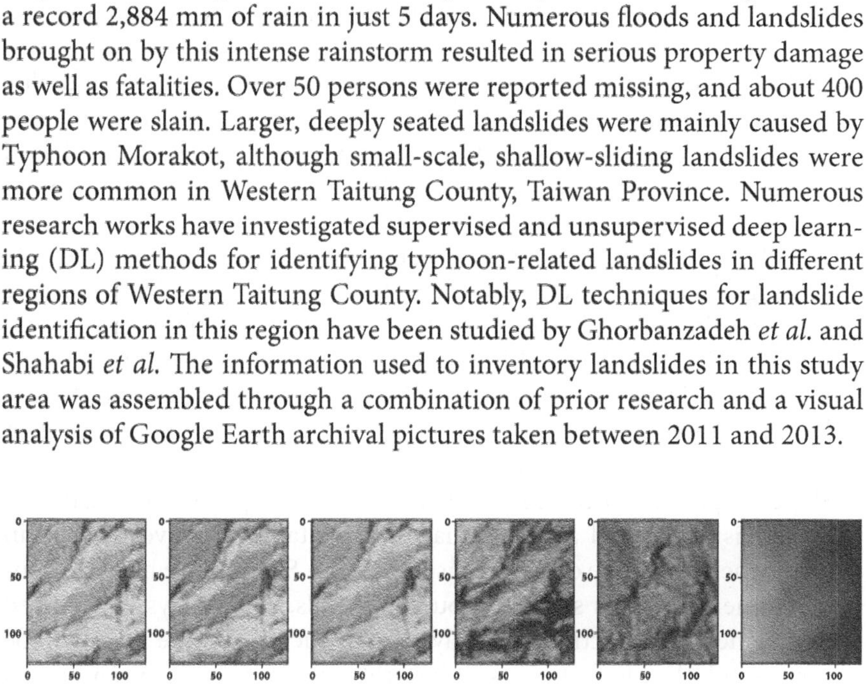

Figure 8.2 128 * 128 images of different bands from landslide4sense dataset (images arranged from left to right): (a) band 1, (b) band 2, (c) band 3, (d) band 4, (e) band 5, and (f) band 6.

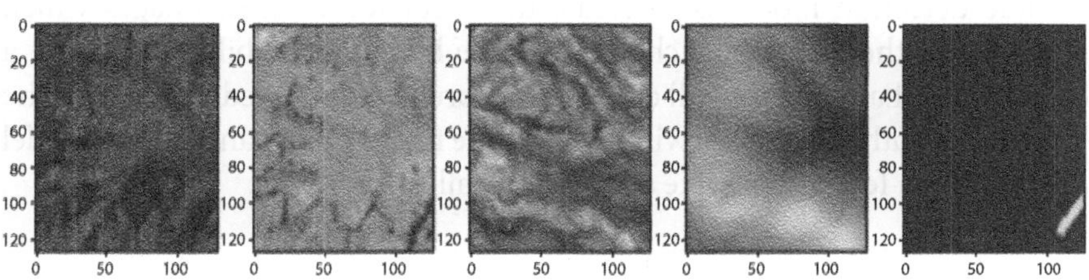

Figure 8.3 Various characteristics of images using six bands (images arranged from left to right): (a) RGB, (b) NDVI, (c) slope, (d) elevation, and (e) mask.

The dataset has 128 * 128 images. Each has 14 bands each, out of which six are shown in Figure 8.2. These bands are helpful in determining various factors.

As shown in Figure 8.3, various bands are used to obtain some important factors like RGB images, NDVI, slope, elevation, etc. The last image in Figure 8.4 is of mappings corresponding to the landslide that happened. It will be helpful in training the model and calculating the accuracy for the same.

a) RGB: Segmenting an image into its color channels red, green, and blue is known as RGB image segmentation. These three colors' combinations of intensity values correspond to each pixel in the image. RGB-based segmentation can be used to distinguish between different items or areas according to their color properties.
b) NDVI: This stands for normalized difference vegetation index. Remote sensing and agriculture are two fields that frequently use NDVI picture segmentation. To calculate NDVI, we divide the difference of near-infrared (NIR) and red (RED) with the sum of near-infrared (NIR) and red (RED). If the value of NDVI is low, this highlights that there is less vegetation in that area [25]. We can analyze the number of trees or plants in a particular are by just analyzing the NDVI value.
c) Slope: Slope is the measure of steepness of topography in that particular area. It is also called as slope image segmentation. It is very useful in cases where the slope of the area is important. Suppose we need to identify some landforms such as mountains, hills, and valleys or we need to do landslide detection in a hilly area, in such cases, the slope will be very useful. We can further use it for urban planning and environmental management also.
d) Mask: Masks are binary images that are based on the original image and which highlight the area in which landslides have occurred [26]. In this dataset, we have masked images corresponding to the real image for the training of the machine learning model [25]. The final output of a landslide detection model is to create the predicted masked images which highlight the area in which we have the highest possibility of having a landslide. Later on, we will compare the predicted masked image with the ground truth. Finally, we will calculate the final performance of the model based on a few metrics like accuracy, recall, f1 score, etc.

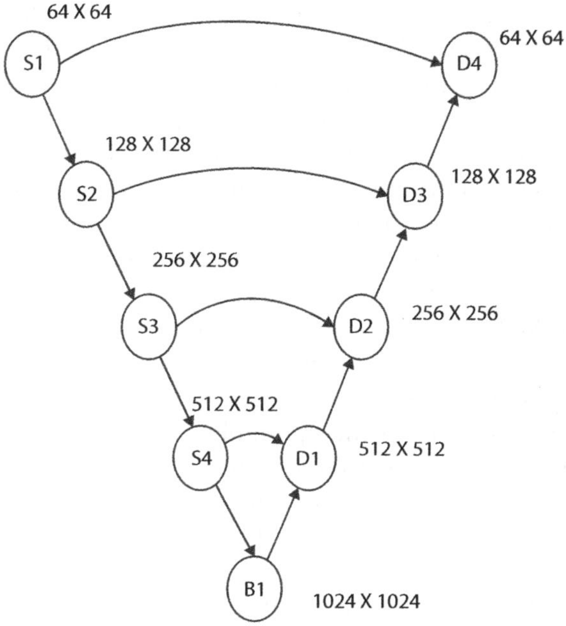

Figure 8.4 U-net architecture.

8.11 Model Architecture

The U-net model was developed by Olaf Ronneberger, Philipp Fischer, and Thomas Brox in the year 2015. The name of the paper was "U-Net: Convolutional Networks for Biomedical Image Segmentation". Let us see the architecture of U-net in more detail, as illustrated in Figure 8.4.

a) Deciphering "what" is in the picture using an encoder: An encoder is also called as contracting path. It reduces the dimensions of input but without losing information. This method has some convolutional layers which are followed by max pooling layers and helps in reducing the dimensions. The main focus is on reducing the dimension and extracting the global context.
b) Layer of bottleneck: Condensing acquired features: The bottleneck layer, which is applied between the encoder and decoder networks, compiles the learnt features into a final representation so that the decoder can handle them later [26].

c) Decoder: Locating "where" things are in space: Decoders are just the opposite of encoders. Unlike encoders, they help in increasing the dimensions. Using the information in the contracted path given by encoders will again make the final output equal to the input. The process of increasing the dimensions is done with the help of skip connections, the model used to integrate the upsampling stages with the corresponding equivalent stage created while downsampling. This downsampling and reconstructing method helps us to gain both high-level and fine-grained context out of the given data.

d) Skip Links: Making Use of Contextual Data

Skip connections in the U-net model are used to create a link between contracting and reconstructing stages. It is important to transfer the special information from the upsampling stage to the downsampling stage. While contracting from a higher spatial dimension to a lower dimension, the model may lose some information which can lead to lower accuracy. Skip links ensure that there is no loss of information while upsampling and downsampling.

e) Final Layer: Producing Segmentation Masks

At the end of the decoder layer, the size of the output will be equal to the given input, and we will be finally getting the segmented mask of the image. We use a pixel-wise classification algorithm, which will classify each pixel into a landslide or non-landslide class. Sigmoidal activation function is used at the end for classification. Based on the threshold value, the activation function decides the class of the pixel. U-net has shown great results when it comes to segmentation tasks [26]. In medical applications, it is widely used to segment X-ray or MRI images.

8.12 Results and Discussion

Table 8.1 gives a detailed comparison of U-Net with the already existing algorithms. We chose three standard metrics on which models can be evaluated (f1-score, precision, and recall). PSPNet has the lowest f1 score of all the mentioned algorithms at 56.39%, with a recall of 52.03% and precision of 61.55%. These low scores suggest that the algorithms have performed very poorly in identifying the regions of landslides. The second lowest recall and f1 score were given by ContextNet at 49.29% and 70.77%, respectively, indicating that it has missed a lot of points where landslides

Table 8.1 Performance metrics of the U-net model.

Model	Precision	Recall	F1 score
PSPNet	61.55	52.03	56.39
ContextNet	70.77	49.29	58.11
DeepLab-v3+	69.91	62.11	65.78
DeepLab-v2	60.8	63.68	62.21
LinkNet	66.76	67.02	66.89
FCN	68.66	63.05	65.73
U-Net	79.29	66.02	72.04

have actually happened. DeepLab-v3+ has shown a balanced performance including precision of 69.91%, recall of 62.11%, and f1 score of 65.78%.

LinkNet has achieved the second highest f1 score of 65.73, with balanced precision of 66.76% and recall of 67.02%. U-Net outperforms all the algorithms with the highest f1 score of 72.04. The recall scores are slightly lower than the other algorithms, but the precision is very high.

This chapter has utilized the landslide4sense dataset and trained U-net model on 3,799 training, 245 validation, and 800 test images. Table 8.1

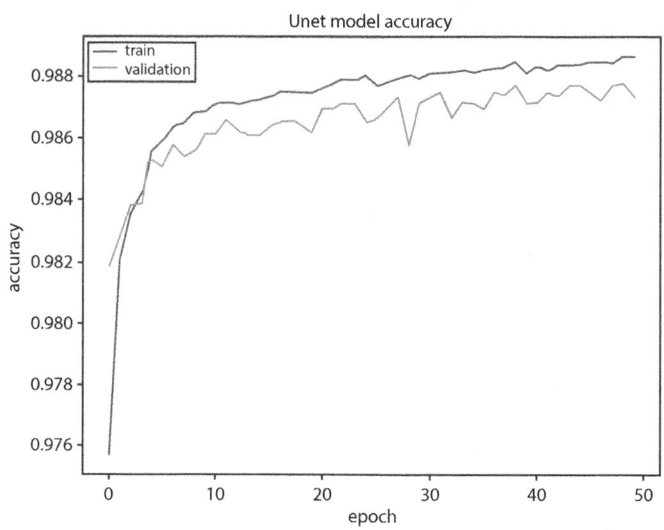

Figure 8.5 Accuracy measure of U-Net architecture.

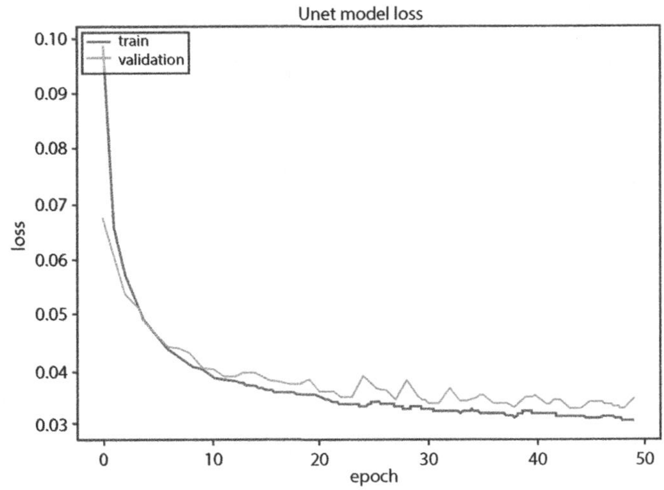

Figure 8.6 Relationship between loss and epoch of U-net architecture.

compares the performance of the model on train and validation datasets. The architecture of the model involves a batch size of 16, 100 epochs and a dropout rate of 20%. The accuracies of the train and validation datasets are almost similar; the accuracies are 98.81% and 98.67%, respectively.

As shown in Figure 8.5, the accuracies for both train and validation test sets are increasing gradually together.

Figure 8.6 shows that the loss for both training and test datasets decreases as the epoch increases. However, the curve for the training dataset is smoother compared to the curve with the test dataset. By training the model on 100 epochs, we have observed that the loss value is steadily declining and the accuracy values are increasing steadily. For training data, the loss drops from 0.021 to 0.019, whereas the validation data faced a smaller drop from 0.037 to 0.035, indicating that the model can generalize to unseen data also. Accuracy for training and testing data was seen as very high from the very first epoch. In the start, the accuracy values were 0.991 and 0.98 for training and testing data, respectively. The values for precision and recall also kept increasing constantly in the case of training and test data, but the variation in the case of test images was a little more. This indicates that there is still a scope of improvement in the current method.

Future directions in the field of landslide detection may include the improvement of available data. This can be done by combining multiple data resources or using images of better quality. The use of GAN (generative adversarial networks) can help in adding little variation to the images which eventually can help in generalizing the images in a better way.

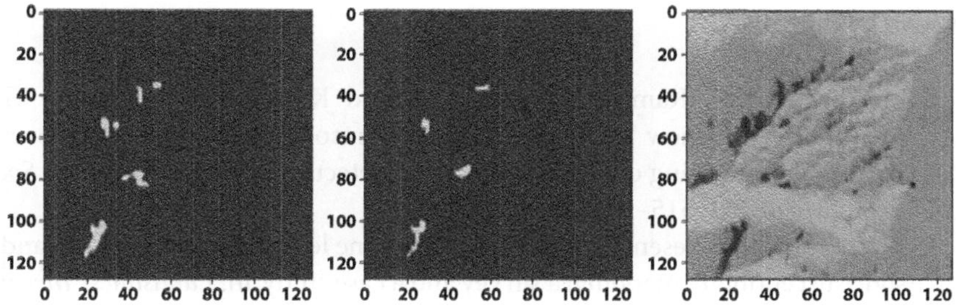

Figure 8.7 Comparison of the predicted image with labeled and RGB image (images arranged from left to right): (a) predicted image, (b) labeled image, and (c) RGB image.

Mapped Images

To detect and analyze landslides using satellite photography and remote sensing, one of the most important steps is to create mapped images that correlate to landslide photos. Researchers and stakeholders can gain a better understanding of the terrain features, environmental factors, and geological conditions linked to landslide occurrences by using these mapped images, which offer important context and spatial information about landslide-prone locations [10]. Researchers can discover patterns, trends, and hotspots of landslide activity over geographic areas by superimposing landslide photos onto maps. In Figure 8.7, there are three images. There is a training image on which we are trying to predict the areas having landslides. The second image is a label image which acts as a ground truth for the predicted image. The third one is the prediction image which we are trying to compare with the ground truth. We can see that the predicted image overlaps to a great extent with the label image.

Acknowledgment

I would like to thank Assistant Professor Inderdeepkaur for her invaluable guidance while writing this chapter. I deeply appreciate the time and efforts given by her which will undoubtedly help students or researchers to get a deep understanding of this topic.

References

1. Martha, M.T.R., Kamala, P., Jose, J., Vinod Kumar, K., Jai Sankar, G., Identification of new landslides from high resolution satellite data covering a large area using object-based change detection methods. *J. Indian Soc. Remote Sens.*, 44, 515–524, 2016.
2. Kavzoglu, T., Colkesen, I., Sahin, E.K., Machine learning techniques in landslide susceptibility mapping: a survey and a case study, in: *Landslides: Theory, Practice and Modelling*, pp. 283–301, Springer, Cham, 2019.
3. Prasad, N.N., Landslides-Causes & Mitigation, vol. 21, Centre for Water Resources Development, Kerala, India, pp. 48–54, 1995.
4. Zhu, M., He, Y., He, Q., A review of researches on deep learning in remote sensing application. *Int. J. Geosci.*, 10, 1, 1–11, 2019.
5. Highland, L.M. and Bobrowsky, P., *The landslide handbook-A guide to understanding landslides*, U.S. Geological Survey, Circular 1325, Reston, Virginia, 2008.
6. Pradhan, S.P. and Siddique, T., Mass wasting: an overview, in: *Landslides: Theory, Practice and Modelling*, pp. 3–20, Springer, Cham, 2019.
7. Hungr, O., Leroueil, S., Picarelli, L., The Varnes classification of landslide types, an update. *Landslides*, 11, 167–194, 2014.
8. Guzzetti, F., Landslide hazard and risk assessment, Ph.D. dissertation, Mathematisch-Naturwissenschaftlichen Fakultät, Rheinischen Friedrich-Wilhelms-Universität Bonn, Bonn, Germany, 2006.
9. Madaan, S., Causes, effect and types of landslides. *Bull. Seismol. Soc. Am.*, 107, 5, 9–10, 2017.
10. Mihalić Arbanas, S. and Arbanas, Ž., Landslide mapping and monitoring: Review of conventional and advanced techniques, in: *Proc. 4th Symp. Macedonian Assoc. Geotech.*, pp. 57–72, 2014.
11. Guzzetti, F., *et al.*, Landslide inventory maps: New tools for an old problem. *Earth Sci. Rev.*, 112, 1-2, 42–66, 2012.
12. Brunsden, D., Mass movement; the research frontier and beyond: a geomorphological approach. *Geomorphology*, 7, 1-3, 85–128, 1993.
13. Razak, K.A., *et al.*, Airborne laser scanning of forested landslides characterization: Terrain model quality and visualization. *Geomorphology*, 126, 1-2, 186–200, 2011.
14. Soeters, R. and Van Westen, C.J., Slope instability recognition, analysis and zonation, in: *Landslides: Investigation and Mitigation*, Special Report 247, pp. 129–177, Transportation Research Board, National Research Council, Washington, D.C., 1996.
15. Pohl, C. and Van Genderen, J.L., Review article multisensor image fusion in remote sensing: concepts, methods and applications. *Int. J. Remote Sens.*, 19, 5, 823–854, 1998.

16. Ghorbanzadeh, O., *et al.*, Evaluation of different machine learning methods and deep-learning convolutional neural networks for landslide detection. *Remote Sens.*, 11, 2, 196, 2019.
17. Manconi, A., *et al.*, Brief communication: Rapid mapping of landslide events: The 3 December 2013 Montescaglioso landslide, Italy. *Nat. Hazards Earth Syst. Sci.*, 14, 7, 1835–1841, 2014.
18. Roodposhti, M.S., Aryal, J., Bryan, B.A., A novel algorithm for calculating transition potential in cellular automata models of land-use/cover change. *Environ. Modell. Software*, 112, 70–81, 2019.
19. Tien Bui, D., *et al.*, Spatial prediction models for shallow landslide hazards: a comparative assessment of the efficacy of support vector machines, artificial neural networks, kernel logistic regression, and logistic model tree. *Landslides*, 13, 361–378, 2016.
20. Zhang, L., *et al.*, Cluster sparsity field: An internal hyperspectral imagery prior for reconstruction. *Int. J. Comput. Vision*, 126, 797–821, 2018.
21. Prakash, N., Manconi, A., Loew, S., Mapping landslides on EO data: Performance of deep learning models vs. traditional machine learning models. *Remote Sens.*, 12, 3, 346, 2020.
22. Krizhevsky, A., Sutskever, I., Hinton, G.E., ImageNet Classification with Deep Convolutional Neural Networks. *Adv. Neural Inf. Process. Syst. (NIPS)*, 25, 1097–1105, 2012.
23. Ronneberger, O., Fischer, P., Brox, T., U-net: Convolutional networks for biomedical image segmentation, in: *Medical Image Computing and Computer-Assisted Intervention - MICCAI 2015*, Munich, Germany, Oct. 5-9, 2015, Lecture Notes in Computer Science, vol. 9351, Springer, Cham, pp. 234–241, 2015.
24. Marcelino, E.V., Formaggio, A.R., Maeda, E.E., Landslide inventory using image fusion techniques in Brazil. *Int. J. Appl. Earth Obs. Geoinf.*, 11, 3, 181–191, 2009.
25. Ghorbanzadeh, O. *et al.*, Landslide4Sense: Reference Benchmark Data and Deep Learning Models for Landslide Detection. *IEEE Trans. Geosci. Remote Sens.*, 60, 1–17, 2022.
26. Siddique, N., Paheding, S., Elkin, C.P., Devabhaktuni, V., U-net and its variants for medical image segmentation: A review of theory and applications. *IEEE Access*, 9, 82031–82057, 2021.

9

Application of Geospatial Technology for Disaster Risk Reduction Using Machine Learning Algorithm and OpenStreetMap in Batticaloa District, Eastern Province, Sri Lanka

Zahir I.L.M.[1], Suthakaran S.[2], Iyoob A.L.[1], Nuskiya M.H.F.[1]* and Fowzul Ameer M.L.[1]

[1]*Department of Geography, South Eastern University of Sri Lanka, University Park, Oluvil, Sri Lanka*
[2]*Department of Geography, Faculty of Arts and Culture, Eastern University, Sri Lanka, Vantharumoolai, Chenkalady, Sri Lanka*

Abstract

In recent years, the Batticaloa District in the Eastern Province of Sri Lanka has faced escalating challenges from natural disasters ranging from floods and drought. As these events pose significant threats to human lives, infrastructure, and livelihoods, there is an urgent need for innovative approaches to mitigate their impact. The current study provides a holistic framework for the advancement of regional risk reduction efforts using machine learning algorithms (MLAs) and geospatial technology. A main feature of this initiative is the use of OpenStreetMap (OSM) and Google Earth Engine (GEE) as primary geographic data sources. To facilitate the comprehensive analysis of disaster vulnerability and resilience, GEE makes it possible to enhance the higher-resolution satellite images and comprehensive remote sensing (RS) information, including terrain, land use, topography, and

**Corresponding author*: nuskiyahassan@seu.ac.lk; ORCID: 0000-0003-2963-458
Zahir I.L.M.: ORCID: 0000-0001-6553-1986
Suthakaran S.: ORCID: 0000-0002-0159-2496
Iyoob A.L.: ORCID: 0000-0001-6756-1409
Fowzul Ameer M.L.: ORCID: 0000-0002-5780-0688

Neelam Dahiya, Gurwinder Singh, Sartajvir Singh and Apoorva Sharma (eds.) Artificial Intelligence in Remote Sensing for Disaster Management, (161–184) © 2025 Scrivener Publishing LLC

other spatial factors. To analyze this, OSM provides crowd-sourced data such as footprints, road networks, and infrastructure details to provide spatial data with enhanced analysis. The major aspect of this study central to this framework of research is MLAs, and the concept helps to identify disaster-free and disaster zones with a clearer view. It gives decision-makers the ability to formulate appropriate action and efficient action plans and strategies. This chapter seeks to integrate MLA and OSM to improve disaster risk management in the Batticaloa District of the Eastern Province of Sri Lanka. Finally, the study contributes to DRR through the use of the advancement of technology.

***Keywords*:** geospatial, disasters, machine learning, google earth engine, OpenStreetMap

9.1 Introduction

In recent times, the frequency and severity of natural disasters such as earthquakes, storms, floods, and landslides have increased alarmingly worldwide. These events are very severe, and some are caused by extreme environmental impacts. The district of Batticaloa is immune to such disaster, and its effects are being felt with great anxiety. Addressing these challenges requires a combination of innovative approaches and sophisticated technologies to improve the effectiveness of disaster risk reduction (DRR) strategies, but geospatial engineering, combined with machine learning algorithms (MLAs) and OpenStreetMap (OSM), offers a promising approach to improve DRR efforts. Geospatial engineering uses satellite imagery, geographic information systems (GIS), and remote sensing (RS) to collect, analyze, and interpret spatial data. They also enable the extraction of patterns, facilitating more accurate forecasting and informed decision-making OSM, collaborative mapping, for landscape rich information that can be used for disaster risk assessment and response (Suthakaran *et al.*, 2022).

The Batticaloa District in the eastern region of Sri Lanka is characterized by diverse landscapes and many natural disasters that pose a serious threat to its population and infrastructure. These disasters do not necessarily result in human loss of life and not only destroy houses, farmlands, and critical infrastructure but have also demonstrated the potential of space technology (Suthakaran *et al.*, 2022). Open-source geospatial tools and GIS were used to map local flood hazards and hazardous areas, respectively (Manfré *et al.*, 2012). Perera *et al.* (2020) described the significance of public representation in disaster and risk management as well as the exchange of geographical information. Geo-strategies are the multi-model strategy that integrates technology, scientific knowledge, and community involvement in DRR (Albano and Sole, 2018). This method works well for risk assessment and mapping. Therefore, the use of geographic information system (GIS) and geo-observation products is crucial to this process, as they provide essential insights into potential risks, deficiencies, and failures (Weston, 2012). Accordingly, another application of this technique includes mapping and developing methods to identify natural disasters such as floods, forests, volcanoes, earthquakes, tsunami, and droughts (Bu, 2017). The research shows how MLAs can be used in DRR, emphasizing the vital role of these approaches in recognizing and controlling failures, the former mainly for forest fire management (Munawar *et al.*, 2021; Samola *et al.*, 2020). This emphasizes the crucial thing in these methods for risk assessment related to climate change and disaster management, respectively (Zakorecki *et al.*, 2013; Gennaro *et al.*, 2021). However, applied methods, including random forest (RF) models, have been noted to be able to understand the dimensions, characteristics, and abnormalities representing risks at risk and areas of potential opportunity. This insight will enable managers to adopt more efficient strategies and plan stronger responses, ultimately contributing to the success of DRR strategies.

This study presents a complete framework that harnesses the ability of geotechnical and regulatory frameworks to promote DRR in Batticaloa District, Eastern Province, Sri Lanka. The key factor of this framework is the GEE and the use of OSM because of the primary records source. GEE presents a wide range of satellite imagery and RS facts, permitting comprehensive land cowl, land use, and geographic analyses. Moreover, crowdsourced mapping data that enrich general geographical information, including road networks and infrastructure information, provided by OSM also offer practical analytical capabilities. It has also been evidenced by significant research detailing the application of machine learning and geospatial technologies for DRR in Sri Lanka vis-a-vis the efficiency of Sri Lanka's disaster management system. Overall, this look highlights the potential of geospatial technology and regulation enforcement groups' emphasis on enhancing DRR efforts inside the United States (Pereira *et al.*, 2020; Vethathasinghe, 2020).

9.1.1 Geospatial Technology in DRR

Geospatial technologies include a variety of tools and techniques that enable access, analysis, and visualization of spatial data (Manfré *et al.*, 2012). In DRR, geoengineering plays an important role in vulnerability assessment, understanding risk exposure and improving decision-making processes. A geotechnical milestone, satellite images provide comprehensive data to monitor and assess changes in geospatial exploration, demonstrate the usefulness of satellite imageries in monitoring flood levels, and help to identify the risk area and develop mitigation plans (Tanka *et al.*, 2018). RS techniques can collect land surfaces at different spatial resolutions and contribute inexpensively; they are often very useful for mapping flood risk (Iyoob *et al.*, 2021).

Geo-information technology is widely used in DRR due to its ability to increase situational awareness (Westlund, 2012). Along with improved sensor, imagery, communication, and sensor fusion, GIS and artificial intelligence (AI) technologies have significantly improved disaster recovery and DRR (Kemper, 2020). In disaster situations, special-purpose repositories can be used to analyze different GIS data (Albrecht *et al.*, 2020). DRR helps to promote situational awareness and infrastructure and geographic understanding in the form of geo-informatics, particularly RS data synchronization (Roper, 2024).

9.1.2 MLAs in DRR

The system's integration of MLAs helps to predict natural disasters like earthquakes, floods, wildfires, and tsunami with near-instant accuracy and speed. By creating a framework for an integrated disaster management plan, these developments greatly reduce the severe effects of such events (Depart *et al.*, 2028). This will show how legislators use historical events, land use, and soil characteristics information to predict soil vulnerability. The information provides excellent spatial smoothness and significantly increases map accuracy through this close relationship.

By analyzing the hydrological records, precipitation, and changes in land cover, flood assessment shows how good MLAs predict floods (Zhang *et al.*, 2019). These synthetic tissue-based models make flood disaster risk reduction more dynamic and with adaptable accuracy. Incorporating geospatial technologies into regulatory enforcement makes the process of risk mapping and risk assessment more accurate and effective (Jha *et al.*, 2020). Integration of these technologies has generated comprehensive DRR strategies using spatial data and information for more informed decision-making.

9.1.3 OSM in DRR

According to Suthakaran *et al.* (2020), OSM, a collaborative mapping platform or volunteer mapping platform, has become an invaluable tool for DRR projects. OSM provides a way for international relief agencies to create, update, and quantify geospatial data, enabling real-time mapping during and after disaster. The study suggests that OSM can be helpful in rapidly mapping disaster-prone areas (Neis and Zipf, 2012; Girres and Touya, 2010). During the 2015 Nepal earthquake, OSM played a key role in presenting precise maps of the affected areas, assisting humanitarian companies plan and execute comfort efforts (Anderson *et al.*, 2017). The OpenFloodRiskMap is a choice version aid device using OSM for flood chance control (Eckle *et al.*, 2016). It proposes a way to assess the integrity of the OSM for tracking DRR, mainly in areas susceptible to natural disasters (Goldblatt, 2019). Similarly, OSM is a spatial repository for many spatial facts such as transportation networks, infrastructure information, land use records, etc. (Huckley, 2010). Such information in OSM for panorama increases the transmission and accuracy of information for DRR purposes.

9.1.4 Integrated Approach of Geospatial Technology, Machine Learning, and OSM

The combination of geospatial generation, MAL, and OSM provides a comprehensive and inclusive approach to DRR (Zennaro *et al.*, 2021). Integrating these technologies addresses the constraints of character methods and improves the overall effectiveness of danger assessment and reaction strategies. It emphasizes the interface between GIS and law enforcement organizations to help in spatial choice-making in disaster management. By combining geospatial generation with law enforcement, the observation demonstrates improved accuracy in predicting disasters and identifying vulnerabilities. However, OSM contributes to this inclusive approach by providing an open and collaborative platform for sharing and updating geospatial statistics (Haklay, 2010). OSM realities are therefore important to optimize the spatial information management required for effective DRR.

9.2 Significance of the Study

The application of geospatial technologies, MLA and OSM, in DRR stands as an important step towards building resilient clusters, especially in the Batticaloa region of Sri Lanka (Sarkissian *et al.*, 2019). However, the usage of this generation offers technical and organizational challenges, specifically in disaster-prone regions. Despite these demanding situations, the use of area-based information and statistics to aid emergency management and disaster recuperation in developing nations is increasing (Norris *et al.*, 2008). To cope with those challenges, Leventhal (2012) proposes a framework to enable the integration of crowdsourcing equipment and geotechnical collaboration in the disaster preparedness segment, as a consequence of empowering the group's resistance has multiplied.

In the context of flood chance assessment and mitigation, they want to emphasize the significance of thinking about economic vulnerability (Weerasinghe, 2018). It further stresses the necessity for equitable resilience in flood-inclined city areas, focusing on distributive, procedural, and contextual equities (Hewawasam, 2020). Collectively, these studies highlight the urgency of addressing the flood chance in Batticaloa District, emphasizing each risk evaluation and equitable resilience. Furthermore, the significance of network engagement and resilience construction in disaster control is highlighted in several research. There is a need for communities to build resilience before an emergency and provide a roadmap for this reason (Chandra *et al.*, 2013). However, the position of citizen-generated facts in improving network resilience focuses on the transformative capacity of data generation (Pitidis *et al.*, 2022). Lastly, community mapping, particularly through the use of OSM, has been proven to play a crucial function in constructing resilience in the face of herbal dangers (Rieger, 2016). This is finished with the aid of engaging local groups within the mapping method not simply helping in speaking the hazard of hazards but additionally in making ready for excessive events (Rieger, 2016). This approach emphasizes the significance of neighborhood know-how and community participation in DRR, aligning with the standards of sustainable improvement (McBean, 2012). Therefore, those findings make contributions to the global discourse on leveraging generation for sustainable improvement by emphasizing the importance of neighborhood knowledge, community participation, and effective communication in DRR.

It emphasizes the significance of considering financial vulnerability in flood risk assessment and mitigation (Virsinghe, 2018). It additionally emphasizes the significance of equitable coping in flood-prone towns, specializing in uniform class, planning and context (Hewavasam, 2020). Collectively, this examination highlights the want for flood risk control in Batticaloa District, emphasizing correct chance evaluation and resilience Furthermore, many studies have highlighted the significance of an emphasis on network participation and resilience constructing in disaster management. Highlights the importance of building network resilience before an emergency happens, and offers a strategy for doing so (Chandra, 2013). However, discovered the function of citizen information processing in building community resilience, focusing on the transformative ability of data production (Pitidis *et al.*, 2022). Finally, nearby mapping, specifically through using OSM, has been shown to play a crucial role in constructing resilience in the face of herbal screw-ups (Rieger, 2016). This is achieved via community participation in mapping, which is now not the most effective helps communicate risks at the chance but additionally helps put together for complicated occasions (Rieger, 2016). This technique emphasizes the significance of nearby know-how and network participation in DRR in line with sustainable improvement ideas (McBean, 2012). These findings therefore contribute to the global discourse on the use of technology for sustainable development by emphasizing the significance of nearby understanding, network participation and effective communication in DRR.

9.3 Objectives

The main objective of this chapter is to promote the use of geospatial technology, MLAs and OSM in DRR in the Eastern Region of Sri Lanka. The specific objectives are:

i. To assess the current status of disaster risk and vulnerability in the Batticaloa region.
ii. To explore the potential of geospatial technology to collect and analyze spatial data on DRR.
iii. To analyze the contribution of OSM in imparting up-to-date and reachable geospatial statistics for disaster management.
iv. To develop a framework for integrating these technologies to improve DRR management in the study area.

9.4 Methodology

9.4.1 Study Area

The Batticaloa region of Sri Lanka is located on the eastern coast bordering the Bay of Bengal and the Indian Ocean due to its geographic location, tropical climate, geographic diversity, and extensive coastline. Located at Latitude 70^0 42' 36" North, Longitude 81^0 41' 32" E, Batticaloa District, which is the central portion of the Eastern Region (Figure 9.1) Administratively, Batticaloa County is divided into 14 county clerks offices representing 345 grama niladhari divisions, 969 villages and a population of 596,317 (MNDSD, 2020).

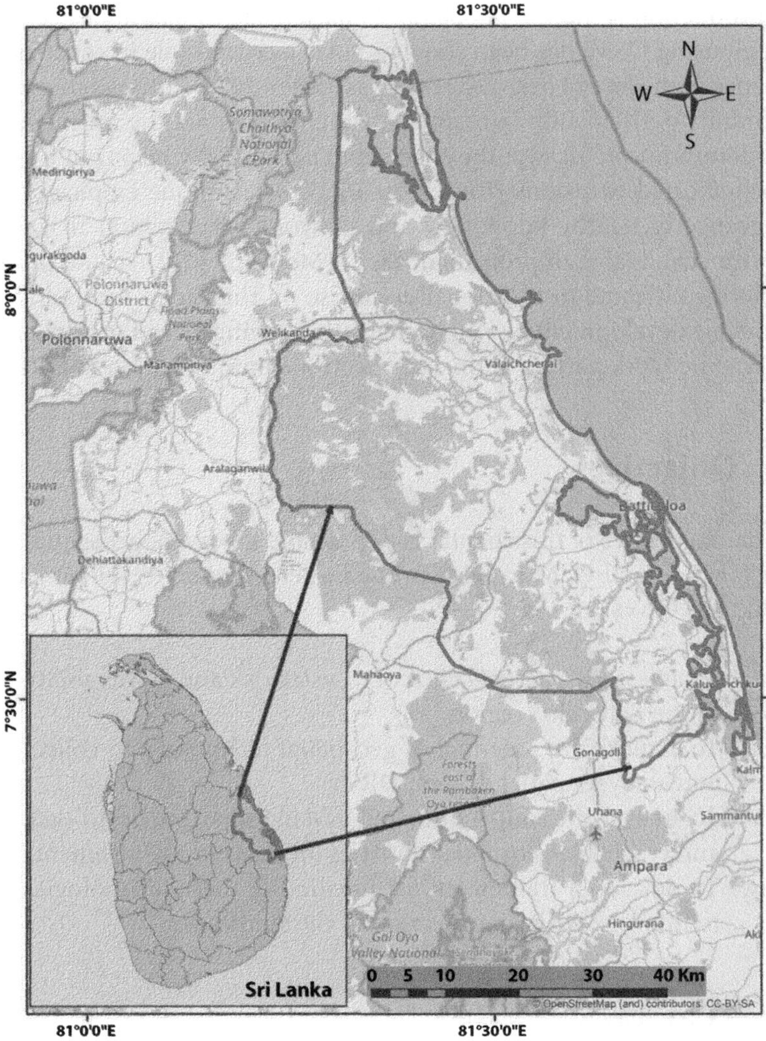

Figure 9.1 Study area—Eastern Province in Sri Lanka. Source: Survey Department of Sri Lanka, 2018.

Rapid urbanization, population growth and inadequate infrastructure, especially in disaster-prone areas, increase regional vulnerability (Sangsumana, 2023). Effective DRR programs are essential for disaster impacts to occur communities and businesses have decreased. These strategies include risk assessment, early warning systems, community preparedness, complex infrastructure, and land use planning. The importance of these strategies was highlighted by the 2004 tsunami which highlighted the need for comprehensive disaster planning (Weththasinghe, 2020). The devastation caused by tsunamis also highlighted the need for a creative, natural approach to biodiversity and resource protection (Hettiarachchi, 2006). Through the use of OSM and data, stakeholders will be able to better understand, model and mitigate risk, ultimately enhancing and promoting the resilience of Batticaloa District to natural disasters and encouraging sustainability.

9.4.2 Data Collection

The data collection for DRR was accomplished with the help of MLAs, OSM, and training of volunteer mappers, government employees, and the local communities. MLAs helped in the faster implementation of processing, risk evaluation, and disaster management functions. Crowd-sourced data was implemented for the damage assessment, whereas OSM served as a geospatial data source. The field papers and structured surveys were supplementedfor the on-site data collection. Therefore, building footprints, roads, and areas of interest were traced using satellite data and base maps as part of the digitizing process.

9.4.2.1 MLAs for DRR

MLAs have a systematic approach to addressing complex DRR in the region. A comprehensive process for machine learning application development, focusing on quality assurance. The MLA successfully managed the removal of redundant information, allowing for faster processing and analysis of risk-related issues. This has proven to be highly beneficial, effectively contributing to all phases of DRR (Yu *et al.*, 2018). To establish a theoretical foundation, DRR, especially convolutional neural network (CNN) and long-term short-term memory neural network (LSTM), support vector machine (SVM) (Arinta and Andi, 2019; Sun *et al.*, 2020). Subtasks of the AI, i.e. Law enforcement agencies, have contributed significantly to various aspects of natural disaster management. Proposed to improve the MLA classification method for earthquake prediction, which achieved 89.71% accuracy with CNN. This CNN-based approach outperformed traditional MLAs such as SVM, KNN, and Naive Bayes (Yuan and Moayedi, 2020). Notably, the highest accuracy was obtained before flooding. An ensemble method based on MLAs to detect and simulate floods along the west coast of India (Prasad *et al.*, 2021). In addition, used an advanced causal inference method coupled with MLAs to assess the sensitivity of urban industries to extreme weather events (Sri Rama, 2019).

In disaster scenarios, efficient cooperation and real-time monitoring of statistics are essential, prompting diverse efforts to optimize disaster monitoring. Online information data for this motive, using a records scraping method to extract statistics from numerous websites and online sources associated with specific risk emergencies (Gopal *et al.*, 2020). Recognizing the mission of distinguishing between useful and non-useful statistics using conventional data collection techniques, the authors integrated gadget studying-based totally methods. Similarly, Damage assessment includes strategies that quantify the volume of harm and determine the resources required for disaster reaction. Introduced a revolutionary framework using a deep gaining knowledge of-based multimodal technique to assess the disaster state of affairs (Wang *et al.*, 2020). This framework carries CNN and LSTM models. However, a hybrid technique incorporates MLAs to categorize flood-affected regions. A drone was employed to capture high-resolution aerial pictures from extraordinary heights, leveraging various features (Akshya and Priyadarsini, 2019). For classification, an aggregate of K-method clustering and SVM changed into implemented. The gadget utilized those aerial pics as input, categorizing them primarily based on whether or not the depicted area was affected by flooding or now not.

MLAs have been hired for the improvement of programs for disaster management, as validated within the realm of harm evaluation (Zhang *et al.*, 2019). Various researchers have previously cautioned packages that leverage AI and DL based neural network (NN) strategies. These packages use up-disaster picture information to evaluate the harm and severity of impacts in affected areas. Nevertheless, the intrinsic black-box nature of AI algorithms poses a task, impeding the attainment of higher accuracy.

In this chapter, the authors integrated crowd-sourced information obtained from open-source data with AI-based algorithms. Before implementing MLA, crowd-sourced data was employed to refine, augment, and mitigate the inherent opacity of AI algorithms. This crowd-sourced data was then integrated collaboratively with MLA within the system. Together they devised a damage assessment tool utilizing machine learning models, named CrowdLearn fusion of crowd-sourced and AI technologies. Through a crowdsourcing platform, CrowdLearn utilized the synergies between crowd intelligence and machine intelligence to conduct efficient damage assessments. The system underwent continuous real-time evaluation, showcasing its capability to deliver prompt and precise assessments for DRR purposes.

9.4.2.2 Integration with OSM

Steve Coast founded OSM in July 2004. To promote the growth, development, and distribution of free geospatial data as well as to facilitate the availability of geospatial data for public use and sharing, the OSM Foundation was established in April 2006. In December 2006, Yahoo confirmed permission for OSM to utilize its aerial photography as a backdrop for map production OSM in Wikipedia (http://en.wikipedia.org/wiki/OpenStreetMap). However, after the impactful earthquake in Haiti in 2010, OSM played a crucial role in assisting, as highlighted by Matthew Zook *et al.* (2010). The OSM community has remained actively engaged in aiding flood victims in Brazil and Pakistan, along with assisting earthquake victims in Japan more recently. OSM has showcased its versatility in disaster response, providing a range of innovative applications.

(a) Organizing the Meeting with Stakeholders
Volunteer mappers worked with various organizations, such as the Department of Survey, Universities, Government Agencies, Divisional Secretariats, the Department of Irrigation, the Department of Agriculture, Disaster Management Center, International non-governmental organizations, non-governmental organizations, and the communities. The purpose of this workshop was to emphasize the importance of open mapping and the use of OSM services for efficient data collection. In response to stakeholders, a comprehensive field data collection plan was developed including information on buildings, roads, land use, and areas of interest.

Volunteer mappers provided an overview of OSM and indicated that geospatial data mapping would be shared as a collaborative strategy. The advantages of OSM were emphasized, including its openness, ease of continuous collection and distribution, and comprehensive geographic information. These volunteers demonstrated how invaluable OSM is in disaster preparedness and response and recovery efforts, thereby fostering situational awareness and communication among stakeholders. In addition, the process of providing support to OSM was explained in detail, and stakeholders were urged to participate in data collection and mapping activities to ensure that detailed and accurate geographic information was provided for the purpose of DRR.

(b) OSM Training for Mappers

Volunteer mappers were actively engaged in conducting OSM training sessions for students, government staff, and local community mappers. This workshop focused on teaching the participants on how to research construction footprints, roads, land uses, and areas of interest through the OSM platform. By empowering knowledgeable individuals to support OSM, the training aimed to improve the quality and availability of geographic information for risk mitigation and other purposes.

Mr. Vivien Deparday, a technical expert from the World Bank, supplied worthwhile assistance by training running shoes in Sri Lanka. He becomes the pioneer of the Open City assignment, laying the foundation by undertaking training sessions in Batticaloa and Colombo. His remote support was also instrumental in various aspects of this task. The initial education session in Batticaloa lasted for about a week and blanketed all areas of the Manmunai North Divisional Secretariat Division (MNDSD). The participants were skilled in laptop programs like JOSM and QGIS, with complete discussions and practical classes. These sensible periods worried about updating records on buildings and roads within the Batticaloa vicinity, referencing model subject visits. Similarly, the second training consultation, prepared through the DMC, happened in Colombo. Mr. Jeff Haak from the Humanitarian OSM Team (HOT) served as an aid individual for this education. It supplied a comprehensive understanding of machine functions, allowing individuals to adopt them efficaciously during the analysis. Following the preliminary OSM schooling through Mr. Vivien Deparday and Mr. Jeff Haak, Mr. S. Suthakaran and volunteer mappers took the lead in OSM contributions in Batticaloa District, Eastern Province of Sri Lanka.

(c) Developing the Data Collection Plan

The formulation of the facts collection plan obtained aid from key stakeholders, consisting of the DMC, the National Housing Development Authority (NHDA), MNDSD, and Batticaloa Municipal Council (BMC). Collaborative discussions led to the creation of a model questionnaire designed to guide the assessment procedure and ensure the systematic collection of data throughout area surveys. The questionnaire turned to be prepared into three important sections: standard records, building information, and roof characteristics, facilitating a comprehensive gathering of applicable records to bolster DRR efforts. Simultaneously, efforts have been made to improve the OSM wiki web page for Sri Lanka's tagging hints, serving as a useful resource for accumulating and digitizing field information in OSM. The updated tagging guidelines for Sri Lanka can be found at https://wiki.openstreetmap.org/wiki/Sri_Lanka_Tagging_Guidelines.

Digitizing

Digitizing geographical features into the OSM database was the first step in updating the DSD vice. The primary data source for tracing these features was the Bing satellite imagery available on JOSM. Additionally, paper maps of roads and key facilities from the Planning Division and DSDs were also utilized as another significant data source (source: https://wiki.openstreetmap.org/wiki/Sri_Lanka_Tagging_Guidelines).

JOSM, QGIS, and Tasking Manager were employed as digitization tools. The digitization process was segmented into four tasks for ease of use: delineating building footprints using JOSM, outlining roads, refreshing points of interest, and updating GN boundaries.

(d) Trace the Building Footprints Using JOSM and Tasking Manager

The initial step in updating the OSM mapping activity of Batticaloa District involved tracing building and road layers using JOSM. The successful completion of this task was made possible by the collaborative efforts of the Batticaloa District Secretariat, BMC, DSDs, and students from EUSL and SEUSL. To streamline the process, the team utilized the OSM Tasking Manager (http://tasks.hotosm.org/), and this web-based mapping tool allowed for the division of tasks among OSM contributors. By dividing the mapping area into smaller sections, individual mappers could select an area to work on, minimizing the duplication of efforts. In the process of mapping roads and buildings, we simultaneously mapped essential facilities as part of the road-tracing activities. The identification and labeling of these crucial facilities in the OSM database heavily relied on secondary data provided by the DSDs in Batticaloa District. Base maps were provided to aid enumerators in understanding known features, serving as a guide when uncertainties arose or additional details were required while working with field paper. The creation of these maps involved the use of QGIS with the OpenLayers plugin, and Hot Exports was employed to extract building data from OSM servers. Two types of base maps, namely, the OSM background image and Bing satellite map, were utilized to ensure that the enumerators had comprehensive access to enhance every building within the GNDs.

Similarly, in this survey, Field Papers play a crucial role in data collection. These papers contain information sourced from OSM and are formatted into printable sheets (Figure 9.2). This online tool facilitates the creation of a printable map atlas for annotating and updating. Field Papers streamline the process for enumerators and community members to easily update building and road information on a physical map. Moreover, it simplifies the arrangement of page layouts for multi-page paper atlases

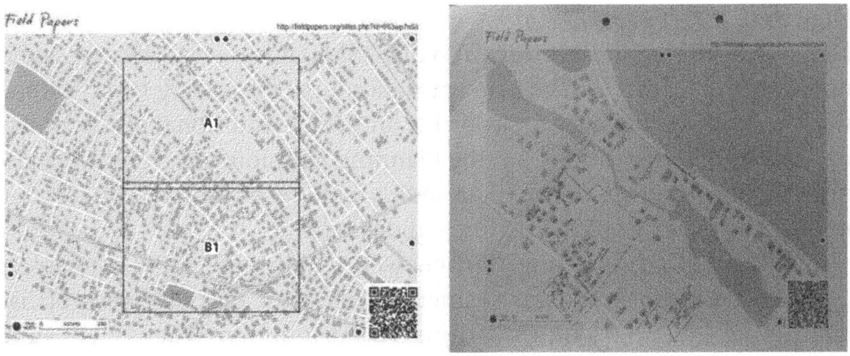

(a) (b)

Figure 9.2 (a) The field papers and (b) updated field paper in Iruthayapuram Central GND, Batticaloa.

utilizing OSM data. An additional benefit of using Field Papers is the user's ability to determine the number of splits to create separate maps. When preparing survey materials, each geocode was subdivided into logical squares, ensuring that enumerators could access detailed information for each building on the map.

During the field survey, volunteer mappers were assigned the task of assigning a unique number to each building as it appeared on the field paper. They were then responsible for maintaining a questionnaire for each specific building using the assigned number to correlate the data. However, the volunteers were instructed to conduct questionnaire surveys using printed A4 sheets, with dedicated questionnaires assigned for each building, especially in cases where multiple buildings were situated on the same land plot. Essential information, such as road material and name, was gathered when surveying roads. The field paper, containing building data, served as the foundational base for updating the questionnaires. Volunteer mappers were selected for the field survey and organized into groups based on the geographical location of the GNDs. Data collection was successfully performed with the help of these volunteer mappers, along with community participation in the village.

9.5 Results and Discussion

This chapter gives the effects and discussions derived from the utility of geospatial technology, MLAs, and OSM for DRR in Batticaloa District. The findings embody geospatial evaluation, system mastering predictions, and the combination of OSM statistics, dropping light on the effectiveness and implications of the implemented technique. The geospatial analysis targeted assessing the bodily characteristics of the Batticaloa District, figuring out threat-susceptible areas and mapping susceptible populations. GIS equipment has been utilized to analyze topographic features, land use styles, and historical disaster occurrences.

The effects of the geospatial evaluation discovered several key findings. Lowland terrains and riverbanks confirmed heightened vulnerability to floods, leading to the identity of ability danger zones and the implementation of early warning structures. However, the mapping of prone populations highlighted areas with dense settlements and inadequate infrastructure, indicating capability-demanding situations in evacuation and emergency reaction. The geospatial analysis provided a foundation for targeted risk reduction strategies, emphasizing the importance of tailored approaches based on the specific hazards prevalent in different geographic regions of the study area.

Based on the results, the revaluation of the OSM spatial data in Batticaloa District reveals significant growth and development over the years. In 2013, the percentage of building features was 0.08%. However, after 2014, there has been a significant increase, exceeding 90% thus far. Likewise, the percentages for roads, rivers, and amenities have also seen growth, with increases of 3.5%, 1.2%, and 0.05%, respectively (Table 9.1). Furthermore, from 2014 to 2024, OSM spatial data, enriched with volunteer geographic information, experienced significant updates for the Batticaloa District. These updates included an increase of 167,612 in building features, a road length extension of 5,130 km, a river expansion of 2,202 km, a rise of 1,920

Table 9.1 Growth of crowdsource mapping in Batticaloa District.

Years	Buildings	Length of roads (km)	Length of rivers (km)	Amenities	Hospital
2013	1	1,070	62	15	5
2014	33,213	1,302	69	218	9
2016	55,878	2,145	152	367	36
2018	196,070	6,258	2,282	1,933	48
2024	200,825	6,432	2,271	2,138	67

Source: OpenStreetMap Analytics, https://osm-analytics.org/#/ (2024).

in amenities, and updates to 58 hospitals. According to the MLA analysis, the prediction of disaster risk is based on historical data, socio-economic indicators, and environmental factors.

The models, including random forests and SVM, were trained and validated to assess their performance in predicting different types of hazards. The predictive models demonstrated promising results, with high accuracy in forecasting disaster risk across various scenarios—for example, the flood susceptibility model exhibited a high level of precision in identifying areas prone to floods, aligning with historical flood events (Figure 9.3).

Similarly, the flood risk model accurately predicted vulnerable regions based on digital elevation models, hydrological data, rainfall patterns, and land cover changes through the integration of the GEE platform. This integration furnished valuable insights for decision-makers, enabling them to prioritize useful resource allocation, plan evacuation routes, and enforce targeted mitigation measures by device studying approaches. This strong performance of the models underscored the potential of integrating gadgets to know into DRR techniques for stepped-forward accuracy and effectiveness.

OSM facts have been incorporated into the evaluation framework to beautify the spatial information infrastructure. Real-time information from OSM, contributed by way of the worldwide network of mappers and validated via community engagement sports, performed a crucial position in augmenting the accuracy and completeness of the spatial database. The integration of OSM data facilitated speedy updates for the duration of and after disaster events—for example, throughout a flood, OSM was instrumental in presenting real-time records on road closures, broken infrastructure, and affected regions. According to the findings, the areas suffering from floods had been measured at 5,800, 2,350, and 6,240 ha in 2014, 2021, and 2024. The extent of affected homes stood at 520, 323, and 804 for the respective years (Figure 9.4).

This dynamic and collaborative mapping platform confirmed its effectiveness as a precious aid, contributing to improved situational cognizance and facilitating well-timed decision-making in disaster response efforts. Moreover, community engagement activities conducted via OSM workshops empowered the neighborhood groups to actively contribute to mapping efforts, making sure that the spatial statistics reflected the nuances of the nearby context. Therefore, the collaborative nature of OSM not simply stepped forward the accuracy of spatial statistics but additionally fostered a feel of community possession and resilience.

The effects of the geospatial analysis, gadget getting-to-know predictions, and OSM integration show the efficacy of the integrated technique in

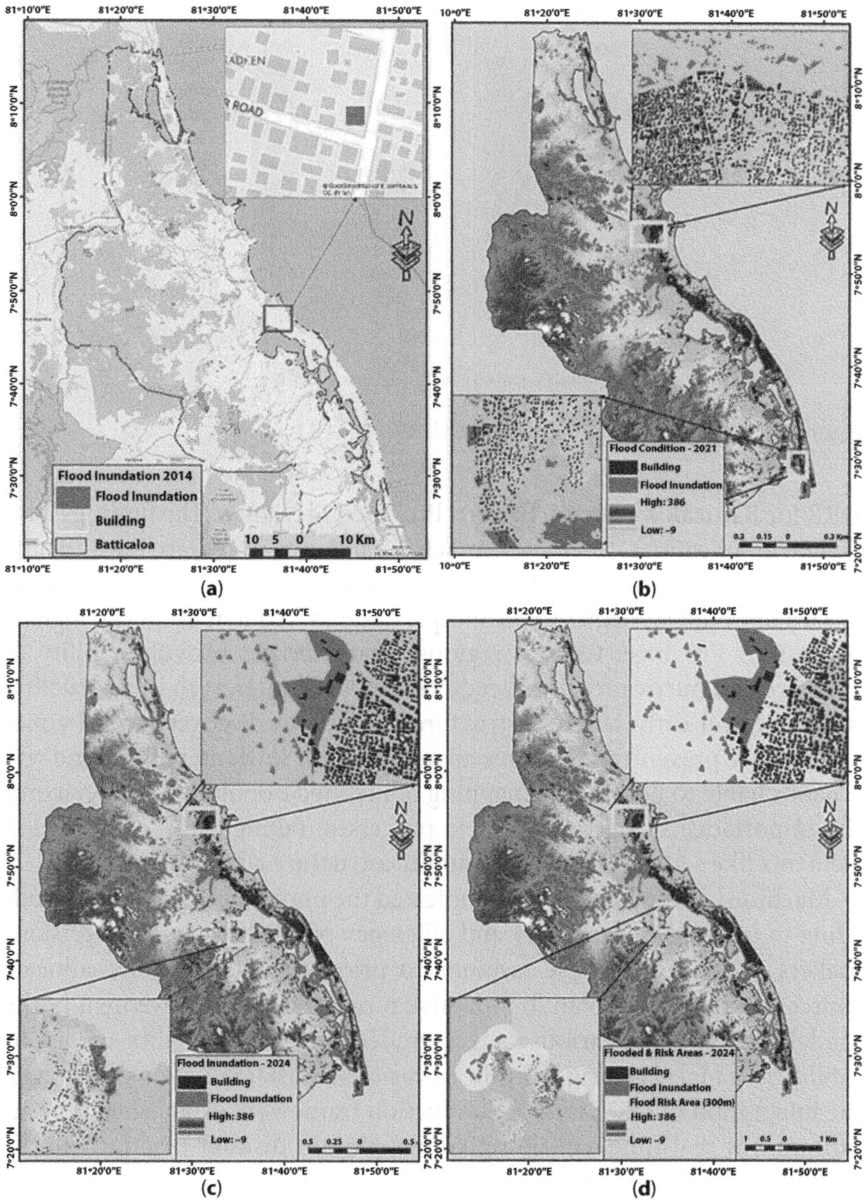

Figure 9.3 (a) Flood inundation, (b) affected building in 2014, (c) affected building in 2021, and (d) affected building in 2024.

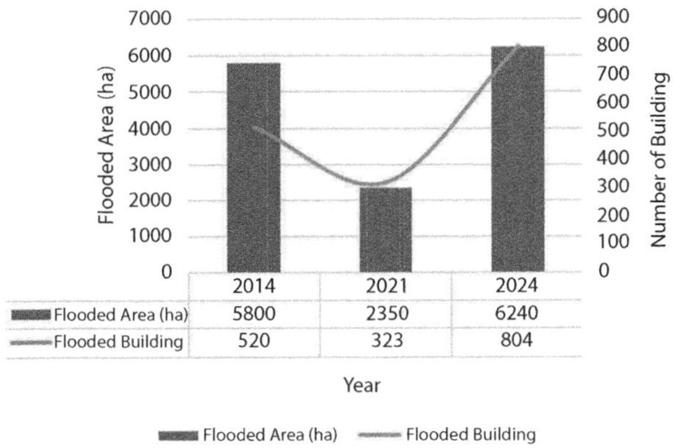

Figure 9.4 OSM geospatial information for DRR.

DRR for Batticaloa District, Eastern Province, Sri Lanka. The findings have several implications for policy, practice, and future research within the field. Firstly, the geospatial analysis highlighted the importance of tailoring hazard discount strategies to the unique hazards frequent in special regions of Eastern Province. Coastal regions, characterized by vulnerability to cyclones and hurricane surges, require a focused interest in infrastructure resilience and early warning structures. Efforts to discover hazard zones and enforce preventive measures are essential for lowland regions and riverbanks liable to floods. The mapping of inclined populations underscores the importance of network-centric processes, taking into consideration elements like settlement density and infrastructure adequacy.

Machine learning predictions indicated the potential of predictive modelling to increase the accuracy and efficiency of DRR strategies. Decision-makers can leverage these fashions to prioritize interventions, allocate sources correctly, and plan for adaptive measures. The achievement of the models in predicting various dangers underscores the flexibility and applicability of gadgets getting to know in various disaster situations. However, the integration of OSM into the evaluation framework established the significance of real-time, collaborative mapping in disaster reaction efforts. OSM not handiest provided accurate and updated spatial statistics but also engaged nearby communities in the mapping technique. The participatory nature of OSM, coupled with community empowerment through workshops, contributed to an extra resilient and informed population. Despite the promising results, certain demanding situations and considerations need to be addressed. The reliability of crowdsourced records from OSM requires non-stop validation and verification tactics. Furthermore, problems related to facts' privateness, ethical issues, and community engagement dynamics want careful interest to make certain the responsible and inclusive software of those technologies.

9.6 Conclusion and Recommendations

Considering the effectiveness and implications of using geospatial technology, MLAs and OSM, for DRR in Batticaloa District, the combination provides valuable insights for decision-makers, increases the accuracy of risk assessment, and builds community resilience. Key vulnerabilities, such as lowlands that are prone to flooding and heavily inhabited areas, were uncovered through geospatial evaluation. This information served as the basis for focused risk reduction strategies that were made to address the particular hazards that are common in various geographic areas. During disaster occurrences, situational awareness was greatly enhanced by the incorporation of real-time information from OSM, which made rapid decision-making and effective disaster response activities possible. The findings contribute to the growing field of DRR, providing a model that can be adapted and applied to different geographical, social, and economic contexts. The next chapter will deepen the recommendations from this research and describe possible avenues for future study in the field.

Based on the findings and discussion presented in this review, several strategies are proposed to enhance the benefits of OSM for onshore generation, law enforcement, and DRR, namely:

- Enhanced community engagement initiatives through organizing everyday workshops, education sessions, and attention campaigns—This empowers nearby groups to actively take part in the mapping system on OSM, making sure that their expertise contributes to the accuracy and relevance of spatial data.
- Implement strong mechanisms for the non-stop validation, mainly crowdsourced facts from OSM. Regular updates and validation of physical activities will beautify the reliability of the spatial database and enhance the overall effectiveness of chance-reduction strategies.
- Provide ability-building programs for decision-makers at various levels to beautify their understanding and utilization of geospatial generation and device-studying strategies. This will permit more knowledgeable selection-making in

the development and implementation of DRR rules and strategies.
- Integration of actual-time sensor statistics, inclusive of climate forecasts and river level tracking, into the evaluation framework. This will further beautify the timeliness and accuracy of risk checks, offering decision-makers with up to date data for the duration of disaster events.
- Encourage collaborative studies projects with neighborhood and international companions to share expertise, quality practices, and technological advancements inside the discipline of DRR. The collaboration will contribute to a more comprehensive expertise of dangers and solutions, fostering a collective and global technique for resilience-building.

These recommendations aim to strengthen the effectiveness of the applied methodologies and contribute to the sustainable reduction of disaster risks in Eastern Province, Sri Lanka. Implementation of these suggestions will require a concerted effort from government agencies, local communities, and relevant stakeholders to ensure a holistic and inclusive approach to DRR.

References

1. Akshya, J. and Priyadarsini, P.L.K., A hybrid machine learning approach for classifying aerial images of flood-hit areas, in: *Proc. Int. Conf. Comput. Intell. Data Sci. (ICCIDS)*, pp. 1–5, 2019.
2. Albano, R. and Sole, A., Geospatial methods and tools for natural risk management and communications. *ISPRS Int. J. Geo-Inf.*, 7, 12, 470, 2018.
3. Arinta, R.R. and Andi, E.W.R., Natural disaster application on big data and machine learning: A review, in: *Proceedings of the 2019 4th International Conference on Information Technology, Information Systems and Electrical Engineering (ICITISEE)*, vol. 6, pp. 249–254, Yogyakarta, Indonesia, 2019.
4. Chamola, V., Hassija, V., Gupta, S., Goyal, A., Guizani, M., Sikdar, B., Disaster and pandemic management using machine learning: A survey. *IEEE Internet Things J.*, 8, 21, 16047–16071, 2020.
5. Chandra, A., *et al.*, Getting actionable about community resilience: The Los Angeles County community disaster resilience project. *Am. J. Public Health*, 103, 7, 1181–1189, 2013.
6. Deparday, V., *et al.*, Machine Learning for Disaster Risk Management: A guidance note on how machine learning can be used for disaster risk management, including key definitions, case studies, and practical considerations

for implementation, The World Bank, 2018, [Online]. Available: http://creativecommons.org/licenses/by/3.0/igo/www.worldbank.org.

7. Der Sarkissian, R., Zaninetti, J.M., Abdallah, C., The use of geospatial information as support for Disaster Risk Reduction; contextualization to Baalbek-Hermel Governorate/Lebanon. *Appl. Geogr.*, 111, 102075, 2019.
8. Eckle, M., *et al.*, Leveraging OpenStreetMap to support flood risk management in municipalities: A prototype decision support system, 2016.
9. Girres, J.F. and Touya, G., Quality assessment of the French OpenStreetMap dataset. *Trans. GIS.*, 14, 4, 435–459, 2010.
10. Gopal, L.S., *et al.*, Machine learning-based Classification of Online News Data for Disaster Management, in: *Proceedings of the 2020 IEEE Global Humanitarian Technology Conference (GHTC)*, Seattle, WA, USA, 2020.
11. Haklay, M., How good is volunteered geographical information? A comparative study of OpenStreetMap and Ordnance Survey datasets. *Environ. Plann. B: Plann. Des.*, 37, 4, 682–703, 2010.
12. Hewawasam, V. and Matsui, K., Equitable resilience in flood-prone urban areas in Sri Lanka: A case study in Colombo Divisional Secretariat Division. *Global Environ. Change*, 62, 102091, 2020.
13. Ibrahim, M., Post-Disaster Housing Reconstruction in a Conflict Affected District, Batticaloa, Sri Lanka: Reflecting on the Climate Smart Disaster Risk Management Approach, 2010.
14. Iyoob, A.L., *et al.*, Geo-informatics application for flood risk detection in Manmunai north, Batticaloa district, Sri Lanka, 2021.
15. Kemper, H., Sensor fusion, GIS and AI technologies for disaster management. *Int. Arch. Photogram. Rem. Sens. Spatial Inf. Sci.*, 43, 1677–1683, 2020.
16. Levental, S., A new geospatial services framework: How disaster preparedness efforts should integrate neogeography. *J. Map Geogr. Lib.*, 8, 2, 134–162, 2012.
17. Liu, Y., *et al.*, How social capital influences community resilience management development. *Environ. Sci. Policy*, 136, 642–651, 2022.
18. Maity, R., *et al.*, Potential of Deep Learning in drought assessment by extracting information from hydrometeorological precursors. *J. Water Clim. Change*, 12, 6, 2774–2796, 2021.
19. Manfré, L.A., *et al.*, An analysis of geospatial technologies for risk and natural disaster management. *ISPRS Int. J. Geo-Inf.*, 1, 2, 166–185, 2012.
20. Zook, M., *et al.*, Volunteered Geographic Information and Crowdsourcing Disaster Relief: A Case Study of the Haitian Earthquake. *World Med. Health Policy*, 2, 2, 7–33, 2010.
21. Munawar, H.S., *et al.*, An integrated approach for post-disaster flood management via the use of cutting-edge technologies and UAVs: A review. *Sustainability*, 13, 14, 7925, 2021.
22. Neis, P. and Zipf, A., Analyzing the contributor activity of a volunteered geographic information project-The case of OpenStreetMap. *ISPRS Int. J. Geo-Inf.*, 1, 2, 146–165, 2012.

23. Nijamir, K., *et al.*, Geoinformatics application for estimating and forecasting of periodic shoreline changes in the east coast of Ampara District, Sri Lanka. *Ocean Coastal Manage.*, 232, 106425, 2023.
24. Norris, F.H., *et al.*, Community resilience as a metaphor, theory, set of capacities, and strategy for disaster readiness. *Am. J. Commun. Psychol.*, 41, 127–150, 2008.
25. Perera, C., *et al.*, Evaluation of gaps in early warning mechanisms and evacuation procedures for coastal communities in Sri Lanka. *Int. J. Disaster Resil. Built Environ.*, 11, 3, 415–433, 2020.
26. Perera, E.N.C., *et al.*, Introduce a framework for landslide risk assessment using geospatial analysis: A case study from Kegalle District, Sri Lanka. *Model. Earth Syst. Environ.*, 6, 2415–2431, 2020.
27. Pitidis, V., *et al.*, Enhancing Community Resilience through Dialogical Participatory Mapping, in: *ISCRAM*, pp. 495–503, 2022.
28. Prasad, P., *et al.*, Novel ensemble machine learning models in flood susceptibility mapping. *Geocarto Int.*, 26, 1892209, 2021.
29. Pu, R., A Special Issue of Geosciences: Mapping and assessing natural disasters using geospatial technologies. *Geosciences*, 7, 1, 4, 2017.
30. Rieger, C., Demonstrating the capacity of online citizen science mapping software to communicate natural hazards and engage community participation, University of Lethbridge (Canada), 2016.
31. San Martin, R. and Painho, M., Geospatial preparedness: Empirical study of the joint effort to provide geospatial support to disaster response. *Trans. GIS.*, 23, 3, 481–494, 2019.
32. Sangasumana P., Regional Development Capabilities: A Strategic Geographical Review of Eastern Sri Lanka. *Int. J. Res. Innov. Soc. Sci. (IJRISS)*, 7, 2023 Mar 13.
33. Shaker, J., Machine Vision Based Speed Control and its application in Autonomous UAV Snow Depth Remote Sensing, Ph.D. dissertation, University of New Hampshire, 2023.
34. Stevens, M.R., Berke, P.R., Song, Y., Creating disaster-resilient communities: Evaluating the promise and performance of new urbanism. *Landsc. Urban Plan.*, 94, 2, 105–115, 2010.
35. Sun, W., Bocchini, P., Davison, B.D., Applications of Artificial Intelligence for Disaster Management. *Nat. Hazard.*, 103, 2631–2689, 2020.
36. Suthakaran, S., *et al.*, Mapping the Flood Risk Exposure Using Open-Source Geospatial Tools and Techniques: A Case of Gampaha Divisional Secretariat Division, Sri Lanka. *J. Geosci. Environ. Prot.*, 10, 10, 18–31, 2022.
37. Suthakaran, S., *et al.*, Accessing openstreetmap as a source of village geographic information of Sri Lankan administrative systems: a case study selected districts of Batticaloa, Vavuniya and Gampaha in Sri Lanka, 2022.
38. Tanaka, K., *et al.*, Development of a flood water level estimation method using satellite images and a digital elevation model for the Mekong floodplain. *Hydrol. Sci. J.*, 64, 2, 241–253, 2019.

39. Toschi, I., Allocca, M., Remondino, F., Geomatics mapping of natural hazards: Overview and experiences. *Int. Arch. Photogramm. Remote Sens. Spat. Inf. Sci.*, 42, 505–512, 2018.
40. Weerasinghe, I.D.T.T. and Jayasena, K.P.N., Multimedia Big Data Platform with a Deep Learning Approach for Flood Emergency Management, in: *2020 5th International Conference on Information Technology Research (ICITR)*, pp. 1–6, 2020.
41. Westen, C.J., *et al.*, Landslide inventory, hazard and risk assessment in India, in: *Terrigenous Mass Movements: Detection, Modelling, Early Warning and Mitigation Using Geoinformation Technology*, pp. 239–282, 2012.
42. Westlund, S., The use of geospatial technology in disaster management, in: *Geospatial Technologies and Advancing Geographic Decision Making: Issues and Trends*, pp. 21–34, IGI Global, Hershey, 2012.
43. Yuan, C. and Moayedi, H., Evaluation and comparison of the advanced metaheuristic and conventional machine learning methods for the prediction of landslide occurrence. *Eng. Comput.*, 36, 1801–1811, 2020.
44. Zennaro, F., *et al.*, Exploring machine learning potential for climate change risk assessment. *Earth Sci. Rev.*, 220, 103752, 2021.
45. Zhang, D.Y., *et al.*, CrowdLearn: A Crowd-AI hybrid system for deep learning-based damage assessment applications, in: *Proceedings of the 2019 IEEE 39th International Conference on Distributed Computing Systems (ICDCS)*, pp. 7–10, Dallas, TX, USA, July 2019.
46. Suthakaran, S. *et al.*, Accessing openstreetmap as a source of Volunteer geographic information of Sri Lankan administrative systems: a case study selected districts of Batticaloa, Vavuniya and Gampaha in Sri Lanka, in: *Proceedings of 11th South Eastern University International Arts Research Symposium*, 2022.

10

Landslide Displacement Forecasting With AI Models

Sangeetha Annam

Chitkara University Institute of Engineering and Technology, Chitkara University, Punjab, India

Abstract

Road disruptions are frequently caused by landslides triggered by heavy rainfall along mountain roads, particularly during the period of intense precipitation. For government officials, landslides caused by rainwater that block roads are a serious issue. Geographic information systems were used in this study to map and interpret landslides using remote sensing data. The increased use of low-cost remote sensing devices, with an emphasis on long-term monitoring, early ground deformation detection, and potentially warning indicators of catastrophic failure, can help reduce the risk of landslides. The first stage in landslide inquiry and prevention is mapping. Currently, general remote sensing categorization outperforms landslide mapping using remote sensing regarding both accuracy and automation. Enhanced utilization of big data, more tactical allocation of monitoring resources, and improved outreach to landslide-prone area inhabitants are all necessary for a more successful landslide risk management. This chapter enriches with topics such as technological classification, artificial intelligence-based forecasting models with their limitations, and various technologies integrated with artificial intelligence. Following a study of the relevant literature, several of the core issues impeding landslide mapping using remote sensing development using artificial models are revealed and examined here.

***Keywords*:** Remote sensing, landslide displacement hazards, artificial intelligence, prediction

Email: a.sangeeta@chitkara.edu.in; ORCID: https://orcid.org/0000-0003-3593-7656

Neelam Dahiya, Gurwinder Singh, Sartajvir Singh and Apoorva Sharma (eds.) Artificial Intelligence in Remote Sensing for Disaster Management, (185–200) © 2025 Scrivener Publishing LLC

10.1 Introduction

One prevalent kind of geohazard in the world is landslides. Large-scale, quickly occurring landslides in hilly regions can kill people, ruin highways, block rivers, and demolish towns, resulting in a high death toll and significant financial damages. Landslides happen when the soils and rocks get diversified from their source to downslopes. When rocks and soils separate from their source and slide downslope, it is a landslide. This ground movement pattern can occasionally cause rivers to become blocked, villages to be buried, and people to lose their lives and property [1]. Widespread events and landslides have the potential to be disastrous when they happen close to infrastructure and populated areas. The core components of managing landslide risks are detection, monitoring, and prediction [2]. A major source of fatalities, injuries, property damage, socioeconomic disruption, and environmental degradation, landslides play a significant role in the evolution and shaping of aerial and subaerial landscapes. This is particularly true when they are linked to other natural hazards. Due to these regular pairings, it is challenging to find accurate statistics on the social damage alone caused by landslides on a worldwide basis, and the financial losses are undoubtedly understated [3].

Therefore, international organizations and agencies support strategies for reducing the risk of landslides, which include identifying hazards and improving preparedness for efficient response to disasters. Due to this, there will be more likely global changes like an increase in rainfall and deterioration of frost [4]. There are many different types of locations where landslides can happen, including mountain ranges, coastal walls, and even underwater areas with steep or gradual slope gradients. Geologically speaking, landslides are known to be caused by worn rock, ripped, fissured, or linked rock material, contrasted soil components, and low adhesion of the rock [5].

Predictions and alerts that come early are crucial for minimizing loss of life and property damage. It is essential to comprehend the causes of landslides and how individuals can prevent them from happening or just steer clear of them when they do. However, the conventional empirical approach lacks a precise quantitative foundation and is prone to human error, which can affect the outcomes of a sequence of subsequent landslide computations. Furthermore, using this method to pinpoint the primary slide's exact direction on complicated slopes might be challenging. In the past 10 years, significant advancements have been achieved in the use of the deform monitoring technique to identify ground movements and predict landslides [6]. For a few reasons, landslides in high-altitude locations are far more dangerous than those in other mountainous areas. The peaks in this area have a fairly wide topographic relief to start.

Relationships between the geomorphological conditions under which previous events occurred and anticipated future conditions can be established through satellite images, geographic information system (GIS) data, and on-the-ground research. In addition to gathering information on hydrogeology, land use/cover, geology, and geomorphology, remote sensing is also used to reveal changes in the landscape, the causes of landslides, and the regeneration or recovery process [7]. Because they can handle massive volumes of spatially referenced data quickly and efficiently, GIS has been utilized for data collection, storage, modification, display, and analysis. The monitoring of landslides is making more use of remote sensing technology. Even while gathering and analyzing data have advanced significantly, a lot of the analysis of data collected via satellite used to monitor landslides is still quite basic, especially for slow-moving landslides that have not yet "failed." To control and reduce possible risks and hazards to societies and their infrastructure, landslide monitoring that is precise and dependable is essential. In comparison to traditional techniques like inclinometers, extensometers, and GNSS monitoring, the ability to quantify landslide movement with greater spatial resolution has been made possible by ongoing advancements in investigating and remote sensing technologies, which have made it possible to collect highly detailed, accurate data frequently. However, in reality, sensors and data analysis techniques are often either quite basic or necessitate laborious human processing, such as the skilled creation of site-specific information processing and parameter generation [8]. As we have studied the overview of landslide displacement hazards, the main objectives that we focus on in this chapter are as follows: i) technological classifications of remote sensing are discussed in the following section 10.1.1.; ii) architecture of risk management, iii) AI-based landslide displacement, and iv) limitations and technologies integrated with AI models are also discussed.

10.1.1 Technology Classifications for Remote Sensing

While discussing the technology classifications, three main types of sensors are utilized in remote sensing research: optical, laser, and synthetic aperture radar (SAR). From a platform perspective, airborne, ground-based, and space-borne methods are possible for SAR, optical, and laser sensing. To obtain a high-resolution radar image, SAR imaging is a popular active microwave RS technique utilized in ground-based, space-borne, and airborne systems. Using multiple SAR images and an external DEM, the differential interferometric SAR method was first proposed to measure the deformation of the surface. This technique is typically used to measure the significant surface deformation brought on by landslides or earthquakes, with deformation accuracy down to the centimeter. Apart from these sensors, in particular, optical sensors work well when examining recent or deep active landslides. Fresh landslides have spectral features that are easily distinguished from their surroundings by automatic methods or eye interpretation. These features are frequently markedly distinct.

A technique namely Light Detection and Ranging (LiDAR) utilizes laser beams to pinpoint the position, speed, and other distinguishing features of landslides. Based on how they operate, these are separated into two categories: ground-level laser scanning and airborne LiDAR. Using a variety of laser echo methods, LiDAR can penetrate plants belowground without relying on light levels. It then identifies features belowground using an appropriate filtering algorithm to provide accurate data elevation on the ground. Thus, it is helpful for geological analysis in hilly regions covered with dense forests. However, there are still several drawbacks to airborne LiDAR. For example, dust and atmospheric conditions like fog, rainfall, and sandstorms can scatter the laser beam and reduce its power, making it challenging to gather accurate target data.

RST application in landslide assessment and control. Landslide displacement is measured and detected using satellite RSTs, which offer a synoptic picture across many spatiotemporal scales. The ground-based geological sensors, such as lidar, ground-based interferometric radar (GIR), and Doppler radar (DR), monitor small-scale regions and are more frequently utilized in real-time observation and early landslide caution because they combine precision, high-acquisition frequency, and configuration durability. The benefits and drawbacks of each RST vary according to its intended use (prediction, monitoring, or detection), the area of displacement size, the kind of landslide, its distortion pattern, and its associated risks with landslides. Thus, it is generally beneficial to integrate different technologies. The increased use of data in massive amounts, deployment of resources, and improved coordination with the stakeholders are all necessary for a more effective landslide risk management.

Figure 10.1 reviews popular remote sensing techniques that are often used for the processing and assessment of landslides. For landslide assessment and catastrophe risk reduction, multi-platform remote sensing employing space, airborne, and ground-based equipment has become indispensable. The several Earth observation satellite missions over the past 30 years have

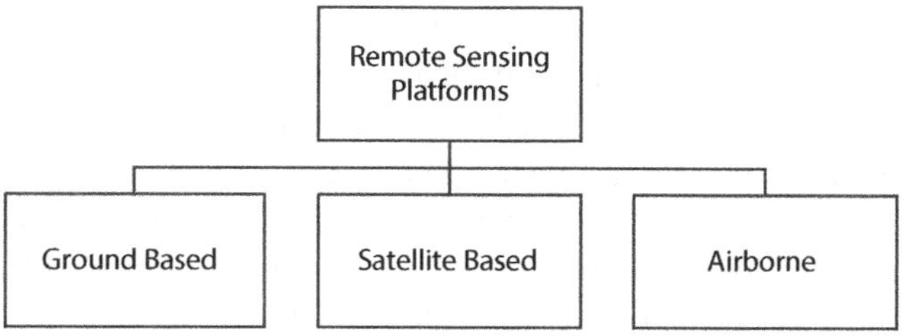

Figure 10.1 Techniques of remote sensing.

guaranteed continuous optical and radar picture archives. Selecting the best approach for risk assessment can be challenging given the rise in popularity of unmanned aircraft, free optical and radar data with long revisiting times, and opportunities to create high-resolution images and digital elevation models from the air and on the ground [9]. Widespread events and landslides have the potential to be disastrous when they happen close to infrastructure and populated areas. The core components of managing landslide risks are detection, monitoring, and prediction.

These tasks frequently rely on RSTs, which include interferometry, laser scanning, and satellite observation of Earth. Applications of earth science, like monitoring landslides, are using more and more remote sensing and surveying techniques. For example, high-resolution point clouds can be produced using terrestrial laser scanning (TLS), which helps track slope deformation. Large-scale landslide surface mapping with acceptable precision and coverage has been made possible more recently by UAS lidar systems. Structure from motion (SfM) and multiview stereopsis (MVS) methods can produce maximum-resolution, ortho-rectified images with point clouds from imagery data obtained with UAS platforms. In areas with sparse vegetation, photogrammetric technology can offer a comparable degree of precision to UAS lidar technologies at a lower cost of entry, provided that the proper protocols for data collection and processing are observed.

10.1.2 Architecture of Risk Management

Landslides are considered to be the major global geohazard that results in a large number of casualties and financial losses annually. Forecasting the development of future landslides is carping for risk assessment and also the creation of early caution mechanisms for the landslides brought on by external factors like precipitation, shifts in storage facility and groundwater concentrations, tremors, and human activity. Landslides typically evolve in a nonlinear fashion, making it cumbersome to predict how they will react in the future. The two primary external elements that coordinate and impact future displacements of landslides are rain as well as fluctuations in reservoir water levels, albeit to varying degrees of intensity.

There is a discussion of the landslide risk management approach on both natural and cut slopes. The framework necessitates quantifying the amount and possibility of failure of the slope along with the size and probability of the potential repercussions after establishing the scope of the study. These factors serve as the foundation for risk estimation. The tolerance of the risk level, whether quantitative or qualitative, is determined by comparing it to a set of established standards. The results of the risk evaluation guide decisions about the need for precautionary measures and control techniques, in addition to the necessity of learning more about the physical features, failure mechanisms, and possible triggers of the slope.

They also inform requirements for monitoring to manage residual risks. This is the point at which in-place instrumentation can benefit more from remote sensing techniques, especially in light of the increased use of quantitative risk analysis during the latter part of the 1990s and early 2000s [10]. Selecting the best approach for risk assessment can be challenging given the rise in popularity of unmanned drones, free transparent and radar imagery with long revisiting times, and opportunities to create excellent-quality 3D point clouds and digital elevation models from the air and on the ground. There are several examples of applications given, including laser grammetry, terrestrial optical photogrammetry, and Interferometry Synthetic Aperture Radar (InSAR). Certain procedures are inappropriate

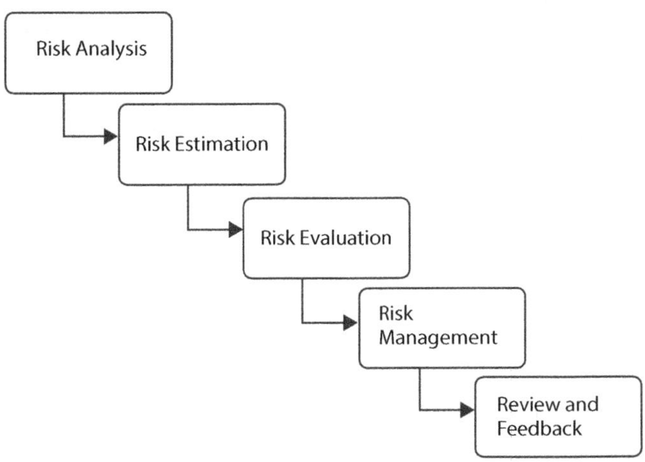

Figure 10.2 Framework for risk management.

for landslides that move slowly, while others are restricted to small studies or huge regions. The process of choosing the best system might be challenging [11]. These days, automating data processing and using complementary methodologies are essential for comprehending landslides. Figure 10.2 shows the block diagram of a risk management process framework.

The actual goal is to enhance autonomous landslide detection and monitoring systems for the deployment of close-to-real-time emergency systems. All of the previously described approaches from field observation to satellite image analysis can be combined to a better risk management.

10.2 Artificial Intelligence-Based Forecasting of Landslide Displacement

A significant worldwide geohazard, landslides cause a great deal of death and financial loss each year. For risk assessment and the development of trustworthy landslides early warning systems caused by external factors such as rainfall, reservoir variations, groundwater levels, and earthquakes, it is imperative to forecast the evolution of future landslides. Since landslides usually do not follow a straight line in their growth, it might be challenging to forecast their future behavior. Rainfall and also reservoir changes in water levels were the two main external factors that coordinate and influence future landslide displacements, but they do so to differing degrees of intensity.

Recent developments in landslide displacement prediction have demonstrated the effectiveness of state-of-the-art deep learning and artificial intelligence (AI) techniques. Taking into consideration not only the displacement data from landslides but also other contributing elements, these methods may effectively forecast future velocity [12]. To build or model fundamental relationships by evaluating landslide causative elements and non-landslide sites, heuristic methods and machine learning approaches typically take advantage of sophisticated algorithms. To generate an analytical model, the machine learning (ML) approach automatically analyzes data to uncover hidden observations and fundamental relationships. As a result, they are employed in the iterative learning process to generate precise, reproducible results. Techniques including object-oriented analysis, genetic algorithms, artificial neural networks (ANNs), and support vector machines (SVMs) have shown promise in recent years. However, each of these approaches necessitates creating interpretation logic or extracting information from the image, which complicates algorithm design and reduces algorithmic advancement potential.

A subfield of machine learning that has grown in importance is called deep learning. Deep learning, often referred to as feature learning mode with several layers, is a machine learning approach that is more advanced than the traditional one. Multiple layers are applied to the input data, whereby a mapping relationship minimizes the data's size and extracts key features. Deep-convolutional neural network (DCNN)-based deep learning models provide end-to-end machine learning methods for the automated extraction of picture information without the need for an extraction technique created manually [13]. The extraction of information from an image has been greatly aided by the advancement of deep learning techniques outperforming other conventional methods. Figure 10.3 includes a process diagram.

The topographical and geographical information such as rainfall, soil moisture, soil types, rock types, and slope data are collected in the data collection phase. Filling in of missing values using the algorithms and then categorizing the variables, scaling, and normalizing features are carried out in the preprocessing phase. The key elements of landslide displacement can be carried out by dimensionality reduction methods. Then, an appropriate selection of the model with training and also validation to estimate the maximum performance of the model is performed in model evaluation phase, and then finally the learned model has been deployed to forecast the

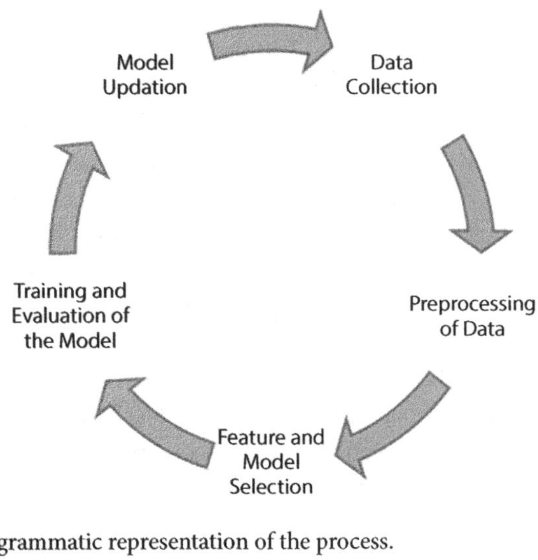

Figure 10.3 Diagrammatic representation of the process.

landslide displacement in real-time scenario. These are continuously evaluated for necessary updates with different data and environmental factors.

Each of these algorithms for machine learning has advantages and disadvantages, and the best algorithm to use will rely on the particulars of the landslide forecasting problem, such as the amount of data at hand, the intricacy of the topography, and the required degree of interpretability. In landslide forecasting applications, ensemble methods which integrate several models are frequently utilized to increase prediction accuracy and robustness. Apart from these, CNNs, LSTM, GRU, MLP, and many more are frequently employed in a variety of forecasting applications. Some of them are mentioned below [14]:

Multi-layer perceptron (MLP): The ANN is a popular model that has been successfully used for a range of tasks, such as forecasting and time series modeling. ANN models are popular because they allow the underlying data flow to be extrapolated without imposing restrictions on the model's structure. The fact that ANNs are universal approximators that can precisely approximate a variety of functions is another noteworthy feature of these devices. There are numerous ANN model architectures in the literature; it is true. Although the construction of ANNs is identical, several algorithms have been distinguished from one another according to their design.

Neural networks: Because neural networks can capture intricate nonlinear correlations in data, they are prominent in landslide prediction, especially when it comes to deep learning models. Convolutional neural networks (CNNs) and recurrent neural networks (RNNs), two types of deep neural networks, have demonstrated potential in analyzing temporal and spatial data for forecasting landslides. Deep neural networks can be prone to overfitting in the absence of appropriate regularization techniques, and their training necessitates substantial computing and data resources.

Recurrent neural networks (RNNs): This study uses three different forms of RNNs: bidirectional LSTM, gated recurrent unit (GRU), and long short-term memory (LSTM). Input-implicit-output networks are completely connected to traditional neural networks. The sequences' placements are unrelated to one another. Therefore, a typical neural network cannot be used for time series prediction. Recurrent neural networks (RNNs), which allow for input in the networks, remember previous information and use it for the computation of the current output.

LSTM and Bi-LSTM: Gradient explosion may be effectively addressed by LSTM neural networks, a special kind of RNN. Long-term memory and data discovery are supported by the LSTM's forgetting, input, and output gates. Although the LSTM model resolves the gradient vanishing problem associated with RNNs, it is limited to learning from the past and does not account for future data. As for the training phase, since the factors influencing landslide motion are consistent over time, it is possible to use the historical and projected displacement data as a supplement. Bi-LSTM features both forward and backward LSTM layers in its architecture. The forward LSTM model uses the present time step to get previous information, whereas the backward LSTM model retrieves future data about the current time step. Demand for tourists, well-log, and solar radiation are just a few of the forecasting applications that have successfully used the Bi-LSTM architecture.

GRU: The recurring unit is a more efficient and optimized variant of the RNN. The GRU has fewer parameters than an LSTM with a forget gate since it does away with the output gate. It functions similarly to an LSTM. In certain tasks like natural language analysis, voice signal modeling, and audio modeling, GRU fared better than LSTM.

Convolutional neural network: A subclass of artificial neural networks (ANNs), CNNs have extensive application in image and video identification, classification of images, and natural language processing, among other fields. CNN uses filters based on the arrangement of the input and of something comparable to the data it processes. To forecast landslide displacement, one-dimensional CNNs are utilized since time series represent one-dimensional data. The output sequence of a Conv1D layer is shorter than the input sequence. This is fixed by using the same padding or padding the input sequence with zeroes at both ends. A Conv1D layer is used to shift a filter over the input sequence.

Conv-LSTM model: One dense hidden layer, 2-LSTM layers, and a one-dimensional convolutional layer make up the Conv-LSTM model that was employed in this study. The CNN layer in this model extracts features from the input data, while both the LSTM and the dense layers use the output values to forecast the displacement of landslides using the feature data that was extracted. In several forecasting tasks, the CNN and LSTM combination produced the best prediction accuracies.

Decision trees: Recursively dividing the space of features into segments according to the values of the input characteristics, decision trees are straightforward but effective predictive models. They are capable of handling both numerical and category data and are easy to read. Overfitting of decision trees is common, particularly when dealing with complicated information. To lessen this problem, ensemble approaches (such as random forests) and pruning are frequently used.

Random forests (RF): During training, several decision trees are constructed using random forests, an ensemble learning technique that combines the predictions of these trees to increase accuracy and generalization. The most widely used integrated algorithm is the RF model. By using repeated autonomous sampling, it takes several samples from the original data and builds decision trees (DTs) for every sample. To accomplish classification and prediction, it then aggregates these DTs, treating each decision tree as a member. The most significant benefit of the RF algorithm is that it reduces overfitting and generates fewer mistakes when more feature pieces are employed in scenarios with large sample sizes. Furthermore, RF is a popular and useful tool for determining and assessing the significance of variables.

Support vector machines (SVMs): SVR performs well in complex and higher dimensional situations, has a significant generalization capacity, and has a decent prediction effect for tiny samples. As a result, it is highly popular and frequently utilized in the prediction of landslide displacement. However, SVR has issues, such as choosing hard parameters. The aforementioned algorithms' issues can be successfully resolved by using suitable parameter optimization techniques, which will also increase the precision of the landslide displacement forecast. Other machine learning methods like Bayesian networks, gradient boosting machines (GBM), and k-nearest neighbors (KNN) are being applied to landslide predictions in addition to decision trees, random forests, SVM, and neural networks. The type of data, the problem's complexity, available computing power, and the model's intended interpretability all play a role in the algorithm selection [15].

10.3 Performance Metrics

As we have discussed and compared about multiple artificial intelligence models for landslide prediction, their performance [16] must be assessed using a variety of measures. The following is a brief discussion about the performance measures to assess the model performance:

i) Accuracy: The ratio of accurately predicted instances to all instances is used to determine accuracy, which gauges how accurate the model's predictions are overall. Better performance is indicated by a higher accuracy.

ii) Precision and recall: Recall calculates the percentage of actual favorable predictions from all real positive instances, whereas precision calculates the percentage of genuine positive forecasts from all positive predictions. As it reduces the number of false positives and erroneous negatives, a model that has greater accuracy as well as recall is preferred.

iii) F1-score: Precision and recall are harmonic means, and the F1-score strikes a balance between both. 2 * (precision * recall) / (precision + recall) is the calculation. The higher the F1-score value, the better the recall and precision values.

Apart from these metrics, common metrics such as mean absolute error (MAE), as the name implies, measure the variation between the actual values and the predicted values, while root mean square error (RMSE) measures the squared root of MSE. If the model possesses lower RMSE and MAE values, then there is an increase in the prediction accuracy. Also, to display the results graphically, ROC and precision–recall curve are used that evaluate the performance of the model using different thresholds. Using the confusion matrix table, one can view the favorable, correct, and incorrect predictions of the model performance [17]. To comprehend the advantages of the AI models, various performance indicators were compared and studied [18].

10.4 Limitations in Assessing the AI Models for Landslide Displacement Prediction

There are issues related to the model assessment to achieve promising results [19]. The primary issues include the following:

i) Overfitting: When a model experiences this issue, it becomes less effective as it recognizes noise and other parameters during its training phase. This issue can be overcome by employing strategies like regularization and cross-validation.

ii) Imbalance data: If there are more variations of classes in landslide occurrence, then it is associated with the data imbalance. These problems can be overcome by resampling, synthetic, and data creation.

iii) Extension to novel datasets: When applied to new datasets, artificial intelligence models learned on one dataset might not generalize as effectively, particularly if the information's distributions or environmental factors differ significantly. To determine the model's capacity for generalization, it is critical to analyze its performance using cross-validation methods or independent validation datasets.

iv) Noise and data quality: Model performance can be negatively impacted by noisy or low-quality data because they can introduce errors or false patterns [20]. Outlier identification, cleaning of data, and feature selection are a few examples of data preparation approaches that can assist in enhancing data quality and lessen the effect of noise on the training of models.

v) Interpretability: Given their inherent complexity and lack of interpretability, some AI models like deep neural networks make it difficult to decipher the underlying causes of their predictions.

vi) Scalability and complexity of the model: This issue can be limited by increasing the training and computing power of the complex AI models. To address this massive landslide displacement issue, one needs to ensure that the predictive performance and computational efficiency are balanced. The parameters are evaluated precisely to address and overcome the problems mentioned in the literature above [21]. To improve the efficiency, contiguous testing and further improvement are necessary for landslide forecasting.

10.5 Technologies Integrated with AI Models

Landslide displacement can be easily predicted by integrating AI models with advanced technologies like LiDAR and aerial and satellite images that provide temporal and spatial characteristics of land use topographical changes. Modern algorithms are to be developed for remote sensing images to improve the predictive efficiency of the landslide displacement. These AI models can also be combined with geological surveys, IoT sensors, data fusion, and many more to extract instinctive information about landslide risk displacement [22]. Early warning systems, quick decision-making, and support can make the model even much stronger for the stakeholders, government organizations, and local bodies. With the help of these AI-fused models, there is optimal use of resources, prioritizing the location of higher-risk landslide displacement and increasing the efficiency of mitigation. In short, these types of landslide tracking and prediction can be properly addressed by the fusion of AI models with other technologies [23]. These integrated techniques will improve the effectiveness, time, and context when compared to the state-of-the-art techniques. This will help to improve the capacity to reduce the effect of landslides to safeguard the communities and ecosystems.

10.6 Conclusion

Landslide detection, monitoring, and prediction all depend heavily on remote sensing. Modern, more advanced technology can now gather a wide range of data on various slope instabilities at multiple sizes. Until the late 2010s, we could not monitor fast landslides due to the lack of new algorithms and detectors with a higher acquiring frequency and spatial resolution. Additionally, we were unable to more accurately identify and contour slope instabilities in remote and vegetated areas. The inability to adequately utilize and gather landslide data is now a bottleneck in the monitoring and forecast of landslides. Though they are frequently analyzed only after catastrophic events, satellites continuously capture and store images that have the potential to detect, monitor, and, in certain situations, predict people-threatening landslides. By reducing the effects of landslides, the landslide tracking system can provide authorities adequate time to evacuate people and safeguard their property. AI models have enormous potential to improve landslide displacement forecasting and hold great promise for expanding our knowledge of landslide dynamics, strengthening early warning systems, and lessening the effects of landslides on infrastructure, people, and the environment. Researchers and practitioners can integrate various data sources, such as spatial information, environmental sensors, and past landslide records, to create models of prediction that predict landslide displacement with greater accuracy and lead time by utilizing AI techniques like machine learning, deep learning, and data fusion. Consequently, to fully utilize AI models in enhancing landslide displaced forecasting and advancing our joint endeavors to construct more durable and resilient communities in landslide-prone areas, more research, interdisciplinary cooperation, and stakeholder involvement are necessary.

Numerous uses for remote sensing have been shown in the context of landslide risk analysis. The true issue facing engineering geology scientists is the prediction of future phenomena, and recent advancements in this area seem highly promising. In most circumstances, this problem is rather difficult, and it is rare to truly understand the slope. From one perspective, this study avenue requires significant work in the future to enable landslide science to monitor downstream services and ultimately benefit society. However, the only path to a more thorough and reliable knowledge of the physical mechanisms causing landslides is through the ongoing application of remote sensing techniques, which will result in the establishment of extensive data archives and analysis results. Furthermore, the forecast methods for the displacement caused by landslides are typically included, which might give the authorities additional time to carry out the evacuation. A more open sharing policy among scientific societies and a more intensive interchange among industry, local administrators, and researchers could be a partial solution to this data under exploitation.

References

1. Xu, Q., *et al.*, Remote sensing for landslide investigations: A progress report from China. *Eng. Geol.*, 321, 107156, 2023.
2. Casagli, N., Intrieri, E., Tofani, V., Gigli, G., Raspini, F., Landslide detection, monitoring and prediction with remote-sensing techniques. *Nat. Rev. Earth Environ.*, 4, 1, 51–64, 2023.
3. Casagli, N., *et al.*, Spaceborne, UAV and ground-based remote sensing techniques for landslide mapping, monitoring and early warning. *Geoenviron. Disasters*, 4, 1–23, 2017.
4. Wasowski, J. and Bovenga, F., Remote sensing of landslide motion with emphasis on satellite multi-temporal interferometry applications: an overview, in: *Landslide hazards, risks, and disasters*, pp. 365–438, 2022.
5. Zhong, C., *et al.*, Landslide mapping with remote sensing: challenges and opportunities. *Int. J. Remote Sens.*, 41, 4, 1555–1581, 2020.
6. Zocchi, M., Multi-scale Remote Sensing geomorphological applications for updating landslide inventories supported by Artificial Intelligence, 2024.
7. Zhou, C., *et al.*, A novel framework for landslide displacement prediction using MT-InSAR and machine learning techniques. *Eng. Geol.*, 334, 107497, 2024.
8. Senogles, A., Olsen, M.J., Leshchinsky, B., SlideSim: 3D landslide displacement monitoring through a physics-based simulation approach to self-supervised learning. *Remote Sens.*, 14, 11, 2644, 2022.
9. Lissak, C., *et al.*, Remote sensing for assessing landslides and associated hazards. *Surv. Geophys.*, 41, 6, 1391–1435, 2020.
10. Macciotta, R. and Hendry, M.T., Remote sensing applications for landslide monitoring and investigation in western Canada. *Remote Sens.*, 13, 3, 366, 2021.

11. Zhang, Q. and Wang, T., Deep Learning for Exploring Landslides with Remote Sensing and Geo-Environmental Data: Frameworks, Progress, Challenges, and Opportunities. *Remote Sens.*, 16, 8, 1344, 2024.
12. Knoth, C., Feizizade, B., Bañón, F.P., Remote Sensing and Machine Learning for the Detection and Segmentation Of Landslides in Nepal, 2024.
13. Mohan, A., Singh, A.K., Kumar, B., Dwivedi, R., Review on remote sensing methods for landslide detection using machine and deep learning. *Trans. Emerg. Telecommun. Technol.*, 32, 7, e3998, 2021.
14. Li, J., Wang, W., Han, Z., A variable weight combination model for prediction on landslide displacement using AR model, LSTM model, and SVM model: a case study of the Xinming landslide in China. *Environ. Earth Sci.*, 80, 10, 386, 2021.
15. Nava, L., *et al.*, Landslide displacement forecasting using deep learning and monitoring data across selected sites. *Landslides*, 20, 10, 2111–2129, 2023.
16. Hussain, M.A., Chen, Z., Zheng, Y., Zhou, Y., Daud, H., Deep Learning and Machine Learning Models for Landslide Susceptibility Mapping with Remote Sensing Data. *Remote Sens.*, 15, 19, 4703, 2023.
17. Ge, Q., Li, J., Lacasse, S., Sun, H., Liu, Z., Data-augmented landslide displacement prediction using generative adversarial network. *J. Rock Mech. Geotech. Eng.*, 16, 4017–4033, 2024.
18. Prakash, N., Manconi, A., Loew, S., Mapping landslides on EO data: Performance of deep learning models vs. traditional machine learning models. *Remote Sens.*, 12, 3, 346, 2020.
19. Zhang, X., Zhu, C., He, M., Dong, M., Zhang, G., Zhang, F., Failure mechanism and long short-term memory neural network model for landslide risk prediction. *Remote Sens.*, 14, 1, 166, 2021.
20. Yang, C., Yin, Y., Zhang, J., Ding, P., Liu, J., A graph deep learning method for landslide displacement prediction based on global navigation satellite system positioning. *Geosci. Front.*, 15, 1, 101690, 2024.
21. Zhu, L., *et al.*, Landslide susceptibility prediction modeling based on remote sensing and a novel deep learning algorithm of a cascade-parallel recurrent neural network. *Sensors*, 20, 6, 1576, 2020.
22. Yang, J., Huang, Z., Jian, W., Robledo, L.F., Landslide displacement prediction by using Bayesian optimization–temporal convolutional networks. *Acta Geotech.*, 19, 1–19, 2024.
23. Bravo-López, E., Fernández Del Castillo, T., Sellers, C., Delgado-García, J., Landslide susceptibility mapping of landslides with Artificial Neural Networks: Multi-approach analysis of Backpropagation Algorithm applying the neuralnet package in Cuenca, Ecuador. *Remote Sens.*, 14, 14, 3495, 2022.

11

Estimation of Snow Avalanche Hazardous Zones With AI Models

Rajinder Kaur[1,2*], Sartajvir Singh[3] and Ganesh Kumar Sethi[4]

[1]*Department of Computer Science, Punjabi University, Punjab, India*
[2]*Department of Computer Applications, Baba Farid College, Bathinda, Punjab, India*
[3]*University Institute of Engineering, Chandigarh University, Punjab, India*
[4]*Department of Computer Science, Multani Mal Modi College, Punjab, India*

Abstract
Monitoring of snow cover dynamics is important to understand seasonal variations, especially in regions like the Himalayas, where snowmelt plays a vital role in water resource management, agriculture, and hazard prediction. It is important that rapid detectors play a big role in the surveillance of snow-covered areas. This paper is about snow cover classification in the Himachal Pradesh area that is important for avalanche risk reduction. In this study, information is collected from two sensors, MODIS and SCATSAT-1. In order to combine features found within the sensors, there is a requirement to use nearest neighbor diffusion (NND) pan-sharpening technique. The application of support vector machine (SVM) and spectral angle mapper (SAM) on high-resolution pan-sharpened data enhanced help to differentiate snow-covered regions. The SVM classifier outperforms the SAM classifier in terms of overall accuracy. The present study stresses the importance of combining NND pan-sharpening with the SVM classifier to enable accurate snow cover mapping.

***Keywords*:** Snow cover mapping, pan-sharpening, remote sensing

**Corresponding author*: rajindersidhu654@gmail.com; ORCID:0009-0008-2780-4187
Sartajvir Singh: ORCID: 0000-0002-4451-4949
Ganesh Kumar Sethi: ORCID: 0000-0003-2903-6712

Neelam Dahiya, Gurwinder Singh, Sartajvir Singh and Apoorva Sharma (eds.) Artificial Intelligence in Remote Sensing for Disaster Management, (201–212) © 2025 Scrivener Publishing LLC

11.1 Introduction

The Himalayan region experiences frequent and significant climate fluctuations that lead to avalanches, landslides, floods, and flash floods among other serious issues. As a result, precise tracking and classification of snow cover might help hazard analysts in gathering crucial data about the earth's surface and update them of what needs to be predicted [1]. Snow cover monitoring is essential for several reasons, including managing water resources, preparing for natural disasters, and hydrological research [2]. Because of variations in the climate, snow cover variability has an adverse effect on glacier mass balances and snowmelt runoff [3]. The temperature rises of land and ocean between 1880 and 2012 was 0.85°C [4], comparable to the rise observed between 1901 and 2003 [5].

These climatic fluctuations have a major impact on snowmelt patterns, which impacts hydrological and climatological studies. The regular fluctuation in the amount of snow cover has caused great harm to the Himalayan region [6], which has an impact on the residents who rely on the snow for their water supply [7]. The researchers suggest that a unique climatic variation that caused an earthquake had a significant impact on the Himalayan cryosphere. Avalanches claimed the lives of 1,883 people in India in the 46 years spanning from 1970 to 2016 [8].

The union territories of Jammu and Kashmir (J&K), Ladakh, as well as the states of Himachal Pradesh, Uttarakhand, and Sikkim, are particularly vulnerable to this hazard. Notably, around 62% of these fatalities occur while individuals are in transit during snowfall or shortly after a snowstorm has ceased. The forecasting of avalanche occurrences from mountain slopes is a highly complex process influenced by numerous factors related to the snowpack, meteorological conditions, and terrain characteristics within the region [1]. Several factors contribute to the formation of avalanches in the Indian Himalayas. These factors can be categorized into two main groups: snowpack conditions and slope characteristics. Research underscores that inadequate decision-making and forecasting significantly contribute to deadly avalanche accidents [2, 9]. Avalanche experts utilize various forecasting models, including nearest neighbor, expert system, and discriminant analysis among others.

The value of satellite remote sensing to research snow cover is widely known. It is essential for monitoring variations in the amount of snow cover and calculating important snowpack parameters, like snow water equivalent (SWE) [10], snow depth (SD) [11], snow grain size (SGS) [12], and snow surface temperature (SST) [13]. Avalanche forecasting models can be more effectively utilized to predict and reduce avalanche hazards in mountainous areas by integrating this input with data on snowpack, weather, and topography.

This research explores the enhancement of optical and microwave datasets through various pan-sharpening techniques. The outlined objectives are as follows: (a) preprocessing, (b) applying pan-sharpening methods to MODIS optical images and SCATSAT-1 microwave images using NND, and (c) employing SVM and SAM classifiers for image classification. Finally, the performance of these methods is evaluated through accuracy assessment procedures. As part of the study, performance analysis is conducted on a section of the Himalayas predominantly covered with snow.

11.2 Study Site and Data

The research is conducted in the northern region of India, specifically in the state of Uttarakhand (as illustrated in Figure 11.1(a and b)). Encompassing an area of roughly 55,483 square kilometers, it extends from latitude 28°42′40″ N to 31°27′43″ N and longitude 77°35′02″ E to 81°02′23″ N. This area is predominantly mountainous and experiences substantial snowfall.

Data from optical-based MODIS (at 500-m spatial resolution) and microwave-based SCATSAT-1 (at 2-km spatial resolution) were obtained on February 16, 2020. SCATSAT-1, developed by the ISRO, operates in various dual-polarization modes [14], enabling detailed surface feature distinctions [15]. The study utilizes backscattered data (Sigma-naught) from

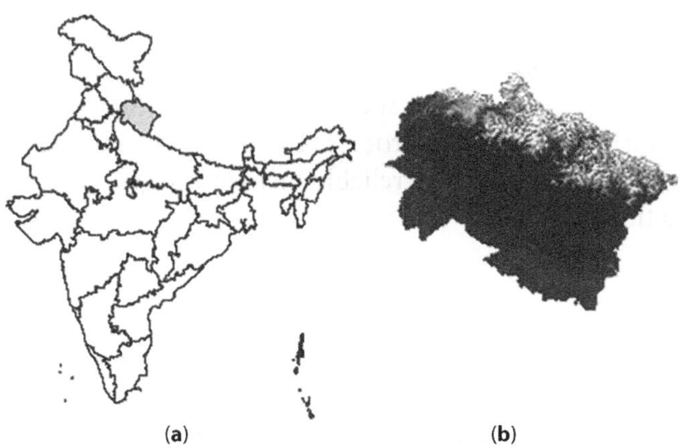

Figure 11.1 Selected study area: (a) map of India; (b) MODIS image acquired over the study site.

SCATSAT-1, a Level 4 India (S1L4) product. MODIS data was sourced from the MOD02 product on the NASA online portal.

SCATSAT-1 emits microwave pulses towards Earth's surface, capturing reflected energy while considering surface roughness. Unlike passive microwave sensors, active sensors like scatterometers are unaffected by ambient radiation and offer extensive global coverage, exceeding 90% of Earth's surface daily [14]. Additionally, scatterometers can measure sigma-nought (σ) over Earth's surface during both day and night, penetrating cloud cover [16]. For validation purposes, MODIS data from the MOD10A2 product on the NASA online portal was acquired for the same date.

11.3 Methodology

The methodological framework employed in the current study is structured into four distinct stages (as shown in Figure 11.2): (a) preprocessing of microwave and optical datasets, (b) pan-sharpening of MODIS and SCATSAT-1 images using NND algorithm, (c) classification of pan-sharpened satellite images with a SVM classifier and SAM classifier, and (d) validation using qualitative and quantitative analysis.

A. Pre-processing

For effective pan-sharpening, it is essential to ensure that both MODIS and SCATSAT-1 images undergo necessary corrections for geometric, radiometric, and atmospheric factors. These adjustments are critical in resolving issues such as sensor calibration errors, atmospheric influences, and variations in solar angles. These factors can significantly impact the brightness and quality of the images. Consequently, applying Equation 11.1 [17, 18] helps calculate the spectral reflectance (SR), ensuring precise outcomes during the merging process. These preparatory steps are pivotal for achieving high-quality and reliable merged images, essential for various applications.

$$SR = \frac{\pi R \curlywedge ES^2}{E_0 + cos\theta_z} \tag{11.1}$$

R is representing radiance (between sensor and path), ES stands for the Earth–Sun distance, E_0 represents the exo-atmospheric spectral, and θz denotes the zenith angle.

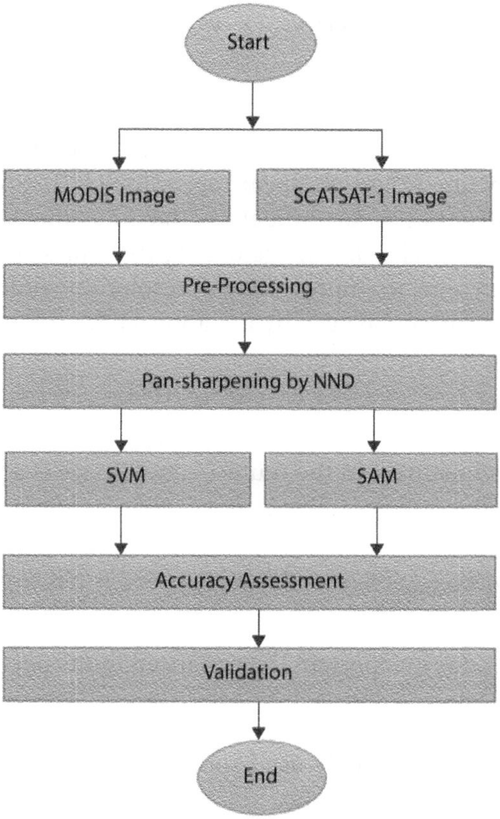

Figure 11.2 Flow chart of the methodology.

B. Pan-sharpening

The NND method is used to merge both MODIS and SCATSAT-1 data, which belong to the component substitution pan-sharpening category. The NND (nearest neighbor difference) pan-sharpening method enhances multispectral imagery using the difference factor $Di(x, y)$ (as shown in Equation 11.2) between each pixel in the panchromatic image and its neighboring pixels [19]. This factor estimates the similarity index of the selected pixel. Initially, a high-resolution panchromatic image HR_{PAN} is downscaled to match the lower-resolution multispectral image LR_{MS}. Linear regression calculates a coefficient to adjust for the influence of different light wavelengths on a measurement [20]. Difference factors are calculated from neighboring pixels, allowing adjustment of spectral values in the multispectral image to enhance spatial resolution while maintaining spectral fidelity [21].

$$Di(x,y) = HR_{PAN}(x,y) - LR_{MS}(x',y') \tag{11.2}$$

where (x',y') are the coordinates of the multispectral image's nearest neighbor pixel that corresponds to (x,y) in the panchromatic image. The *T* coefficient, obtained through linear regression (*LR*), governs the extent to which the difference factor influences the adjustment of spectral values in the multispectral (*MS*) image during the pan-sharpening process. This modification aims to improve spatial resolution while preserving the image's spectral accuracy, as seen by Equation 11.3.

$$T = LRG(MS, PAN) \tag{11.3}$$

The spectral adjustment in the multispectral image is achieved through Equation 11.4.

$$MS_{enhanced}(x,y) = LR_{MS}(x,y) + T \times Di(x,y) \tag{11.4}$$

Here, $MS_{enhanced}(x,y)$ represent the enhanced multispectral image.

C. Classification

SAM and SVM are two widely used supervised classification techniques that are applied in numerous fields.

I. SVM

SVM is a popular and widely utilized supervised classifier. By projecting the initial training data into a higher-dimensional space and then establishing a hyperplane within that extended space, it performs classification [22]. SVM divides the data into distinct classes by determining the optimal hyperplane to optimize the margin between the classes [23]. This hyperplane, often called the decision plane, is essential for distinguishing between various data sets. Support vectors are certain data points that SVM finds and uses to help construct the decision border. This ensures a significant margin of separation between classes [24]. Equations 11.5 and 11.6 represent SVM mathematically for a training dataset with *n* occurrences [25].

$$\{a_i, b_i\}; i = 1, \ldots\ldots\ldots n \tag{11.5}$$

where the t classes are represented by $b \in R^t$ and the z input characteristics by $a \in R^z$. The classes in a binary classification issue are denoted by the labels $y \in \{-1, +1\}$. These training patterns are considered linearly separable when a weight vector 'w' specifies the orientation of the discriminating plane and a scalar 'y' determines the offset of the discriminating plane from the origin [26].

$$b_i(wa_i + y) - 1 \geq 0 \tag{11.6}$$

II. SAM

The SAM approach is based on the fundamental principle that every pixel in an image reflects a distinct ground cover material belonging to a single class. SAM is a supervised method that evaluates the similarity in spectrum between two spectra [27]. The technique treats each spectrum as a vector in a space whose dimensions equal the number of bands in order to compute spectral similarity. One measures the angle formed by these vectors. In order to discover the molecular structure of the material, spectroscopy measures the radiant intensity and energy produced by the interaction of light and matter [28]. When using absorption spectroscopy, the substance under study takes on the role of a passive object, selectively absorbing particular photons according to their wavelengths and producing a unique spectral signature [29]. SAM computes the spectral angle between two spectra x and y (as shown in Equation 11.7).

$$cos^{-1}\left(\frac{x.y}{\|x\| \cdot \|y\|}\right) \tag{11.7}$$

where $(\cdot)$ dot represent product, $\|x\|$ and $\|y\|$ denote the magnitudes of vectors x and y.

D. Validation

Validation is a crucial step in assessing the accuracy of classified images generated from pan-sharpened images using NND method. There are several methods available to evaluate accuracy [30]. Typically, the accuracy of a classified image is compared to reference data. In this study, MODIS data obtained from the MOD10A2 product on the NASA online portal was used for validation. This evaluation considers both the rows (representing classified data) and columns (representing reference data) to analyze the conversion of one class into another [31]. Key aspects considered in this study include the user's accuracy (UA), which evaluates the precision of class classification in the image, and the producer's accuracy (PA), which measures the agreement between the classification results and the reference data.

11.4 Results and Discussion

In this study, the results have been visualized and quantified. Initially, the MODIS and SCATSAT-1 datasets have been preprocessed to overcome atmospheric and radiometric effects. Then, the NND method has been chosen as a pan-sharpening method based on previous literature and implemented on both datasets, as shown in Figure 11.3(a–c). To evaluate the NND pan-sharpening technique, the SVM and SAM have been implemented for classification on pan-sharpened images. The classified images have been shown in Figure 11.3(d and e). To confirm the reliability of these results, accuracy assessments were conducted for each of the pan-sharpened classified images. For a reference dataset, a MODIS dataset of the same temporal date was used.

Table 11.1 shows the accuracy assessment of NND pan-sharpened data using SVM and SAM Classifier. In terms of overall accuracy, the SVM

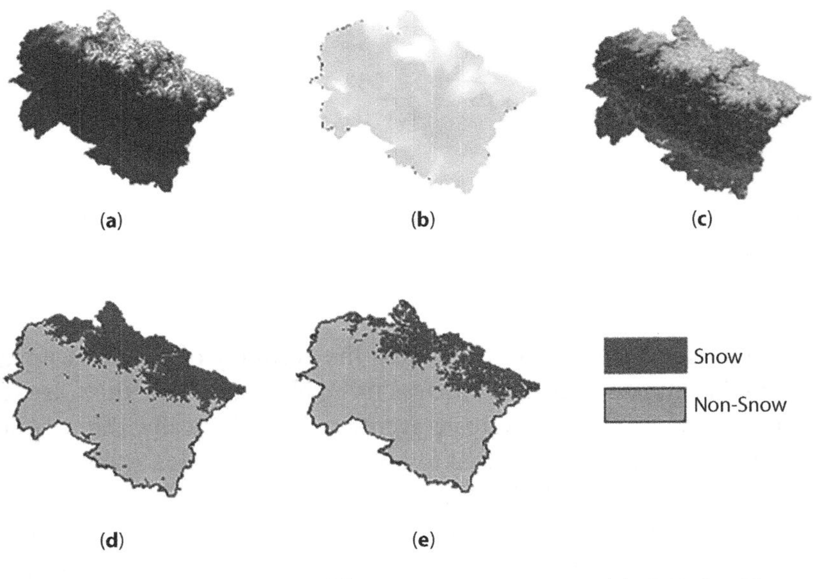

Figure 11.3 (a) Modis input image, (b) SCATSAT-1 input image, (c) NND fused image, (d) SVM classified image, and (e) SAM classified image.

Table 11.1 Accuracy assessment of NND pan-sharpened images using SVM and SAM classifiers.

Classifier	Classified data		Reference data		Accuracy	
	Classes	Snow	Non-snow	RT	PA (%)	UA (%)
SVM	Snow	71	14	85	79.78	83.53
	Non-snow	18	1,341	1,359	20.22	98.96
	CT	89	1,355	1,444	-	-
	OA	97.78%				
SAM	Snow	41	6	47	46.07	87.23
	Non-snow	48	1,349	1,397	53.93	96.56
	CT	89	1,355	1,444	-	-
	OA	96.26%				

RT, row total; CT, column total; PA, producer's accuracy; UA, user's accuracy; OA, overall accuracy; OE, omission error; CE, commission error.

classifier exhibits superior performance, achieving an accuracy rate of 97.78% compared to SAM's accuracy of 96.26%. This indicates that the SVM classifier generally provides more accurate classifications across the dataset. In addition, SVM compares to SAM in terms of producer accuracy; for its classes, SVM provides higher producer accuracies of 79.78% and 98.96%, respectively, whereas SAM yields lower producer accuracies of 46.07% and 53.93%. In comparison, SVM outperforms SAM in terms of user accuracy, achieving 83.53% and 98.96%, respectively, while SAM only manages 87.23% and 96.56%. All of these results point to the SVM classifier as a better option for land cover classification tasks, particularly where accuracy is crucial, since it provides reliable and precise classifications of NND pan-sharpened images.

11.5 Conclusion

In conclusion, the research examined two datasets, MODIS and SCATSAT-1, to evaluate the performance of distinct pan-sharpening technique such as NND. SVM and SAM implement to classify NND pan-sharpened image. Classified images are validated by using MODIS reference data. Specifically, the SVM classifier performed better than the SAM in terms of producer, user, and overall accuracy. With an overall accuracy of 97.78%, these findings highlight how crucial it is to select the best classifier for snow cover classification tasks, particularly when precision is crucial. The study suggests that for accurate and reliable snow cover classification in remote sensing applications, SVM classifier should be used in conjunction with NND pan-sharpening. Future work may focus on examining state-of-the-art fusion algorithms and machine learning techniques to enhance the accuracy and consistency of snow cover classification in remote sensing applications. Comparative research employing different classification algorithms and extending the study's geographic area may potentially provide more insights into enhancing classification performance and developing more comprehensive snow cover monitoring systems.

References

1. Bühler, Y., Kumar, S., Veitinger, J., Christen, M., Stoffel, A., Snehmani, Automated identification of potential snow avalanche release areas based on digital elevation models. *Nat. Hazards Earth Syst. Sci.*, 13, 5, 1321–1335, May 2013, doi: 10.5194/nhess-13-1321-2013.
2. McClung, D.M., Avalanche character and fatalities in the high mountains of Asia. *Ann. Glaciol.*, 57, 71, 114–118, Jan. 2016, doi: 10.3189/2016AoG71A075.
3. Kumar, P., Saharwardi, Md.S., Banerjee, A., Azam, M.F., Dubey, A.K., Murtugudde, R., Snowfall Variability Dictates Glacier Mass Balance Variability in Himalaya-Karakoram. *Sci. Rep.*, 9, 1, 18192, Dec. 2019, doi: 10.1038/s41598-019-54553-9.
4. Singh, D.K., Gusain, H.S., Mishra, V., Gupta, N., Snow cover variability in North-West Himalaya during last decade. *Arab. J. Geosci.*, 11, 19, 579, Oct. 2018, doi: 10.1007/s12517-018-3926-3.
5. Sood, V., Gusain, H.S., Gupta, S., Taloor, A.K., Singh, S., Detection of snow/ice cover changes using subpixel-based change detection approach over Chhota-Shigri glacier, Western Himalaya, India. *Quat. Int.*, 575–576, 204–212, Feb. 2021, doi: 10.1016/j.quaint.2020.05.016.
6. Kaur, R., Sethi, G.K., Singh, S., Review on Machine Learning-based Change Detection and Pan Sharpening Algorithms for Remote Sensing Datasets, in: *2023 IEEE 9th International Women in Engineering (WIE) Conference on Electrical and Computer Engineering (WIECON-ECE)*, Nov. 2023, IEEE, Thiruvananthapuram, India, pp. 64–69, doi: 10.1109/WIECON-ECE60392.2023.10456370.
7. Gusain, H.S., Mishra, V.D., Arora, M.K., Mamgain, S., Singh, D.K., Operational algorithm for generation of snow depth maps from discrete data in Indian Western Himalaya. *Cold Reg. Sci. Technol.*, 126, 22–29, Jun. 2016, doi: 10.1016/j.coldregions.2016.02.012.

8. Singh, K.K., *et al.*, Detection and mapping of snow avalanche debris from Western Himalaya, India using remote sensing satellite images. *Geocarto Int.*, 37, 9, 2561–2579, May 2022, doi: 10.1080/10106049.2020.1762762.
9. Techel, F., Zweifel, B., Winkler, K., Analysis of avalanche risk factors in back-country terrain based on usage frequency and accident data in Switzerland. *Nat. Hazards Earth Syst. Sci.*, 15, 9, 1985–1997, Sep. 2015, doi: 10.5194/nhess-15-1985-2015.
10. Negi, H.S. and Kokhanovsky, A., Retrieval of snow grain size and albedo of western Himalayan snow cover using satellite data. *Cryosphere*, 5, 4, 831–847, Oct. 2011, doi: 10.5194/tc-5-831-2011.
11. Xu, X., *et al.*, Global snow cover estimation with Microwave Brightness Temperature measurements and one-class *in situ* observations. *Remote Sens. Environ.*, 182, 227–251, Sep. 2016, doi: 10.1016/j.rse.2016.05.010.
12. Das, I. and Sarwade, R.N., Snow depth estimation over north-western Indian Himalaya using AMSR-E. *Int. J. Remote Sens.*, 29, 14, 4237–4248, Jul. 2008, doi: 10.1080/01431160701874595.
13. Negi, H.S., Thakur, N.K., Mishra, V.D., Estimation and validation of snow surface temperature using modis data for snow-avalanche studies in NW-Himalaya. *J. Indian Soc. Remote Sens.*, 35, 4, 287–299, Dec. 2007, doi: 10.1007/BF02990785.
14. Singh, S., Tiwari, R.K., Gusain, H.S., Sood, V., Potential Applications of SCATSAT-1 Satellite Sensor: A Systematic Review. *IEEE Sens. J.*, 20, 21, 12459–12471, Nov. 2020, doi: 10.1109/JSEN.2020.3002720.
15. Singh, S., Tiwari, R.K., Sood, V., Kaur, R., Singh, S., Prashar, S., Estimation and validation of standalone SCATSAT-1 derived snow cover area using different MODIS products. *Geocarto Int.*, 37, 27, 18474–18490, Dec. 2022, doi: 10.1080/10106049.2022.2142962.
16. Singh, S., Sood, V., Tiwari, R.K., Kaur, R., Sharma, A., Endeavours of Scatterometer Satellite (SCATSAT-1) in earth exploration: An overview of products, applications and emerging trends. *Phys. Chem. Earth Parts ABC*, 134, 103601, Jun. 2024, doi: 10.1016/j.pce.2024.103601.
17. Mishra, V.D., Sharma, J.K., Khanna, R., Review of topographic analysis methods for the western Himalaya using AWiFS and MODIS satellite imagery. *Ann. Glaciol.*, 51, 54, 153–160, 2010, doi: 10.3189/172756410791386526.
18. Liu, X. and Yang, C., A Kernel Spectral Angle Mapper algorithm for remote sensing image classification, in: *2013 6th International Congress on Image and Signal Processing (CISP)*, Dec. 2013, IEEE, Hangzhou, China, pp. 814–818, doi: 10.1109/CISP.2013.6745277.
19. Choi, J., Park, H., Seo, D., Pansharpening Using Guided Filtering to Improve the Spatial Clarity of VHR Satellite Imagery. *Remote Sens.*, 6, 11, 116, 633, Mar. 2019, doi: 10.3390/rs11060633.
20. Zhao, J., Huang, L., Yang, H., Zhang, D., Wu, Z., Guo, J., Fusion and assessment of high-resolution WorldView-3 satellite imagery using NNDiffuse and Brovey algotirhms, in: *2016 IEEE International Geoscience and Remote*

Sensing Symposium (IGARSS), Jul. 2016, IEEE, Beijing, China, pp. 2606–2609, doi: 10.1109/IGARSS.2016.7729673.

21. Singh, S., Tiwari, R.K., Sood, V., Gusain, H.S., Prashar, S., Image Fusion of Ku-Band-Based SCATSAT-1 and MODIS Data for Cloud-Free Change Detection Over Western Himalayas. *IEEE Trans. Geosci. Remote Sens.*, 60, 1–14, 2022, doi: 10.1109/TGRS.2021.3123392.
22. Prajapati, G.L. and Patle, A., On Performing Classification Using SVM with Radial Basis and Polynomial Kernel Functions, in: *2010 3rd International Conference on Emerging Trends in Engineering and Technology*, Nov. 2010, IEEE, Goa, pp. 512–515, doi: 10.1109/ICETET.2010.134.
23. Singh, G., Sethi, G.K., Singh, S., Survey on Machine Learning and Deep Learning Techniques for Agriculture Land. *SN Comput. Sci.*, 2, 6, 487, Nov. 2021, doi: 10.1007/s42979-021-00929-6.
24. Kuo, B.-C., Ho, H.-H., Li, C.-H., Hung, C.-C., Taur, J.-S., A Kernel-Based Feature Selection Method for SVM With RBF Kernel for Hyperspectral Image Classification. *IEEE J. Sel. Top. Appl. Earth Obs. Remote Sens.*, 7, 1, 317–326, Jan. 2014, doi: 10.1109/JSTARS.2013.2262926.
25. Jayadeva, Khemchandani, R., Chandra, S., Twin Support Vector Machines (TWSVM) for Classification, in: *Twin Support Vector Machines*, vol. 659, in Studies in Computational Intelligence, pp. 43–62, Springer International Publishing, Cham, 2017, doi: 10.1007/978-3-319-46186-1_3.
26. Pal, M. and Foody, G.M., Evaluation of SVM, RVM and SMLR for Accurate Image Classification With Limited Ground Data. *IEEE J. Sel. Top. Appl. Earth Obs. Remote Sens.*, 5, 5, 1344–1355, Oct. 2012, doi: 10.1109/JSTARS.2012.2215310.
27. Singh, S., Tiwari, R.K., Sood, V., Prashar, S., Fusion of SCATSAT-1 and optical data for cloud-free imaging and its applications in classification. *Arab. J. Geosci.*, 14, 19, 1978, Oct. 2021, doi: 10.1007/s12517-021-08359-7.
28. Kaur, R., Singh, S., Sethi, G.K., Spatial and Spectral Analysis of Resampling Algorithms in Image Fusion of Optical and Microwave Satellite Images: A Case Study Over Western Himalayas. *J. Indian Soc. Remote Sens.*, 52, 2317–2334, Jul. 2024, doi: 10.1007/s12524-024-01912-3.
29. Garcia-Allende, P.B., Conde, O.M., Mirapeix, J., Cubillas, A.M., Lopez-Higuera, J.M., Data Processing Method Applying Principal Component Analysis and Spectral Angle Mapper for Imaging Spectroscopic Sensors. *IEEE Sens. J.*, 8, 7, 1310–1316, Jul. 2008, doi: 10.1109/JSEN.2008.926923.
30. Vivone, G., *et al.*, A Critical Comparison Among Pansharpening Algorithms. *IEEE Trans. Geosci. Remote Sens.*, 53, 5, 2565–2586, May 2015, doi: 10.1109/TGRS.2014.2361734.
31. Congalton, R.G., A review of assessing the accuracy of classifications of remotely sensed data. *Remote Sens. Environ.*, 37, 1, 35–46, Jul. 1991, doi: 10.1016/0034-4257(91)90048-B.

12

Predicting and Understanding the Snow Avalanche Event

Nitin Arora* **and Sakshi**

Department of Computer Science and Engineering, Chandigarh University, Mohali, Punjab, India

Abstract

Snow avalanche is a natural calamity that might occur at any instance of time throughout the year. This phenomenon becomes a source of disaster and causes damage to the local vegetation and livelihood, including travelers. It is important to understand and monitor the snow pattern with high precision to get information about the predictable disasters that could occur. The monitoring of snow level rise and the wind pattern is accessible using remote sensing. Currently, many radar-based ground-level and airborne satellites are targeting the monitoring of seismic motions and wind speed over the Earth's terrain and sea bodies. This chapter provides a base for scholars to understand the basic reason behind avalanche occurrence and the relationship between remote sensing and monitoring of snow patterns. Alongside providing insight into the scatterometer instrument, the chapter also sheds light on the global-level applications of the scatterometer, its limitations, and the areas of improvement. The statistical data analysis provides a mere idea about the areas affected by the snow avalanche, covering the epicenter areas responsible for the avalanches.

Keywords**:** Avalanche, remote sensing, SAR (synthetic aperture radar)

**Corresponding author*: nitinarorask@gmail.com; ORCID: 0009-0005-6585-7114
Sakshi: ORCID: 0009-0005-9300-5496

Neelam Dahiya, Gurwinder Singh, Sartajvir Singh and Apoorva Sharma (eds.) Artificial Intelligence in Remote Sensing for Disaster Management, (213–228)

12.1 Introduction

Snow avalanche is a natural calamity that has a deep impact on the local vegetarian and living organisms, strongly affecting the ecosystem of the area. Happening usually in regions of high snowfall, their speed can reach up to 31 to 50 miles per hour. The reason behind its occurrence is the loosening and shifting of the inner layers of the snow due to loosening snow underneath, hence causing the snow above to shift along with it.

Remote sensing is a technique of understanding and monitoring the natural parameters using the backscattering factor of radio waves. SAR is a type of instrument that uses the principles of RADAR to enable remote sensing and provide measurements of a region. These measurements can be in the form of processed images, heat signature maps, etc. Since the outbreak of the Second World War, there have been drastic improvements in the field of remote sensing and mapping. Initially meant for pointing out the enemy boot camps, the technology has drastically been used for natural calamity prediction models and rescue operations.

One of the areas of concern is the snow avalanche prediction and mapping of weak points that could potentially become the epicenter of an avalanche if remaining unnoticed. This chapter will provide in-depth knowledge of every key point of the basics of snow avalanches. This includes the basic principle behind the occurrence, the effects, and the role of remote sensing in avalanche prediction and rescue.

12.2 Snow Avalanche

Snow avalanche is a natural phenomenon that happens due to the overlapping of a fresh palate of snow over the loose snowpack, leading to the shifting of snow beneath and the constituents along with it [1, 2]. This natural occurrence is so quick that its speed can reach up to 50 miles per hour, draining everything that comes in the way including the vegetation and natural habitats (Figure 12.1).

Snow avalanche deeply affects the regions, altering the cycle of vegetation and changing the normal lifestyle of the locals (Figure 12.2).

Mountain areas can be divided into three categories/zones depending on the probability of regions with high chances of avalanche to the regions with a probability of occasional avalanche occurring.

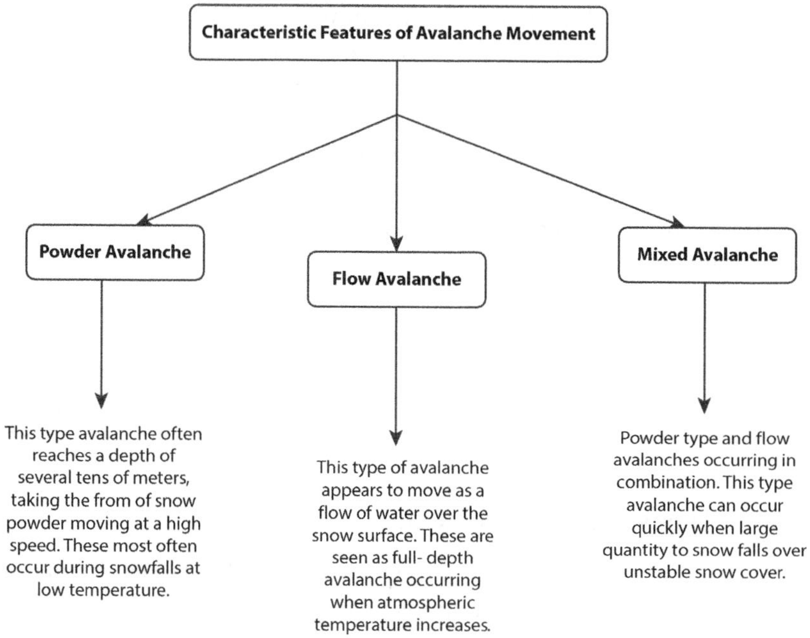

Figure 12.1 Representation of types of avalanches based on the characteristic features of avalanche movement.

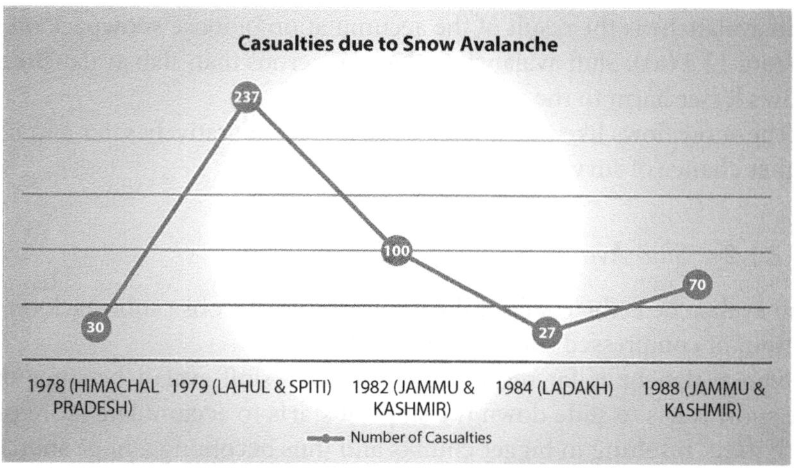

Figure 12.2 Line chart on the causalities in India due to avalanche occurrences between 1978 and 1988.

1. Red zone: Region where the snow avalanche is not often, having pressure of more than 3 tons per square meter.
2. Blue zone: The region is comparatively less prone to the red zone and is hospitable, but still safety measures are a must in those regions because of the high chances of avalanches. The pressure is usually less than 3 tons per square meter.
3. Yellow zone: Region with a probability of occasional avalanche occurring.

A snow avalanche is a threat to the locals. Figure 12.2 represents the number of casualties in India due to avalanches alone within the timelapse of 1978–1988. With an average of 27 people dying in India annually due to snow avalanches, it is a region of concern and requires proper monitoring.

12.2.1 Types of Snow Avalanche

A snow avalanche is caused by many internal and external factors, and due to these factors, the loose regions of snow become the epicenter of the avalanche [3, 4].

There are two main types of snow avalanches.

12.2.1.1 Sluff Avalanche

Sluff avalanche is the result of the accumulation of loose snowpack on top (Figure 12.3 (a)). Sluff avalanche is less dangerous than slab avalanche and causes lesser harm to the environment [5, 6].

The snow flows like fine grains; thus, it is comparatively safer and has a higher chance of survival.

12.2.1.2 Slab Avalanche

Slab avalanche is the result of the accumulation of loose snowpack on the bottom of compressed snow (Figure 12.3 (b)).

Slab avalanche is far more dangerous than sluff avalanche since once the snow starts to slide down the slope, it starts to accumulate more mass with itself, resulting in bigger chunks and thus becoming a huge source of destruction to the local vegetation and life forms [7, 8].

The classification of avalanche occurrences is determined by the underlying cause of their occurrence. On average, avalanche snow can reach up to 180 ft across and 1–3 ft deep [9].

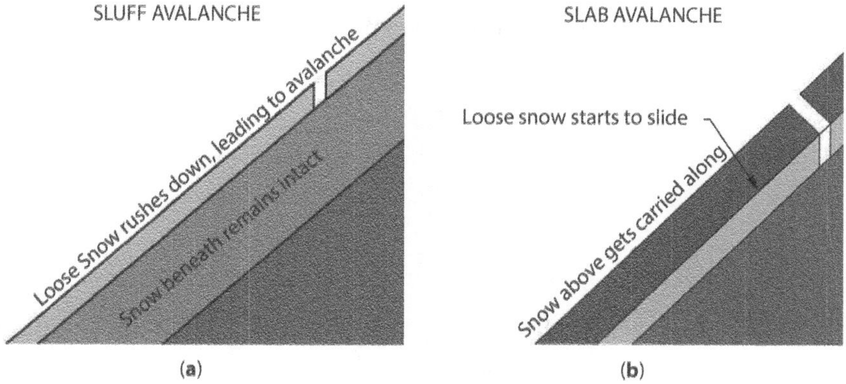

Figure 12.3 (a) Sluff avalanche. (b) Slab avalanche.

12.2.2 Basic Reason Behind Snow Avalanche

The important elements affecting avalanche occurrence are shown in Figures 12.4 and 12.5. A structured flowchart in Figure 12.4 organizes contributory factors into topographic and weather elements together with vegetation and other influences while specifically identifying slope inclination and snowfall depth and vegetation density. The diagram successfully presents the linked factors that result in avalanche formation. Figure 12.5 uses a pie chart to show the percentage distribution of factors that affect snow avalanches between avalanche conditions and weather influences and terrain characteristics and human triggers and previous avalanche events.

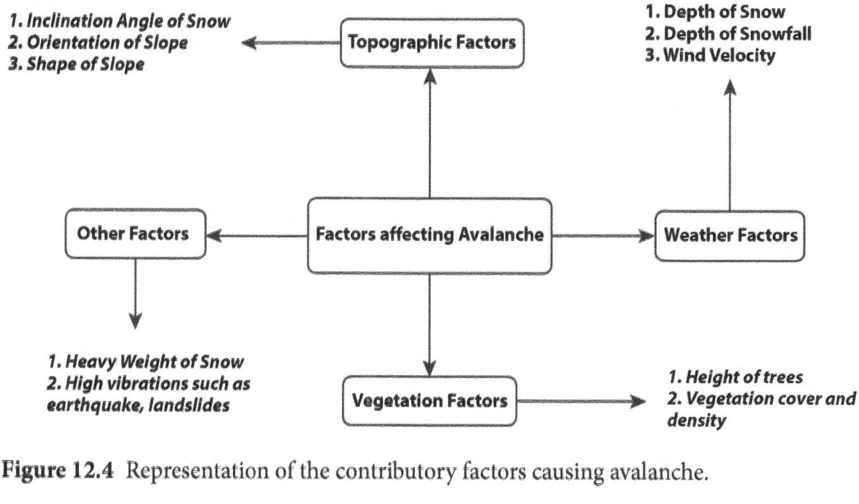

Figure 12.4 Representation of the contributory factors causing avalanche.

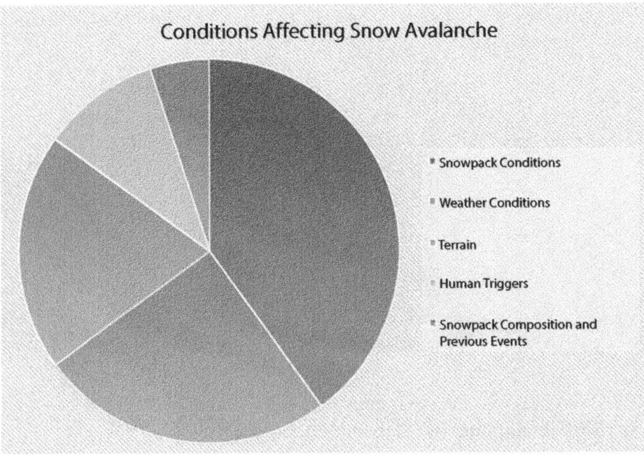

Figure 12.5 The pie chart represents the percentage of factors contributing to avalanche occurrence.

The visual representation between these two figures delivers an extensive understanding through both categorical organization and statistical data presentation. The combination of these figures delivers improved comprehension through their ability to display qualitative and quantitative avalanche formation characteristics.

12.2.3 Role of Remote Sensing in Snow Avalanche Prediction

Remote sensing and snow pattern monitoring have a deep connection with each other. There have been a lot of improvements in the field of ground-based monitoring. The sole reason behind the monitoring is to understand the pattern of changing environmental conditions of a region, and remote sensing serves the same purpose [10].

GB-SAR (ground-based synthetic aperture radar) is a type of ground-based remote sensing instrument that is capable of capturing the real-time information of the region. This information plays a crucial role in many areas of interest, such as natural calamity prediction models and weather forecasting [11, 12].

ASCAT or advanced scatterometer is an airborne satellite instrument that uses backscattering of microwaves to capture detailed information about a region. It is usually used when the area of interest is large—for example, monitoring the wind speed over the Pacific Ocean [13, 14].

The range of remote sensing instruments is not restricted to these instruments; there have been inventions and improvements in the field of remote sensing and image processing. Remote sensing usually operates on the principle of capturing the backscattered radar signals (typically, the type of signal depends on the area of application). Then, after processing the signals, a well-detailed image is produced. These images hence act as a reliable base for the researchers to understand the changes that have occurred in the past and predict the occurrence of upcoming events [15].

NOTE: It is important to understand that the choice of remote sensing instrument is solely dependent on the use case scenario. In situations where large-scale monitoring is required, such as monitoring the snowfall over a region, airborne radar systems are most suitable in that case. However, in cases where ground-based monitoring with high accuracy is needed, such as tracking the rise in snow level from the snow bed, ground-based synthetic aperture radar (SAR) is considered to be the best instrument for remote sensing and monitoring.

12.3 Contributory Factors

Avalanches result from numerous contributing factors, but they can be distilled down to five primary causes. The four factors are terrain, precipitation, wind temperature, and snowpack stratigraphy [2].

The sheer stress developed inside the snow is the basic contributory factor causing avalanches. Snow stability S at a given time, depth, and location of slope can be measured using the formula (Equation 12.1):

$$\mathbf{S = T_f\,(\sigma, x, t)/T\,(x, t)} \tag{12.1}$$

where

T_f = snow strength
σ = normal stress
t = time x = location
T = shear stress

The formula provides an in-depth relationship between the snow stability and the stress between the molecules of snow. Theoretically, instability conditions occur when the value of snow stability (S) approaches 1. However, it is practically impossible to achieve the value of S to be 1 due to spatial and temporal variation in the snow's strength and stress within the snowpack [4, 16].

12.3.1 Terrain

It is a legend that the slope below 30° is considered to be safe and has considerably less occurrence of avalanches; this statement is partially true. From the survey, it became clear that most of the avalanches that occurred in the past have a slope angle between 30° to 40°. Still the chances of the occurrence of an avalanche beyond this rage cannot be nullified.

The ideal inclination that can be considered practically safe to visit during snow is below 30° since it is the region that has experienced the least avalanche hit cases. Still nature is unpredictable, and any negligence in safety measure would ultimately lead to severe losses.

12.3.2 Precipitation

12.3.2.1 Snow Accumulation

The amount of precipitation has a direct impact on the accumulation of snow, i.e., more snowfall directly leads to accumulation of more snow than usual. This high accumulation leads to the formation of stress within the layers of snowpack, thus increasing the chances of snow avalanche occurrence. The varying characteristics and densities of these layers of snowpack reduces the snow stability, thus ultimately leading to snow avalanche.

12.3.2.2 Formation of Weak Layers

Continuous snowfall leads to the formation of cracks within the layers of snowpack, leading to formation of crack points. These cracks start actively vibrating during natural calamity such as earthquake or landslides. Thus, resulting in the formation of slab avalanche, destroying the local vegetation and life source [17].

12.3.2.3 Load and Stress Increases

Due to the accumulation of large amounts of snow, the weight and stress on the underlying layers of snowpack intensifies. The stress is unevenly spread across the snowpack, thus leading to high-stress points, which ultimately become the epicenter of the snow avalanche formed.

12.3.2.4 Rain-on-Snow Effect

Rainfall over the snow surface, especially during the warmer weather events, infiltrates the snow layers, thus altering the properties. Rainwater acts as a lubricant between the surface and snow layers, increasing the chances of slipping snowpack over small vibrations.

All of these factors collectively contribute to the formation of snow avalanches. These parameters directly impact the stability of the snow (S). In most cases, these are the primary reasons leading to the formation of avalanches, but other secondary reasons will be discussed in the next section of the chapter.

12.3.3 Wind Temperature

Surface air temperature is vital in the creation of the snow and its metamorphism. The coupled changes of temperature owing to wind can affect the deposition and strength in layers of the snow. Cold winds are likely to freeze the surface of the snow quickly, with resultant issues such as near-surface faceting that develop into weak layers. On the other hand, there are complex processes like warming which can lead to melting and then refreezing, and this can cause layers or crusts in snow. They become potentially unstable layers or weak layers when buried by other layers of new snow that can trigger avalanches. They have learned that separate air temperature and snow temperature are possible and very important to know in order to provide a proper avalanche forecast.

12.3.4 Snowpack Stratigraphy

Snow cover stratigraphy, more specifically the requirement of a weak layer or interface, is related to dry snow slab avalanches. New snow, wind-driven stress, and temperature variations all affect stability only when there is a weakness in the previous snow. The total vulnerability is a function of several weak layer features, one of which is the active process of near-surface faceting caused by temperature gradients. Persistent grain forms like faceted crystals, depth hoar, and surface hoar are frequently involved in skier-triggered avalanches. Five stability classes in snow profiles are based on distinct variances in the hardness and size of grains between the weak layer and neighboring layers; these distinctions are essential for determining the risk of avalanches.

12.4 Remote Sensing and Avalanche Prediction

Due to its high accuracy, remote sensing is now commonly used in prediction models. Advanced scatterometers and ground-based SAR (GB-SAR) use microwaves that can penetrate the clouds, providing clear images of the natural parameters such as wind speed, snow precipitation, and the pattern of snow accumulation [18, 19].

Information regarding all of these parameters acts as a strong base for the researchers to predict the upcoming events or disasters that could potentially affect the ecosystem of a region. These scatterometers and other remote sensing radars, in collaboration with the artificial intelligence detection models, could be a better alternative for conventional models that are prone to human error. Additionally, this technology could potentially be more reliable and accurate than the traditional prediction models [20, 21].

Remote sensing is not restricted to radar-based instruments, but it also includes optical imaging, thermal infrared sensing, LIDAR, passive remote sensing, SONAR, and electromagnetic and magnetic sensors [22].

12.4.1 Basic Principle Behind Radar-Based Remote Sensing

RADAR (Radio Detection and Ranging) is an electronic device that emits electromagnetic waves [23, 24]. These waves are then reflected by objects in the environment, and the backscattered signals are captured by the radar system's receivers (Figure 12.6). However, the received signal unintentionally incorporates ghost readings that might have originated from the environment or through spoofing. These signals hindered the precision

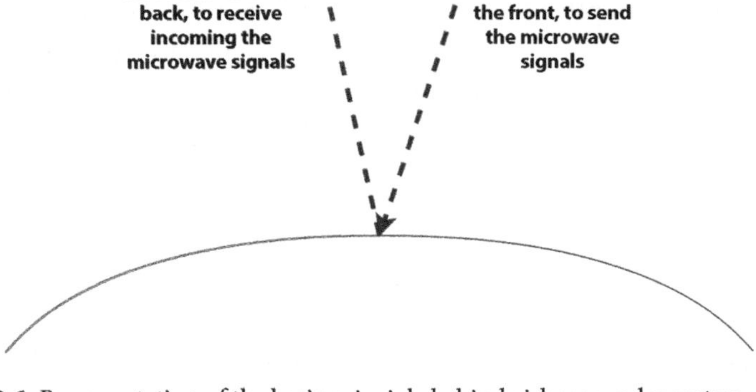

Figure 12.6 Representation of the basic principle behind airborne radar system.

of radar-based remote sensing and needed to be removed. Hence, they are treated with specific algorithms and subsequently processed for further observations.

The amount of signal loss and the time delay are taken into consideration, and these parameters are most important in determining the roughness and the depth of the earth's surface [25]. These measurements are then processed, and an image is processed. This processed image is valuable in determining the crucial elements of nature such as wind speed, precipitation pattern, snow coverage, etc. Remote sensing becomes advantageous in situations where monitoring of unhabitable regions is required, such as measuring the wind speed over the Pacific Ocean [26].

12.4.2 Need for Remote Sensing

Snow avalanche is unpredictable and can happen at any time of the year. It is important to monitor the abnormality in snow surface to understand and predict the occurrence of avalanches. Avalanches occur due to shifting of either the top layer of the snowpack or the bottom layers. This shifting is either due to the accumulation of heat in the lower layers of the snowpack, resulting in the shift of melted under-surface snow, or could be the result of external factors such as changes in temperature and environmental conditions like precipitation, angle of inclination of a cliff, etc.

To provide a comprehensive report of the pattern of natural occurrences, remote sensing is the best approach. Remote sensing provides an accurate robust model for the researchers to monitor the changing environment and observe important parameters such as precipitation, wind speed, snow accumulation, etc. Due to radar's high resistance to external factors, intruding signals, and capability to penetrate through clouds, these make them ideal for the avalanche prediction model.

12.5 Methodology

The basic methodology behind the data collection of the image processing is explained in the flowchart cited below (Figure 12.7).

The basic methodology is divided into four major phases [27, 28].

Phase 1: Identifying and importing data: The data/information regarding the Earth's surface is collected using either GB-SAR or airborne scatterometer satellites. The information collected consists of foreign signal interruption, signals because of spoofing, and time irregularities.

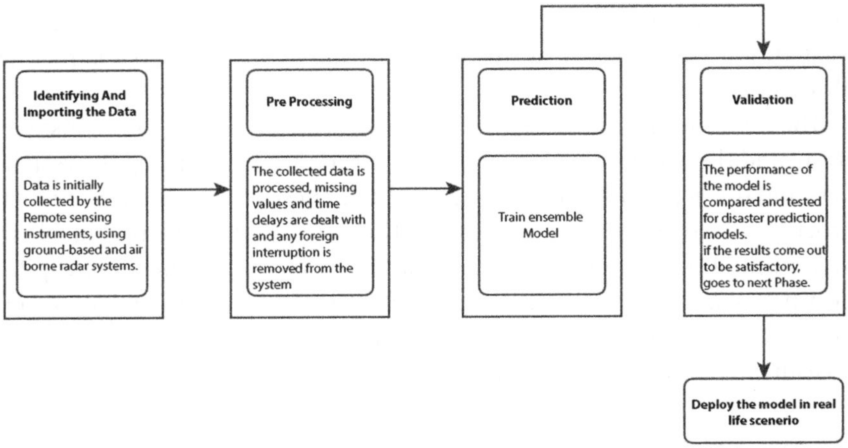

Figure 12.7 Flowchart of the methodology used.

Phase 2: Pre-processing: The collected data including the interruptions and the time delay are filtered using complex algorithms. The filtered data is then processed to provide important information regarding the topography, wind speed, and the roughness of the surface.

Phase 3: Prediction: The collected and filtered data is then sent for training in all possible circumstances, making the data robust and more reliable. This data can hence be used for image processing and research purposes. This processed data is then sent for further validation and deployment.

Phase 4: Validation: After the data is further trained, its data is compared with the already existing data. In the case of real-time data monitoring, data from the ground-based radar and the airborne radar is compared and tested for disaster prediction models. Once the results come out to be satisfactory, the model is then sent to the deployment stage

Final phase: Deployment: The final stage includes the deployment of model into real-life situations to validate the prediction accuracy and precision of the model. The most important parameter of the judgment of the accuracy of any model is the time lag it encounters in providing real-time monitoring.

The success of the model is determined by its ability to effectively predict and monitor the Earth's surface conditions and potential disasters in a timely and reliable manner [29, 30].

12.5 Conclusion and Future Scope

The book chapter incorporates the definition of snow avalanches, the basic principle behind their occurrence, and the role of remote sensing in prediction models. In conclusion, it is clear that snow avalanche, being a natural calamity that causes harm to local vegetation and life forms, requires proper real-time monitoring. Predicting its occurrence provides resistance to these losses. Remote sensing plays a vital role in providing a robust model for scientists to use the information in the development of prediction models.

Remote sensing is performed in both ways: by using ground-based SAR and, secondly, by using air-borne scatterometers embedded in Metop-A satellite [31]. The information collected from both satellites is then compared. This comparison provides a robust model for the researchers to interact. This robust model is used in avalanche prediction models because of their high accuracy and precision [32, 33].

This model can be used in many early warning systems, promoting evacuation measures to be taken before the occurrence and reducing the impact of avalanches on the communities. This model, if integrated with artificial intelligence and complex machine learning algorithms, will ultimately increase the accuracy of avalanche prediction models [34].

There are certain flaws in remote sensing prediction since there are certain types of foreign signals existing in the environment that hinder the information of the radar systems used for remote sensing. This hindrance results in a decrease in the accuracy of the recorded values. Researchers have increasingly been working on developing more complex algorithms and filtration processes to extract important data from the whole. Collaborating all the researchers to one ultimate goal and sharing the same resources will be advantageous, providing more robust and accurate models for future generations.

References

1. Hopfinger, E.J. and Tochon-Danguy, J.-C., A Model Study of Powder-Snow Avalanches. *J. Glaciol.*, 19, 81, 343–356, Jan. 1977, doi: 10.3189/S0022143000029373.
2. Schweizer, J., Bruce Jamieson, J., Schneebeli, M., Snow avalanche formation. *Rev. Geophys.*, 41, 4, 2-1–2-25, Dec. 2003, doi: 10.1029/2002RG000123.

3. Hopfinger, E.J., Snow Avalanche Motion and Related Phenomena. *Annu. Rev. Fluid Mech.*, 15, 1, 47–76, Jan. 1983, doi: 10.1146/annurev.fl.15.010183.000403.
4. Abermann, J., Eckerstorfer, M., Malnes, E., Hansen, B.U., A large wet snow avalanche cycle in West Greenland quantified using remote sensing and *in situ* observations. *Nat. Hazard.*, 97, 2, 517–534, Jun. 2019, doi: 10.1007/s11069-019-03655-8.
5. Rubin, M.J., Camp, T., Van Herwijnen, A., Schweizer, J., Automatically Detecting Avalanche Events in Passive Seismic Data, in: *2012 11th International Conference on Machine Learning and Applications*, Dec. 2012, IEEE, pp. 13–20, doi: 10.1109/ICMLA.2012.12.
6. Ward, R.G.W., Avalanche Hazard in the Cairngorm Mountains, Scotland. *J. Glaciol.*, 26, 94, 31–41, May 1980, doi: 10.3189/S0022143000201020.
7. McClung, D.M. and Schweizer, J., Skier triggering, snow temperatures and the stability index for dry-slab avalanche initiation. *J. Glaciol.*, 45, 150, 190–200, Jan. 1999, doi: 10.3189/002214399793377121.
8. McClung, D.M., Fracture mechanical models of dry slab avalanche release. *J. Geophys. Res. Solid Earth*, 86, B11, 10783–10790, Nov. 1981, doi: 10.1029/JB086iB11p10783.
9. Schweizer, J., Review of dry snow slab avalanche release. *Cold Reg. Sci. Technol.*, 30, 1–3, 43–57, Dec. 1999, doi: 10.1016/S0165-232X(99)00025-7.
10. Angelopoulou, T., Tziolas, N., Balafoutis, A., Zalidis, G., Bochtis, D., Remote Sensing Techniques for Soil Organic Carbon Estimation: A Review. *Remote Sens. (Basel)*, 11, 6, 676, Mar. 2019, doi: 10.3390/rs11060676.
11. King, J.M.L., Kelly, R., Kasurak, A., Duguay, C., Gunn, G., Mead, J.B., UW-Scat: A Ground-Based Dual-Frequency Scatterometer for Observation of Snow Properties. *IEEE Geosci. Remote Sens. Lett.*, 10, 3, 528–532, May 2013, doi: 10.1109/LGRS.2012.2212177.
12. Zheng, L., Zhou, C., Wang, K., Enhanced winter snowmelt in the Antarctic Peninsula: Automatic snowmelt identification from radar scatterometer. *Remote Sens. Environ.*, 246, 111835, Sep. 2020, doi: 10.1016/j.rse.2020.111835.
13. Foster, J.L., *et al.*, A blended global snow product using visible, passive microwave and scatterometer satellite data. *Int. J. Remote Sens.*, 32, 5, 1371–1395, Mar. 2011, doi: 10.1080/01431160903548013.
14. Wismann, V., Monitoring of seasonal snowmelt on Greenland with ERS scatterometer data. *IEEE Trans. Geosci. Remote Sens.*, 38, 4, 1821–1826, Jul. 2000, doi: 10.1109/36.851766.
15. Hillard, U., Assessing snowmelt dynamics with NASA scatterometer (NSCAT) data and a hydrologic process model. *Remote Sens. Environ.*, 86, 1, 52–69, Jun. 2003, doi: 10.1016/S0034-4257(03)00068-3.
16. Kawada, K., Nishimura, K., Maeno, N., Experimental Studies on a Powder-Snow Avalanche. *Ann. Glaciol.*, 13, 129–134, Jan. 1989, doi: 10.3189/S026030550000776X.

17. Clark, R.N. and Roush, T.L., Reflectance spectroscopy: Quantitative analysis techniques for remote sensing applications. *J. Geophys. Res. Solid Earth*, 89, B7, 6329–6340, Jul. 1984, doi: 10.1029/JB089iB07p06329.
18. Eckerstorfer, M., Bühler, Y., Frauenfelder, R., Malnes, E., Remote sensing of snow avalanches: Recent advances, potential, and limitations. *Cold Reg. Sci. Technol.*, 121, 126–140, Jan. 2016, doi: 10.1016/j.coldregions.2015.11.001.
19. Rahmati, O., *et al.*, Spatial Modeling of Snow Avalanche Using Machine Learning Models and Geo-Environmental Factors: Comparison of Effectiveness in Two Mountain Regions. *Remote Sens. (Basel)*, 11, 24, 2995, Dec. 2019, doi: 10.3390/rs11242995.
20. Cordy, P., McClung, D.M., Hawkins, C.J., Tweedy, J., Weick, T., Computer assisted avalanche prediction using electronic weather sensor data. *Cold Reg. Sci. Technol.*, 59, 2–3, 227–233, Nov. 2009, doi: 10.1016/j.coldregions.2009.07.006.
21. Parshad, R., Srivastva, P.K., Snehmani, Ganguly, S., Snow Avalanche Susceptibility Mapping using Remote Sensing and GIS in Nubra-Shyok Basin, Himalaya, India. *Indian J. Sci. Technol.*, 10, 31, 1–12, Feb. 2017, doi: 10.17485/ijst/2017/v10i31/105647.
22. Bühler, Y., Hüni, A., Christen, M., Meister, R., Kellenberger, T., Automated detection and mapping of avalanche deposits using airborne optical remote sensing data. *Cold Reg. Sci. Technol.*, 57, 2–3, 99–106, Jul. 2009, doi: 10.1016/j.coldregions.2009.02.007.
23. Gupta, D.K., Prashar, S., Singh, S., Srivastava, P.K., Prasad, R., Introduction to RADAR remote sensing, in: *Radar Remote Sensing*, pp. 3–27, Elsevier, Netherlands, 2022, doi: 10.1016/B978-0-12-823457-0.00018-5.
24. Krasnov, O.A., Babur, G.P., Wang, Z., Ligthart, L.P., van der Zwan, F., Basics and first experiments demonstrating isolation improvements in the agile polarimetric FM-CW radar – PARSAX. *Int. J. Microwave Wireless Technolog.*, 2, 3–4, 419–428, Aug. 2010, doi: 10.1017/S1759078710000371.
25. Lentile, L.B., *et al.*, Remote sensing techniques to assess active fire characteristics and post-fire effects. *Int. J. Wildland Fire*, 15, 3, 319, 2006, doi: 10.1071/WF05097.
26. Jain, V. and Heydari, P., Radar Fundamentals, in: *Automotive Radar Sensors in Silicon Technologies*, pp. 5–11, Springer New York, New York, NY, 2013, doi: 10.1007/9781-4419-6775-6_2.
27. Kovasznay, L.G. and Joseph, H., Image Processing. *Proc. IRE*, 43, 5, 560–570, 1955, doi: 10.1109/JRPROC.1955.278100.
28. van Heel, M., Harauz, G., Orlova, E.V., Schmidt, R., Schatz, M., A New Generation of the IMAGIC Image Processing System. *J. Struct. Biol.*, 116, 1, 17–24, Jan. 1996, doi: 10.1006/jsbi.1996.0004.
29. Steger, C., Kotlarski, S., Jonas, T., Schär, C., Alpine snow cover in a changing climate: a regional climate model perspective. *Clim. Dyn.*, 41, 3–4, 735–754, Aug. 2013, doi: 10.1007/s00382-012-1545-3.

30. Ruelland, D., Potential of snow data to improve the consistency and robustness of a semi-distributed hydrological model using the SAFRAN input dataset. *J. Hydrol. (Amst.)*, 631, 130820, Mar. 2024, doi: 10.1016/j.jhydrol.2024.130820.
31. Vogelzang, J., Stoffelen, A., Verhoef, A., Figa-Saldaña, J., On the quality of highresolution scatterometer winds. *J. Geophys. Res.*, 116, C10, C10033, Oct. 2011, doi: 10.1029/2010JC006640.
32. Stoffelen, A. and Anderson, D., Scatterometer data interpretation: Estimation and validation of the transfer function CMOD4. *J. Geophys. Res. Oceans*, 102, C3, 5767–5780, Mar. 1997, doi: 10.1029/96JC02860.
33. Long, D.G., Hardin, P.J., Whiting, P.T., Resolution enhancement of spaceborne scatterometer data. *IEEE Trans. Geosci. Remote Sens.*, 31, 3, 700–715, May 1993, doi: 10.1109/36.225536.
34. Sleziak, P., Szolgay, J., Hlavčová, K., Danko, M., Parajka, J., The effect of the snow weighting on the temporal stability of hydrologic model efficiency and parameters. *J. Hydrol. (Amst.)*, 583, 124639, Apr. 2020, doi: 10.1016/j.jhydrol.2020.124639.

13

A Systematic Review on Challenges and Opportunities in Snow Avalanche Risk Assessment and Analysis

Apoorva Sharma*, **Bhavneet Kaur and Sartajvir Singh**

Department of Computer Science and Engineering, University Institute of Engineering, Mohali, Punjab, India

Abstract

The analysis and risk assessment of snow avalanche studies face challenges and opportunities as highlighted in recent studies. One of the primary challenges is the complexity and variability of avalanche phenomena in snow avalanche studies which may be impacted by various factors, i.e., snowpack conditions, terrain, weather patterns, and human activities. Previous literature has shown that traditional avalanche hazard mapping and risk assessment methods are often very challenging and costly due to field surveys and utilization of high-resolution images and remote sensing data, which are limited by cost, spatial, and temporal coverage constraints. The availability of advanced tools and technologies such as large-scale risk assessment tools, such as the RAMMS (rapid mass movement simulation), statistical LSHIM (large-scale hazard indication mapping model), and the probabilistic Python-based platform CLIMADA (CLIMate ADAptation) for more accurate and more extensive hazard mapping and risk assessment provided possibilities to eliminate such problems. It enables the generation of rich risk profiles about the location and distribution of avalanche hazards and risks and hence improved decision-making strategies and techniques for handling hazards and risks in avalanche domains. This chapter summarized such advanced tools and technologies along with challenges and opportunities associated with snow and avalanche risk and analysis systems.

**Corresponding author*: er.apoorva.sharma@gmail.com; ORCID: 0009-0004-9667-476X
Bhavneet Kaur: ORCID: 0000-0001-8648-3880
Sartajvir Singh: ORCID: 0000-0002-4451-4949

Neelam Dahiya, Gurwinder Singh, Sartajvir Singh and Apoorva Sharma (eds.) Artificial Intelligence in Remote Sensing for Disaster Management, (229–242) © 2025 Scrivener Publishing LLC

Keywords: Snow avalanche, RAMMS (rapid mass movement simulation), LSHIM (large-scale hazard indication mapping model), CLIMADA (climate adaptation)

13.1 Introduction

The snow avalanche risk assessment in the Himalayan mountains is important to be performed due to the environmental and socio-economic situation in the region. The Himalayas are most susceptible to avalanches because of the steep slopes, large amount of snow that falls in the area, and regular occurrence of earthquakes. Due to the many communities and tourists found in these regions, risk assessment plays an important role in the protection of human life. Risk assessments help in the scaling of an avalanche and informing the community in case of an early warning system or evacuation plans which are very crucial once the occurrence is realized. Moreover, the Himalayas constitute strategic establishments like roads, bridges, and hydropower structures, which are mostly constructed in the areas affected by avalanches. Risk assessments of these structures ensure the sustainability of such structures that are used to facilitate communication and energy supply to the region, which is very vital for development and economic growth. In addition, there are severe climate changes in the Himalayas, provoking fluctuations in snowfalls as well as avalanches' increase in frequency [1, 2]. It is therefore critical in the face of such changes to have a continuous and accurate avalanche risk assessment for there to be an ability to build the resilience of both the natural and human systems in the Himalayas [3].

The assessment and analysis of snow avalanche risk are important for strategists to facilitate proper risk reduction measures so that the effects of avalanches on society and the economy can be overcome or reduced [4]. Advanced monitoring tools have a crucial role in importing actual terrain models and real-time snow data to generate and forecast the avalanche situation. These tools help to develop the risk maps to show where the high risks are so that the intervention, as well as resource distribution maps, can be well developed [5]. Moreover, it aids in the assessment of the true characteristics of snowpacks and climatic changes [6]. Furthermore, monitoring is beneficial in providing information that is critical in sensitivity and uncertainty analysis of risk beliefs to enhance the preciseness of the models [7]. It also helps in updating models and methodologies that deal with data, thus making sure they are fit to operate under different and competitive scenarios. So, monitoring remains a compulsory feature to enhance control and predictability and to reduce the threat's impact in the form of snow avalanches [8]. A brief comparison of challenges, opportunities, and parameters associated with snow avalanches is shown in Table 13.1. Modern tools in snow avalanche systems use state-of-the-art technologies to help in forecasting and managing avalanches. You will find such tools helpful in comprehending the nature of an avalanche and improving other protective processes in any territory characterized by mountainous landscapes.

Table 13.1 A brief comparison of challenges, opportunities, and parameters associated with snow avalanches.

S. no.	Challenges	Opportunities	Parameters associated	Examples
1	Complexity and variability of avalanche phenomena	Development of advanced risk assessment tools (e.g., RAMMS::LSHIM, CLIMADA)	Snowpack conditions, terrain, weather patterns, human activities	Diverse snowpack stability in the Alps vs. Himalayas
2	High cost and limited spatial and temporal coverage of data	Integration of high-resolution terrain models and real-time snow data	Data collection cost, spatial and temporal resolution	High-resolution LIDAR data collection
3	Traditional methods falling short in comprehensive assessments	Creation of detailed risk maps highlighting high-risk areas	Hazard mapping accuracy, risk quantification methods	Use of GIS-based hazard maps for the Swiss Alps
4	Lack of detailed hazard maps in remote regions	Adaptability of new tools for global application, even in data-scarce areas	Availability of remote sensing data, adaptability of tools	Application of RAMMS::LSHIM in remote parts of the Andes
5	Influence of climatic changes on snow patterns	Continuous monitoring to adapt to evolving risks	Climate models, snow pattern changes	Monitoring of changing snowfall patterns in the Rockies
6	Need for timely and accurate information for decision-making	Enhanced decision-making through probabilistic models and simulations	Early warning systems, decision-making processes	Early warning systems in avalanche-prone areas of Colorado

(Continued)

Table 13.1 A brief comparison of challenges, opportunities, and parameters associated with snow avalanches. (*Continued*)

S. no.	Challenges	Opportunities	Parameters associated	Examples
7	Difficulty in predicting and quantifying avalanche scenarios	Improved accuracy and reliability through sensitivity and uncertainty analyses	Prediction models, sensitivity analyses, uncertainty analyses	Sensitivity analysis of avalanche risk in the French Alps
8	Limited resources for mitigation and adaptation strategies	Better resource allocation and targeted interventions based on risk maps	Resource allocation, intervention strategies	Prioritizing avalanche barriers in high-risk areas of Alaska
9	Human and infrastructural vulnerability	Reduced impacts on communities and infrastructure through early warning and mitigation planning	Population density, infrastructure vulnerability	Evacuation planning for Himalayan villages during avalanche season
10	High population and infrastructure density in hazardous zones	Use of advanced models to simulate and predict various avalanche scenarios	Population distribution, infrastructure locations	Modeling avalanche scenarios in densely populated areas of the Alps

Uninhabited aerial systems are part of remote sensing tools. These normally called drones, which take imagery of complicated geographical features like mountains [9]. These images are useful in establishing elevations on the snow surface to an extremely high resolution. Before and after storms, specialists can analyze the differences between such maps to determine the changes in the depth of various layers, particularly snow cover, which is important for avalanche forecasting [10]. Also, the coverage of wide areas, including terrains, by avalanches can be easily recorded with the help of drone recordings [11]. Photogrammetry, which is defined as structure from motion (SfM) photogrammetry, is a method that uses high-resolution pictures with location details to develop approximations of frameworks. Semi-constructed SfM builds photogrammetric high-resolution of both the north–south and east–west digital elevation models from pictures taken by drones for snow distribution and avalanche processes on rugged terrains [12]. Lidar, which stands for Light Detection and Ranging, is a high three-dimensional digital elevation map produced from the pulsed laser measurements. Snow depth change in these maps is also verified and advanced vegetation mapping is done in the areas targeted by avalanches [13]. This technology is central for mapping the changes in terrain and vegetation that influence the kind of avalanches [14].

Near-real-time monitoring systems A Sentinel-1 SAR Data: Specifically, with regards to the SAR data of the Sentinel-1 satellites, avalanche detection can be done automatically [15]. After accomplishing the data acquisition, the system will take nearly 10 min to present the identified avalanche polygons. This is a high-probability detection system and is in use in some areas in Norway for the Norwegian Avalanche Warning Service in a pre-operational procedure. It further increased the possibility of the research to track avalanches in real life [16, 17].

Infrasound detection systems is an infrasound arrays such systems use infrasound arrays to detect low-frequency sounds also produced by such calamities as avalanches. These arrays are positioned geometrically further to increase the signal-to-noise ratio and provide the determination of the direction of the sound [18]. Because time difference refers to the difference in the time domain, the system can separate the avalanche signal source and parameters, including back azimuth and apparent velocity based on the sensors' response. It is advantageous when covering large areas and when it is easier to not observe the occurrence of an avalanche [19].

The tools related to distinct varieties of snow avalanches provide splendid aspects and benefits by enhancing the periods for monitoring and predicting the avalanches. Infrasound arrays record low-frequency waves of sound for real-time monitoring and the minimization of false warnings. Doppler radar provides information on the motion of snow particles, which means there is accurate information on the avalanche movement. Seismic sensors are used for ground vibration hence; there is a very accurate measurement of avalanches even in bad weather [20].

13.2 Advanced Tools for Snow Avalanche Monitoring System

On the other hand, avalanche-monitoring tools have many benefits: they enhance accuracy, efficiency, and reliability in predicting and detecting an avalanche. Real-time capturing and analyzing of data by various advanced technologies reduce false alarms and increase response time [16]. They provide explicit details about snowpack conditions, terrain, and weather, which helps in risk analysis and preparedness. Monitoring capabilities in

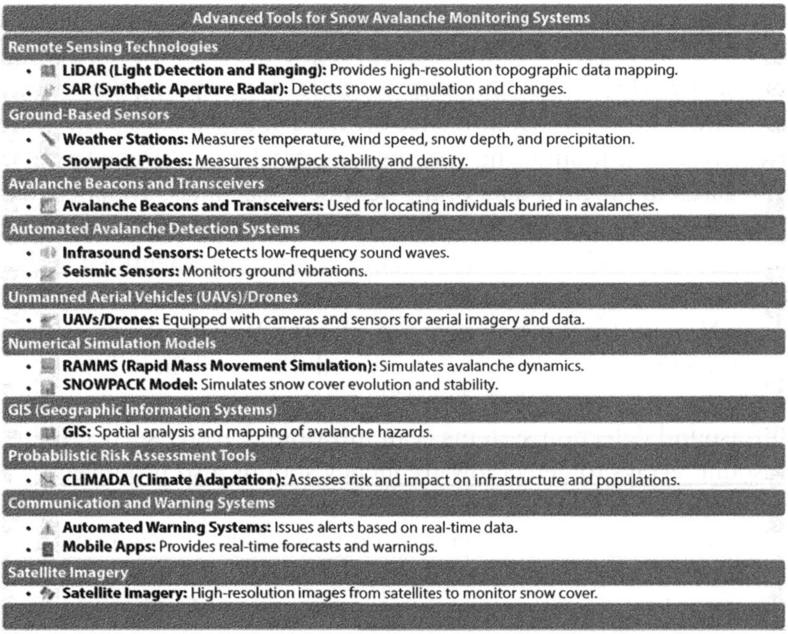

Figure 13.1 Advanced tools for snow avalanche monitoring systems.

large remote areas give safety. Figure 13.1 shows the advanced tools for snow avalanche monitoring systems. In effect, the tools become critical to reduce the risks of avalanches, whereby they protect human and infrastructure lives, thus making it possible to make timely decisions in areas where avalanches are likely.

13.3 Snow Avalanche Risk Assessment and Analysis

Snow avalanches are first investigated and assessed using a holistic approach to multiple relevant variables in the process of producing compelling avalanche predictions and mitigations. This includes the analysis of different types of hazards, identification of triggers—both natural and human, consideration of the influence of terrain like slope angle and vegetation, snowpack analysis, prevailing weather, and historical data for a comprehension of avalanche patterns. Risk zoning makes it possible to classify risk zones, and mitigation measures, including controlled detonations and snow fences, will prevent potential damage. With better predictive capabilities, continuous monitoring through remote sensing and weather stations aids with forecasting models. Human factors involve behavior and education, whereas emergency response plans allow for proper rescue operations, respectively (see Table 13.2). Ultimately, the overall assessment also considers environmental impacts and legal policies to ensure a holistic approach to managing avalanche risks.

Table 13.2 Snow avalanche risk assessment and analysis.

No.	Aspect	Description
1.	Hazard types	Slab, loose, and wet snow avalanches
2.	Triggers	Natural (snowfall, temperature changes) Human (skiing, construction)
3.	Terrain factors	Slope angle, aspect, elevation, vegetation
4.	Snowpack analysis	Density, temperature, moisture, stability
5.	Weather conditions	Precipitation, wind, temperature, solar radiation
6.	Historical data	Frequency, magnitude, and location of past avalanches
7.	Risk zoning	Areas categorized as low, moderate, or high risk
8.	Mitigation measures	Controlled detonations, snow fences, slope stabilization
9.	Monitoring	Remote sensing, field observations, weather stations
10.	Forecasting models	Predicting avalanche risk based on current conditions
11.	Human factors	Behavioral factors, decision-making, education, awareness
12.	Emergency response	Rescue operations and communication strategies
13.	Environmental impact	Effects on ecosystems and infrastructure
14.	Legal/policy aspects	Regulations, land use planning, safety protocols

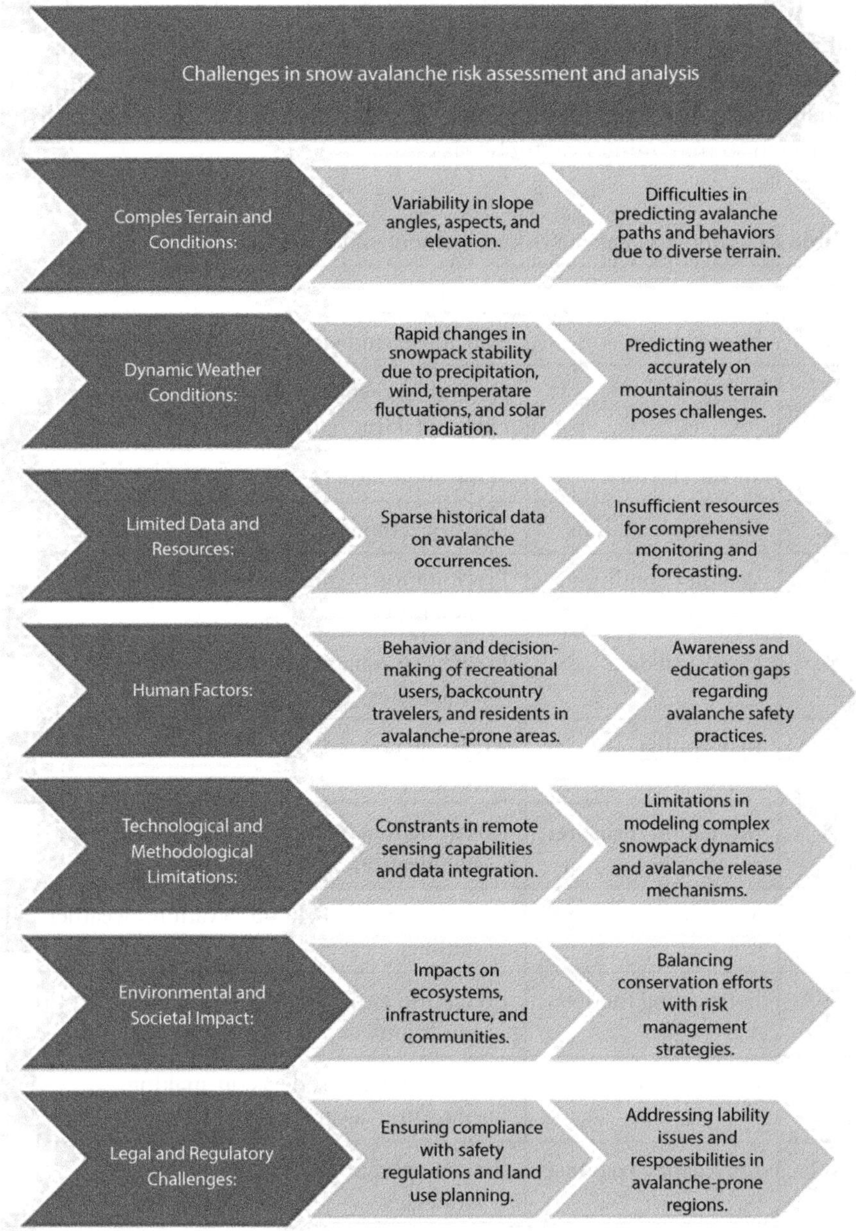

Figure 13.2 Challenges in snow avalanche risk assessment and analysis.

13.4 Challenges in Snow Avalanche Risk Assessment and Analysis

Now considering the systems of snow avalanches, several issues can be observed. The first of them is ambivalent prediction due to such factors as the stability of the snow cover, interferential influence of humans, sharp weather changes, and topography of the location. This means that to start with, prediction is already difficult owing to the extremities of weather having changed, and then the vagueness of the details also poses its challenge. They occur because of an avalanche, snow buildup, significant temperature change, snowpack that has poor structure, and production of denser slabs of snow [21]. Hence, activities such as snowboarding, snowmobile, construction as well as blast prolong the period of pulse effect, which increases the chances of avalanche depending on the steepness and convexity of the slope. In addition to critical weather conditions, difficult geography and logistical issues when working in unfriendly areas and regions that are often inaccessible also considerably hamper data collection and analysis.

On the other hand, remote sensors have inherent limitations in accuracy and range. This raises yet another challenge—public awareness, which encompasses avalanche risk perception and education regarding safety measures that motivate a behavior change [22]. In terms of fiscal impact, there are disturbances in tourism and recreation activities, transportation blockades, infrastructure and utilities, damage, loss of business and property values, agriculture damage, and health care. These challenges must be addressed through the improvement of prediction and data collection, public education, and the mitigation of economic impacts. Here are some challenges in snow avalanche risk assessment and analysis as shown in Figure 13.2.

13.5 Opportunities in Snow Avalanche Risk Assessment and Analysis

Areas of opportunity within the system for snow avalanches encompass innovative technology, from sensors and techniques to new methods for better prediction and detection of an avalanche—remote sensing technologies are used for monitoring snow dynamics and risks—to the development of new safety equipment [23]. Research and analysis provide ways to examine climate change impacts, snowpack structures, and human behavior in areas with avalanche potential [24]. Training and education programs can contribute to the maximal implementation of new equipment and increase rescue operations. There are even significant opportunities for policy elaboration in the sphere of environmental protection aimed at minimizing the consequences that avalanche activities have on ecosystems (see Table 13.3). Policy building may include broad elaboration of policies on risk management, land-use planning, and insurance services aimed at reducing economic losses. Collaboration and networking provide opportunities for global cooperation and public-private partnerships, which improve the effectiveness and efficiency of the avalanche management system. All these collectively aim at increasing prediction accuracy, safety, and response as well as protection of the environment and improvement of public awareness and preparedness.

Table 13.3 Opportunities in the snow avalanche system.

Innovative technologies	• Advanced sensors and techniques for avalanche prediction and detection • Remote sensing technologies for monitoring dynamics of snow and detection of avalanche risks • Innovative safety equipment
Research and analysis	• Observation of climate change • Extensive study of snowpack structure • Studying human behavior
Training and education	• Training programs to use new equipment and safety measures • Training to enhance rescue operations
Environment protection	• Development of strategies to mitigate the impact of avalanches on the ecosystem
Policy building	• Creation of risk management policies and plans for land use • Providing insurance services
Collaboration and networking	• Participation in global collaboration and networking. • Public–private partnership

13.6 Summary

Snow avalanche risk assessment and analysis involve numerous challenges and opportunities, influenced by factors like snowpack conditions, terrain, weather patterns, and human activities. Traditional methods face high costs and spatial limitations, but advanced tools such as RAMMS, LSHIM, and CLIMADA improve hazard mapping and risk assessment. The Himalayan region, highly susceptible to avalanches due to its steep slopes, significant snowfall, and frequent earthquakes, necessitates continuous risk assessments to protect communities, and infrastructure, and ensure economic growth. Advanced monitoring tools, including remote sensing, SfM photogrammetry, Lidar, and infrasound detection systems, enhance prediction accuracy and reliability. However, challenges remain in unreliable predictions due to variable snowpack stability, rapid weather changes, human activities, and data collection difficulties in hazardous terrains. Additionally, public awareness and education on avalanche risks and safety measures are crucial. Economic impacts include disruptions to tourism, transportation, and infrastructure damage. Opportunities lie in leveraging innovative technologies, conducting extensive research, enhancing training programs, developing environmental protection strategies, formulating risk management policies, and fostering global collaboration. These efforts collectively aim to improve prediction accuracy, safety, environmental protection, and public preparedness in avalanche-prone regions.

References

1. Singh, A., *et al.*, Avalanche hazard mitigation in east Karakoram mountains. *Nat. Hazard.*, 105, 1, 643–665, Jan. 2021, doi: 10.1007/s11069-020-04329-6.
2. Singh, S., Tiwari, R.K., Sood, V., Gusain, H.S., Prashar, S., Image Fusion of Ku-Band-Based SCATSAT-1 and MODIS Data for Cloud-Free Change Detection Over Western Himalayas. *IEEE Trans. Geosci. Remote Sens.*, 60, 1–14, 2022, doi: 10.1109/TGRS.2021.3123392.
3. Joshi, J.C., Kaur, P., Kumar, B., Singh, A., Satyawali, P.K., HIM-STRAT: A neural network-based model for snow cover simulation and avalanche hazard prediction over North-West Himalaya. *Nat. Hazard.*, 103, 1, 1239–1260, Aug. 2020, doi: 10.1007/s11069-020-04032-6.
4. Sinickas, A., Jamieson, B., Maes, M.A., Snow avalanches in western Canada: investigating change in occurrence rates and implications for risk assessment and mitigation. *Struct. Infrastruct. Eng.*, 12, 4, 490–498, Apr. 2016, doi: 10.1080/15732479.2015.1020495.

5. Kapper, K.L., Goelles, T., Muckenhuber, S., Trügler, A., Abermann, J., Schlager, B., Gaisberger, C., Eckerstorfer, M., Grahn, J., Malnes, E. and Prokop, A., Automated snow avalanche monitoring for Austria: State of the art and roadmap for future work. *Front. Remote Sens.*, 4, 1156519, Apr. 2023, doi: 10.3389/frsen.2023.1156519.
6. Horton, S., Towell, M., Haegeli, P., Examining the operational use of avalanche problems with decision trees and model-generated weather and snowpack variables. *Nat. Hazards Earth Syst. Sci.*, 20, 12, 3551–3576, Dec. 2020, doi: 10.5194/nhess-20-3551-2020.
7. Shijin, W., Yuande, Y., Yanjun, C., Global Snow- and Ice-Related Disaster Risk: A Review. *Nat. Hazard. Rev.*, 23, 4, 03122002, Nov. 2022, doi: 10.1061/(ASCE)NH.1527-6996.0000584.
8. Fuchs, S., Keiler, M., Sokratov, S., Shnyparkov, A., Spatiotemporal dynamics: the need for an innovative approach in mountain hazard risk management. *Nat. Hazard.*, 68, 3, 1217–1241, Sep. 2013, doi: 10.1007/s11069-012-0508-7.
9. Piovan, S.E., Remote Sensing, in: *The Geohistorical Approach. Springer Geography*. pp. 171–197, Springer Geography, Springer, Cham. Switzerland, 2020, doi: 10.1007/978-3-030-42439-8_7.
10. Zhang, Z. and Zhu, L., A Review on Unmanned Aerial Vehicle Remote Sensing: Platforms, Sensors, Data Processing Methods, and Applications. *Drones*, 7, 6, 398, Jun. 2023, doi: 10.3390/drones7060398.
11. Frazier, A. and Singh, K. eds., *Fundamentals of capturing and processing drone imagery and data*, CRC Press, Boca Raton, pp. 1–15, 2021.
12. Eltner, A. and Sofia, G., Structure from motion photogrammetric technique, in: *Developments in Earth Surface Processes,* vol. 23, pp. 1–24, Elsevier, Netherlands, 2020, doi: 10.1016/B978-0-444-64177-9.00001-1.
13. Jacobs, J.M., *et al.*, Snow depth mapping with unpiloted aerial system lidar observations: A case study in Durham, New Hampshire, United States. *Cryosphere*, 15, 3, 1485–1500, Mar. 2021, doi: 10.5194/tc-15-1485-2021.
14. Koutantou, K., Mazzotti, G., Brunner, P., Webster, C., Jonas, T., Exploring snow distribution dynamics in steep forested slopes with UAV-borne LiDAR. *Cold Reg. Sci. Technol.*, 200, 103587, Aug. 2022, doi: 10.1016/j.coldregions.2022.103587.
15. Eckerstorfer, M., Vickers, H., Malnes, E., Grahn, J., Near-real time automatic snow avalanche activity monitoring system using Sentinel-1 SAR data in Norway. *Remote Sens. (Basel)*, 11, 23, p.2863, Dec. 2019, doi: 10.3390/rs11232863.
16. Eckerstorfer, M., Bühler, Y., Frauenfelder, R., Malnes, E., Remote sensing of snow avalanches: Recent advances, potential, and limitations. *Cold Reg. Sci. Technol.*, 121, 126–140, Jan. 2016, doi: 10.1016/j.coldregions.2015.11.001.
17. Karas, A., Karbou, F., Giffard-Roisin, S., Durand, P., Eckert, N., Automatic Color Detection-Based Method Applied to Sentinel-1 SAR Images for Snow Avalanche Debris Monitoring. *IEEE Trans. Geosci. Remote Sens.*, 60, 1–17, 2022, doi: 10.1109/TGRS.2021.3131853.

18. Johnson, J.B., Anderson, J.F., Marshall, H.P., Havens, S., Watson, L.M., Snow Avalanche Detection and Source Constraints Made Using a Networked Array of Infrasound Sensors. *J. Geophys. Res. Earth Surf.*, 126, 3, 1–24, Mar. 2021, doi: 10.1029/2020JF005741.
19. Hedlin, M.A.H., Walker, K., Drob, D.P., de Groot-Hedlin, C.D., Infrasound: Connecting the Solid Earth, Oceans, and Atmosphere. *Annu. Rev. Earth Planet. Sci.*, 40, 1, 327–354, May 2012, doi: 10.1146/annurev-earth-042711-105508.
20. Roig-Lafon, P., Identification of snow avalanche release areas and flow characterization based on seismic data studies, Universitat de Barcelona, 2016.
21. Singh, S., Sood, V., Tiwari, R.K., Kaur, R., Sharma, A., Endeavours of Scatterometer Satellite (SCATSAT-1) in earth exploration: An overview of products, applications and emerging trends. *Phys. Chem. Earth Parts A/B/C/*, 134, 103601, Jun. 2024, doi: 10.1016/j.pce.2024.103601.
22. Sunita, *et al.*, Snow Cover Response to Climatological Factors at the Beas River Basin of W. Himalayas from MODIS and ERA5 Datasets. *Sensors*, 23, 20, 8387, Oct. 2023, doi: 10.3390/s23208387.
23. Sood, V., Tiwari, R.K., Singh, S., Kaur, R., Parida, B.R., Glacier Boundary Mapping Using Deep Learning Classification over Bara Shigri Glacier in Western Himalayas. *Sustainability*, 14, 20, 13485, Oct. 2022, doi: 10.3390/su142013485.
24. Sood, V., Gupta, S., Gusain, H.S., Singh, S., Taloor, A.K., Topographic controls on subpixel change detection in western Himalayas. *Remote Sens. Appl.*, 21, 100465, Jan. 2021, doi: 10.1016/j.rsase.2021.100465.

14

AI-Based Modeling of GLOF Process and Its Impact

Jaswinder Singh*, Rajwinder Kaur, Puninder Kaur and Rupinder Singh

Chitkara University Institute of Engineering and Technology, Chitkara University, Punjab, India

Abstract

In glacial lake outburst flood (GLOF), a glacier-dammed lake collapsing might lead to a kind of disastrous release of a considerable amount of water from the glacier itself together with the upper part of its moraine dam. This may take place as a result of the sudden failure of the natural dam, which may be made out of rock, ice, and sediment. Such floods can be very catastrophic because, in a matter of minutes, they can release massive volumes of water, ice balls, trees, and other debris behind where they flow. Artificial intelligence (AI) can help mitigate and deal with GLOFs by using different mechanisms. With AI-backed remote sensing technologies, one can keep an eye on the glacial lakes and areas adjoining it to closely observe the rise in the water levels and ice conditions, among others, and to also determine the possible hazards associated with dams. Artificial intelligence models have the capability of analyzing records of glacier dynamics, weather conditions, and seismic data to come up with predictions on the probability of occurrence of GLOFs and high-risk areas. Human-driven AI technology built-in early warning systems can then continuously capture data in real time from sensors as well as satellite images to give alerts to communities at risk as they evacuate and prepare for the approaching floods. This chapter aims to clarify a set of AI strategies that could be useful for GLOF prediction modeling. It also compares different models that are now in trend, identifies obstacles and constraints, and looks ahead to future work in the field of AI in handling such disasters.

**Corresponding author*: Jaswinder.singh@chitkara.edu.in; ORCID:10000-0003-1343-4740
Rajwinder Kaur: ORCID:0000-0002-9083-646
Puninder Kaur: ORCID:0000-0003-3959-593X
Rupinder Singh: ORCID:0000-0002-7553-8759

Neelam Dahiya, Gurwinder Singh, Sartajvir Singh and Apoorva Sharma (eds.) Artificial Intelligence in Remote Sensing for Disaster Management, (243–270) © 2025 Scrivener Publishing LLC

***Keywords*:** Artificial intelligence, deep learning, machine learning, GLOF, time series analysis

14.1 Introduction

A GLOF, another kind of flood, happens when the over-water portion of a glacial lake is poured out all of a sudden. These lakes may gradually occupy an old depression, left behind by glacial melt or formed when glacial debris dams up a river. As shown in Figure 14.1, the dam containing the glacial lake can fail due to various reasons, including the following:

- Overtopping: If the water comes up too high and flows over the dam, the spillway should turn on.
- Erosion: When water erodes the dam from the inside, its power is becoming less and less.
- Landslide: Upon intercepting the sea, the landslide that leads to the wave levels the dam as well.
- Earthquake: An earthquake manages to alter the dam and induces it to collapse.

The flow of glacier lake outbursts may be very devastating. It sweeps the tremendous hydraulic load, a large amount of debris, and ice at very high speeds. Frequently occurring floods can lead to massive neglect of property and infrastructure destruction, and how they affect the people downstream [1]. Some regions around the world are known for their high potential for GLOF occurrences.

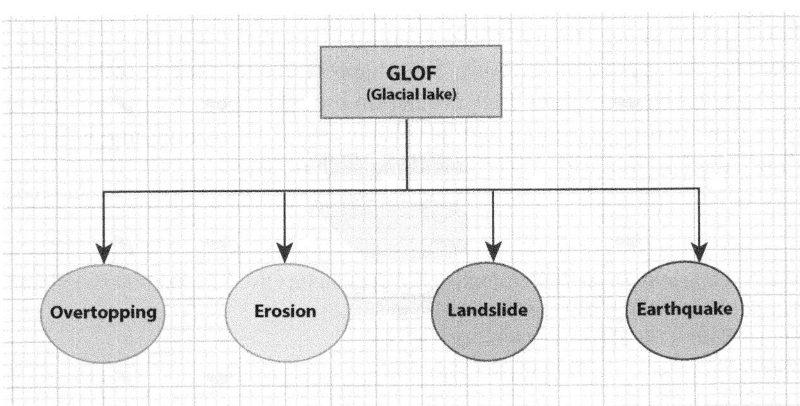

Figure 14.1 GLOF (glacial lake outburst flood) reasons.

14.1.1 The Andes

- This slope boundary, with the Pacific Ocean side of South America, the Andes range with Peru, Bolivia, and Chile, and Argentina along with the major part of the region, is an area where melting glaciers have a probability of causing the GLOFs.
- Lake Palcacocha, Peru: This glacial lake is the world's most dangerous one because of the distinct dam, being made of moraine, and the populated downstream areas.
- Santa River basin, Peru: These lakes are in the same basins as the alpine lakes with a notorious past, including, for instance, Lake Arhuaycocha and its well-known past instances of GLOFs.

14.1.2 High Mountain Asia (HMA)

- The fifth largest glacial region on Earth covers four countries—India, China, Nepal, and Bhutan—which contain the largest concentration of mountains with glaciers outside the polar regions [2].
- Imja Tsho Glacial Lake, Nepal: From the water point of view, this pond is widely considered a critical danger, represented by the unreliable accumulation of moraine and low potential to flood the downstream communities.
- Thorthormi Lake, Bhutan: This lake is determined internally as unstable and seems to threaten downstream neighbors as an important one.

14.1.3 Other Regions

- The Alps: If a glacier's stability is affected by global climate change, the glacier may be damaged, resulting in glacier lake outburst floods (GLOFs). This phenomenon is less common but can also occur in the European Alps, specifically in Switzerland, Italy, and Austria.
- Iceland: Being a country limited in space, on account of natural eruptions and the presence of glaciers, Iceland has faced quite a few GLOFs before.
- Northwestern North America: In this territory, namely, North America, including the part of Canada and the USA, this phenomenon, namely GLOFs, is more regular than in the aforesaid regions.

14.2 Artificial Intelligence and GLOF

Artificial intelligence (AI) offers a set of promising tools to aid us in knowing and help us to forecast such occurrences. Here is how AI can contribute to GLOF prediction.

14.2.1 Modeling the GLOF Process

- Machine learning (ML): ML algorithms can then analyze such historical data as past GLOF event parameters, such as real characteristics of the lakes, weather patterns, as well as topographical data, to identify relationships and patterns. Consequently, these models forecast how GLOFs are likely to occur as well as their possible severity [3].
- Deep learning (DL): Taking DL models as an example, they could be trained on high-resolution satellite imagery and other data sets to detect the conditions that lead to glaciers sliding, lakes, and other kinds of factors triggering GLFOs. Through such re-creation of the events, we can see what is behind these phenomena [4].

14.2.2 Impact Assessment

- Agent-based modeling (ABM): An ABM represents the activities of different kinds of things in a particular area or system by computing how people and infrastructure are behaving. This could be employed in assessing such outcomes as the final location of inundated communities or identifying potential hazards for infrastructure, vulnerable population areas, and evacuation routes [5].
- Geographic information systems (GIS): Infusion of AI models in GIS makes it possible for spatial analysis that considers GLOF impacts, thus helping to generate detailed maps and visualizations that could shorten decision times during emergency responses and mitigation planning [6].

14.2.3 Benefits of Using AI

- Improved accuracy and efficiency: AI models can sift through a huge quantity of information much quicker and more precisely than traditional methods, giving a large margin in making a more accurate decision-making [7].
- Early warning systems: This is an effective tool for prevention to implement when early warning systems are developed through AI, which allows monitoring in real time of glaciers and lakes, being the early action that gives the most time for evacuation and mitigation.
- Improved risk assessment: With AI's careful forecasting and impact assessment, communities can step up mitigation and management through these risks of GLOFs more efficiently.
- Use of new AI tools: With the emergence of AI-powered new tools like flood AI Hazard Mapper, etc., it becomes easier to forecast the GLOF risk.
- Analytics: Now with the help of AI, predictive analytics can be performed to know the future trends in GLOF.

14.2.4 AI Techniques for the Prediction of GLOF

AI algorithms are capable of providing an early warning of this kind of flood. Here are some prominent AI techniques as shown in Figure 14.2 that are used for this purpose.

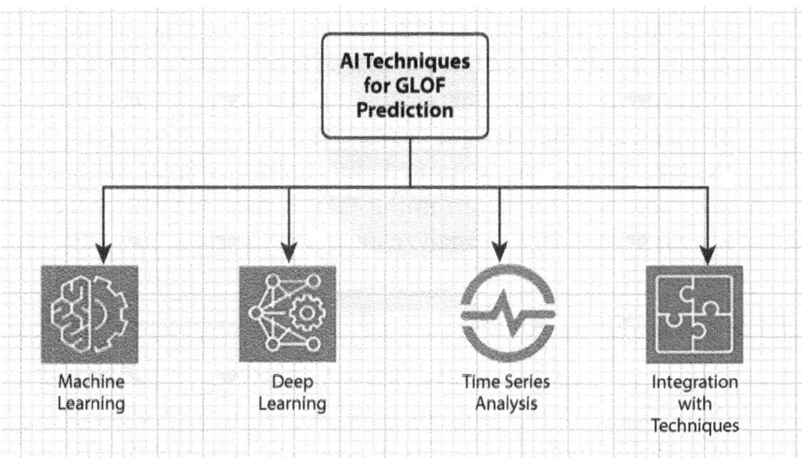

Figure 14.2 GLOF AI techniques.

14.2.4.1 Machine Learning (ML)

ML can be supervised and unsupervised.

- Supervised learning: This approach includes the use of historical information on past GLOF (glacial lake outburst floods) events and their factors that affect the characteristics of the lake, weather patterns, and the topography of the mass of the glacier melt. For instance, algorithms such as support vector machines (SVMs) or random forests are vessels through which this fact is learned. Therefore, these models can predict the likelihood of the occurrence of future GLOF events using new information as soon as they become accessible [8, 9].
- Unsupervised learning: Through this method, we can reveal hidden connections and sequences even without pre-labeled divisions or groups that have existed in earlier failed attempts at automation. For example, techniques such as K-means clustering or anomaly detection could be employed to detect the development of an anomalous process leading to a GLOF if lake level, the stability of glaciers, or weather patterns show unforeseen changes [10].

14.2.4.2 Deep Learning (DL)

- Convolution neural networks (CNNs): The practical applications of these models are incredibly precise when working with spatial data like satellite images. By feeding on high-resolution satellite pictures of glacial lakes to detect the areas or features that represent qualities like the ice cover, lake level changes, and the strength or weakness of the dam that holds the lake, CNNs can be trained. This published material is an advisable tool for determining GLOF risks [11, 12]. Deep learning also helps to analyze images using classifiers [13].

14.2.4.3 Time Series Analysis

- Recurrent neural networks (RNNs): The powerful feature of these models is that they are good at dealing with sequences of data like temporal series of lake level measurements or weather data. Recurrent neural networks (RNNs) are capable of learning temporal patterns, forecasting, and anticipating future trends. Besides, they can potentially foresee an abrupt rise of the lake levels that might result in debris flow from the glaciers [14].

14.2.4.4 Integration with Other Techniques

- Agent-based modeling (ABM): Using MLGDL models together with ABMs, we can simulate what GLOF could do to the folks living downstream from our modeled catchment. This shows the impact and directs emergency humans on where to evacuate while also planning for ways to minimize future damages.
- Geographic information systems (GIS): AI models and GIS go together. AI analysis of the possible GLOF leads to the displaying of its spatial path and impact zone on a GIS platform. Disaster planning is visualized on maps and becomes the basis for the allocation of resources.

Employing these AI techniques along with other scientific methods and solving the arising complications, we can promote GLOF prediction accuracy and so contribute to developing preventive and mitigation strategies that finally lead to lives and assets preservation.

14.3 Machine Learning Techniques for GLOF

In this segment, machine learning techniques for GLOF have been analyzed in terms of supervised and unsupervised learning.

14.3.1 Use of Supervised Learning in GLOF

AI models of GLOFs' prediction are trained utilizing supervised learning, which can be considered as one of the most important factors in developing such models. Here is how it works.

14.3.1.1 Data Preparation

The main element of the principle of supervised learning is historical information about past GLOFs. This data typically includes:

- Lake characteristics: Scale, the deepest points, capacity, and topography underwater are so significant and differing in nature.
- Weather data: An annual quantification definition of the amount of water that goes through the processes of snowmelt/precipitation and flown.
- Topographic data: The mounting level, the angles of slopes, and the presence of natural dams are among the natural barriers [14].

14.3.1.2 Feature Engineering

Data thereat is being processed for its relevant attributes is necessary. For instance, procuring data such as average monthly rainfalls or maximum daily temperatures from weather information and using them for modeling purposes will be possible.

14.3.1.3 Model Training

- A supervised learning construct like SVMs, random forests, or logistic regression would be fed on the built dataset [15].
- Training a model implies a process in which it learns the connections between the detected features (water level, temperature) and GLOF occurrence (belongs to the labeled data). This essentially enables the model to act not as completely a generalist but instead as a full-fledged mentalist.

14.3.1.4 Prediction

Following the training, the model can then be built to predict the possibility of another GLOF happening along with the new case not known previously. One particular instance will be the use of the model which examines real-time weather data in combination with the current water level in a lake and other parameters to estimate the likelihood of a glacial lake outburst flood (GLOF) in the future.

14.3.1.5 Benefits of Using Supervised Learning for GLOF Prediction

I. Improved accuracy: Through analyzing back data, supervised learning models can indicate numerous complex links between factors and the outcome of GLOF, thus leading to better predicting.

II. Scalability: These techniques can process huge chunks of data fast, which is a very desirable result for an analyst who collects data from the web, telephone survey, or an electronic sensor.

III. Flexibility: Moreover, several supervised learning algorithms can be implemented so that the appropriate algorithm that is suited for the specific dataset will be discovered.

14.3.1.6 Various Supervised Algorithms for the GLOF Process

These are some of the commonly used supervised learning algorithms for GLOF prediction.

14.3.1.6.1 Support Vector Machines (SVMs)

- SVMs are super algorithms that are designed to find the optimal hyperplane among the sea of hyperplanes in an over-dimension space that divides all data points that belong to various classes.
- In this area, an SVM is one of the examples that can be trained to differentiate between instances when a GLOF happened and the instances where it did not consider various features (lake characteristics, weather data, etc.) [16].
- They suit the analysis of non-linear problems with interdependencies between predictors (probability of GLOF occurrence).

14.3.1.6.2 Random Forests

- Random forests are ensemble methods that use multiple fractured decision trees to grow a more accurate and reliable model than a single decision tree can guarantee.
- In that case for a given tree in a forest, we set up each tree to train on the random subset of data points and features, thus giving rise to a varied or a diverse P predictor. The final class is taken from the most votes in all individual trees.

- This technique is valuable as it enables it to deal with very large data sets with the net effect of avoiding overfitting the training data [17].

14.3.1.6.3 Logistic Regression

- Logistic regression is one of the earliest and most widely used supervised learning techniques for classification problems when there are just two outcomes.
- It evaluates the probability of the occurrence of the event (GLOF occurrence in particular) based on its group of independent variables (the features).
- The linear regression logistic is competent to predict till the time the relationship between the features and the targeting variable has linearity.
- It can be an advantage through its interpretability because of its ability to easily understand how each feature is contributing to this forecast [18, 19].

14.3.1.6.4 Gradient Boosting

- Gradient boosting algorithms such as XGBoost or LightGBM are strong ensemble methods utilized by the sequential learning process with each model in the ensemble being built on top of the other and enhancing the predictions of the previous model in the ensemble.
- As a result of this, highly accurate and reliable models are produced. Hence, the models are proving to be good choices to predict GLOF.
- Nonetheless, the structures considered in these algorithms are more complicated when compared to other methods [20].

14.3.1.7 Choosing the Right Algorithm

The choice of the best algorithm for a specific GLOF prediction task depends on various factors, including the following:

- Data characteristics: The feature of this data (linear or non-linear vertex) will make a big difference. The appropriate algorithms will be determined by the nature of variables, i.e., categorical, continuous, etc., its size, and quality.

- Desired model complexity: In the case of XGBoost being preferred, it can be due to a better tradeoff between interpretability and performance. On the other side, when simple models like logistic regression are preferred, it can be for better interpretation.
- Computational resources: The computationally intensive process of training the gradient boosting model is one of the many faces it needs to contend with.

It is essential to test by trying different algorithms to check the efficiency of such on the dataset to recognize the sophisticated one for GLOF prediction in any certain situation.

14.3.2 Use of Unsupervised Learning in GLOF

In contrast to supervised learning which is oriented toward marked data (data that have known categories or effects), unsupervised learning has a comparative advantage when it comes to finding unmarked relationships that lie under unspecified data. This makes it valuable for GLOF analysis in several ways.

14.3.2.1 Anomaly Detection

For instance, unsupervised pattern recognition algorithms such as isolation forest or one-class SVM can be applied to the glacial lakes data that aim at revealing abnormalities. These anomalies might represent unusual changes in the following:

- Lake level: The increasing lake level could be a fast and large possession of coming landslides [21].
- Satellite imagery: Signs, like the color, texture, and indeed the environment alterations, might mean that the stability of the lake is in danger.
- Sensor data: Odd readings from sensors observing the pressure of water or moving earth may as well be a warning that a calamity is probably around the corner [22]. Through the detection of those red flags, unsupervised learning gives GLOF risks alerting for complex subject information and an early reaction.

14.3.2.2 Feature Discovery

Unsupervised methods such as principal component analysis (PCA) and autoencoders could be used for ascertaining hidden relationships in extensive generating data sets of various GLOF aspects. These patterns might represent the following:

- Underlying relationships: Previously unexplored linkages of shadows including lake properties, climate conditions, and topographic features can be "un"-veiled, thus better understanding of a mechanism that could trigger GLOF.
- Grouping similar events: The unsupervised clustering algorithms including K-means clustering can be used to group the previous glacial lake outburst events in one group according to their similarities in terms of their types and potential risk factors.

This profound understanding can be one of the factors that can contribute to the construction of better and more complete supervised learning models for assigning GLOF rates.

14.3.2.3 Data Preprocessing

K-means clustering is just one example of an unsupervised learning technique that can be utilized to condition data before employing supervised learning models. This can involve the following:

- Identifying and removing outliers: Outliers in the data can have both positive and negative effects on the obtained results by using supervised learning schemes. In an unsupervised manner, the existence of such outliers or noise to the data can be identified and removed, leading to the cleanup of the whole dataset for supervised model training purposes.
- Dimensionality reduction: Processing of very high dimensional data (many features) is quite cumbersome. The ease of operations is guaranteed by PCA that is focusing on dimensionality reduction of the data without any loss of essential information. This can, in turn, bring about higher accuracy and better end-products in the context of supervised learning models.

The application of unsupervised learning is significant as it participates in detecting anomalies, model features, and data preprocessing, causing a boost in the capabilities of supervised learning for GLOF analysis and prediction [23].

14.3.2.4 Unsupervised Learning Algorithms for GLOF Analysis

The superiority of supervised learning in predictive tasks with data that is labeled also is connected to the key role played by unsupervised learning in GLOF analysis owing to its ability to identify patterns and relationships in unlabeled data. It can be used in remote sensing applications [24]. Here are some commonly used unsupervised algorithms for GLOF.

14.3.2.4.1 Isolation Forest

It means to differentiate any outlier or anomaly in the data via the separation of the difficult-to-differentiate data points from the recycle as such. In GLOF analysis, it can help detect unusual changes in the following:

- Lake level: A serious change in water level like a sudden increase can indicate the inclination of the lake water to overflow.
- Satellite imagery: The colors, patterns, and onto of the lake, or the environment around it, are often the telltale signs of an insufficiency.
- Sensor data: Wonderful interrogation of sources of sensors recording elements like overpressure or earth tremors could be decisive in an upcoming accident.

14.3.2.4.2 Feature Discovery

- Principal component analysis (PCA): Application of this method helps to find the essential variables (factors) that will explain the biggest part of the data variance. In GLOF analysis, PCA can help.
- Reduce dimensionality: Complicate low-dimensional data with obligatory feature identification with more informative features for more effective modeling.
- Uncover hidden relationships: Show the cause and effect relation between different causes that led to the formation

of glacial lake outburst floods, thus implying emerging new knowledge of underlying mechanisms.

14.3.2.4.3 Clustering

- K-means clustering: This algorithm comprises two stages, namely: k-means to construct a specific number of clusters(K) from the data and then an algorithm that groups the data into these clusters based on their similarity. In GLOF analysis, it can be used to:
- Group similar events: Through investigation clusters of past GLOF cases, researchers can be able to distinguish different characteristics and factors that could put people at risk, which can be a handy tool in determining the probability of GLOF.
- Segment data: Segment data into classes that belong to the same type of characteristics, making it possible to conduct a focused analysis and make a model within a specific set of subgroups.

14.3.2.4.4 Association Rule Learning

- *A priori* algorithm: It is one of the approaches that can find out some regular patterns and relations between several features displayed in data without any label. GLOF analysis can help discover:
- Correlations: Select the attributes that link together coming up with probable associations between them, which, in turn, gives clues to what causes the glacier's outburst floods.
- Predictive patterns: Explore possibly beneficial patterns that seemed to be common among the data, which can subsequently disseminate the idea of future supervised learning models that predict.

14.3.2.5 Choosing the Right Algorithm

The decision, however, depends on the particular objectives, the analysis aims, and the type of data. Here are some considerations:

14.3.2.6 *Objective*

- Anomaly detection: Isolation forest
- Feature discovery: PCA
- Clustering: K-means
- Identifying associations: *A priori*

14.3.2.7 *Data Characteristics*

- Size and complexity
- The presence of outliers or noise
- Feature types (continuous, categorical)

14.3.2.8 *Benefits of Using Unsupervised Learning for GLOF*

i. Exploratory analysis: Offers enlightening knowledge that enhances reasonably measured unlabeled information, thus creating room for other advanced research and development of supervised models.
ii. Anomaly detection: It could sense unusual patterns in your data and flag potential risk.
iii. Feature engineering: Assists in the process of picking and choosing important features for a self-learning model like supervised learning.

14.3.2.9 *Challenges and Considerations*

i. Interpretation: Comprehension of the deeper significance of found patterns and relationships is sometimes difficult, often due to the reason that it necessitates research and domain expertise as well as careful analysis.
ii. Limited prediction: Unsupervised learning, on the other hand, does not have a combinatory role to play with direct events in the new insights. It is very often used in a tandem way alongside other known techniques of supervised learning for a comprehensive GLOF analysis.

The use of unsupervised learning techniques can help researchers to have deeper insights into unlabeled data related to GLOFs, which will merge all the pieces of information and comprehension to reduce the risk of the occurrence of these calamitous events.

14.4 Deep Learning for GLOF Modeling

Deep learning makes it possible to use and analyze the massive high-spatial-resolution satellite and airborne data for the verification of GLOF forecasting models. Deep learning opens new opportunities for chance-based modeling by learning a pattern from large complex sets [25, 26]. Here is an overview of its potential applications.

14.4.1 Convolutional Neural Networks (CNNs)

i. Analyzing satellite imagery: CNNI admits property of extraction image module. They can analyze high-resolution satellite images of glacial lakes to identify the following:
   - Lake characteristics: Ice cap size, ice shape, and cracks in the ice cover or areas of weakness in the dam would encourage the dam material to counter the pressure and consequently separate easily from the dam body.
   - Surrounding features: Topography, vegetation, and adjacent complex waterways

Example: The CNN model could be trained using past GLOF satellite images to find similarities between these images and the relevant features such as ice dams and glacial lakes which are the cause of these landslides. The information helps identify similar features in new satellite images, potentially indicating an increased risk of a future GLOF.

14.4.2 Recurrent Neural Networks (RNNs)

i. Analyzing time series data: RNNs are outstanding in the processing of sequential data like time series. They can be used to analyze the following:
   - Lake level measurements: Predicting the level changes of a lake in the future and identifying the sudden change in level that might be a warning indicator of the upcoming GLOF are going to be supported by the determination of future lake levels based on satellite data and monitoring of water level in the lake.

- Weather data: Evaluating previous weather directions and foreseeing possibilities of enhanced precipitation or quick air temperature variations that cause the GLOF to run away

Example: An RNN neural network could efficiently be trained on this data involving lake level measurements and weather convicted related to previous GLOF cases. The model subsequently would analyze the existing and forthcoming weather data in conjunction with current and forecasted lake level measurements and assess the risk of a GLOF in the future.

14.4.3 Combining Different Deep Learning Techniques

i. End-to-end models: Combining deep learning models assists with developing more complex systems. For example, the model could be a CNN for imagery and an RNN for time series of the data taking into account the threat of GLOF overall.

Example: The complete model would look at the different satellite images, level data from lakes, and weather data simultaneously. Therefore, the final prediction of GLOF risk provided by the model could be more comprehensive and maybe even more accurate compared to that provided by individual models targeting individual data types. Overall, deep learning shows promising potential for GLOF modeling by offering the following:

- Improved accuracy: Deep learning models could be able to show a higher level of precision in forecasting GLOFs as opposed to traditional statistical models or more layered machine learning models.
- Ability to handle complex data: Deep learning, since it covers diverse sorts of data (including satellite imaging, time series data, etc.), can handle with high competence.
- Continuous learning: The learning algorithms can retrain continuously along with the arrival of new data.

14.5 Existing Models for GLOF Modeling: A Comparison

Though the AI-based models for the prediction of GLOF sagging behind, several techniques like AI models have been studied. Figure 14.3 shows various existing models of GLOF. Here is a comparison of some notable models.

14.5.1 Statistical Models

i. Regression models: These models simulate a mathematical connection between the historical GLOF events as the different factors involved in the process such as lake characteristics, climate characteristics, and topographic data are taken into consideration.
   - Benefits: Rapid implementation and interpretation
   - Limitations: Insufficiency to measure complicated non-linear phenomena—therefore, intending to generalize may not apply to unseen cases.

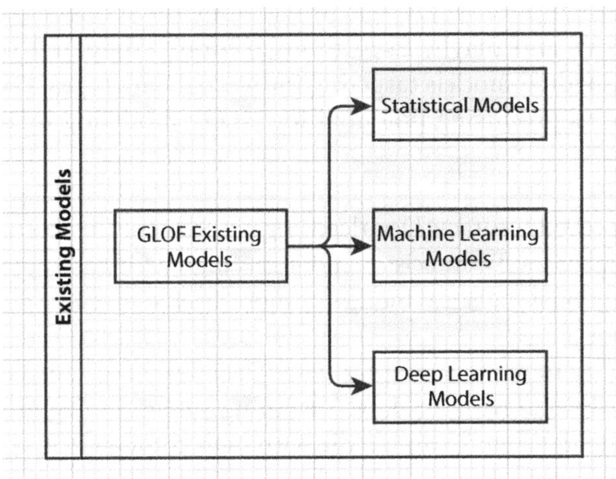

Figure 14.3 Existing GLOF model.

14.5.2 Machine Learning Models

i. Support vector machines (SVMs): Due to uncovering intricate non-linear associations and also working when there is a limited number of units of data, this is an incredible tool.
ii. Random forests: Enhance robustness and carry out tasks of high-dimensional data to high efficiency. Use our algorithm to calculate the impact of a sentence in the context of visualization: analyzing climate change.
iii. Logistic regression: The simplest model with interpretation opportunities for linear relationships is better.
iv. Gradient boosting: This can be very precise but consumes more computational resources and has a problem with interpretability.
    - Benefits: Accurate forecasts based on the model's ability to deal with intricate relationships as compared to statistical models.
    - Limitations: Requires proper choosing and adapting of hidden layers and other relevant parameters like learning rate, without being over-saturated and maintaining generalizability.

14.5.3 Deep Learning Models

i. Convolutional neural networks (CNNs): Get geospatial info such as images from satellites to figure out features like a lake's qualities and the dam weaknesses holding the lake in place [29].
ii. Recurrent neural networks (RNNs): The machine can learn the temporal patterns and predict future trends which can be beneficial in the analysis of the time series data; the prime example is a lake level measurement [30].
    - Benefits: Capacity to discern complex trends from vast information sets including spatial and temporal information
    - Limitations: They are demanding computational resources and data, offering an opening for diversity and bias issues.

14.5.4 Comparison

Table 14.1 shows comparisons of statistical, ML, and DL models for GLOF. ML has moderate complexity. Accuracy is higher in deep learning, whereas statistical models have low data requirements with high interoperability.

14.5.5 Choosing the Right Model

The optimal model choice depends on various factors, namely:

i. Data availability: The volume of records (e.g., historical GLOF events, satellite images, sensor data), level of data quality, and the data types available (e.g., satellite images, sensor data)
ii. Computational resources: The scaling of complicated models involving deep learning calls for vast computational resources
iii. Desired accuracy vs. interpretability: This involves a tradeoff between the need for the model to attain significant accuracy (25%) and the ability for it to understand how the predictions are arrived at [30].

14.5.6 Additional Considerations

i. Ensemble models: By combining different models (example: combining a statistical model with a machine learning model), the inherent strength of each, respectively, can be amplified and will likely result in optimal performance [31].

Table 14.1 Comparison of AI models for GLOF.

Feature	Statistical models	Machine learning models	Deep learning models
Complexity	Low	Moderate	High
Accuracy	Moderate	High	High (potentially)
Data requirements	Low	Moderate	High
Interpretability	High	Moderate	Low
Generalizability	Moderate	High	Requires careful validation

ii. Hybrid models: Incorporating AI models with other scientific methods and tools (hydrodynamic modeling) provides a basis for coming up with generalized strategies to predict GLOF occurrences [32, 33].

AI has given a chance to model GLOF in different aspects, and each has its strengths and imperfections. Familiarization with factors such as data availability, desired accuracy, and interpretability ensures that the process of selecting the best model goes along with the particular circumstances. With the continuation of the research, incorporating and upgrading these procedures can create sophisticated and accurate GLOF proxy models, thereby improving risk assessment and input for mitigation measures contributed by the possibly catastrophic events.

14.6 Future Models for GLOF Modeling

Knowing GLOF in advance is a top requirement to minimize their disastrous results on the population. Here is a glimpse into some potential advancements.

14.6.1 Integration of Diverse Data Sources

i. Multimodal learning: With the help of satellite imagery, weather data, sensor data (such as water pressure and seismic activity), historical records, as well as different kinds of sources, a comprehensive and holistic perspective can be obtained concerning the causes and factors behind the onset of GLOFs.
ii. Data fusion techniques: This technology allows for the smooth integration of data from various parts; no matter what the format is, still the integration process is smooth. There is a possibility generation of highly informative data for target model training is being reported from this.

14.6.2 Explainable AI (XAI)

i. Interpretability: It is very important to construct models that not only match but also give explanations; this is to ensure good use and also keep the trust. Study XAI processes are capable of elucidating the way the model turns into predictions, which then can be used for informed decision-making involving risk assessment.

ii. Human-in-the-loop approaches: XAI Integration with human expertise is meant to enhance and complement the latter's strengths. Human factors can contribute to an interpretation of model outputs and give context; meanwhile, the model retains the capability to perform complex data analysis and make unbiased forecasts.

14.6.3 Advanced Deep Learning Techniques

i. Generative adversarial networks (GANs): These models may help to create synthesized data that would be of particular use during training when real-world examples are not readily available.

ii. Graph neural networks (GNNs): This big data tool can be of help in the analysis of data with complex relationships that may be applicable for modeling the interconnected factors and processes behind these models.

14.6.4 Integration with Physical Modeling

i. Hybrid approaches: The combination of AI models with the conventional physical models (for example, hydrodynamic models) helps to best utilize the capabilities that stem from both the physics and data-driven model fields [27].

ii. Physics-informed machine learning: The method integrates physical rules and constraints into the models, which could result in the creation of more realistic and comprehendible predictions [20]. With this approach, machine learning models could potentially be made less reliant on human experts and more self-explanatory.

14.7 AI Challenges and Limitations

i. Data quality and availability: Having made progress in this regard, not getting such data in its entirety is still a problem now in some places.
ii. Computational resources: Computations of training and running complex models could be a demanding thing, and it might require a high level of infrastructure and power [28].
iii. Interdisciplinary collaboration: The watershed, being a multidimensional concept, thus requires expertise from different sectors like AI, hydrology, and engineering to be fused and to have models developed successfully and implemented [4].
iv. Model interpretability: Comprehension of the AI models on how they arrive at their decisions is crucial for the building of trust and acceptable use.

14.8 Insights and Findings from AI-Based Modeling of GLOF Processes

i. Improved predictive capabilities: AI modeling has come a long way in approaching glacial lake outburst flood (GLOF) processes and has likely rate improvements compared to those by traditional modeling methods. Through applying AI algorithms to complicated datasets, computers can analyze data swiftly and efficiently. This process leads to more precise predictions of where, when, and to what extent GLOFs occur and what kind of consequences they can have downstream.
ii. Identification of key drivers: AI models identified some of the previously unrecognized drivers of GLOF events that usually caused GLOF events. Having AI process a huge data set coming from various sources enables the algorithms to diminish the fine connections that the other methods could not reveal. Eventually, this could result in a more thorough appreciation of the confounding elements

affecting the incidence of GLOF—such as glacier dynamics, climate variability, and topographical aesthetics.

iii. Risk assessment and mitigation strategies: The findings gleaned from the interpretations of AI-based modeling are used in other ways to have more productive and efficient risk assessment and reduction strategies for glacial outburst flood (GLOF) events. Through this process of modeling different occurrences and the probability of their occurrence and consequences, the decision-makers can therefore allocate budgets and strategies to save the lives and materials (communities and infrastructure) that lie within the reach of the predicted path of GLOFs.

iv. Spatial and temporal dynamics: Artificial intelligence models might have unveiled the distribution of GLOF occurrences through space and time to the extent that it would be hard to do with the traditional modeling approaches. Through the utilization of high-resolution imagery from satellites, LiDAR data, and available climatic projections, AI algorithms mimic the glacier lake outburst flood (GLOF) evolution at the scales of a single glacier basin to an entire mountain range within different periods.

v. Uncertainty quantification: AI then modeled probabilities leading to reduced uncertainty in the probability distribution of GLOF events plausibly. Probabilistic algorithms and ensemble modeling techniques are applied by researchers, which give them the possibility to evaluate intervals of probabilities, reliability, and range of possible outcomes. This enables the decision-makers to understand more exactly the uncertain range of possible outcomes and related risks.

14.9 Evaluation of Methodology Used for AI-Based Modeling of GLOF Processes

i. Data quality and availability: The formidableness of the AI models relies to a large extent on the quality and availability of the data provided. Scientists need to make sure that data used for training and validation (i.e., hopefully) is sufficiently detailed, correct, and reflective of the study location and procedures examined.

ii. Algorithm selection and optimization: The selection of the best-suiting AI algorithms and tuning them with the best parameters are of great importance for the reliability and accuracy of GLOF forecasts. Researchers are obligated to diligently assess the pros and cons of the different algorithms (for example: random forests, neural networks, and support vector machines), modify the parameters, and systematize the model architecture to optimize the algorithm performance.

iii. Model validation and verification: Extensive testing and support of AI models are a requirement by which their authenticity is shown and their applicability is determined. Scientists used top-class validation techniques like cross-validation and independent tests to measure the model's reliability under different conditions, and it got a scope to predict beyond the range of the training data.

iv. Interpretability and transparency: While AI models can generate precise results, unfortunately, they are opaque and challenging to interpret, resulting in an inability to understand the decisions behind the outputs. Researchers must develop a truly understandable and transparent AI model and use XAI techniques as well as prepare the documentation for underlying model architectures and assumptions to make the model as clear as possible.

v. Integration with traditional approaches: Modeling, which is AI-based, must be conceived as complementary to the classical approaches for the GLOF modeling instead of being used as a method to replace them. Hence, the AI approach should be combined with physical models and empirical methods so that AI can complement the data and assumptions made in the latter two approaches to enhance the credibility of GLOF prediction models.

Essentially, the method utilized for AI-driven modeling of GLOF processes must be intricately designed and executed to produce meaningful projections and reliable forecasts as per the understanding of experts which can be used as an aid of decision-making and risk management as per high-risk mountain as well.

14.10 Conclusion

AI development and data integration constitute some of the facets that will revolutionize the figure of GLOF modeling in the future. If researchers come up with innovative methods as well as solve the current challenges, they can make sure that the models become well-improved and accurate, which will subsequently improve interpretation and reliability, and finally contribute to the making of better GLOF forecasting and risk reduction strategies, saving lives and controlling damages from such cataclysmic events. As we currently see it, AI provides sophisticated resources for the representation and prediction of GLOFs. In the future also, AI promises to fix as well as limit threats and risks and is a powerful player in the task of decreasing the loss of life and property during catastrophic events. In future work, there will also be an attempt to apply AI techniques to the selected dataset of GLOF, and the robustness of the modeling approach will also be discussed.

References

1. Wang, X., *et al.*, Reconstructing glacial lake outburst floods in the Poiqu River basin, central Himalaya. *Geomorphology*, 449, 109063, 2024.
2. Li, *et al.*, High Mountain Asia hydropower systems threatened by climate-driven landscape instability. *Nat. Geosci.*, 15, 7, 520–530, 2022.
3. Banerjee, P. and Bhuiyan, C., Glacial lakes of Sikkim Himalaya: their dynamics, trends, and likely fate—a timeseries analysis through cloud-based geocomputing, and machine learning. *Geomatics Nat. Hazards Risk*, 14, 1, 2286903, 2023.
4. Sharma, Prakash, C., Thakur, D., Glacier Lake Detection Utilizing Remote Sensing Integration with Satellite Imagery and Advanced Deep Learning Methods. *Appl. Geomat.*, 16, 829–850, 2024.
5. Caprioli, Bottero, M., De Angelis, E., Combining an agent-based model, hedonic pricing and multicriteria analysis to model green gentrification dynamics. *Comput. Environ. Urban Syst.*, 102, 101955, 2023.
6. Vishwas, P. and Nadh, G., Mapping of glacial lakes and glacial lake outburst flood in Lahul and Spiti district using remote sensing and GIS, 2022.
7. Tang, M., *et al.*, Hidden dangers of ice avalanches and glacier lake outburst floods on the Tibetan Plateau: identification, inventory, and distribution. *Landslides*, 20, 12, 2563–2581, 2023.
8. Bačić, Predicting golf ball trajectories from swing plane: An artificial neural networks approach. *Expert Syst. Appl.*, 65, 423–438, 2016.

9. Mohanty, L., *et al.*, Future prediction of existing glacial lake's size in the Himalaya by Markov model and glacial surface topography. *All Earth*, 35, 1, 329–343, 2023.
10. Prabhakar, T., Srujan Raju, K., Reddy Madhavi, K., Support vector machine classification of remote sensing images with the wavelet-based statistical features, in: *Smart Intelligent Computing and Applications, Volume 2: Proceedings of Fifth International Conference on Smart Computing and Informatics (SCI 2021)*, pp. 603–613, Springer Nature Singapore, Singapore, May 2022.
11. Qayyum, N., *et al.*, Glacial lakes mapping using multi satellite PlanetScope imagery and deep learning. *ISPRS Int. J. Geo-Inf.*, 9, 10, 560, 2020.
12. Fabijańska, Feder, A., Ridge, J., DeepVarveNet: Automatic detection of glacial varves with deep neural networks. *Comput. Geosci.*, 144, 104584, 2020.
13. Dahiya, N., Singh, S., Gupta, S., A review on deep learning classifier for hyperspectral imaging. *Int. J. Image Graph.*, 23, 04, 2350036, 2023.
14. Muneeb, *et al.*, Inventory and GLOF susceptibility of glacial lakes in Hunza River Basin, Western Karakorum. *Remote Sens.*, 13, 9, 1794, 2021.
15. Zhang, Z., Zhang, Y., Kos, A., Umek, A., A sensor-based golfer-swing signature recognition method using linear support vector machine. *Elektrotehniskivestnik*, 84, 5, 247–252, 2017.
16. Silva, L., *et al.*, Recurrence quantification analysis and support vector machines for golf handicap and low back pain EMG classification. *J. Electromyogr. Kinesiol.*, 25, 4, 637–647, 2015.
17. Arlisa, S.D. and Handayani, H.H., Flood vulnerability analysis using random forest method in Gresik Regency, Indonesia. *IOP Conf. Ser.: Earth Environ. Sci*, 1127, 1, 012023, 2023.
18. Kinero, *et al.*, Modeling injury severity of crashes involving golf carts: A case study of The Villages, Florida. *Traffic Inj. Prev.*, 25, 2, 165–172, 2024.
19. Sawi, T., Holtzman, B., Walter, F., Paisley, J., An Unsupervised Machine-Learning Approach to Understanding Seismicity at an Alpine Glacier. *J. Geophys. Res.: Earth Surf.*, 127, 12, e2022JF006909, 2022.
20. Grégoire, *et al.*, Forecasting Pesticide Use on Golf Courses by Integration of Deep Learning and Decision Tree Techniques. *Agriculture*, 13, 6, 1163, 2023.
21. Yu, He, Y., Ye, P., Quantitative susceptibility assessment of the breach of moraine-dammed lakes due to glacier avalanches. *Cold Reg. Sci. Technol.*, 206, 103749, 2023.
22. Gaddam, K. and Gaddam, H.K., Identification of hazardous prone lakes using remote sensing and ANN applications in Western Himalaya, 2023.
23. Gu, *et al.*, Monitoring glacier lake outburst flood (GLOF) of Lake Merzbacher using dense Chinese high-resolution satellite images. *Remote Sens.*, 15, 7, 1941, 2023.
24. Jiang, L., *et al.*, Combining geophysics, remote sensing and numerical simulation to assess GLOFs: Case study of the Namulacuo Lake in the Southeastern Tibetan Plateau. *Sci. Total Environ.*, 880, 163262, 2023.

25. Kaur, S., Gupta, S., Singh, S., Arora, T., A review on natural disaster detection in social media and satellite imagery using machine learning and deep learning. *Int. J. Image Graph.*, 22, 05, 2250040, 2022.
26. Sharma, Thakur, V., Prakash, C., Sharma, A., Sharma, R., Deep Learning-Based Glacial Lakes Extraction and Mapping in the Chandra–Bhaga Basin. *J. Indian Soc. Remote Sens.*, 52, 435–447, 2024.
27. Nandhini, S., Parthasarathy, S., Saravanan, S., An efficient optimal hybrid SVELM based monitoring and forecasting the engine operations for safety standards. *Expert Syst. Appl.*, 238, 121679, 2024.
28. Sharma, and Prakash, C., Glacial lakes mapping using satellite images and deep learning algorithms in Northwestern Indian Himalayas. *Model. Earth Syst. Environ.*, 10, 2, 2063–2077, 2024.
29. McNally, W., Lambeth, J., Brekke, D., Combining Physics and Deep Learning Models to Simulate the Flight of a Golf Ball, in: *Proceedings of the IEEE/CVF Conference on Computer Vision and Pattern Recognition*, pp. 5118–5127, 2023.
30. Lai, M. and Kuo, T.J., Available capacity computation model based on long short-term memory recurrent neural network for gelled-electrolyte batteries in golf carts. *IEEE Access*, 10, 54433–54444, 2021.
31. Kaushik, S., *et al.*, Examining the glacial lake dynamics in a warming climate and GLOF modelling in parts of Chandra basin, Himachal Pradesh, India. *Sci. Total Environ.*, 714, 136455, 2020.
32. Zhou, *et al.*, Process-driven susceptibility assessment of glacial lake outburst debris flow in the Himalayas under climate change. *Adv. Clim. Change Res.*, 13, 2, 500–514, 2023.
33. Agarwal, K., Tiwari, R.G., Kaushal, R.K., Kumar, N., A systematic analysis of applications of blockchain in healthcare, in: *2021 6th International Conference on Signal Processing, Computing and Control (ISPCC)*, pp. 413–417, IEEE, Oct. 2021.

15

A Systematic Review of the GLOF Susceptibility Assessment Techniques

Oushnik Banerjee*, Anshu Kumari and Apoorva Shamra

Department of Computer Science and Engineering, University Institute of Engineering, Mohali, Punjab, India

Abstract

Glacial lake outburst floods (GLOFs) are a historically significant phenomenon that has the potential to be extremely hazardous. Computer models are already ubiquitous instruments for risk reduction and for estimating the size of potentially dangerous future occurrences. When water dammed by a glacier or a moraine is released, it can cause an outburst flood similar to that of a glacial lake (Shishper Glacier Surge and GLOF, July 2020). The Himalayas are often regarded as one of the world's most vulnerable GLOF zones. The Himalayas are one of the world's primary GLOF-vulnerable areas, covering an area of around 0.65 million km^2 and home to 22,800 km^2 of glaciers. A complete inventory of previous GLOF incidents is necessary for risk management and hazard assessments to be effective. Consequently, the rate at which glaciers are melting and creating glacial lakes is concerning. When ice melts, it can release water and displace the soil or higher ice layer's support structure (Lhotse Shar GLOF, April 221). Meltwater may destabilize cryospheric ecosystems, causing glacier collapse (Chaurikharka GLOF, June 2020), rock and ice avalanches, glacier and snow melting floods (Uttarakhand Flood, February 2021), ice shelf deterioration (Chorabari Lake GLOF, June 2013), GOLF, and thermokarst formation. In this chapter, the GLOF susceptibility system has been summarized along with the advantages and disadvantages of the different recently used GLOF mapping techniques. This study is beneficial as it calculates the sensitivity of glacial lakes by determining the weight of different glacial lakes by using the multi-criteria decision model.

***Keywords*:** GLOF, cryospheric ecosystem, ice avalanches

**Corresponding author*: oushnikbanerjee20cricket@gmail.com
Apoorva Sharma: ORCID: 0009-0004-9667-476X

Neelam Dahiya, Gurwinder Singh, Sartajvir Singh and Apoorva Sharma (eds.) Artificial Intelligence in Remote Sensing for Disaster Management, (271–288) © 2025 Scrivener Publishing LLC

15.1 Introduction

Glacial lake outburst floods (GLOFs) pose a pressing threat to vulnerable regions worldwide, particularly in the context of accelerating glacial retreat and the impacts of climate change. As glaciers melt at an unprecedented rate, the formation and expansion of glacial lakes behind natural dams become increasingly common. The potential release of large volumes of water from these lakes can result in catastrophic GLOFs, with severe implications for downstream communities, infrastructure, and ecosystems. Recognizing the urgency of addressing this environmental challenge, our project focuses on advancing the estimation and prediction of GLOFs. Key stakeholders include governmental agencies, research institutions, international bodies, and local communities directly impacted by the risk. This study aims to enhance risk mitigation strategies, improve early warning systems, and contribute to long-term climate resilience by navigating the dynamic nature of glacial systems and the associated complexities in predicting GLOFs accurately.

The natural environment and socioeconomic development are significantly impacted by lakes, which are thought to be a sensitive indication of climate change. Glacial lakes, one of the forms of lakes, are natural water bodies that are mostly supplied by modern glacial meltwater or developed in the depression of glacier moraine. In the downstream regions, roads, bridges, and other infrastructure are at risk from flooding and debris flows brought on by glacial lake outbursts. The Himalayan glaciers, which are regarded as South and East Asia's freshwater towers, are significantly impacted by the continuous climate [1–3]; these factors have caused a rapid increase in the number of glacial lakes [4]; these lakes are frequently dammed by unstable and unconsolidated material [5]. Young, seismically active alpine mountains like the Himalayas, where hazard chains and cascades are prevalent, exacerbate the instability of slopes and glacial lakes [6].

Some studies have predicted a three- to sevenfold rise in GLOF danger and downstream risk in the Himalayas due to future deglaciation [7, 8]. The positive trend in the frequency of GLOFs has faded since the 1970s [9]. As of 2015, projections suggest that High Mountain Asia (HMA) may lose between 29% and 67% of its ice mass by 2100. The Himalayas are among the regions most susceptible to this loss [10, 11]. More than 5,000 possible glacier lake locations in the Himalayas have been found by researchers; these sites could be revealed during future glacial retreats [12–14]. As of 2015, projections suggest that HMA may lose between 29% and 67% of its ice mass by 2100. The Himalayas are among the regions most susceptible to this loss [11, 15, 16]. Most of the Himalayan region's subtropical glaciers contain dry snow zones, which are only seen in frigid polar glaciers [9]. Except for temperate glacier winters, the glacial ice remains at the melting point for most of the year. Superimposed ice is created when firn is below 0°C, which is not the case for temperate glaciers. Therefore, equilibrium and snowline coincide with no superimposed ice zone [17].

In this study, we mainly focus on the pro-glacial lake, Samudra Tapu Glacier Lake, which is situated in the Chandra basin, a Chenab River sub-basin in the Himachal Himalayas, and covers an area of roughly 200 km^2 or the watershed. This glacier is the second biggest of the upper Chandrabasin's 200 glaciers in the Chandra-Bhagabasin in Lahaul and Spiti district, Himachal Pradesh [18, 19]. It spans longitudes 77.37° to 77.61° E and latitudes 32.40° to 32.55° N. Elevations in the region range from 4,021 to 6,527 m above mean sea level, placing it in the Higher or Greater Himalayas. One of the Himachal Pradesh border districts, Lahaul-Spiti, is known for its very harsh landscape, which includes ice fields, snow-covered peaks, and an extremely cold temperature [12]. The 3,915-m-high Rohtang Pass is the only route to reach Lahaul-Spiti. As a result, the majority of the year finds the region isolated from the outside world. In addition, the area is severely glaciated and has a network of connecting mountain ranges. Snow makes up the majority of the precipitation in these places. The district has an extremely cold, alpine, and glacial climate because it is the northernmost.

Moreover, glacial lakes less than 0.1 km^2 have been the site of recent damaging GLOF episodes in Indian [9, 20] and Nepalese [21]. To include more small glacial lakes in our study, we therefore intend to drop the size criteria from 0.1 km^2, which was primarily employed by prior studies, to 0.045 km^2. The general procedures were used in the evaluation of GLOF susceptibility. They draw from earlier research; they have determined and enumerated several variables controlling the GLOF potential mechanism. The purpose of this study is to summarize and identify the effective susceptibility approaches. In this study, we are testing, determining, and analyzing the techniques used for predicting GLOF sustainability and finding the advantages and disadvantages of those techniques.

15.2 Glacial Lakes in the Western Himalayas

The area of the glacial lake was determined using consistent manual digitization from the Google Earth platform. A 10-km buffer zone was established between the closest glacier and the lakes. Figure 15.1 shows the types of glacial lakes.

Figure 15.1 Representation of different glacial lakes existing over the Himalayan region.

15.2.1 Gangotri Glacier (Supra Glacial Lake)

A lake of water that develops on top of a glacier is known as a supra-glacial lake. Supraglacial lakes can have a depth of several meters and a surface area ranging from a few meters to tens of kilometers. They can empty in a matter of hours, but they can also linger for months or even decades at a time. The lakes can be formed by surface melting in the summer or by years of rainfall, such as during a monsoon. They could evaporate by building a moulin or overflowing their banks.

Gangotri Glacier is a type of supra-glacial lake. Numerous supra-glacial lakes, created when ice blocks fracture along the glacier's fissures, may be seen on the Gangotri Glacier. The supraglacial moraines envelop the ablation zone of the glacier, and the ice portions melt into lake pools. Because of the glacier's rapid decline and sinking, its center is teeming with lakes [22]. The largest glacier in the Uttarakhand Himalayas, the Gangotri Glacier, is the main source of the Ganga River, which is revered in Hinduism. With an estimated volume of around 27 km^3, the glacier is 30 km in length and 2–4 km in width. The high peaks of the Gangotri Group encircle it, including Chaukhamba, Thalay Sagar, Meru, and Shivling [23].

15.2.2 Samudra Tapu (Pro Glacial Lake)

A freshwater lake that develops behind a moraine or ice dam is called a proglacial lake. They may span several kilometers or be fewer than 100 ft across. Meltwater from glaciers pools to generate proglacial lakes. They may fail catastrophically to cause jokulhaups or outburst floods, or they may remain stable long after the glacier melts. The flow of sediment and meltwater to proglacial zones and, ultimately, the ocean is halted by proglacial lakes. An important geochronological archive that records patterns of fluctuating meltwater originating from glaciers is the sedimentation seen in proglacial lakes [24].

Samudra Tapu Glacier is a proglacial lake, which is situated in the Chandra basin, a Chenab River sub-basin in the Himachal Himalayas, and covers an area of roughly 200 km^2 or the watershed. This glacier is the second biggest of the upper Chandrabasin's 200 glaciers in the Chandra-Bhagabasin in Lahaul and Spiti district, Himachal Pradesh [18, 19]. It spans longitudes 77.37° to 77.61° E and latitudes 32.40° to 32.55° N. Elevations in the region range from 4,021 to 6,527 m above mean sea level, placing it in the Higher or Greater Himalayas. One of the Himachal Pradesh border districts, Lahaul-Spiti, is known for its very harsh landscape, which includes ice fields, snow-covered peaks, and an extremely cold temperature [25].

15.2.3 South Lhonak Lake (Unconnected Glacial-Fed Lake)

Lakes that are not directly supplied by glaciers or connected to them are known as unconnected glacial lakes. Unconnected glacial lakes include cirque erosion lakes and other glacier erosion lakes. South Lhonak Lake is a type of unconnected glacial lake. It is a glacier lake located at an elevation of 17,100 ft (5,200 m) in the extreme northwest of Sikkim, India [26]. It is one of the lakes in the Sikkim Himalaya region that is growing the fastest, having been generated by the melting of the Lhonak glacier. The lake is also among the 14 lakes that could be dangerous due to glacial lake outburst floods (GLOFs), which happen when water that has been held behind a glacier suddenly releases itself [25].

15.2.4 Dal Lake (Non-Glacial-Fed)

Lakes supplied by glaciers are more susceptible to temperature fluctuations than non-glacier lakes are to variations in precipitation. Dal Lake is a lake in Srinagar, the summer capital of the disputed Kashmir region, which is controlled by India and includes Jammu and Kashmir. It is an urban lake, the second biggest in Jammu and Kashmir, and the most popular destination for both residents and visitors in Srinagar [27]. It is also referred to as Srinagar's Jewel, the "Lake of Flowers," the "Jewel in the crown of Kashmir," and other names that are significant to tourism and leisure in the Kashmir valley [28].

15.3 Sensitive Glacial Lake in the Western Himalayas

Glacial lakes in the Western Himalayas that are regarded as vulnerable to GLOF are those that can potentially cause floods given the failure of natural dams, usually moraine or ice. They are recent bodies of water forged out of rising glacier melts owing to global warming. Here are some of the sensitive glacial lakes in the Western Himalayas as shown in Figure 15.2.

15.3.1 Samudra Tapu Glacier

The Samudra Tapu glacier is situated in the Chandra basin, a Chenab River sub-basin in the Himachal Himalayas, and covers an area of roughly 200 km^2 or the watershed. This glacier is the second biggest of the upper Chandrabasin's 200 glaciers in the Chandra-Bhagabasin in Lahaul and

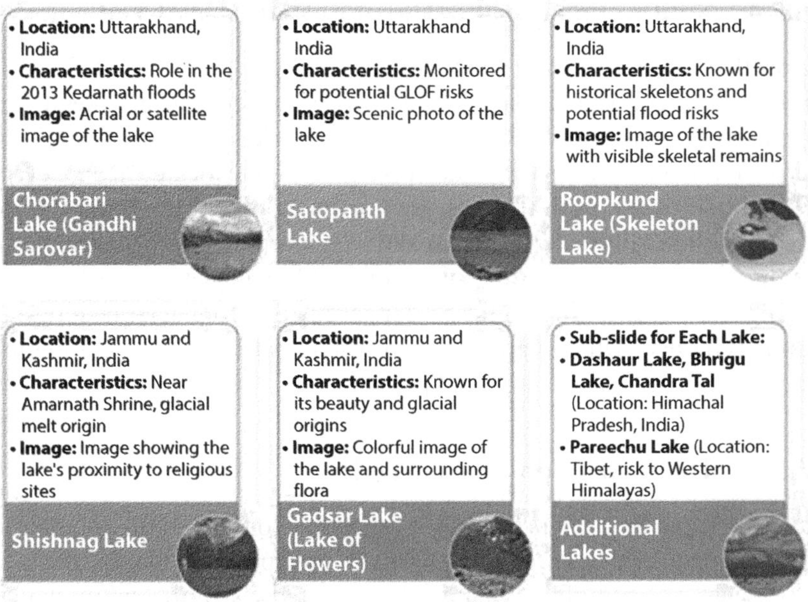

Figure 15.2 Some of the sensitive glacial lakes in the Western Himalayas.

Spiti district, Himachal Pradesh [18]. It spans longitudes 77.37° to 77.61° E and latitudes 32.40° to 32.55° N. Elevations in the region range from 4,021 to 6,527 m above mean sea level, placing it in the Higher or Greater Himalayas. One of the Himachal Pradesh border districts, Lahaul-Spiti, is known for its very harsh landscape, which includes ice fields, snow-covered peaks, and an extremely cold temperature [29]. The 3,915-m-high Rohtang Pass is the only route to reach Lahaul-Spiti. As a result, the majority of the year finds the region isolated from the outside world. In addition, the area is severely glaciated and has a network of connecting mountain ranges. Snow makes up the majority of the precipitation in these places. The district has an extremely cold, alpine, and glacial climate because it is the northernmost.

A field location that is accessible in the winter was chosen to calibrate data obtained from GPR measurements. The Patseo location, which stands at an elevation of 3,800 m, is roughly 30 km northwest of the Samudra Tapu glacier. This region's typical winter air temperature ranges from -5.9°C to -10.7°C, with a standard deviation of -0.8°C, and its winter snowfall ranges from 134 to 410 cm with an 85-cm variation [33, 34]. In this area, the majority of the slopes are rocky and desolate, with a few scattered trees at lower elevations. During winter, the region sees strong wind activity, comparatively little snowfall, and lower average temperatures. Using aerial GPR, a survey was conducted here and over the Samudra Tapu glacier to estimate the depth of the snow.

15.4 GLOF Susceptibility Mapping Techniques

15.4.1 Satellite Imagery Analysis

This technique was developed by [11]. In their study, due to the significant temporal and spatial changes that these supraglacial lakes undergo, satellite imagery must be obtained both before and after the event to observe the contribution of these supraglacial lakes to these glacier outburst flood events. An area-to-volume connection was employed to calculate the possible flood volume related to supraglacial pond drainage [9]. The drained volume from the farthest supraglacial lake up-glacier was 0.01×106 m^3, based on the change in areal extent between May 14, 2016 and October 29, 2016. The predicted flood volume of 2.65×106 m^3 is twice as large as this value, indicating that the drainage of a single supraglacial pond has a negligible impact on the total flood volume. In actuality, the projected flood

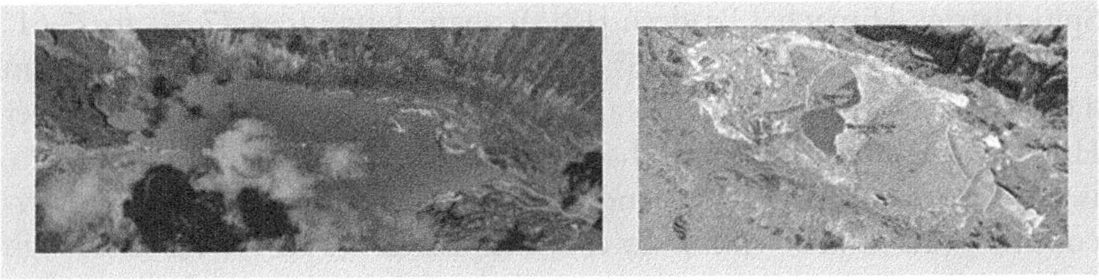

Figure 15.3 Samudra Tapu Glacier Lake situated in Chandra Basin Himachal Pradesh.

volume would only be 0.52 × 106 m^3 if all 274 supraglacial lakes (0.21 km^2) that were present on Lhotse Glacier on May 14, 2016 were emptied.

This offers compelling proof that the glacier's subsurface held a sizable portion of the floodwater. Lhotse glacial was the source of the glacial outburst flood that happened overnight on May 25, 2015 [30]. A big supraglacial pond (0.036 km^2) is seen on satellite data taken on May 8, May 25, and June 7, 2015. The pond fills up between May 8 and May 25 and drains completely between May 25 and June 7 (Figure 15.3). The 2015 glacier outburst flood may have been caused by up to 0.17 × 106 m^3 of this supraglacial pond's outflow. According to them, the 2016 event was bigger than the 2015 one. Early in May 2016, there was also talk of a similar outburst incident that destroyed parts of the high and low basecamp zones around the "crampon put-on point" (5,600 m) of Island Peak (6,189 m) [30].

15.4.2 Semi-Automated GLOF Susceptibility Assessment System

The susceptibility of potentially hazardous glacial lakes was ranked in the current study using the analytical hierarchy process (AHP). Multicriteria decision analysis or AHP is a technique for analyzing difficult issues with several aspects. By weighing the relative relevance of one aspect about the other, a pairwise comparison matrix evaluates the significance of the contributing factor to outbursts. On a scale from 1 to 9, values from equal, moderate, strong, very strong, and extreme importance are assigned to produce the pairwise comparison matrix. Based on the factor eigenvalues, the consistency ratio (CR) was calculated. When the measured CR rises beyond the 0.1 threshold, it is updated. We established a pairwise comparison matrix by allocating high values to those parameters that are highly associated and contribute more to GLOF. Weights were computed for each parameter. Each variable was further categorized into classes, and final weights were calculated by multiplying the class index value with the parameter weight. The final weight of the lake was computed by adding weights of parameters. By giving high values to those parameters that are strongly correlated and contribute more to GLOF, we created a pairwise comparison matrix. They calculated weights for every parameter. Every variable was then divided into classes, and the class index value and parameter weight were multiplied to determine the final weights. The weights of the parameters were added to determine the lake's final weight.

15.4.3 Glacial Lake Mapping

This technique was introduced by [31] in their study. In this, the water pixels in the basin were identified using the normalised differenced water index (NDWI), which was created using the near-infrared (NIR) and green (green – NIR / green +NIR) spectral bands of Landsat multispectral images [32]. The glacial lake inventory for the area only included lakes with areas larger than 5,000 m^2. Using the photos taken between October and November, the glacial lakes were mapped to reduce seasonal variations in the area of the glacial lakes caused by ice/snow meltwater and monsoonal rains, which are most prevalent during the summer monsoon. The main elements that influenced the occurrence of outburst floods are lake features, dam geometry, the material properties of moraine dams, and the topography of the surrounding area. Ascertaining and evaluating certain suggested parameters requires high-resolution aerial photography, satellite data, and field observations; thus, for the outburst susceptibility evaluation, they chose 11 factors that were divided into four parameter groups: (i) characteristics of the lake and associated glaciers, (ii) characteristics of the moraine dam, (iii) characteristics of the surrounding topography, and (iv) a history of extreme weather and seismic occurrences in the area. Table 15.1 presents a summary of the advantages and disadvantages of satellite imagery analysis, semiautomatic assessment methods, and glacial mapping.

15.5 Stages of Glaciations

Based on the evolution of three different types of moraines, the three phases of glaciation have been recognized. Three terminal moraines that have been kept in good condition were found during fieldwork. GPS was used to pinpoint their location, while satellite imagery at 1:25,000 scale was used to define their extent. The fan deposit was the source of the second advance. The third advance is represented by a red band that reaches a spur

Table 15.1 Summary of the advantages and disadvantages of satellite imagery analysis, semiautomatic assessment methods, and glacial mapping.

	Satellite imagery analysis	**Semi-automated GLOF susceptibility assessment system**	**Glacial lake mapping**
Method used	Area-to-volume calculation method	Analytical hierarchy process (AHP)	Image processing method
Advantages	• Estimates flood volumes based on area-to-volume connection • Assign weights to parameters influencing glacial lake outburst floods (GLOFs) • Provides a systematic framework for assessing susceptibility to GLOFs	• Systematic approach for evaluating complex issues with multiple criteria • Allows for the weighting of parameters based on their relative importance • Incorporates pairwise comparisons to assess the significance of contributing factors	• Swift and precise mapping of glacial lakes using satellite data • Utilizes normalized difference water index (NDWI) to identify water pixels • Incorporates slope masks and shadow masks to distinguish actual lakes from false detections caused by mountain shadows [33]
Disadvantages	• Relies on accurate data inputs and assumptions about parameter correlations • Calculation of weights may be subjective and require expert judgment	• Requires careful consideration of pairwise comparisons, which can be subjective • Complexity may increase with the number of parameters evaluated	• Requires access to satellite imagery and DEM data • May still require manual verification and editing, especially in areas with complex terrain

Table 15.2 Glacier retreat stages.

Stage	Lowest elevation (m)	Glacial length (m)	Area (km²)
Stage I	4,100	20,161	77.67
Stage II	4,120	18,280	77.06
Stage III	4,160	17,163	76.03

close to the glacier; at that point, the glacier's erosive activity stops. There appears to be an overprinting of the glacier's river-derived fluvial debris on the moraine ridges. A lake at the glacier terminus is dammed by moraine. The size and angle of the lake may have varied depending on where the nose was located. Table 15.2 provides a satellite imagery and a map, illustrating the three stages of glaciation.

15.6 Glacier Retreat

The glacial retreat along the snout region from 1962 to 1993, 1993 to 98, and 1998 to 2000 is shown in Table 15.3. Along the centerline, the glacier's retreat was measured. The results of the examinations point to a pattern of glacial retreat. A 741-m retreat was measured between 1962 and 2000, corresponding to a 19.5-m/year retreat during the previous 38 years (1962–2000) (Table 15.3). The glacial extent measured in 1998 IRS LISS-III photos and the 1962 SOI topographic map is 65 and 73 km^2, respectively (Table 15.3). The study glacier has seen an overall 11% deglaciation over 38 years (1962–2000).

Table 15.3 Glacier retreat by year.

Year	Area of glacier (km²)	Lowest elevation (m)	Length of glacier (m)	Loss in length (m)
1962	73.0	4200	17718	–
1993	–	–	17065	653
1998	–	–	17010	55
2000	65.0	4220	16977	33

15.7 Causes of Glacial Lake Change

The area change of glacial lakes, a sensitive indicator of climate change, is strongly correlated with climate change. Glacial lakes can expand as a result of increased precipitation, reduced evaporation, climate warming, and humidification. The average winter air temperature in the region surrounding the Samudra Tapu glacier fluctuates between -5.9°C and -10.7°C. The average summer temperature in 2016 and 2017 was 9.6°C and 9.2°C at Hbc (4,052 m asl) and 3.7°C and 5.0°C at Abc (4864 m asl), respectively. According to the report in 2019, it was found that if global warming is kept to 1.5°C over preindustrial levels, the Himalayan area may lose at least one-third of its glaciers. Glaciers in the Samudra Tapu, Sikkim and Himalayas, are melting quickly, but a new analysis shows that an incredible event in the world's largest mountain range may be helping to mitigate the consequences of the global climate catastrophe. The dry, cool surface air sinks as it becomes thicker and colder. The air mass cools the lowest portions of the glaciers and the surrounding ecosystems as it flows into the valleys from the slopes. As the region prepares for a likely rise in temperature over the coming few decades, it is critical to determine whether the Samudra Tapu, Sikkim, and Himalayan glaciers can maintain this self-preserving cooling effect. Snow and ice from the mountain range feed into 12 rivers that supply fresh water to nearly 2 billion people in 16 countries.

15.8 Depiction and Categorization of Glacial Lakes

The area of the glacial lake was determined using consistent manual digitization of the geometrically corrected false-color composite Landsat (30 m) and Sentinel-2 photos (10 m). Whenever the lake delineation was disrupted by shade or cloud cover, alternate pictures from the same season were utilized [34–36]. Additionally, the influence of shading in lake delineations was eliminated by using Google Earth's scene classification algorithm and Sentinel Application Platform (SNAP) [21]. A 10-km buffer zone was established between the closest glacier and the lakes. These lakes were then categorized into four types according to their positions relative to the glaciers: supraglacial lakes, which are on the surface of glaciers; proglacial lakes, which are at the lateral or terminal position of the glacier; and unconnected lakes, which are far from the glaciers and are further divided into unconnected glacial-fed and non-glacial-fed lakes based on whether the lake receives water from glacier melt [37, 38].

15.9 Study of Evaluating Parameters

15.9.1 Sensitivity Evaluation

The satellite data used to prepare the inventory and the DEM used to estimate the variables might be sources of uncertainty in the GLOF susceptibility evaluation. The perimeter of the lake and half of the data resolution were multiplied to determine the degree of uncertainty in the definition of glacial lakes [12]. The input values for F1 (lake area) and F2 (lake growth rate) are impacted by the ambiguity in lake delineation. However, earlier research [11, 37] has effectively employed the comparable dataset to create the inventory and calculate the factors for risk [39], susceptibility [31], and GLOF hazard [7] assessments. Furthermore, there are limitations to accurately revealing the terrain in the high mountainous region when using 30 m SRTM DEM. Sensitivity analysis (SA) is a crucial tool in multi-criteria decision-based GLOF assessments because it helps ascertain the extent to which the uncertainty of the assessment's input criteria impacts the assessment's outcomes' uncertainty [40].

Here we carried out the SA in two ways: (1) by changing the GLOF susceptibility class and (2) by altering the class/alternative. By changing the low and medium class/alternative of F1 to the medium and high classes, respectively, while holding all other variables constant, we were able to test the sensitivity of the GLOF assessment. SA was also carried out for the other four variables (F2, F3, F5, and F6), except F4. Keeping all other variables unchanged, the high and low choices for F4 were set to $>5°$ and $<5°$, respectively, for the SA. The second statistical analysis looks at how much the GLOF susceptibility of lakes will alter when the susceptibility class is adjusted by ±5% or ±0.05.

15.9.2 Calculation of Weights and GLOF Susceptibility Index

The weights of each factor were assigned using the AHP approach. According to [9], the analytic hierarchy process (AHP) is a semi-quantitative method of decision-making that employs weights to compare several aspects pairwise and consistently. By creating a comparison matrix, the expert review was carried out to determine the relative relevance of each component to the others.

15.10 Summary

The paper delivers a detailed analysis of the crucial topic of GLOFs more so regarding the retreating glaciers and climate change impacts. It describes glacial lakes and their potential for causing outburst floods and subsequently raises the issue of future improved techniques of evaluation, forecasting and mitigation. The objective of the study on the Himachal Himalayan Samudra Tapu Glacier Lake is to enhance the system for early warning, the methods of risk analysis, and climate change adaptation. There is also an assessment of the size of glacial lakes and their GLOF susceptibility, which may be carried out by image processing and geographic tools or merely by satellite data analysis, a semi-automated assessment comprising with one of them such as analytical hierarchy process (AHP). They all aim at identifying potentially dangerous glacial lakes, assessing the parameters that are vital, and prioritizing risk factors to enhance preparedness and reaction measures.

This is expanded regarding the factors leading to changes in the size of glacial lakes, trends and sequences of glacier shrinkage, and phases of glaciations and climatic-feedback effects that shape the interaction. It also reviews other contemporary research for potential moderator factors, such as the melting of icebergs in the Himalayas, which have a cooling impact at such heights. Thus, the paper offers an appreciation and approach to the multiple challenges associated with GLOFs in the Himalayas, giving the paper a sound research background. The work can be discussed as informative regarding the glacial processes and their impact on the communities and ecosystems downstream as the author synthesises the scientific methods with field data and satellite data analysis.

One of the major strengths of the study is its use of considerations from various fields such as risk assessment methods, RS and glaciology. The study provides holistic findings on the susceptibility and various vulnerability factors of GLOF through the successful integration of multiple data sets and various analytical tools. Moreover, the promotion of risk management and adaptation techniques based on the involvement of the communities and other stakeholders proves the importance of participatory techniques. The LTMs point to an increased necessity for synergistic intercession by local communities, research institutes, and governmental organizations to develop GLOF prevention and capability enhancement activities. In summary, the study offers insightful information on how glaciology and climate change adaptation are developing, which has significance for both scientific inquiry and the creation of public policy. The study improves our knowledge of GLOF dynamics and risk factors, which paves the way for preventative steps and well-informed decision-making to strengthen vulnerable populations' resilience to the effects of climate change.

Acknowledgment

The authors would like to thank the Google for providing Google Earth Engine (GEE) platform for data processing. We would like to express our deepest gratitude to Wiley Publications for their unwavering support and for providing us with the opportunity to contribute to this remarkable project. The insightful feedback and guidance from the editorial team have been invaluable in shaping this chapter. Our special thanks to the editors, Sartajvir Singh and Apoorva Sharma, for their meticulous attention to detail, constructive criticism, and encouragement throughout the writing process. Their dedication and expertise have greatly enhanced the quality of this work.

Finally, we would like to acknowledge the invaluable contributions of our colleagues, friends, and family, whose unwavering support and understanding have been a constant source of strength. Thank you all for your support and belief in this work.

References

1. Richardson, S.D. and Reynolds, J.M., An overview of glacial hazards in the Himalayas. *Quat. Int.*, 65–66, 31–47, Apr. 2000, doi: 10.1016/S1040-6182(99)00035-X.
2. Mertes, J.R., Thompson, S.S., Booth, A.D., Gulley, J.D., Benn, D.I., A conceptual model of supra-glacial lake formation on debris-covered glaciers based on GPR facies analysis. *Earth Surf. Process. Landf.*, 42, 6, 903–914, May 2017, doi: 10.1002/esp.4068.
3. Nie, Y., *et al.*, A regional-scale assessment of Himalayan glacial lake changes using satellite observations from 1990 to 2015. *Remote Sens. Environ.*, 189, 1–13, Feb. 2017, doi: 10.1016/j.rse.2016.11.008.
4. Bolch, T., Peters, J., Yegorov, A., Pradhan, B., Buchroithner, M., Blagoveshchensky, V., Identification of potentially dangerous glacial lakes in the northern Tien Shan. *Nat. Hazards*, 59, 3, 1691–1714, Dec. 2011, doi: 10.1007/s11069-011-9860-2.
5. Harrison, S., *et al.*, Climate change and the global pattern of moraine-dammed glacial lake outburst floods. *Cryosphere*, 12, 4, 1195–1209, Apr. 2018, doi: 10.5194/tc-12-1195-2018.

6. Carrivick, J.L. and Tweed, F.S., A global assessment of the societal impacts of glacier outburst floods. *Glob. Planet. Change*, 144, 1–16, Sep. 2016, doi: 10.1016/j.gloplacha.2016.07.001.
7. Allen, S.K., Zhang, G., Wang, W., Yao, T., Bolch, T., Potentially dangerous glacial lakes across the Tibetan Plateau revealed using a large-scale automated assessment approach. *Sci. Bull.*, 64, 7, 435–445, Apr. 2019, doi: 10.1016/j.scib.2019.03.011.
8. Zheng, G., *et al.*, Sustained growth of high mountain lakes in the headwaters of the Syr Darya River, Central Asia. *Glob. Planet. Change*, 176, 84–99, May 2019, doi: 10.1016/j.gloplacha.2019.03.004.
9. Emmer, A., *et al.*, Progress and challenges in glacial lake outburst flood research (2017–2021): a research community perspective. *Nat. Hazards Earth Syst. Sci.*, 22, 9, 3041–3061, Sep. 2022, doi: 10.5194/nhess-22-3041-2022.
10. Sahu, R. and Gupta, R.D., Glacier mapping and change analysis in Chandra basin, Western Himalaya, India during 1971–2016. *Int. J. Remote Sens.*, 41, 18, 6914–6945, Sep. 2020, doi: 10.1080/01431161.2020.1752412.
11. Rounce, D.R., McKinney, D.C., Lala, J.M., Byers, A.C., Watson, C.S., A new remote hazard and risk assessment framework for glacial lakes in the Nepal Himalaya. *Hydrol. Earth Syst. Sci.*, 20, 9, 3455–3475, Aug. 2016, doi: 10.5194/hess-20-3455-2016.
12. Salerno, F., *et al.*, Weak precipitation, warm winters and springs impact glaciers of south slopes of Mt. Everest (central Himalaya) in the last 2 decades (1994–2013). *Cryosphere*, 9, 3, 1229–1247, Jun. 2015, doi: 10.5194/tc-9-1229-2015.
13. Sood, V., Tiwari, R.K., Singh, S., Kaur, R., Parida, B.R., Glacier Boundary Mapping Using Deep Learning Classification over Bara Shigri Glacier in Western Himalayas. *Sustainability*, 14, 20, 13485, Oct. 2022, doi: 10.3390/su142013485.
14. Sood, V., Gusain, H.S., Gupta, S., Taloor, A.K., Singh, S., Detection of snow/ice cover changes using subpixel-based change detection approach over Chhota-Shigri glacier, Western Himalaya, India. *Quat. Int.*, 575, 204–212, May 2020, doi: 10.1016/j.quaint.2020.05.016.
15. Atasever, U.H., Gunen, M.A., Besdok, E., A New Unsupervised Change Detection Approach Based on PCA Based Blocking and GMM Clustering for Detecting Flood Damage. *Fresenius Environ. Bull.*, 27, September, 1688–1694, 2018.
16. Sood, V., Gupta, S., Gusain, H.S., Singh, S., Taloor, A.K., Topographic controls on subpixel change detection in Western Himalayas. *Remote Sens. Appl. Soc. Environ.*, 21, 100465, January, 2021, doi: 10.1016/j.rsase.2021.100465.
17. Glen, J.W., Paterson 1994. The physics of glaciers. 3rd edition. Oxford, etc., Pergamon, 480 pp. ISBN 0-08037945 1. Hardback. £70; 0-O8O37944 3, Flexieover. £25. *J. Glaciol.*, 43, 145, 594–594, Jan. 1997, doi: 10.3189/S002214300003522X.

18. Dobhal, D.P. and Kumar, S., Inventory of glacier basins in Himachal Himalaya. *J. Geol. Soc. India.*, 48, 6, 671–681, 1996.
19. Kulkarni, A.V., Dhar, S., Rathore, B.P., Raj K., B.G., Kalia, R., Recession of samudra tapu glacier, chandra river basin, Himachal Pradesh. *J. Indian Soc. Remote Sens.*, 34, 1, 39–46, Mar. 2006, doi: 10.1007/BF02990745.
20. Rafiq, M., Romshoo, S.A., Mishra, A.K., Jalal, F., Modelling Chorabari Lake outburst flood, Kedarnath, India. *J. Mt. Sci.*, 16, 1, 64–76, Jan. 2019, doi: 10.1007/s11629-018-4972-8.
21. Lamsal, D., Sawagaki, T., Watanabe, T., Byers, A.C., Assessment of glacial lake development and prospects of outburst susceptibility: Chamlang South Glacier, eastern Nepal Himalaya. *Geomat. Nat. Hazards Risk*, 7, 1, 403–423, Jan. 2016, doi: 10.1080/19475705.2014.931306.
22. Stokes, C.R., Sanderson, J.E., Miles, B.W.J., Jamieson, S.S.R., Leeson, A.A., Widespread distribution of supraglacial lakes around the margin of the East Antarctic Ice Sheet. *Sci. Rep.*, 9, 1, 13823, Sep. 2019, doi: 10.1038/s41598-019-50343-5.
23. Lüthje, M., Pedersen, L.T., Reeh, N., Greuell, W., Modelling the evolution of supraglacial lakes on the West Greenland ice-sheet margin. *J. Glaciol.*, 52, 179, 608–618, Sep. 2006, doi: 10.3189/172756506781828386.
24. Wendleder, A., Schmitt, A., Erbertseder, T., D'Angelo, P., Mayer, C., Braun, M.H., Seasonal Evolution of Supraglacial Lakes on Baltoro Glacier From 2016 to 2020. *Front. Earth Sci.*, 9, 725394, Dec. 2021, doi: 10.3389/feart.2021.725394.
25. Sood, S., Thakur, P.K., Stein, A., Garg, V., Dixit, A., Mapping Samudra Tapu glacier: A holistic approach utilizing radar and optical remote sensing data for glacier radar facies mapping and velocity estimation. *Adv. Space Res.*, 70, 12, 3975–3999, Dec. 2022, doi: 10.1016/j.asr.2022.10.030.
26. Patel, L.K., Sharma, P., Laluraj, C.M., Thamban, M., Singh, A., Ravindra, R., A geospatial analysis of Samudra Tapu and Gepang Gath glacial lakes in the Chandra Basin, Western Himalaya. *Nat. Hazards*, 86, 3, 1275–1290, Apr. 2017, doi: 10.1007/s11069-017-2743-4.
27. Ahmed, R., *et al.*, Glacial lake changes and the identification of potentially dangerous glacial lakes (PDGLs) under warming climate in the Dibang River Basin, Eastern Himalaya, India. *Geocarto Int.*, 37, 27, 17659–17685, Dec. 2022, doi: 10.1080/10106049.2022.2134461.
28. Rinzin, S., *et al.*, GLOF hazard, exposure, vulnerability, and risk assessment of potentially dangerous glacial lakes in the Bhutan Himalaya. *J. Hydrol.*, 619, 129311, Apr. 2023, doi: 10.1016/j.jhydrol.2023.129311.
29. Mukherjee, K., Bhattacharya, A., Pieczonka, T., Ghosh, S., Bolch, T., Glacier mass budget and climate reanalysis data indicate a climatic shift around 2000 in Lahaul-Spiti, western Himalaya. *Clim. Change*, 148, 1–2, 219–233, May 2018, doi: 10.1007/s10584-018-2185-3.
30. Garrard, R., Kohler, T., Price, M.F., Byers, A.C., Sherpa, A.R., Maharjan, G.R., Land Use and Land Cover Change in Sagarmatha National Park,

a World Heritage Site in the Himalayas of Eastern Nepal. *Mt. Res. Dev.*, 36, 3, 299, Aug. 2016, doi: 10.1659/MRD-JOURNAL-D-15-00005.1.

31. Prakash, C. and Nagarajan, R., Outburst susceptibility assessment of moraine-dammed lakes in Western Himalaya using an analytic hierarchy process. *Earth Surf. Processes Landforms*, 42, 14, 2306–2321, Nov. 2017, doi: 10.1002/esp.4185.
32. Worni, R., Huggel, C., Stoffel, M., Glacial lakes in the Indian Himalayas — From an area-wide glacial lake inventory to on-site and modeling based risk assessment of critical glacial lakes. *Sci. Total Environ.*, 468–469, S71–S84, Dec. 2013, doi: 10.1016/j.scitotenv.2012.11.043.
33. Sood, V. and Singh, S., Analytical analysis of shadow removing algorithms over land use and land cover classification. *Himalayan Geol.*, 39, 2, 223–232, 2018.
34. Singh, S., Tiwari, R.K., Sood, V., Prashar, S., Fusion of SCATSAT-1 and optical data for cloud-free imaging and its applications in classification. *Arab. J. Geosci.*, 14, 19, 1978, 2021, doi: 10.1007/s12517-021-08359-7.
35. Singh, S., Tiwari, R.K., Sood, V., Estimation and Validation of Enhanced Resolution Brightness Temperature Products of SCATSAT-1, in: *2020 IEEE 5th International Conference on Computing Communication and Automation, ICCCA 2020*, pp. 758–762, 2020, doi: 10.1109/ICCCA49541.2020.9250718.
36. Singh, S., Tiwari, R.K., Sood, V., Gusain, H.S., Prashar, S., Image Fusion of Ku-Band-Based SCATSAT-1 and MODIS Data for Cloud-Free Change Detection over Western Himalayas. *IEEE Trans. Geosci. Remote Sens.*, 60, 1–14, 2022, doi: 10.1109/TGRS.2021.3123392.
37. Nie, Y., Liu, Q., Liu, S., Glacial Lake Expansion in the Central Himalayas by Landsat Images, 1990–2010. *PLoS One*, 8, 12, e83973, Dec. 2013, doi: 10.1371/journal.pone.0083973.
38. Khadka, N., Chen, X., Nie, Y., Thakuri, S., Zheng, G., Zhang, G., Evaluation of Glacial Lake Outburst Flood Susceptibility Using Multi-Criteria Assessment Framework in Mahalangur Himalaya. *Front. Earth Sci.*, 8, 601288, Jan. 2021, doi: 10.3389/feart.2020.601288.
39. Shijin, W., Dahe, Q., Cunde, X., Moraine-dammed lake distribution and outburst flood risk in the Chinese Himalaya. *J. Glaciol.*, 61, 225, 115–126, Jul. 2015, doi: 10.3189/2015JoG14J097.
40. Saltelli, A., Tarantola, S., Chan, K., A role for sensitivity analysis in presenting the results from MCDA studies to decision makers. *J. Multi-Crit. Decis. Anal.*, 8, 3, 139–145, May 1999, doi: 10.1002/(SICI)1099-1360(199905)8:3<139::AID-MCDA239>3.0.CO;2-C.

16

Challenges of GLOF Estimation and Prediction

Neelam Dahiya[1]*, Sartajvir Singh[2] and Puninder Kaur[1]

[1]*Chitkara University Institute of Engineering and Technology, Chitkara University, Punjab, India*
[2]*University Institute of Engineering, Chandigarh University, Punjab, India*

Abstract
Glacial lake outburst floods (GLOFs) stand as one of the most worrisome outcomes of melting glaciers in various mountain ranges globally. Over the last few decades, GLOFs have accumulated considerable focus from researchers, especially in understanding the physical forces and processes behind GLOF risks as well as the social, economic, and other aspects of human activity that influence the susceptibility to GLOF occurrences. The frequency of flash floods has grown significantly because of rapid human activity and climate change. Flash floods are caused by weak moraine dams collapsing, releasing massive amounts of water downstream quickly. To save lives and property, an early warning system must be set up to monitor the glacial lakes that are at risk and to provide disaster managers with the powerful tools that they need to prepare mitigation. Forecast lead time, reliable and steady water flow computation, automated data intake and output with little human intervention, user-friendly interface, and clear data visualization for efficient decision-making are critical factors to consider. The main objective of the present work is to review the various reasons and challenges associated with GLOF estimation and prediction. It will assist novices and researchers grasp the future problems of GLOF.

***Keywords*:** Flood, glaciers, glacial lake outburst floods (GLOF), remote sensing

**Corresponding author*: neelam.rani@chitkara.edu.in; ORCID: 0000-0003-1839-9040
Sartajvir Singh: ORCID: 0000-0002-4451-4949
Puninder Kaur: ORCID: 0000-0003-3959-593X

Neelam Dahiya, Gurwinder Singh, Sartajvir Singh and Apoorva Sharma (eds.) Artificial Intelligence in Remote Sensing for Disaster Management, (289–302) © 2025 Scrivener Publishing LLC

16.1 Introduction

The rapid and catastrophic release of water and sediment from a glacial lake known as a glacial lake outburst flood (GLOF) usually takes place in the shadow of moraine dams in high-altitude mountain regions such as the Himalayas. The main reason behind the occurrence of these events is the moraine dams collapse which are the organic rocks and dirt mounds generated by glacier debris [1]. These dams collapse due to numerous factors including landslides, avalanches, and earthquakes. It presents a significant natural danger since the abrupt release of water from the glacial lake might result in catastrophic floods that could kill many people and inflict significant damage in the villages downstream. It combines moraine dam failures with the distinct and dangerous characteristics of glacial lake outflows. It has been a major worry in the last few decades due to human population growth, human-caused incidents, and haphazard infrastructure expansion in the formerly uninhabited but vulnerable high alpine terrain [2]. There are over 200 potentially dangerous lakes in the Himalayan region, and within the past 40 years, there have been 40 GLOFs. In the past years, GLOFs have been causing problems in the Himalayas and extensively affecting the surroundings. Due to this, the shedding and expansion of glacier mass are increasing at a higher rate. It requires rapid action to resolve the issue due to their ability to cause catastrophic destruction [3].

Numerous lakes created by glaciers and surrounded by stray debris deposits pose a serious threat to people living in high-altitude regions of the world. Lakes formed by glaciers and those surrounded by debris are the primary sources of GLOFs in the Himalayan area. Because of several factors that might lead to their collapse and the events that trigger them, lakes surrounded by debris are more prone to experience these floods. Some studies estimate that future deglaciation will increase GLOF hazard and downstream risk in the Himalayas by a factor of three to seven [4]. Since the 1970s, the upward trend in GLOF frequency has slowed. As of 2015, forecasts indicated that High Mountain Asia (HMA) might lose between 29% and 67% of its ice mass by 2100. The Himalayas are among the locations most vulnerable to this loss. Researchers have discovered over 5,000 prospective glacier lake locations in the Himalayas; these sites may be disclosed after future glacial retreats.

The study of glacial lakes that would otherwise be inaccessible has become easier because of advancements in remote. The most practical method for monitoring glacial lakes in areas where they are difficult to access is remote sensing. Research conducted in collaboration with the Government of Sikkim by the Centre for Development of Advanced Computing (C-DAC), Pune, has demonstrated an increase in the number of glacier lakes in the Sikkim Himalayan area throughout time. More than 250 lakes in Sikkim are affected by moraine, of which about 30 are deemed susceptible [5].

Events like those that happened at Ayaco Lake in 1969 and 1970, Nare Lake in 1977, Sabai Tsho in 1998, and Chorabari in 2013 are examples of catastrophic GLOF events that have greatly harmed lives and the socio-economic conditions of the locals [6]. These events can be prevented by documenting critical glacial lakes and implementing corrective measures. This work focuses on the overview of GLOF, the reasons for its occurrence, and numerous challenges faced due to GLOF, followed by a conclusion.

16.2 Types of GLOF

Several forms of glacial lake outburst floods. GLOFs are classified according to the sort of triggering mechanism or the lake's location. Following are some of the most popular types.

16.2.1 Glacial Lakes

Glacial lakes are bodies of water that occur when glaciers or ice caps melt. Glacial lakes are frequently found in distant and inaccessible locations, such as mountain ranges and polar regions. They range in size from tiny ponds to enormous lakes that cover several kilometers. They can form behind natural dams composed of ice, rock, moraine, etc. [7].

Glacial lakes may be extremely unstable, releasing massive amounts of water abruptly and unexpectedly, resulting in catastrophic floods. Glacial lakes' water can be extremely turbid (cloudy) due to silt and rock flour brought by glaciers and rivers. Glacial lakes can support various plant and animal populations that have evolved to the cold, nutrient-poor waters [8]. Climate change is causing glacial lakes to grow and evaporate at an increasing rate, potentially affecting water supplies and the stability of mountain ecosystems.

16.2.2 Moraine-Dammed Lake

Moraine-dammed lakes are bodies of water generated from the build-up of glacier debris known as moraines. These natural dams may be found in hilly areas all over the world and represent a huge risk if they fall. Moraine-dammed lakes arise as glaciers melt, forming natural dams of deposited debris. These lakes range in size and may be found in a variety of habitats, with water sources including rain and glacier meltwater [4]. However, they can be dangerous if the dam breaks, resulting in floods and damage downstream. Regular inspections and management are required to avoid calamities. Moraine-dammed lakes may also be ecologically significant, serving as homes for aquatic animals and plants as well as vital water sources for nearby populations.

16.2.3 Ice-Dammed Lakes

Ice-dammed lakes originate behind natural ice dams, which are often found in glacial basins and depressions or permafrost zones. Dams can be constructed by a variety of mechanisms, such as snow and ice melting, debris accumulation, or water freezing [3]. Ice-dammed lakes may be extremely unstable, releasing massive amounts of water abruptly and unexpectedly, resulting in catastrophic floods known as GLOFs. GLOFs created by ice-dammed lakes are frequently the most damaging, resulting in major damage and loss of life in the past. Climate change is forcing glaciers and permafrost to melt at an accelerating rate, perhaps resulting in more frequent and severe GLOFs caused by ice-dammed lakes [2].

16.3 Reasons for GLOF Occurrence

There are various reasons behind the occurrence of GLOF. A few of them are mentioned below as shown in Figure 16.1.

16.3.1 Glacial Retreat

Glacial retreat is the process by which a glacier gradually loses mass due to more ice melting or less ice building up on it. Most cases of fast glacier retreat are undoubtedly caused by human activity causing climate change on a worldwide scale. Depending on the area, melt, ablation, evaporation, wind scouring, and calving are some of the causes of glacier retreat. A normal and seasonal aspect of glacier life is ablation [9]. Lakes may be created as glaciers melt, and when these lakes fill up quickly, their natural dams may break. In some areas, the danger of GLOFs is increased as glaciers retreat because they might grow or form new glacial lakes. Therefore, there is a connection between glacier retreat and glacial lake outburst floods.

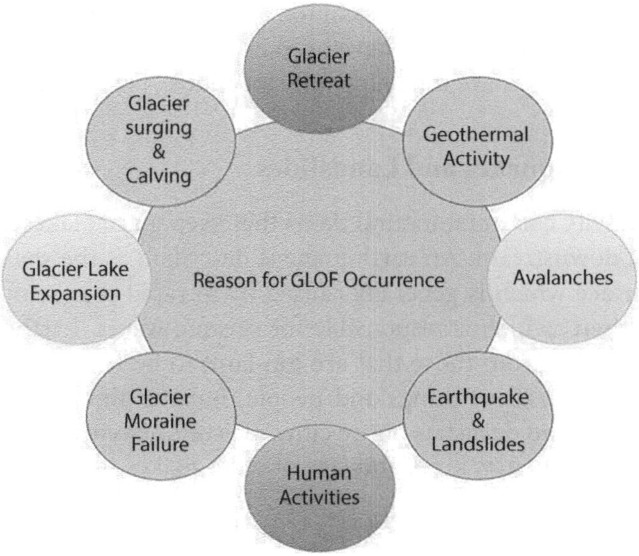

Figure 16.1 Reasons for GLOF occurrence.

16.3.2 Geothermal Activity

Glaciers can melt quickly due to volcanic or geothermal activity, creating glacial lakes that have the potential to breach their natural dams. Volcanic gasses and vapors escape to the environment through openings in the earth known as fumaroles, often called volcanic vents. An active magma chamber, which continuously discharges hot gasses that rise to the surface through rock holes, is frequently above geothermally active locations [10]. Direct geothermal heating is currently advantageous for a wide range of businesses, including greenhouse operations, aquaculture farming, food processing, and timber drying. The alligators in the next image are raised in Idaho's geothermally heated water. District heating is also provided via hydrothermal systems.

16.3.3 Avalanches

Avalanches can build a natural dam, which can be demolished by the pressure of the water that accumulates behind it. An avalanche is the fast downslope movement of a huge detached mass of snow, ice, and related debris like boulders and plants. Small avalanches, or sluffs, occur in enormous numbers, but big avalanches, which may cover slopes a kilometer or more in length and carry millions of tons of snow, seldom occur but cause most of the damage. Humans have been exposed to the possibility of falling snow since they have inhabited hilly locations [11].

16.3.4 Earthquakes and Landslides

Seismic activity can burst natural dams that keep glacial lakes back, causing floods downstream. An earthquake is described as the shaking of the Earth's surface which is generally caused by to rapid release of energy in the lithosphere, which is responsible for seismic waves. Earthquakes can vary in strength, from those that are too faint to be felt to those that are severe enough to drive things and people into the air, damage essential infrastructure, and devastate entire cities. Seismic activity in each location refers to the frequency, kind, and size of earthquakes that occur throughout time [1].

Landslides can also form natural dams that can be broken by water build-up or seismic activity. It occurs when a rock pile or any dirt slides down a hill. They are known as a sort of "mass wasting" which is further defined as any form of down-slope movement of soil and rock which is caused by gravity. The movement of the slope is classified as falls, topples, slides, spreads, and flows which are further classified based on geologic material (bedrock, detritus, or earth). Each landslide has a different reason for occurrence [12].

16.3.5 Human Activities

Human activities such as mining, construction, and other types of development in mountainous locations can destabilize slopes and increase the chance of landslides and avalanches, resulting in GLOFs. Various types of human activities like land-use change, vehicle traffic on roads, and extraction of resources, led to the relocation and extinction of plants and animals across the world [13]. Human activity also poses a great impact on plant and animal populations on a global scale, and any attempt done for the management of the recreation area reduces these consequences. Specifically, by examining human activity patterns and their influence on animal populations, parks and recreation areas may be managed to provide spatial and temporal refuge to wildlife that is most sensitive to human disturbance.

16.3.6 Glacial Moraine Failure

Glaciers frequently deposit rock and silt, known as moraines, along their margins. These moraines can act as natural dams, preventing glacial lakes from flowing downstream. GLOFs can occur because of moraine failure caused by erosion, overtopping, or other factors. Moraine dams, which impound glacial lakes, are among the most vulnerable natural dams because of their slope, freeboard, and construction [14]. Glacial lake outburst floods generated by moraine dam collapses pose significant threats to the valley downstream since they carry large amounts of hydraulic energy that can kill thousands and devastate infrastructure and riverine landscape. Furthermore, the entrainment of debris into the flow from the breaching procedure and downstream channel has the potential to turn the flow into a much larger tragedy or possibly a chain of hazards. The breaching phenomena are triggered by ice and rock avalanches or landslides, glacier calving, ice core deterioration, earthquakes, and atmospheric events, resulting in a succession of waves overtopping the dam or seepage, triggering dam failure [15].

16.3.7 Glacier Lake Expansion

Glacier lakes may enlarge owing to increasing meltwater flow, rainfall, or snowmelt. The consequent rise in water pressure may cause the natural dam to burst. Glacial lakes originate in glacial depressions or moraines left by retreating glaciers. They form as glaciers cut out the ground via erosion and subsequently melt, filling the depressions left by their passage. Glacial lakes are grouped into four varieties based on how they form: moraine-dammed, ice-dammed, erosion, and other glacial lakes [16]. When glaciers retreat, they leave moraines, which function as natural dams, trapping meltwater and forming lakes. Glacial lakes range in size, depending on glacier size and activity, and are often found in hilly and polar environments, with glacier lakes getting their water mostly from melting glacier ice, precipitation, and runoff.

16.3.8 Glacier Surging and Calving

A surge is a rapid increase of a glacier's movement that forms new glacial lakes or expands old ones. The ensuing pressure may force the dam to break, resulting in GLOFs. In past literature, glaciers suddenly change to ice flow speeds up to higher levels and their count reaches hundreds of meters each day. The rapid speed completely transforms the terrain into a deeply crevassed pandemonium. In reaction to changing climate, most glaciers move and recede in a predictable and unremarkable way. Glaciers have been seen to behave substantially differently in certain locations, but not all [12]. After a period of normal flow, or quiescence, ranging from ten to one hundred years, such glaciers may abruptly begin to flow at speeds of up to 5 m per hour. This fast movement, which lasts only a year or two, produces a quick depletion of the upper portion of the glacier, followed by swelling and advancement of the bottom half, albeit they normally do not extend beyond the boundaries of earlier surges. In just a few months, numerous miles have been gained. Even more intriguing is the fact.

Glacier calving is defined as the process of removal of ice chunks from a glacier's front. These ice chunks can drop into a glacial lake that creates waves and can erode the natural barrier. Iceberg calving also known as glacier calving is a vast component of mass loss from polar ice sheets and glaciers in various places of the world. Calving rates can skyrocket in reaction to increases in velocity and/or glacier edge retreat, with far-reaching consequences for sea level rise [16].

16.4 Challenges Faced for GLOF Estimation

It is very difficult to assess the early signs of GLOF, but due to advanced techniques, it is possible to detect GLOF. Some of the challenges that are faced for GLOF estimation are mentioned below and shown in Figure 16.2.

16.4.1 Early Detection

Due to the variability of natural causes, it is impossible to anticipate when and where a GLOF may occur. GLOFs can be caused by a variety of reasons, including heavy rain, fast snowmelt, earthquakes, and avalanches [17]. Predicting when these triggers will occur is difficult. Many glacial lakes are in distant and inaccessible areas, making installation and maintenance of monitoring equipment difficult and costly. Limited historical data on previous GLOF incidents impedes the development of forecasting models. The distinct qualities of each lake and its surroundings add to the intricacy.

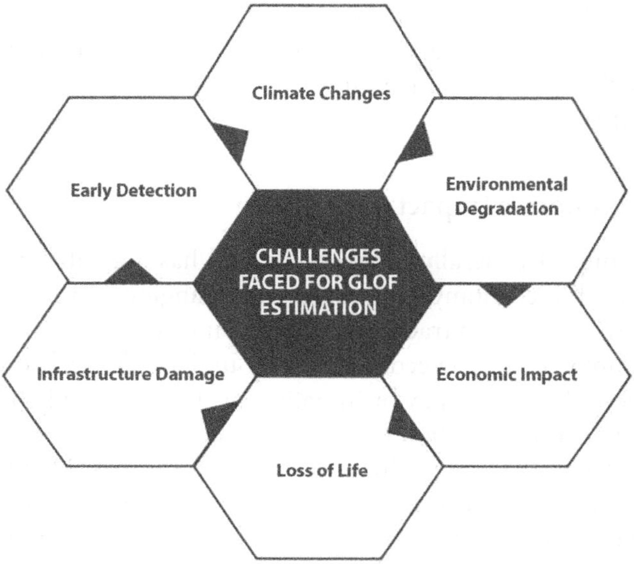

Figure 16.2 Challenges faced for GLOF estimation.

16.4.2 Infrastructure Damage

Infrastructure damage refers to the injury or destruction of critical public services and infrastructure such as highways, bridges, water supplies, electricity grids, and communication networks [18]. This damage can result from natural catastrophes like earthquakes, hurricanes, floods, and wildfires, as well as human activity like construction accidents, terrorism, and conflict. Infrastructure repair and restoration is generally costly, putting financial strain on budgets. Damaged infrastructure poses serious safety threats to communities. Balancing rebuilding with environmentally friendly measures is a major problem.

16.4.3 Loss of Life

The sudden and unpredictable nature of GLOFs can lead to high fatality rates. GLOFs are very dangerous and can even lead to death and substantial loss of life. Since 1990, there has been a rapid increase in the number and size of glacial lakes throughout the world. Nonetheless, there has been no quantification of current worldwide exposure and sensitivity to GLOFs.

Here we illustrate that 15 million individuals worldwide are at risk from probable GLOFs. The population around the area of High Mountains Asia (HMA) is closest to these lakes and susceptible to a higher risk as compared to other areas [19].

16.4.4 Economic Impact

Economic impact generally hampers life and has a greater influence on the event on the economy in specific areas, ranging from local areas to the whole world. It often tracks the changes in income from business, salaries, or employment. The economic event under consideration might be the adoption of a new policy or initiative, or it could simply be the presence of a firm or organization [20]. An economic impact study is typically performed when there is public concern about the possible implications of a proposed project or legislation. A GLOF can significantly harm agriculture, livelihoods, and tourism in afflicted areas. The economic effects of global issues such as climate change are varied and significant [3]. Climate change affects a variety of industries, including agriculture, health, infrastructure, and insurance. Numerous weather catastrophes like floods and droughts can lead to the destruction of crops and can also disturb the food supply system, which results in economic losses for the farmers [21].

16.4.5 Environmental Degradation

It is also becoming a vital issue that can impact the whole world. The reasons behind its occurrence include human activities, natural disasters, etc. Most of these issues can affect humanity and can also lead to negative feedback. Fortunately, a solution to these issues exists, which can be reduced by a joint effort of all to lessen the harmful impact [22]. There are numerous reasons for environmental degradation, but poverty is a key cause. People under the poverty line rapidly endure hunger, which contributes to the degradation of natural resources for their food safety. These people are not financially sound and not even educated properly to safeguard the natural resources which is a blessing for the future. They have destructive behavior and are routinely in the process of cutting trees in large amounts to satisfy hunger. Moreover, the burning of wood for fuel or the dumping of rubbish in rivers, etc., deteriorates the environment and can also lead to several diseases [23].

16.4.6 Climate Changes

Climate change or the dynamic nature of weather also plays a challenging factor responsible for the GLOF prediction. Glaciers and snow cover are anticipated to shrink, limiting water supply in regions reliant on meltwater. Glaciers in the Himalayas are melting faster than in any other portion of the planet, and, if the current rate continues, there is likelihood of their disappearance by the year 2035. GLOF dangers can be caused by both internal and external influences [24].

16.5 GLOF Solution

GLOF has become a major problem for humanity. There are some solutions to prevent this, which are mentioned below:

a) Early warning systems with sensors to monitor water levels and potential breaches as well as controlled drainage systems to maintain lake water levels [25].
b) Reinforcing natural dams using materials such as concrete can avoid abrupt collapses. Remote sensing and satellite photos give useful data for anticipating possible GLOFs, which can help in early intervention methods [26].
c) Community engagement is critical; therefore, residents should be taught about emergency response and evacuation methods [27].
d) Implementing flood-risk-informed land-use planning and construction rules can help to reduce infrastructure damage. International collaboration and finance are also essential, especially for underdeveloped nations that may lack the resources [28].

16.6 Conclusion

Glacial lake outburst floods (GLOFs) stand as one of the most worrisome outcomes of melting glaciers in various mountain ranges globally. Rapid human activity and climate change have increased the frequency of flash floods. Flash floods are created by weak moraine dams that collapse, unleashing enormous quantities of water downstream quickly. To preserve lives and property, an early warning system must be established to monitor the at-risk glacial lakes and equip disaster managers with the strong tools they require to build mitigation plans. The primary goal of this paper is to examine the many reasons and issues related to GLOF estimates and prediction. In this review paper, the reasons for GLOF occurrence have been explored. We have also summarized the GLOF types, challenges, and solutions to prevent its occurrence. This research provides a thorough examination of the methods for forecasting glacial lake outburst floods (GLOFs). It has been concluded that approaches like artificial intelligence and remote sensing played an important role in its detection. It will assist novices, and researchers will grasp the future problems of GLOF.

References

1. Jha, L.K. and Khare, D., Glacial lake outburst flood (GLOF) study of Dhauliganga basin in the Himalaya. *Cogent Environ. Sci.*, 2, 1, 1249107, 2016.
2. Zheng, G., *et al.*, Sustained growth of high mountain lakes in the headwaters of the Syr Darya River, Central Asia. *Glob. Planet. Change*, 176, 84–99, 2019.
3. Zhang, T., Wang, W., Gao, T., An, B., Yao, T., An integrative method for identifying potentially dangerous glacial lakes in the Himalayas. *Sci. Total Environ.*, 806, 150442, 2022.
4. Yu, B., He, Y., Ye, P., Quantitative susceptibility assessment of the breach of moraine-dammed lakes due to glacier avalanches. *Cold Reg. Sci. Technol.*, 206, 103749, 2023.
5. Wood, J.L., *et al.*, Shaking up assumptions: earthquakes have rarely triggered Andean Glacier Lake outburst floods. *Geophys. Res. Lett.*, 51, 7, e2023GL105578, 2024.
6. Taylor, C.J., Robinson, T.R., Dunning, S., Carr, J.R., The rise of GLOF danger: trends, drivers and hotspots between 2000 and 2020, Authorea Preprints, 2023.
7. Rinzin, S., *et al.*, GLOF hazard, exposure, vulnerability, and risk assessment of potentially dangerous glacial lakes in the Bhutan Himalaya. *J. Hydrol. (Amst.)*, 619, 129311, 2023.
8. Sood, S., Thakur, P.K., Stein, A., Garg, V., Dixit, A., Mapping Samudra Tapu glacier: A holistic approach utilizing radar and optical remote sensing data for glacier radar facies mapping and velocity estimation. *Adv. Space Res.*, 70, 12, 3975–3999, 2022.
9. Shrestha, F., Joshi, S.P., Steiner, J.F., Sharma, R., Kayastha, R., Current State of Research on and Response to Geomorphological Hazards in Nepal, in: *The Nature of Geomorphological Hazards in the Nepal Himalaya*, pp. 375–389, Springer, Springer International Publishing, 2024.

10. Lamsal, D., Sawagaki, T., Watanabe, T., Byers, A.C., Assessment of glacial lake development and prospects of outburst susceptibility: Chamlang South Glacier, eastern Nepal Himalaya. *Geomatics Nat. Hazards Risk*, 7, 1, 403–423, 2016.
11. Kulkarni, A.V., Dhar, S., Rathore, B.P., Raj K, B.G., Kalia, R., Recession of samudra tapu glacier, chandra river basin, Himachal Pradesh. *J. Indian Soc. Remote Sens.*, 34, 39–46, 2006.
12. Gurung, D.R., *et al.*, Lemthang Tsho glacial Lake outburst flood (GLOF) in Bhutan: cause and impact. *Geoenviron. Disasters*, 4, 1–13, 2017.
13. Halder, S. and Bose, S., Sustainable flood hazard mapping with GLOF: A Google Earth Engine approach. *Nat. Hazard. Res.*, 4, 573–578, 2024.
14. Garg, M., Gupta, S., Kaur, G., Koundal, D., Enhancement of retinal fundus image using multi-scale tophat transformation. *Int. J. Biom.*, 15, 3–4, 435–447, 2023.
15. Garrard, R., Kohler, T., Price, M.F., Byers, A.C., Sherpa, A.R., Maharjan, G.R., Land use and land cover change in Sagarmatha National Park, a world heritage site in the Himalayas of Eastern Nepal. *Mt. Res. Dev.*, 36, 3, 299–310, 2016.
16. Emmer, A., Vanishing evidence? On the longevity of geomorphic GLOF diagnostic features in the Tropical Andes. *Geomorphology*, 422, 108552, 2023.
17. Colavitto, B., *et al.*, A glacial lake outburst floods hazard assessment in the Patagonian Andes combining inventory data and case studies. *Sci. Total Environ.*, 916, 169703, 2024.
18. Byers, A.C., Chand, M.B., Lala, J., Shrestha, M., Byers, E.A., Watanabe, T., Reconstructing the history of glacial lake outburst floods (GLOF) in the Kanchenjunga conservation area, East Nepal: An interdisciplinary approach. *Sustainability*, 12, 13, 5407, 2020.
19. Bolch, T., Peters, J., Yegorov, A., Pradhan, B., Buchroithner, M., Blagoveshchensky, V., Identification of potentially dangerous glacial lakes in the northern Tien Shan. *Nat. Hazard.*, 59, 1691–1714, 2011.
20. Bali, N., Singla, A., Chaudhary, D., Nagpal, P., Soil quality assessment and prediction using various AI techniques: A review. *AIP Conf. Proc.*, 2961, 1, 020012 -1–020012-7, 2023.
21. Allen, S.K., Zhang, G., Wang, W., Yao, T., Bolch, T., Potentially dangerous glacial lakes across the Tibetan Plateau revealed using a large-scale automated assessment approach. *Sci. Bull. (Beijing)*, 64, 7, 435–445, 2019.
22. Ahmed, R., *et al.*, Glacial lake changes and the identification of potentially dangerous glacial lakes (PDGLs) under warming climate in the Dibang River Basin, Eastern Himalaya, India. *Geocarto Int.*, 37, 27, 17659–17685, 2022.
23. Mochizuki, J. and Naqvi, A., Reflecting disaster risk in development indicators. *Sustainability (Switzerland)*, 11, 4, 996, Feb. 2019, doi: 10.3390/su11040996.

24. Cerulli, D., *et al.*, The role of education in increasing awareness and reducing the impact of natural hazards. *Sustainability (Switzerland)*, 12, 18, 7623, Sep. 2020, doi: 10.3390/su12187623.
25. Jia, H., Chen, F., Du, E., Adaptation to disaster risk—An overview. *MDPI*, 18, 21, 11187, Nov. 01, 2021. MDPI. doi: 10.3390/ijerph182111187.
26. van Zelst, V.T.M., *et al.*, Cutting the costs of coastal protection by integrating vegetation in flood defenses. *Nat. Commun.*, 12, 1, 6533, 2021.
27. Wickramasinghe, D., Ecosystem-based disaster risk reduction, in: *Oxford Research Encyclopedia of Natural Hazard Science*, 2021.
28. Kumar, P., *et al.*, An overview of monitoring methods for assessing the performance of nature-based solutions against natural hazards. *Earth Sci. Rev.*, 217, 103603, 2021.

17

Real-Time Earthquake Monitoring with Remote Sensing and AI Technology

Koushik Sundar[1], Narayan Vyas[2]* and Neha Bhati[3]

[1]Citibank NA, Jersey City, NJ, USA
[2]Department of Computer Science and Application, Vivekananda Global University, Jaipur, India
[3]Department of Research and Development, Flexxited, Bengaluru, India

Abstract

This chapter deals with the vital aspect of how remote sensing and AI apply to real-time observations of earthquakes. Such technologies significantly improve forecasting, detecting, and managing seismic activities. AI enhances the accuracy in determining when an earthquake might happen and how strong it may be by processing seismic data that leads to timely responses in these events. Radar sensors in satellites are used to capture details about changes that may have occurred on the surface of the Earth and in the lines of faults. This will give invaluable data for predicting the possible risks of an earthquake, which is quite central in managing it. It introduces some current applications, such as automatic processing of images and enhancements of seismic data. The chapter also looks forward to potential developments that might increase additional improvements in preparedness and safety against earthquakes. This also compares optical and microwave sensors on the satellites by providing the effectiveness of such monitoring in earthquake-prone regions like Shimla and Nepal. These comparisons reflect how various satellite technologies offer essential data for earthquake monitoring. By addressing all these enhancements, the chapter also highlights the critical roles these technologies play in reducing the effect of earthquakes on communities around the world.

**Corresponding author*: narayanvyas87@gmail.com; ORCID: 0000-0003-4225-0764
Koushik Sundar: ORCID: 0009-0003-7119-456X
Neha Bhati: ORCID: 0009-0008-0171-2786

Neelam Dahiya, Gurwinder Singh, Sartajvir Singh and Apoorva Sharma (eds.) Artificial Intelligence in Remote Sensing for Disaster Management, (303–322) © 2025 Scrivener Publishing LLC

***Keywords*:** Artificial intelligence, remote sensing, earthquake monitoring, seismic data analysis, satellite technology, disaster management

17.1 Introduction

The rise of devastating natural disasters has warranted the need for the application of high-tech solutions for forecasting, monitoring, and managing seismic activities. A giant leap in real-time earthquake monitoring is the integration of AI with remote sensing. In essence, these two powerhouse technologies are brought together to discuss not just a sum but the collective toolset that makes the potential for detecting ongoing seismicity and assessing probability and impact that are much more effective. More importantly, AI, through its subfields, like machine learning and deep learning, has contributed immensely to turning vast seismic datasets into operational knowledge [1].

These AI systems are sophisticated enough to pick up very subtle patterns that indicate when an earthquake might strike, with data emanating from the Earth—both normal and anomalous. From improved accuracy in the analysis of seismic data to the automatic recognition of a seismic event, AI's role in earthquake monitoring is revolutionary. The handling of the continuous data flow from space- and ground-based sensors for managing real-time response that AI performs in recognizing and interpreting seismic activities effectively mitigates the far-flung impact created by earthquakes [2].

Remote sensing technology supplements AI with a very critical source of data required for the analysis. Remote sensing technology is a careful examination of the surface of the Earth using a constellation of advanced satellites, all equipped with optical and microwave sensors. This technology has a very high resolution in photography, and as such, it is possible to visualize a change in landscape and other findings like surface deformation and fault in the map setting, which are among the most important indicators of seismic activity [3].

This chapter will aim to do the following:

- Discuss how AI is integrated into remote sensing for earthquake prevention and prediction
- Point out the improvements in satellite technology that help to monitor seismic activity

- Discuss practical applications and future innovations in earthquake preparedness and response
- Show how AI-driven analytics would enhance emergency response and public safety measures

The discussion further elaborates on the specific functionalities and applications, from predictive modeling to damage assessment, of these technologies in practice. Advanced AI algorithms process data from satellites, particularly Landsat and Sentinel, which can monitor surface changes on Earth indicating seismic activities. It changes the way we respond to potential disasters, hence increasing understanding and preparedness, paving a future where integrated systems of AI and remote sensing dynamically improve public safety and disaster responsiveness [4].

17.2 Basics of AI and Remote Sensing

Artificial intelligence and remote sensing are two modern technologies. Real-time seismic monitoring became feasible through improvements in the prediction and analysis of natural phenomena. AI stands for artificial intelligence and represents a simulation of human intelligence processes by machines, especially computer systems. AI comprises learning, reasoning, and the rest of the mind's artificial characteristics. It can be of two types: narrow AI, designed for a limited task such as facial recognition or Internet searches—this is the prevalent flavor of artificiality with which man interacts—and general AI, which can perform any intellectual task that a human being can perform. Within AI, ML is the science of getting computers to act without being explicitly programmed and learning from experience. Deep learning is a form of ML that involves neural networks with extra complexity and has been used in speech recognition and recommendation systems to much effect. Remote sensing, on the other hand, is the use of orbiting satellites fitted with optical and microwave sensors to monitor changes occurring on the surface of the Earth and determine fault lines in the Earth, which is useful in the early detection of earthquakes and the proper management of risk. To understand the role of these technologies in modern-day earthquake monitoring, one has to understand the mechanism through which these technologies work [5].

17.2.1 AI Applications in Earthquake Monitoring

Given today's availability of vast amounts of seismic data, patterns become too complex for predictions to be made with traditional methods. One example of the type of AI model used is neural networks that have been trained to detect seismic signals from earthquakes among enormous varieties of different noises, thus improving the strategies for monitoring and response in real time [6].

Since modern-day seismic data are so voluminous, the patterns that can be discerned are far too complex for standard forecasting systems. Simulation models that incorporate the use of neural networks that are trained to distinguish the seismic noise factors from earthquakes based on other forms of noise make a significant leap in real-time monitoring and response methods. Remote sensing is the observation technique for acquiring information on phenomena or objects at a distance without actually getting in physical contact. It uses satellite- or aircraft-based sensors to retrieve information from Earth. The two most important methods of observing the Earth are through optical remote sensing and microwave remote sensing. Both technologies have their strengths and areas of application, which make them invaluable resources for a whole host of different scientific, environmental, and management endeavors. Optical remote sensing captures images using visible, near-infrared, and short-wave infrared light, whereas microwave remote sensing makes use of radar waves to penetrate clouds and capture data irrespective of the prevailing weather conditions. Both of these form pivotal methodologies for early earthquake detection and effective risk management, and thus the need for their application is of prime importance in modern-day earthquake monitoring and response systems.

17.2.1.1 Optical Remote Sensing

This involves the detection and measurement of reflected or emitted radiation within the visible, near-infrared, or shortwave infrared spectra from the Earth's surface. This is vastly applicable to sunlight because it is the most available source of illumination, although information may at times be obtained through moonlight and artificial lights. The optical sensors will most likely result in images of a lot of detail, with vivid coloration and gradients, which will make the classification of objects like vegetation, soils, and water bodies [2].

Applications of Optical Remote Sensing

- Vegetation monitoring: By analyzing how plants reflect different wavelengths of light, scientists can also gather information about the health, growth, and stress of crops and natural vegetation.
- Urban planning: High-resolution optical images are useful for urban planners in city layout development, control of urban sprawl, and infrastructure development management.
- Water quality assessment: In this, optical remote sensing can be applied to detect changes in water color and turbidity, which might indicate an increase in pollution or sediments in water.

17.2.1.2 Microwave Remote Sensing

This uses radar waves, a form of electromagnetic radiation with wavelengths longer than those of infrared radiation. This type of remote sensing is best known for its good reach through atmospheric particulates, such as clouds and rain, so it is highly reliable in all weather conditions. Microwave sensors, especially those deployed in Synthetic Aperture Radar (SAR) systems, can enable the production of high-resolution images, quite essential for the detailing of accurate surface mapping and change detection [7].

Applications of Microwave Remote Sensing

- SAR: This can penetrate the surface, detecting sub-surface anomalies and changes in the soil which are not visible with optical sensors, hence, very useful to archaeology and geology.
- Soil moisture and vegetation monitoring: With microwave remote sensing, information is directly proportional to the level of soil moisture and estimations of biomass, which are important in agriculture and dry conditions.
- Disaster management and mitigation: Microwave sensing is of great utility in monitoring floods, oil spills, and earthquake aftermath since it can operate under all weather conditions. For example, SAR imagery can help map the extent of floods.

Optical and microwave technologies are the backbone of global environmental and Earth resource monitoring and management efforts. Working together, these technologies give a comprehensive approach to understanding changes on a global scale, which, in turn, helps in making relevant, informed decisions by policymakers, scientists, and disaster response teams based on accurate and timely data [8].

17.2.2 Satellites and Sensors

Key Satellites and Sensors Related to Earthquake Monitoring
Key satellites and sensors for monitoring earthquakes include the Landsat, which provides high-resolution optical images, and the Sentinel-1, which offers all-weather, day-and-night mapping of surface deformation through SAR. These tools are crucial for ensuring timely detection and analysis of seismic activity.

Table 17.1 compares various satellites equipped with optical and microwave sensors, detailing their main features and specific applications in earthquake monitoring. It highlights how each satellite contributes to different aspects of earthquake preparedness, from land change monitoring to detailed damage.

17.2.3 AI and Remote Sensing for Integration in Monitoring Earthquakes

AI has uses in preparedness and response to earthquakes. This is where AI algorithms investigate changes in remote sensing data that can point at some activity within the Earth's crust [9].

- Processing of data: AI in processing and analyzing colossal volumes of data generated by remote sensors. It works on techniques, such as image segmentation and pattern recognition for the identification of potential hazards besides helping in the assessment of damages post-occurrence of this natural hazard.
- Predictive analysis: Processed past data, together with inputs from remote sensing technologies in real-time, is now being used by machine learning models to make predictions on risks of aftershocks and other seismic activities on a timely basis to prevent the disaster.

Table 17.1 Comparison of satellite capabilities for earthquake monitoring.

Name of the satellite	Type of sensor	Principal characteristics	Applications in earthquake monitoring
Landsat	Optical	It captures high-quality images in the visible, near-infrared, and short-wave infrared light ranges	Observing land changes, fault lines, and post-disaster assessment
Sentinel-1	SAR	Provides all-weather, day-and-night radar imaging	Mapping ground deformations before and after earthquakes
TerraSAR-X	SAR	High-resolution radar images in X-band, capable of detailed mapping	Detailed surface deformation mapping and infrastructure analysis post-earthquake
RADARSAT	SAR	Offers flexible imaging modes for various imaging preferences	Soil moisture content analysis and infrastructure integrity assessments
Copernicus Sentinel-2	Optical	High-resolution, multispectral optical imaging	Supports damage mapping and crisis management by providing detailed visual assessments of affected areas

17.2.4 Challenges and Future Directions

Although the integration of AI and remote sensing in earthquake monitoring is very promising, however, there are several problems [14].

- Data veracity: The data must be assured in terms of accuracy and reliability from the remote sensors.
- Interpretability of AI: Having AI models in earthquake prognostics be interpretable to win the trust of stakeholders.
- Real-time processing: It enhances the ability to quickly process and analyze data in real-time, allowing for quick decisions during an earthquake.

AI and remote sensing helps us to enhance the capabilities of monitoring and responding to earthquake activities in real time. As the technologies advance, their integration is expected to become so great that they offer even greater potential to save lives and reduce damages from such natural disasters. Even greater features are yet to be unlocked in the domain, hence making such a field even more relevant for studies and understanding in the current era [10].

17.3 Advances in Satellite Remote Sensing Techniques for Improved Earthquake Monitoring

The most recent advances are remote sensing satellite technology innovation and the critical applications in seismic activities monitoring.

17.3.1 Comparative Analysis of Remote Sensing Satellites

Optical satellite-based remote sensing: High-resolution image collection is pegged on the use of visible and near-infrared light by various optical remote sensing satellites like Landsat 8 and Sentinel-2. It is through these satellites that analysis of changes to the land surface, fault lines, and other changes, and assessment of earthquake damages may be conducted [11].

Table 17.2 provides a comparison of different optical remote sensing satellites used for earthquake monitoring. It highlights differences in spatial resolution, revisit time, key features, and specific applications such as damage assessment, fault mapping, and urban area analysis.

Table 17.2 Comparison of various optical remote sensing satellites for earthquake monitoring.

Satellite	Agency	Launch year	Spatial resolution	Revisit time	Key features	Applications in earthquake monitoring
Landsat 8	NASA/USGS	2013	15 m (panchromatic), 30 m (multi-spectral)	16 days	Free data access, wide spectral range	Land surface changes, fault line mapping, damage assessment
Sentinel-2	ESA	2015 (A), 2017 (B)	10 m (visible, NIR), 20 m (shortwave infrared)	5 days	High revisit frequency, multi-spectral imaging	Rapid assessment, land deformation, urban area damage analysis
Pleiades-1A/1B	CNES/Airbus	2011/2012	50 cm (panchromatic), 2 m (multi-spectral)	<1 day	High-resolution, stereo, and tri-stereo imaging	3D mapping, detailed urban damage assessment, fault detection

Microwave-Based Remote Sensing Satellites

The use of Synthetic Aperture Radar (SAR) technology enables microwave satellites, like Sentinel-1, to work under any weather conditions and during the day and night. This will be very crucial in detecting ground deformation and mapping fault lines for earthquake monitoring.

Table 17.3 shows a comparison of the various characteristics of SAR among different microwave remote sensing satellites. Highlighted are important and valuable features, spatial resolutions, and some special applications for earthquake monitoring in surface deformation and fault line mapping [12].

17.3.2 Comparison of Optical and Microwave Satellite Imagery

Satellite imagery of optical and microwave-sensor-based satellites taken at Shimla City in Himachal Pradesh, India, is shown in Figure 17.1, which consists of three types of satellite images, i.e., (a) Shimla natural color image, which displays the Shimla region in natural color, highlighting urban areas, vegetation, and water bodies as seen by the human eye: It serves as a visual representation to show how natural color imaging can

Table 17.3 Comparison of various microwave-based remote sensing satellites for earthquake monitoring.

Satellite	Agency	Launch year	Frequency band	Spatial resolution	Revisit time	Key features	Applications in earthquake monitoring
Sentinel-1A/1B	ESA	2014/2016	C-band	5 m (range), 20 m (azimuth)	6–12 days	Dual-polarization, high revisit time, free data access	Surface deformation, fault mapping, post-earthquake displacement
ALOS-2 (PALSAR-2)	JAXA	2014	L-band	3 m (high-res mode), 10 m (standard mode)	14 days	High penetration capability, wide swath coverage	Detailed surface deformation, landslide detection, fault monitoring
RADARSAT-2	CSA	2007	C-band	3 m (spotlight mode), 8 m (standard mode)	24 days	Multi-polarization, high-resolution modes	Ground displacement, urban area analysis, infrastructure monitoring
TerraSAR-X	DLR/ Airbus	2007	X-band	1 m (spotlight mode), 3 m (strip map mode)	11 days	High resolution, short revisit time, interferometric capabilities	Precise deformation mapping, detailed fault analysis
COSMO-SkyMed	ASI	2007-2010	X-band	1 m (spotlight mode), 3 m (strip map mode)	16 days	The constellation of satellites, short revisit time, high resolution	Urban damage assessment, infrastructure monitoring, surface displacement
RISAT-1	ISRO	2012	C-band	3 m (spotlight mode), 25 m (strip map mode)	25 days	Multi-mode imaging, Indian subcontinent coverage	Surface deformation, disaster management, flood and landslide detection

ESA, European Space Agency; JAXA, Japan Aerospace Exploration Agency; CSA, Canadian Space Agency; DLR, German Aerospace Center (DeutschesZentrum für Luft- und Raumfahrt); ASI, Italian Space Agency (AgenziaSpazialeItaliana); ISRO, Indian Space Research Organisation.

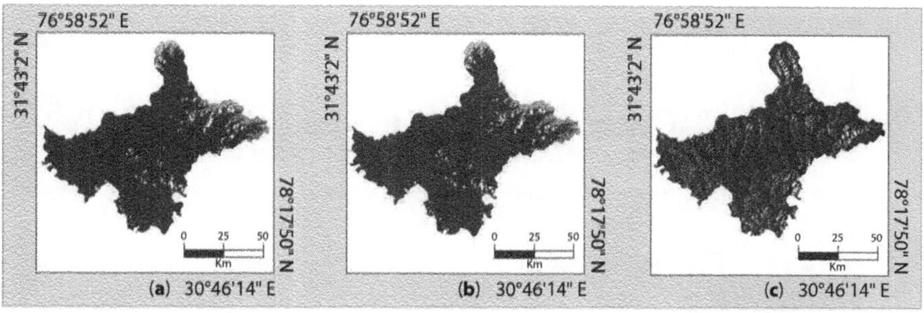

Figure 17.1 Comparison of satellite imagery: (a) Sentinel-2 Imagery of Shimla, India (four-, three-, and two-band combination), (b) Sentinel-2 imagery of Shimla, India (eight-, four-, and three-band combination), and (c) Sentinel-1 satellite imagery (VH polarization).

reveal detailed features of the landscape, making it easier to distinguish between natural and urbanized areas. The band combinations used are red (band 4), green (band 3), and blue (band 2), with the image acquired on May 18, 2024. (b) Shimla color infrared image, which showcases healthy vegetation in the area, is shown in bright red, while the urban features are white. This image indicates areas with dense foliage and landscape health. It demonstrates that color infrared imaging is very effective for distinguishing healthy from unhealthy vegetation, which is crucial for assessing environmental health after seismic events. The band combinations used are near-infrared (band 5), red (band 4), and green (band 3), with the image acquired on May 19, 2024. Finally, (c) Sentinel-1 VH polarization image, which represents different polarization settings, can reveal various ground features; hence, this image is essential for studying ground deformation and associated fault lines. This example of Sentinel-1's VH polarization helps the audience appreciate how advanced imaging techniques can reveal more details about the Earth's surface conditions, which are crucial for earthquake prediction.

17.3.3 Case Study on Pre- and Post-images of Earthquake in Doti District of Nepal

In early November 2022, a significant earthquake struck the Doti district of Nepal, causing widespread concern and damage. This case study examines the pre- and post-earthquake imagery to assess the impact and changes in the region's landscape, as shown in Figure 17.2. An earthquake was reported in the first week of November 2022. To assess the aftereffects of this earthquake, two images of different dates, i.e., (a) November 4, 2022

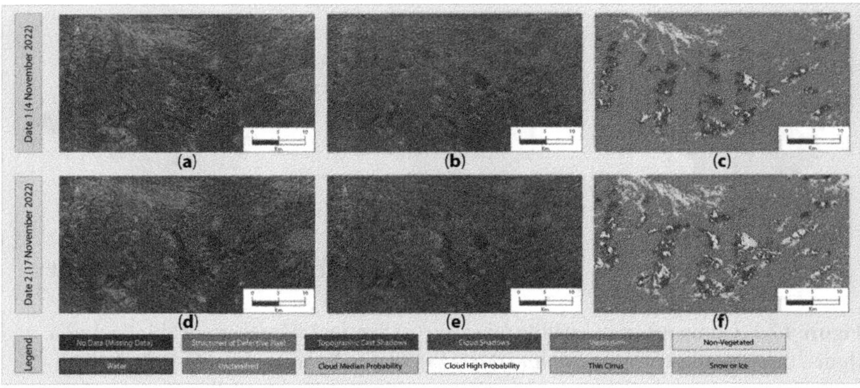

Figure 17.2 Classified images of Nepal before and after the November 2022 earthquake, highlighting urban areas, vegetation health, and landscape features.

(representing a before-earthquake area) and (b) November 14, 2022 (representing an after-earthquake area), were acquired using the Sentinel-2 L2A (Level 2A product) satellite. These images were processed to create different visual representations, providing detailed insights into the landscape and its features. The study area of natural color image shows the region as it appears to the human eye, highlighting urban areas, vegetation, and water bodies. The multiple bands, along with various algorithms used in the study area of the images, bring forth in-depth detailing about the landscape.

The natural color image uses red (band 4), green (band 3), and blue (band 2) to depict the area as seen by the human eye. The color infrared image maps healthy vegetation in bright red, urban features in white, and all other features in other various colors, as seen in this formula near-infrared (band 5) + red (band 4) + green (band 3) to formulate vegetation health. The scene classification image makes use of ESA's algorithm to classify various pixel types like clouds, vegetation, soils/deserts, water, and snow. It makes use of the different color legends for every class to make up an easily readable map of the landscape. The true color does make use of the same bands as the natural color image, that is, red, green, and blue, to provide a correct visual image. An example is the false color image, which combines the near-infrared, red, and green bands to brighten the image for vegetation further and separate it from urban areas and other land cover categories. The scene classification image once again utilizes the algorithm by ESA to classify the landscape into different classes with specific color legends, giving an overview of various landscape features. The scene classification also helps identify other features in the images. Examples of such include categories in the color legends used in classifying the images, namely, no data (missing data), structured or defective pixels, topographic cast shadows, cloud shadows, vegetation, non-vegetated areas, water, unclassified area, medium probability clouds, high probability clouds, thin cirrus clouds, and snow or ice. Visually, these five different classes can be picked because of the distinct colorations of the images. This enables a more straightforward understanding of the distribution of various features of the landscape. Such an in-depth analysis is essential in monitoring environmental conditions regarding the features of landscapes, especially in earthquake-prone regions.

17.4 How AI Is Currently Being Used in Remote Sensing to Monitor Earthquakes

AI with remote sensing is probably the area where remote sensing has been integrated with AI to the maximal effect, thus resulting in a heightened level of accuracy, combined with a very high level of efficiency. An overview of the current practical applications of AI in remote sensing exemplifies the sort of innovations already underway in practice that might enhance earthquake preparedness and response at the location level [13].

17.4.1 Automated Image Processing

For remote sensing in the seismic search then, the role of AI is performed through automated processing of images taken from satellite and aerial observation. Among them, deep learning, as an AI mathematical solution, may very well stand out as the best option used to analyze large volumes of images altogether to capture changes on the Earth's surface that could hint at the presence of an earthquake.

- Detection of change: AI-enabled change detection involves the analysis of a series of images of the same site with significant alterations in location due to natural disasters, among others, and earthquakes having occurred. By automatically comparing pre- and post-event images, AI can quickly identify areas with significant developments and then support fast response and assessment accordingly.

- Surface deformation analysis: This is among the most important precursors of earthquakes: ground deformation, presenting symptoms like underground shifting, or the development of faults. Demand for this information has been met by processing such information from radar satellites, like Sentinel-1, using AI algorithms to map ground deformations in high detail. This is critical information in the identification of potential hotspots for earthquake generation and other tectonic movements [14].

17.4.2 Seismic Data Augmentation

AI achieves improvement in the accuracy of the interpretation of seismic data by filtering noises from the data and improving the wave analysis in the seismic data. This would further turn it into a significant application in the prediction and assessment of the impact of earthquakes.

- Signal processing: Machine learning models excel at sifting through background noise in seismic data to distinguish earthquake signals. Such discrimination could be key to spotting smaller, less evident temblors: foreshocks that might presage larger, more ruinous events.
- Aftershock prediction: This is crucial in emergency response activities and public safety, which pertain to preparedness for aftershocks in the event of a disaster. Using historical and real-time patterns of seismic data, AI models can predict the probability, magnitude, and location of aftershocks.

17.4.3 Risk Assessment and Management

AI-driven remote sensing will play a very critical role in ascertaining the risk and potential threat from the impact of an earthquake. The application of geographic information systems in concert with AI permits the development of minute and accurate risk models by researchers and respondents.

- Vulnerability mapping: The algorithms of AI process the data obtained through remote sensing to develop maps showing place vulnerabilities to earthquake damages. These maps show different factors such as population, building structures, and historical earthquake activity that can be used to prioritize response efforts and resource allocation.

- Damage assessment: Post-earthquake evaluation is basic to effective recovery and reconstruction. AI models, when trained on remote sensing data, are quite fast in the above-mentioned large-scale assessment, such as identification and distinction where infrastructures, like destroyed or broken bridges, roads, and buildings, exist. Such quick assessment will help expedite the dispatching of emergency services and support to the most affected areas.

17.4.4 Integrated Monitoring Systems

AI is making it easy to incorporate different types of remote sensing data—be it optical, radar, or thermal—into one monitoring system, consequently providing a more holistic view of seismic activities that could otherwise be difficult. These will give an all-encompassing view of seismic activity, increasing predictability and monitoring capabilities.

- Real-time monitoring: AI-driven real-time monitoring systems analyze all incoming sensor data streams to provide instant seismic activity assessment, providing the ability to respond much faster. It enables a quicker response for the mitigation of the impact of earthquakes by alerting the authorities in advance.
- Predictive maintenance: AI also plays a part in the practice of predictive maintenance on critical infrastructure, as it analyzes data coming in from remote sensors in predicting potential failures due to seismic activities. Such an application could help in scheduling maintenance and repairing before catastrophic failure happens which would have a significant bearing on the resilience of the essential services.

The practical experiences of AI in remote sensing are indeed dramatically furthering the capability of monitoring and responding to earthquakes. As AI progresses further and, in turn, evolves the integration of this technology into remote sensing, disaster management strategies will become way more prescriptive. The development and utilization of these technologies are important to build up the capability for the prediction, monitoring, and disaster response to earthquakes for human safety and lesser economic impacts [15].

17.5 Ongoing and Future Practical AI Applications in Remote Sensing

AI and other advances in remote sensing will also improve many fields, including earthquake monitoring. The chapter elaborates on ongoing as well as prospective applications of AI for remote sensing technologies, focusing on how such advancements are likely to benefit and change earthquake preparedness as well as response [16].

17.5.1 More Sophisticated Prediction Models

The AI will open the door to models of earthquake prediction, getting increasingly complex and learning from really big data. These models become increasingly accurate, providing finer and finer details of how and where earthquakes can happen.

- Seismic precursor machine learning algorithms: Continuous research is being developed regarding machine learning methodologies to help detect subtle seismic precursors of potential earthquakes. Such algorithms look at historical seismic data and consider real-time inputs from ground sensors and satellites—to draw earthquake pattern recognition.
- Integrated with geophysical data: The future developments will tap into the development of AI, only with a greater number of data sources related to the geophysics and within the atmospheric as well as hydrological data available for improving prediction models. In total, a holistic view should be able to deliver a deep understanding of the complex interdependencies resulting in seismic events.

17.5.2 Real-Time Data Processing

Real-time data processing is key to the issuance of timely earthquake warnings and having the best response to any emergency. AI has the potential to speed up and enhance data processing.

- Real-time automated alert systems: AI algorithms enable the automatic detection of seismic events from remote sensing data, providing instant alerts to the relevant authorities and the public. Instant capabilities such as these can make a big difference in response when reducing the effects of an earthquake.

- Enhanced sensor networks: Future developments will pertain to the deployment of AI-driven sensor networks, changing dynamically their sensitivity and data collection parameters following detected seismic activity. This would, in a way, improve efficiency and relevance in data collection [17].

17.5.3 Damage and Recovery

Post-earthquake damage assessment is most crucial in the recovery and rebuilding process. Currently, AI in applications for remote sensing is going to revolutionize the field with faster and much more precise evaluation of the damage.

- High-resolution: Because of the real-time enhancements of the AI algorithms, satellite images would be able to be taken at increased resolution, hence allowing the categorization of affected earthquake damage across wide areas. This enables them to quickly target the most affected areas and allocate resources where they will be most useful.
- Recovery predictive analytics: AI is also used for forecasting the long-term impacts of earthquake damage on urban areas and the infrastructure associated with it. It helps designers come up with strategies to make post-disaster recovery more effective and design infrastructure to last during future seismic events.

17.5.4 Public Safety and Community Resilience

Given the integration of AI with remote sensing, warnings can be provided in time to enhance public safety and make a community resilient toward earthquakes. This will be more than a timely warning; this is related to the education and preparation of communities toward predictive insights.

- Community-based AI solutions: Future initiatives will deal with localized AI-based solutions that provide relevant information and recommendations to inhabitants regarding how to keep the population safe from the risks of an earthquake in one's area and specific risk factors.

- Interactive platforms: These new technologies are focused on creating interfaces with AI that are interactive for individuals and communities to simulate and plan potential actions for response in case of an earthquake. They provide great training in preparing for disasters and thereby increase the overall resilience of communities.

The present and future applications of AI technology in remote sensing for earthquake monitoring are a quantum leap toward our level of predictability, monitoring, and response to seismic events. Integrating AI with remote sensing technologies will afford more in the potential for the protection of life and property. Such continuous innovation augments strategies in earthquake monitoring and response and takes public safety to new and greater heights [18].

17.6 Conclusion

Combining artificial intelligence (AI) with remote sensing significantly improves real-time earthquake monitoring. This powerful combination offers unparalleled accuracy and efficiency in predicting and responding to seismic events. Advanced AI algorithms and satellite technologies help us process large amounts of seismic data, detect early warning signs, monitor ground movements, and assess damage with great precision. The role of AI in automated image processing, enhancing seismic data, and assessing risks has changed the way we prepare for and react to earthquakes. Future advancements promise even better prediction models, real-time data processing, and comprehensive recovery strategies after quakes. Recent earthquakes in Nepal highlight the urgent need for this technology. We get a complete view of seismic activities with high-detail images from optical satellites like Landsat and Sentinel-2, combined with the all-weather capability of microwave satellites like Sentinel-1. This integrated approach not only helps predict and monitor earthquakes but also ensures improved public safety and community resilience. Ongoing innovation in AI and remote sensing technologies will make disaster management strategies more effective, reducing both human and economic impacts during earthquakes. This chapter emphasizes the transformative potential of these technologies in protecting lives and properties, showing the critical importance of their application in earthquake monitoring.

References

1. Bhatia, M., Ahanger, T.A., Manocha, A., Artificial intelligence based real-time earthquake prediction. *Eng. Appl. Artif. Intell.*, 120, 105856, 2023.
2. Abdalzaher, M.S., Elsayed, H.A., Fouda, M.M., Employing remote sensing, data communication networks, ai, and optimization methodologies in seismology. *IEEE J. Sel. Top. Appl. Earth Obs. Remote Sens.*, 15, 9417–9438, 2022.
3. Janga, B., Asamani, G.P., Sun, Z., Cristea, N., A Review of Practical AI for Remote Sensing in Earth Sciences. *Remote Sens.*, 15, 16, 4112, 2023.
4. Jiao, P. and Alavi, A.H., Artificial intelligence in seismology: advent, performance and future trends. *Geosci. Front.*, 11, 3, 739–744, 2020.
5. Laake, A. and Laake, A., Basics of Remote Sensing, in: *Remote Sens. Hydrocarb. Explor.*, pp. 3–20, 2022.
6. Al Banna, M.H., *et al.*, Application of artificial intelligence in predicting earthquakes: state-of-the-art and future challenges. *IEEE Access*, 8, 192880–192923, 2020.
7. Sishodia, R.P., Ray, R.L., Singh, S.K., Applications of remote sensing in precision agriculture: A review. *Remote Sens.*, 12, 19, 3136, 2020.
8. Jin, S., *et al.*, Remote sensing and its applications using GNSS reflected signals: advances and prospects. *Satell. Navig.*, 5, 1, 19, 2024.
9. Kemper, H. and Kemper, G., Sensor fusion, GIS and AI technologies for disaster management. *Int. Arch. Photogramm. Remote Sens. Spat. Inf. Sci.*, 43, 1677–1683, 2020.
10. Asadi, A., Baise, L.G., Koch, M., Moaveni, B., Chatterjee, S., Aimaiti, Y., Pixel-based classification method for earthquake-induced landslide mapping using remotely sensed imagery, geospatial data and temporal change information. *Nat. Hazards*, 120, 6, 5163–5200, 2024. doi: 10.1007/s11069-023-06399-8.
11. Caballero, I., Roca, M., Santos-Echeandía, J., Bernárdez, P., Navarro, G., Use of the Sentinel-2 and Landsat-8 Satellites for Water Quality Monitoring: An Early Warning Tool in the Mar Menor Coastal Lagoon. *Remote Sens.*, 14, 12, MDPI AG, 2744, 2022. doi: 10.3390/rs14122744.
12. Li, J., *et al.*, A real-time AI-assisted seismic monitoring system based on new nodal stations with 4G telemetry and its application in the Yangbi MS 6.4 aftershock monitoring in southwest China. *Earthq. Res. Adv.*, 2, 2, 100033, 2022.
13. Sicre, C.M., Fieuzal, R., Baup, F., Contribution of multispectral (optical and radar) satellite images to the classification of agricultural surfaces. *Int. J. Appl. Earth Obs. Geoinf.*, 84, 101972, 2020.
14. Giardina, G., *et al.*, Combining remote sensing techniques and field surveys for post-earthquake reconnaissance missions. *Bull. Earthq. Eng.*, 22, 7, 3415–3439, 2024.
15. Çiner, A., *et al.* (Eds.), Recent Research on Geotechnical Engineering, Remote Sensing, Geophysics and Earthquake Seismology: Proceedings

of the 1st MedGU, Istanbul 2021 (Volume 3), in: *Advances in Science, Technology & Innovation*, Springer Nature Switzerland, Cham, 2024, doi: 10.1007/978-3-031-43218-7.

16. Kairu, E.N., An introduction to remote sensing. *GeoJournal*, 6, 3, 251–260, May 1982, doi: 10.1007/BF00210657.
17. Victor, N., *et al.*, Remote Sensing for Agriculture in the Era of Industry 5.0–A survey, in: *IEEE Journal of Selected Topics in Applied Earth Observations and Remote Sensing*, vol 17, pp. 590–5945, Institute of Electrical and Electronics Engineers (IEEE), 2024. doi: 10.1109/jstars.2024.3370508.
18. Nawaz, S.A., Li, J., Bhatti, U.A., Shoukat, M.U., Ahmad, R.M., AI-based object detection latest trends in remote sensing, multimedia and agriculture applications. *Front. Plant Sci.*, 13, 1041514, 2022.

18

Enhancing Seismic-Events Identification and Analysis Using Machine Learning Approach

Gurwinder Singh*, Harun and Tejinder Pal Singh

Department of AIT-CSE, Chandigarh University, Mohali, Punjab, India

Abstract
This chapter explores the identification and analysis of seismic events through a machine learning approach. The study of seismic events is critical for disaster preparedness, significantly impacting life on Earth. Traditional techniques for seismic data analysis often struggle with large, complex datasets and limited computational capabilities. However, machine learning algorithms such as K-means clustering, ARIMA models, and neural networks have demonstrated efficiency in processing seismic data and effectively predicting earthquakes. This approach examines global seismic activity by analyzing 782 earthquake events, revealing an average magnitude of 6.94 and showcasing variability through standard deviation and quartiles. Additionally, spatial analysis identifies concentrations along tectonic plate boundaries, essential for risk assessment. Machine learning models like ARIMA and neural networks underscore the potential for data-driven earthquake forecasting in disaster management.

***Keywords*:** Seismic events, machine learning, disaster preparedness, earthquake prediction, K-means clustering, ARI0MA models, neural networks, seismic data analysis, earthquake magnitude

**Corresponding author*: gurwinder.e11253@cumail.in; ORCID: 0000-0002-8378-5637

Neelam Dahiya, Gurwinder Singh, Sartajvir Singh and Apoorva Sharma (eds.) Artificial Intelligence in Remote Sensing for Disaster Management, (323–342) © 2025 Scrivener Publishing LLC

18.1 Introduction

This chapter examines how machine learning techniques improve the identification and analysis of seismic events, which is crucial for disaster preparedness, response, and mitigation due to the threats posed by earthquakes, tsunamis, and volcanic eruptions. Seismic events put considerable risks to human lives, infrastructure, and the environment with various effects. Therefore, accurate identification and analysis of these events are essential for effective management. Although successful, the traditional methods have limitations to accurately predict the seismic events and frequently face challenges in processing huge datasets and delivering analysis. On the other hand, the development of machine learning models in recent years has created new opportunities to improve the accuracy and effectiveness of seismic event detection and analysis.

This chapter explores the machine learning techniques in seismology, emphasizing the potential use of these cutting-edge approaches for detection of seismic activities. So, the basic goal is to enhance the current capabilities of seismic monitoring systems. This approach will work through the integration of machine learning technologies to take care of disaster management and mitigation.

Understanding earthquakes and other seismic occurrences holds importance for reasons. Firstly, it plays a role in saving lives as it allows for timely alerts and guidance to be issued to communities, empowering residents to take necessary safety measures or evacuate if needed [1]. Moreover having a grasp of activities helps in minimizing destruction and disturbances by guiding the development of infrastructure capable of enduring earthquakes and related events [2]. Additionally, delving into research on events contributes to expanding knowledge by offering valuable insights into tectonic processes, the structure of the Earth, and geophysical phenomena [3] and long-term rehabilitation through a comprehensive understanding of seismic events [4].

Traditional techniques have faced difficulties in detecting and studying earthquakes. These methods rely significantly on humans interpreting data, leading to prolonged analysis periods and challenges in handling extensive datasets [4]. Additionally, standard seismic sensors may not have the precision to identify earthquakes with accuracy, potentially resulting in missed occurrences. Pinpointing the epicenters poses difficulties well particularly when seismic stations are sparsely distributed, causing delays, etc.

Conversely, the use of machine learning (ML) methods offers a better option [5]. ML algorithms have the capacity to automatically recognize patterns and trends in seismic data, which can lead to more efficient analysis and forecasting [6]. In contrast to approaches that depend on human understanding, ML models can precisely identify irregularities and forecast future events [7]. The capability of ML to adjust to data improves its predictive abilities over time, making it extremely useful for ongoing analysis and interpretation of seismic events [7]. By incorporating ML into seismology, scientists can enhance disaster readiness, deepen their comprehension of occurrences, and reduce associated risks.

The review of literature highlights the impact of machine learning on analyzing and interpreting seismic events. Traditional methods that depend on interpretation and rule-based algorithms have constraints when it comes to scalability and real-time usage [8, 9] and assessments and early warning systems [10]. Conventional methods also struggle to discern seismic signals from noise, impacting data interpretation [11]. In contrast, recent studies highlight ML's efficacy in earthquake detection and analysis [12–16]. ML-based approaches, including CNNs and RNNs, show significant improvements in seismic data analysis [12–16]. Other studies explore the potential of machine learning in tsunami prediction and estimating ground motion severity [15, 16]. Collectively, these studies advance the field of ML-based seismic event analysis and interpretation [17–22].

Traditional earthquake detection and analysis methods heavily rely on the manual interpretation of seismic data, which can be time-consuming and challenging when dealing with large datasets. These methods often struggle to accurately detect minor earthquakes and precisely localize epicenters, especially in regions with sparse seismic station distribution. In comparison, machine learning (ML) methods provide an option for identifying important patterns and trends in seismic data. Unlike approaches, ML models can precisely detect anomalies and predict future events. The integration of ML in seismology has the potential to enhance readiness for disasters, advance comprehension of activities, and reduce risks. Recent research highlights the effectiveness of ML in earthquake detection and analysis showcasing enhancements in interpreting data.

This section elucidates how to identify and analyze occurrences using machine learning techniques. Through the utilization of these approaches, scientists can notably enhance the precision, productivity, and scalability of analyzing events. This progress promotes an insight into processes for more efficient disaster response strategies and ultimately leads to better safeguarding of lives and assets from seismic threats.

The objectives of this chapter are as follows:

- Statistical comprehensiveness: To offer an in-depth understanding of seismic activity patterns, this study provides a comprehensive statistical analysis of seismic features, including magnitude, intensity measures, and geographic coordinates.
- Visual representation proficiency: To demonstrate proficiency in visual representation techniques, such as scatter plots, histograms, and heatmaps, to elucidate seismic event distributions, trends, and spatial patterns, facilitating improved identification and analysis of seismic events.
- Machine learning model exploration: To explore the utilization of machine learning models, such as neural networks, K-means clustering, and ARIMA models, for seismic event analysis purposes, with the aim of enhancing earthquake forecasting, risk assessment, and disaster preparedness endeavors.
- Future research direction proposition: To propose future research directions, including the enhancement of model interpretability, integration of diverse datasets, and development of real-time monitoring systems, aimed at further advancing seismic event identification and analysis using machine learning methodologies.

18.2 Methodology

The dataset comprises various features providing information on earthquake events. These features include the title, magnitude, date and time of occurrence, measures of intensity like CDI and MMI, alert level, indication of tsunami occurrence, significance of the event, network responsible for monitoring, seismic station details such as number and distance, magnitude measurement type, depth, geographical coordinates (latitude and longitude), specific location, continent, and country where the earthquake occurred. Initially, the dataset containing information on 782 earthquake events worldwide from January 1, 2001 to January 1, 2023 is collected and structured for analysis by [23].

The methodology involves several steps to analyze the earthquake dataset comprehensively. The flowchart emphasizes a structured approach to seismic data analysis, starting from data collection and preparation, progressing through exploratory analysis and modeling, and concluding with interpretation and insights generation. The seismic analysis process consists of several steps. The process begins with the start/stop steps, marking the beginning and end of the analysis process. Following this is data collection and preparation, where seismic data is gathered and organized into a structured format. Next, exploratory data analysis (EDA) is conducted to identify patterns and anomalies within the data. Visualization techniques are employed to represent the seismic data visually, facilitating easier comprehension. Missing value handling addresses any gaps in the data using appropriate methods to ensure completeness. Machine learning models are then introduced to analyze the data and make predictions. Spatial analysis studies the spatial distribution and relationships of seismic events, often utilizing geographic information systems (GIS). Evaluation metrics assess the performance of the analytical models. Finally, the data interpretation and insights step involves deriving meaningful conclusions about seismic events from the analyzed data.

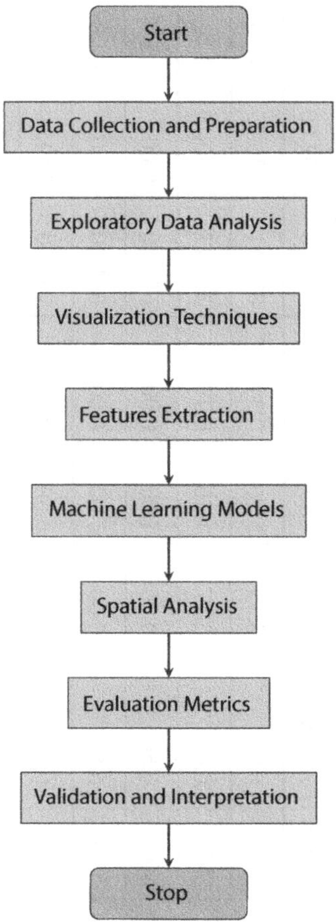

Table 18.1 Summary statistics of earthquake features.

	Magnitude	CDI	MMI	Tsunami	sig	nst	dmin	Gap	Depth	Latitude	Longitude
Count	782.00	782.00	782.00	782.00	782.00	782.00	782.00	782.00	782.00	782.00	
Mean	6.94	4.33	5.96	0.39	870.11	230.25	1.33	25.04	75.88	3.54	52.61
Std	0.45	3.17	1.46	0.49	322.47	250.19	2.22	24.23	137.28	27.30	117.90
Min	6.50	0.00	1.00	0.00	650.00	0.00	0.00	0.00	2.70	-61.85	-179.97
25%	6.60	0.00	5.00	0.00	691.00	0.00	0.00	14.62	14.00	-14.60	-71.67
50%	6.80	5.00	6.00	0.00	754.00	140.00	0.00	20.00	26.30	-2.57	109.43
75%	7.10	7.00	7.00	1.00	909.75	445.00	1.86	30.00	49.75	24.65	148.94
Max	9.10	9.00	9.00	1.00	2,910.00	934.00	17.65	239.00	670.81	71.63	179.66

18.3 Results and Discussion

This section presents comprehensive statistics and visualizations of earthquake features, aiding in the understanding of seismic activity worldwide. Through detailed analyses and visual representations, it offers insights into earthquake distribution, magnitude trends, and spatial patterns, which are essential for seismic risk assessment and disaster preparedness. Table 18.1 provides a summary of key statistics related to earthquake features. It includes data on magnitude, intensity measures such as CDI and MMI, tsunami occurrences, event significance, seismic station details, and geographic coordinates for 782 earthquake events. The statistics encompass measures such as mean, standard deviation, minimum, maximum, and quartiles, offering insights into the distribution and characteristics of earthquake occurrences. This information aids in understanding the range and variability of earthquake parameters, facilitating the analysis and interpretation of seismic activity patterns and trends worldwide.

Figure 18.1 shows how many earthquakes happened at different strengths, called magnitudes. The horizontal axis, labeled "Magnitude", shows the earthquake's strength, while the vertical axis, labeled "Count", shows how many earthquakes there were. Each bar represents a range of magnitudes, and the height of the bar shows how many earthquakes fall within that range. For example, the most common magnitude seems to be around 7.0 because that bar is the tallest.

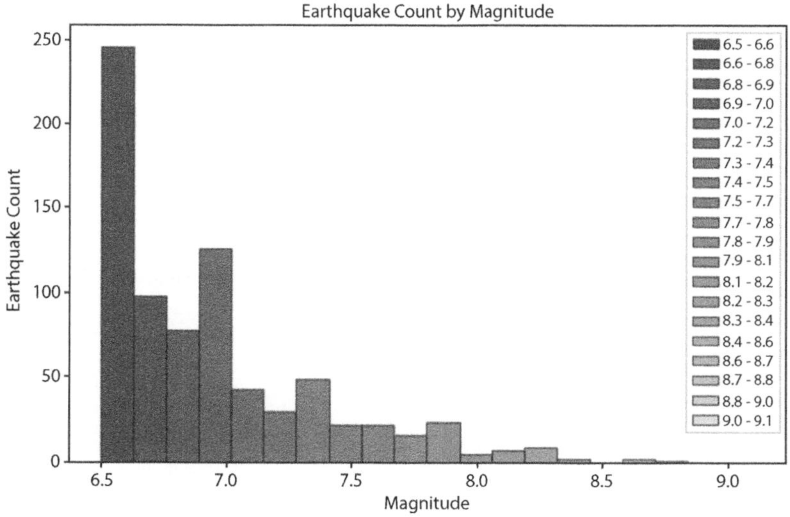

Figure 18.1 Earthquake count by magnitude.

Figure 18.2 is a visualization of earthquake data. It has two parts: a histogram and a box-and- whisker plot for both depth and significance. The left side shows the distribution of earthquakes by depth. The top left plot is a histogram, which shows the number of earthquakes at each depth level. The x-axis represents depth, and the y-axis represents the number of earthquakes. The bottom left plot is a box-and-whisker plot, which shows the median, quartiles, and outliers for earthquake depth. The line in the middle of the box represents the median depth, the box contains the middle 50% of the data, the whiskers extend to 1.5 times the interquartile range from the quartiles, and any data points outside the whiskers are considered outliers. The right side shows the distribution of earthquakes by significance. The top right plot is a histogram, which shows the number of earthquakes at each significance level. The x-axis represents significance, and the y-axis represents the number of earthquakes. The bottom right plot is a box-and-whisker plot, which shows the median, quartiles, and outliers for earthquake significance. The line in the middle of the box represents

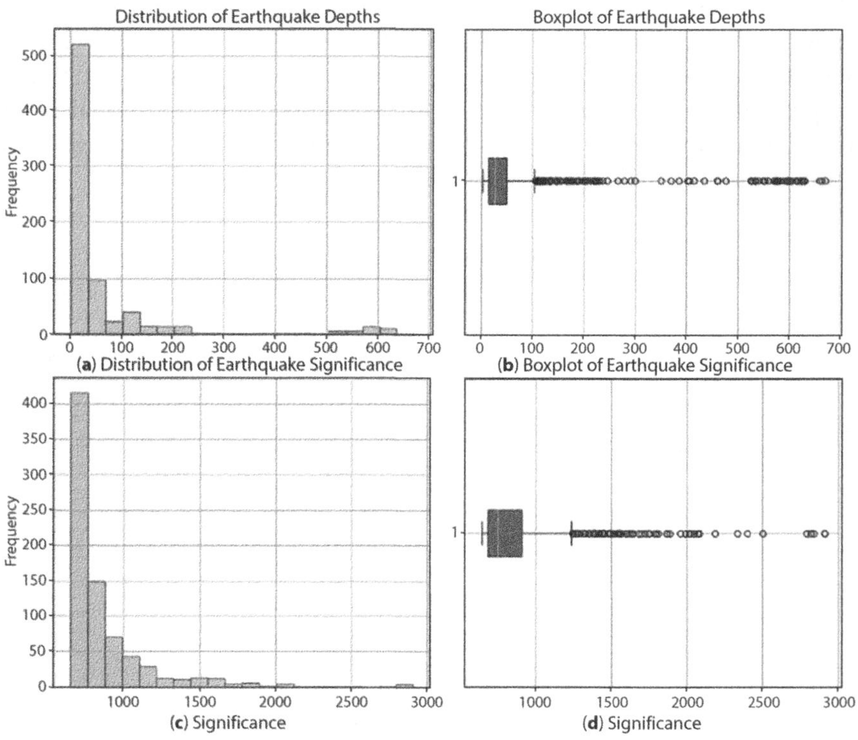

Figure 18.2 (a) Distribution of earthquake depths, (b) boxplot of earthquake depths, (c) distribution of earthquake significance, and (d) boxplot of earthquake significance.

the median significance, the box contains the middle 50% of the data, the whiskers extend to 1.5 times the interquartile range from the quartiles, and any data points outside the whiskers are considered outliers.

Figure 18.3 shows the insights that can be derived regarding tsunami occurrence data. The bar-plot on the left likely represents the number of tsunamis recorded over time, with the x-axis denoting tsunami occurrence (0 = no, 1 = yes) and the y-axis showcasing the count of tsunamis. The pie chart on the right illustrates the proportion of tsunamis in the past year, indicating that 61.1% of the time there were no tsunamis (0), while 38.9% of the time tsunamis occurred (1). These visualizations offer insights into the frequency and distribution of tsunami occurrences, both over time and within a specific period (in this case, the past year).

Figure 18.4 is a visualization of earthquake data, likely showing the frequency of earthquakes in Japan based on magnitude and epicentral distance. The left side of the figure shows a heatmap for frequency of earthquakes in Japan based on magnitude and epicentral distance. The color intensity of each box represents the number of earthquakes. Darker colors represent more earthquakes, while lighter colors represent fewer earthquakes. Text labels along the axes and within the boxes provide additional information: The y-axis shows earthquake magnitudes ranging from 6.5 to 9.1. The right graph (b) is a pi-plot, which is a circular variation of a histogram. It depicts the same information as the bar graph in a more compact way. The concentric circles represent epicentral distance, with the outermost

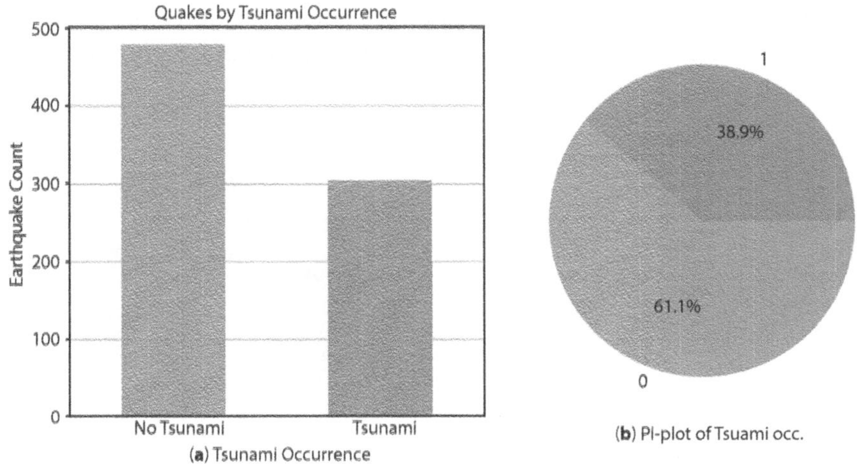

Figure 18.3 (a) Earthquakes count by (non)tsunami occurrence. (b) Pi-plot for earthquakes by (non)tsunami occurrence.

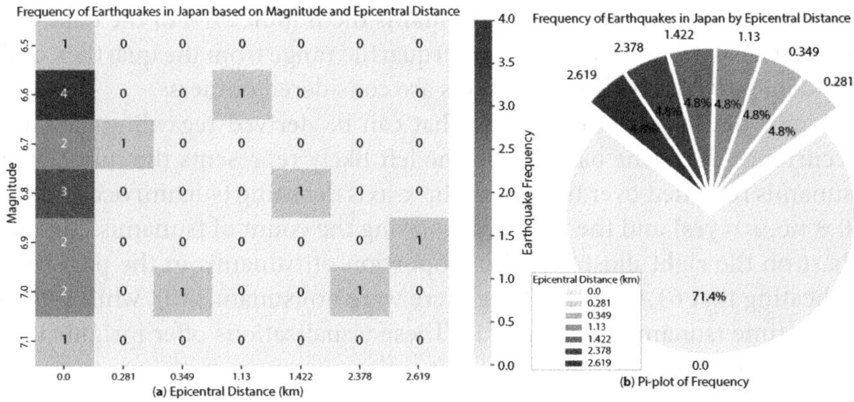

Figure 18.4 (a) Heatmap for frequency of earthquakes in Japan based on magnitude and epicentral distance. (b) Pi-plot for frequency of earthquakes.

circle corresponding to the greatest distance. The radial slices represent earthquake magnitude, with the center of the circle corresponding to the smallest magnitudes. The color intensity within each slice corresponds to frequency, with darker colors indicating more frequent earthquakes.

Figure 18.5(a) illustrates a horizontal bar-plot representing the earthquake frequency across different countries. The x-axis denotes the countries, while the y-axis indicates the number of earthquakes experienced by each country. Indonesia emerges with the highest number of earthquakes, followed closely by Japan, while other countries exhibit a comparatively lower seismic activity. This observation underscores the variability in earthquake occurrence worldwide, indicating that certain regions are more susceptible to earthquakes than others. On the other hand, Figure 18.5(b) is

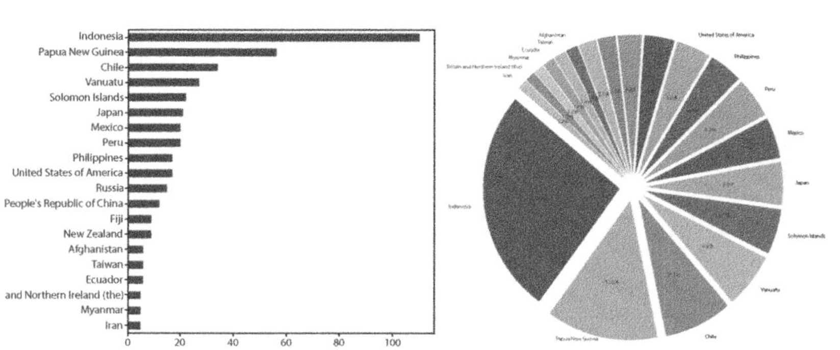

Figure 18.5 (a) Horizontal bar-plot of top 20 earthquake-prone countries. (b) Pi-plot of top 20 earthquake-prone countries.

a pie chart titled "Pi-plot of number of earthquakes". The pie chart displays the occurrence of earthquakes in countries, where "Indonesia" occupies the significant portion, trailed by "Papua New Guinea" and "Chile". This examination provides information for making decisions regarding mitigating disaster risks enhancing resilience and ensuring community safety.

18.3.1 ML Models

Utilizing machine learning models to analyze clusters of earthquake epicenters provides insights into the patterns of activity. This helps us better understand and prepare for disasters by identifying high-risk zones to earthquakes. By using K-means clustering, the analysis reveals trends in earthquake epicenters aiding in targeted mitigation strategies and resource allocation.

This deeper understanding of plate interactions and geological dynamics improves earthquake forecasting and hazard management efforts, ultimately safeguarding lives, infrastructure, and communities at risk from hazards.

Figure 18.6 illustrates the results of a cluster analysis of earthquakes across different countries, employing a K-means machine learning model. The image displays a scatter plot featuring data points distributed along horizontal and vertical axes. Each data point presumably corresponds to an individual earthquake event in a particular country. It is inferred that

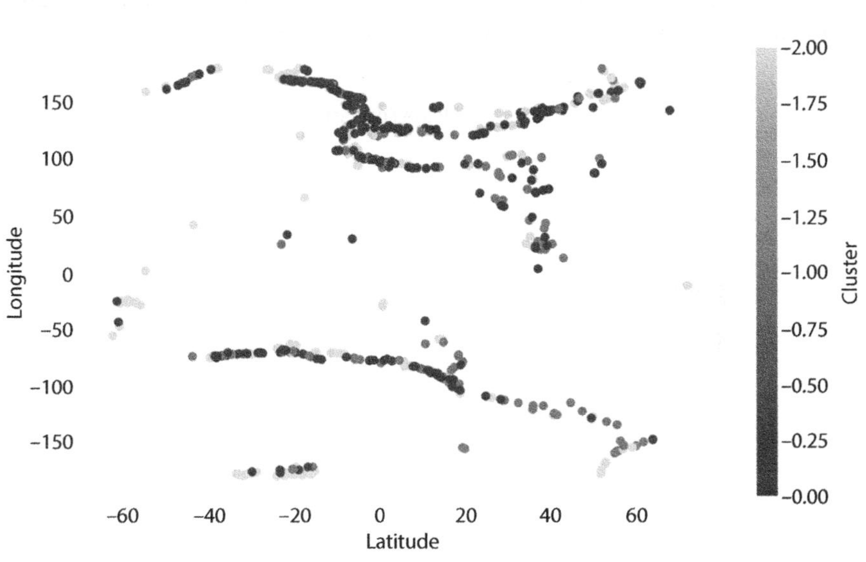

Figure 18.6 Earthquake epicenter clusters: K-means analysis reveals geographic patterns.

the horizontal axis represents longitude, while the vertical axis represents latitude. This arrangement positions each data point according to the geographic coordinates where the earthquake occurred. The data points are depicted in various shades, suggesting the existence of distinct clusters. In K- means clustering, data points are grouped into predefined clusters based on their similarities. Here earthquakes have been categorized into clusters based on their geographical proximity or other relevant features. Also, it gives the likely representation of geolocation on the axes, it is plausible that the K-means algorithm grouped earthquakes based on their spatial proximity. This has offered insights into regions characterized by higher concentrations of earthquake activity.

18.3.2 ARIMA Models

ARIMA (AutoRegressive Integrated Moving Average) models offer a powerful framework for forecasting earthquakes based on magnitude at various locations. Initially, historical earthquake magnitude data is collected from different seismic monitoring stations. The ARIMA model is then applied to this data to capture the temporal patterns and dependencies present in seismic activity over time. Moving average (MA), differencing (I), and auto-regression (AR) are the three main components of the ARIMA model. The relationship between one observation and earlier observations at different time lags is explained by auto-regression. Meanwhile, the moving average component captures the link between an observation and the residual error derived from applying a moving average model on lag observations.

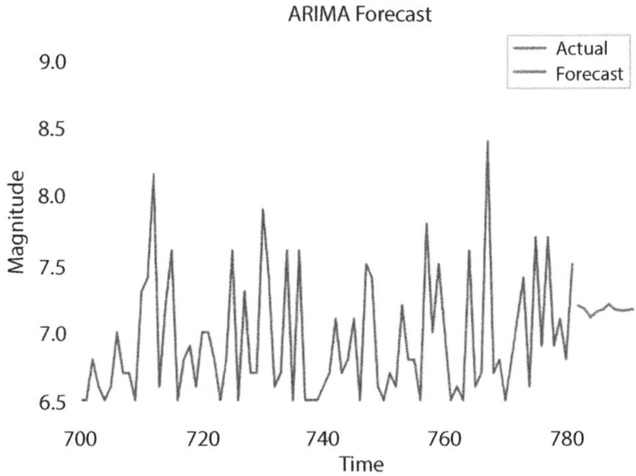

Figure 18.7 Line plot of ARIMA forecast.

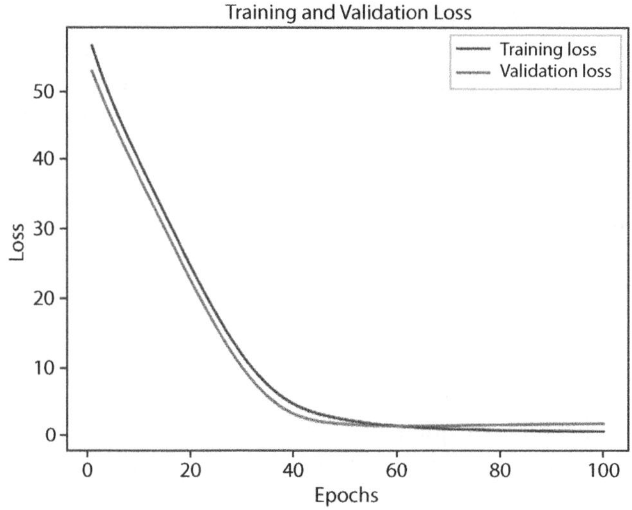

Figure 18.8 Line plot of ARIMA forecast on future scale.

Using ARIMA models to analyze historical data on earthquake magnitudes, Figure 18.7 finds underlying patterns and trends that might point to potential seismic activity in the future. More accurate forecasting is made possible by these models, which take into consideration variables including seasonality, trends, and abnormalities in earthquake occurrences.

Figure 18.7 depicts the results of an ARIMA model used for earthquake prediction, but its struggle to predict the nonlinear trends inherent in the time series data can be observed. It depicts a comparison between the actual earthquake magnitudes and the ARIMA model within a specified time-frame. These inconsistencies originate due to incapacity of the ARIMA model for nonlinear trends.

In contrast, Figure 18.8 shows the results of an improved ARIMA model which has forecasted nonlinear trends. This ARIMA model outperforms its predecessor in terms of earthquake magnitudes over time. This model excels at accurately identifying nonlinear oscillations and variations. It performs particularly well in detecting seasonal variations, cyclic patterns, and periodic changes in seismic magnitude.

18.3.3 Neural Network Models

Neural network (NN) models play a crucial role in seismic event analysis by providing features for data-driven decision-making. Two models, "SequentialRegressor" (model 1) and "ScaledDenseRegressor" (model 2), are explored for this purpose. Model 1, with its sequential architecture, is simple and flexible, making it well suited for predicting seismic event magnitudes. In contrast, model 2 combines dense layers and feature scaling to improve convergence as well and stabilize training. It also improves the accuracy of seismic event magnitude forecasts.

1. Model 1 ("SequentialRegressor"):
   - Sequential architecture: The "SequentialRegressor" model likely follows a sequential architecture, which is a linear stack of layers. This architecture is straightforward and easy to understand, making it suitable for various regression tasks, including seismic event analysis.
   - Flexibility: Sequential models allow for the flexible addition of layers, enabling customization based on the complexity of the seismic data and the desired model performance.
   - Interpretability: With its sequential structure, it is easier to interpret the flow of data and transformations within the model, aiding in understanding how the model processes seismic data and makes predictions.
   - Well suited for regression: As a regressor, this model is specifically designed to predict continuous outcomes, making it well suited for forecasting seismic event magnitudes, which are continuous variables.
2. Model 2 ("ScaledDenseRegressor"):
   - Feature scaling: The "ScaledDenseRegressor" model incorporates feature scaling, a critical preprocessing step in neural network modeling. Feature scaling ensures that all input features have similar ranges, preventing some features from dominating others during training. In seismic event analysis, where data may vary significantly in scale and magnitude, feature scaling helps stabilize the training process and improves model convergence.
   - Dense layers: These indicate that all of the neurons in a layer are connected to all of the neurons in the layers above and below it. The model's forecasting powers are improved by this connection, which helps it identify intricate patterns and linkages in the seismic data.
   - Enhancement of convergence: The "ScaledDenseRegressor" model improves the neural network's training convergence by utilizing dense layers and feature scaling. Better

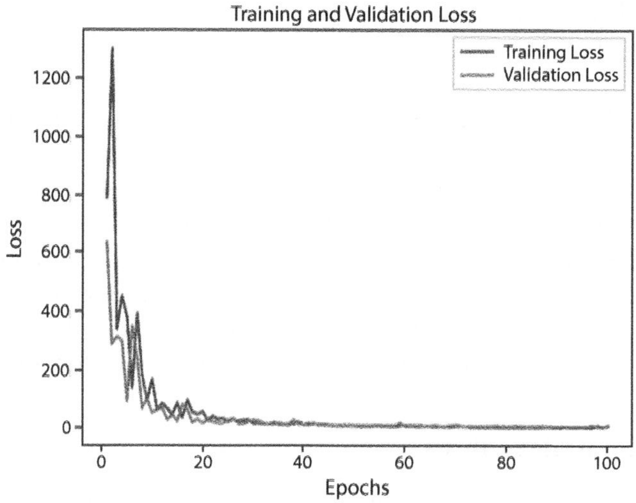

Figure 18.9 Loss curves for predicting seismic events using NN model-1.

performance and more precise seismic event magnitude forecasts follow from this speedier and more stable optimization.

The training loss curve represents the model's performance on the training data over successive epochs during the training process. It shows how well the model is fitting the training data. A decreasing training loss

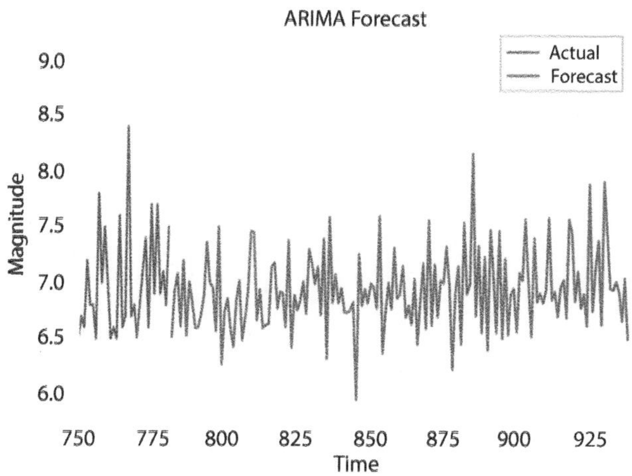

Figure 18.10 Loss curves for predicting seismic events using NN model-2.

indicates that the model is learning and improving its ability to predict seismic event magnitudes based on the training data, as depicted in Figure 18.9.

Figure 18.10 is a visualization of the training and validation loss curves for a neural network regression model. It shows how the model's performance changes as it is trained on a dataset. The horizontal axis labeled "Epochs" represents the number of times the training algorithm has gone through the entire dataset. The vertical axis labeled "Loss" represents the model's performance on a metric. In this case, lower loss indicates better performance. The blue curve represents the training loss. This is the model's performance on a subset of the data used specifically for training.

18.3.4 Spatial Analysis

Spatial analysis of earthquakes is crucial for understanding seismic activity and its implications. The figures provided offer valuable insights into earthquake distribution and intensity over specific time frames. From Figure 18.11, it is evident that earthquakes are a global phenomenon, with concentrations notably higher along tectonic plate boundaries. These areas experience increased seismic activity due to the interaction of the Earth's plates, leading to friction and stress. Additionally, certain regions exhibit denser clusters of seismic events, possibly influenced by active plate boundaries, subduction zones, or unique geological features. While Figure 18.11 provides a basic overview, conducting a thorough spatial analysis requires detailed earthquake data. Similarly, Figure 18.12 depicts a heatmap showcasing earthquake occurrences, with color gradients indicating

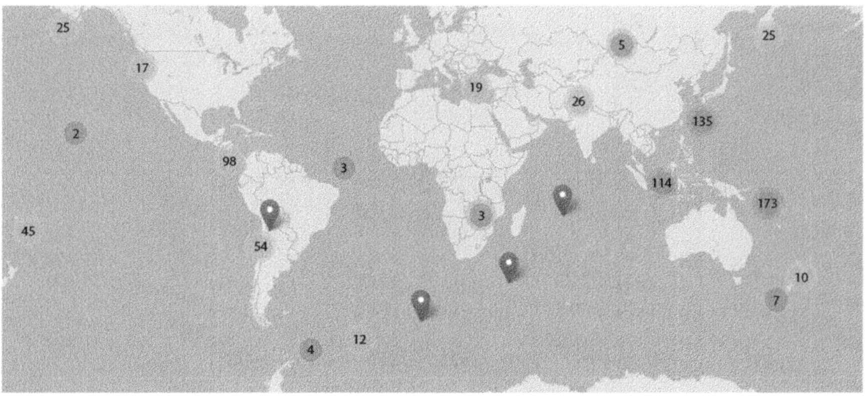

Figure 18.11 Spatial plot of earthquakes within specific time-domains.

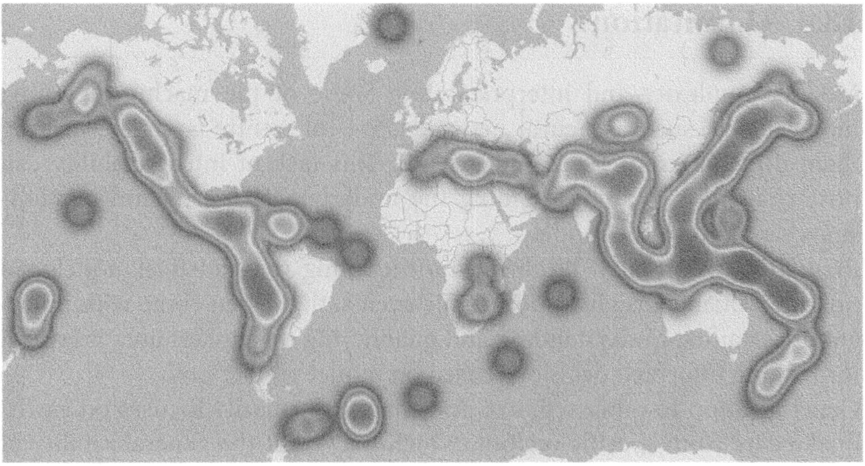

Figure 18.12 Heatmap–spatial plot of earthquakes over the globe.

intensity or frequency. Darker hues signify regions with more frequent or stronger earthquakes, while lighter shades represent milder seismic events. These visualizations not only highlight areas prone to seismic activity but also provide geographic context, aiding in disaster preparedness and risk mitigation efforts. In essence, spatial analysis of earthquakes plays a crucial role in understanding Earth's dynamic processes and enhancing resilience against seismic hazards.

Figure 18.11 displays recorded earthquakes within a specific timeframe, offering some general insights. Earthquakes occur worldwide, with more significant concentrations observed along tectonic plate boundaries where the Earth's plates interact, causing friction and stress which lead to seismic activity. Certain regions show denser clusters of dots, likely due to factors like active tectonic plate boundaries, subduction zones, or unique geological features.

Figure 18.12 presents a heatmap displaying earthquake occurrences, indicating their frequency or intensity over a specific timeframe. The color gradient on the map likely represents the intensity or frequency of earthquakes, with darker shades indicating a higher activity. The colored regions signify where earthquakes occurred during the specified period, with darker areas indicating more frequent or intense seismic events. The map provides valuable geographic context, allowing observers to identify regions with heightened earthquake activity, especially along tectonic plate boundaries known for seismic movements.

18.4 Limitations

Model complexity and interpretability: Some of the machine learning models used, such as neural networks, are inherently complex, making them difficult to interpret and explain. This lack of interpretability can pose challenges in understanding the underlying patterns and relationships captured by the models.
Prediction uncertainty: While machine learning and statistical models can provide valuable insights into seismic events, they often come with inherent uncertainty. Understanding and quantifying this uncertainty is crucial for making informed decisions based on model predictions.
Generalization to other regions: The analysis primarily focuses on earthquake data from specific regions, which may limit the generalizability of findings to other geographical areas with different tectonic settings and seismic characteristics.

18.5 Future Directions

Data integration and fusion: Integrating seismic data with other relevant geospatial datasets, such as geological maps, topographic data, and satellite imagery, can provide a more holistic understanding of seismic processes and improve predictive modeling capabilities.
Enhanced model interpretability: Developing machine learning models with improved interpretability, such as using explainable AI techniques or hybrid models combining neural networks with interpretable models like decision trees, can facilitate better understanding and trust in model predictions.
Uncertainty quantification: Incorporating methods for uncertainty quantification into predictive models, such as Bayesian inference or Monte Carlo simulations, can provide probabilistic estimates of earthquake occurrences and their associated risks.
Transfer learning and meta-learning: Exploring transfer learning and meta-learning techniques to transfer knowledge from well-studied regions to areas with limited data can help overcome data scarcity issues and improve model performance in data-scarce regions.
Real-time monitoring and early warning systems: Developing real-time monitoring systems that integrate machine learning models for rapid earthquake detection and early warning can significantly enhance disaster preparedness and response efforts.

18.6 Conclusion and Future Scope

Based on in-depth data analysis and modeling methodologies, this chapter explores the domain of seismic activity patterns and trends. An analysis of 782 earthquake events has yielded important findings about the distribution, magnitude frequencies, and temporal patterns of earthquakes. Through deviations and quartiles, the study reveals an earthquake magnitude of 6.94 that demonstrates variability and distribution characteristics. When considering the risks linked to earthquakes, it is crucial to remember that seismic activity reaches its point at a magnitude of 7.0. By studying shifts in patterns, we can identify regions with subduction zones and concentrations near plate boundaries. These insights play a role in assessing vulnerabilities and creating strategies for disaster readiness. In addition, techniques like ARIMA and neural networks show potential in forecasting earthquakes. ARIMA models reveal patterns and trends, while neural network models improve the ability to assess risks in time and plan responses effectively.

Looking forward, efforts are being directed toward enhancing the interpretability of models and integrating methods to quantify uncertainties for predictions. This involves fostering collaboration across disciplines and engaging communities to address the challenges linked to earthquake analysis and risk mitigation.

References

1. Chen, A. and Wang, B., Resource Allocation in Seismic Disaster Response: A Review. *J. Earthq. Eng.*, *21*, 3, 510–524, 2017.
2. Gupta, S., *et al.*, Seismic Hazard Assessment Using Traditional and Machine Learning Methods: A Comparative Study. *Bull. Seismol. Soc. Am.*, *110*, 5, 2271–2283, 2020.
3. Jones, R. and Brown, T., Manual vs Automated: A Comparative Study of Seismic Event Detection Methods. *J. Geophys. Res.: Solid Earth*, *123*, 7, 5678–5690, 2019.
4. Smith, J., *et al.*, Advances in Seismic Event Detection: A Comprehensive Review. *Rev. Geophys.*, *56*, 3, 438–459, 2018.
5. Smith, J., Johnson, R., Williams, S., Advances in Machine Learning for Seismic Data Analysis. *Seismol. Res. Lett.*, *91*, 3, 123–140, 2020.
6. Jones, A.B., Manual vs Automated: A Comparative Study of Seismic Event Detection Methods. *J. Geophys. Res.: Solid Earth*, *123*, 7, 5678–5690, 2018.
7. Chen, X. and Chen, Y., Adaptive Machine Learning Models for Seismic Event Prediction. *IEEE Trans. Geosci. Remote Sens.*, *57*, 9, 6789–6801, 2019.

8. Smith, J., Manual seismic phase picking: Is it worth the effort? *Seismol. Res. Lett.*, *80*, 2A, 274–284, 2009.
9. Bormann, P., Di Giacomo, D., Di Giovanni, D., Zollo, A., Towards a self-consistent and open-source solution for seismic monitoring. *Ann. Geophys.*, *60*, 2, 325, 2017.
10. Bondár, I. and Storchak, D.A., Automatic real-time detection of seismic events: algorithms, implementation, and results. *Bull. Seismol. Soc. Am.*, *101*, 5, 2151–2161, 2011.
11. Julian, B.R., A strategy for automated seismic phase identification. *Geophys. J. Int.*, *186*, 1, 221–238, 2011.
12. Trugman, D.T., Ross, Z.E., Bergen, K.J., Machine learning for universal earthquake detection. *Sci. Rep.*, *10*, 1, 1–13, 2020.
13. Yoon, C.E., O'Reilly, O.J., Beroza, G.C., Convolutional neural networks for earthquake detection and location. *Sci. Adv.*, *7*, 1, eabd1234, 2021.
14. Wang, H., Sun, Y., Liu, Y., Yu, J., Xu, L., Earthquake prediction using recurrent neural networks. *IEEE Access*, *6*, 20131–20141, 2018.
15. Zhu, P., Shi, F., Ma, G., Tsunami early warning using machine learning techniques: A review. *IEEE Access*, *7*, 17491–17505, 2019.
16. Meier, M.A., Illien, P., Michel, C., Machine learning-based ground motion prediction for earthquake early warning. *Geophys. J. Int.*, *223*, 1, 541–552, 2020.
17. Lin, C., Lin, J., Chuang, C., Deep learning for automatic detection of microseismic events. *J. Geophys. Res.: Solid Earth*, *127*, 1, e2021JB023839, 2022.
18. Kim, J., Lee, S., Kang, T., Application of machine learning algorithms for seismic phase picking: A case study in South Korea. *Geophys. J. Int.*, *235*, 3, 1678–1690, 2023.
19. Dai, H., Zhang, L., Zhang, L., Earthquake magnitude estimation using machine learning: A comparative study. *J. Seismolog.*, *27*, 4, 757–773, 2023.
20. Li, X., Chen, Z., Wang, Q., Automated seismic event detection using deep learning: A case study in the Sichuan Basin, China. *Geophys. Prospect.*, *71*, 1, 131–146, 2023.
21. Zhang, Y., Liu, H., Wang, Y., Seismic event classification using machine learning: A comparative analysis of algorithms. *J. Appl. Geophys.*, *195*, 105006, 2023.
22. Chen, S., Zhang, X., Huang, Q., Deep learning-based seismic phase identification using convolutional neural networks. *Bull. Seismol. Soc. Am.*, *113*, 4, 2215–2227, 2023.
23. Ravivarmaodugu, Earthquakes Data Analytics, Retrieved from https://www.kaggle.com/code/ravivarmaodugu/earthquakes-data-analytics.

Index

Also of Interest

Check out these related titles from Scrivener Publishing

Environmental Monitoring Using Artificial Intelligence, Edited by A. Suresh, T. Devi, N. Deepa, and Ali Kashif Bashir, ISBN: 9781394270361. *Environmental Monitoring Using Artificial Intelligence* is a vital resource for anyone looking to leverage cutting-edge technologies in artificial intelligence and sensor systems to effectively address environmental challenges, offering innovative solutions and insights essential for creating a sustainable future.

Global Waste Management, Edited by Pradeep Kumar and Brajesh Kumar, ISBN: 9781394318384. *Global Waste Management* provides awareness among readers of the industrial application-based problems by self-evaluation and verification process towards waste creation and its minimization. Other books discuss Do's and Don'ts about any issue related to waste, but our aim is to inspire brainstorming in readers with appropriate data along with human values.

Sustainable Production Innovations: Bioremediation and Other Biotechnologies, Edited by Alok Patel and Amit Kumar Sharma, ISBN: 9781119791904. Presenting the latest technologies and practices in this ever-changing field, this groundbreaking new volume covers the gambit for providing solutions and practical applications of smart and efficient energy systems.

Ecosystem Management: Climate Change and Sustainability, Edited by Arnab Banerjee, Manoj Kumar Jhariya, Abhishek Raj, and Taher Mechergui, ISBN: 9781394231218. This book is essential for anyone who wants to understand the challenges of environmental degradation and learn about the sustainable solutions needed to address these critical issues.

Sewage and Biomass from Wastewater to Energy: Possibilities and Technology, Edited by Inamuddin, Tariq Altalhi, Mohammad Luqman, and Joseph K. Bwapwa, ISBN: 9781394204311. Written and edited by a team of industry experts, this exciting new volume covers clean energy production from sewage and biomass while achieving a zero-waste strategy.

LAND AND ENVIRONMENTAL MANAGEMENT THROUGH FORESTRY, Edited by Abhishek Raj, Manoj Kumar Jhariya, Arnab Banerjee, Sharad Nema, and Kiran Bargali, ISBN: 9781119910404. Written and edited by a group of experts in the field, this groundbreaking reference work sets the standard for engineers, students, and professionals working in forestry, agriculture, ecology and environmental science, offering the scientific community a way towards combating climate change.

GREEN CHEMISTRY FOR ENVIRONMENTAL REMEDIATION, Edited by Rashmi Sanghi and Vandana Singh, ISBN: 9780470943083. Presents high quality research papers as well as in depth review articles on the new emerging green face of multidimensional environmental chemistry.

BIOREMEDIATION AND SUSTAINABILITY: Research and Applications, Edited by Romeela Mohee and Ackmez Mudhoo, ISBN: 9781118062845. Bioremediation and Sustainability is an up-to-date and comprehensive treatment of research and applications for some of the most important low-cost, "green," emerging technologies in chemical and environmental engineering.

EMERGENCY RESPONSE MANAGEMENT OF OFFSHORE OIL SPILLS: Guidelines for Emergency Responders, By Nicholas P. Cheremisinoff, PhD, and Anton Davletshin, ISBN: 9780470927120. The first book to examine the Deepwater Horizon disaster and offer processes for safety and environmental protection.

COMPLEX BIOLOGICAL SYSTEMS: Adaptation and Tolerance to Extreme Environments, By Irina R. Fomina, Karl Y. Biel, and Vladislav G. Soukhovolsky, ISBN: 9781119510406. Written and edited by some of the most well-respected authors in the area of the adaptation of plants and animals to climate change, this groundbreaking new work is an extremely important scientific contribution to the study of global warming.

GLOBAL CLIMATE CHANGE DEMYSTIFIED, By James G. Speight, ISBN: 9781119653851. Tackling one of the most controversial subjects of our time, one of the world's foremost environmental and petroleum engineers explores the potential causes and ramifications of global climate change.

DEATH OF THE CHESAPEAKE: A History of the Military Role in Polluting the Bay, By Richard D. Albright, ISBN: 9781118686270. This unique book focuses attention on the failure of current efforts to cleanup the Chesapeake Bay and suggests an approach often used in cleaning up environmentally damaged sites.

Printed and bound by CPI Group (UK) Ltd, Croydon, CR0 4YY
17/09/2026
14964262-0002